THE RUBBLE YEARS

THE RUBBLE YEARS

The Cultural Roots of Postwar Germany

1945–1948

Hermann Glaser

PARAGON HOUSE PUBLISHERS
New York

Published in the United States by
Paragon House Publishers
2 Hammarskjold Plaza
New York, New York 10017

Translation prepared by Franz Feige & Patricia Gleason

Translators' Note

As mentioned in the introduction, this book is an anthology. Hence the author often supplies extensive quotations or paraphrases from various sources, often without alerting the reader until the footnote. The German text signals the appearance of a direct or indirect quotation by using the subjunctive tense. For clarification in English, variations of "she said" or "he wrote" have been added. Also because the text consists of so many quotations and paraphrases, it contains a variety of styles, tenses and moods. Such is its beauty, but also, at times, its confusing quality

The translators have attempted to ascertain which of the many titles mentioned in the text have actually been translated into English. All titles are given initially in German. If the work has been translated into English, its English title follows in italics. For untranslated works, an English approximation follows in parentheses when a translation seems necessary or appropriate for understanding the text.

Library of Congress Cataloging-in-Publication Data

Glaser, Hermann.
The Rubble Years.

Translation of: Kulturgeschichte der Bundesrepublick Deutschland.
Includes references.
Contents: v. 1. 1945–1948.
1. Germany (West)—Intellectual life. I. Title.
DD259.25.G5713 1986 943.087′4 85-30974
ISBN 0-913729-26-4 (v. 1)

Contents

When Will There Be Peace?

Guilt and Atonement

Period Pieces of Historical Significance

PART TWO

To The Living Spirit

Constant Interchange of Ideas

The Art World

Appendix

INTRODUCTION

Then the son says to the father, "In a letter to the *Frankfurter Allgemeine Zeitung* a reader suggested that we make May 8 a national holiday." The father answers, "The day we were freed from Hitler's regime. Good idea." The son, "But don't you understand? That's the day of the unconditional surrender." The father is startled by the son's objection. "What makes you so thoughtful all of a sudden?" asks the son. The father replies, "That you don't want to celebrate the end of something bad and the beginning of something better." Such dialogues about Germany, this one written by Richard Mathias Mueller in 1965, address an identity crisis which proves highly significant for the democratic-republican self-understanding of the Federal Republic of Germany. Now that a new generation has come of age, critical reflection on the cultural origins of the government is more necessary than ever. Those people who were directly affected by and involved in the activities immediately before and after 1945 are now leaving the social and political arena. The younger generation has for the most part only vague notions of this country's past. Because it brings forth so many painful images, the task of recalling the nation's history is not popular. Yet a feeling of pride is not totally unwarranted. The government and the society which have been developed since, shaped with a consciousness of freedom, deserve high praise.

When these desolate years are referred to as a time of "glorious affliction," no cynicism is intended. Rather, what is being expressed, often unconsciously, at first, is the psychological and spiritual liberation experienced in the midst of the misery of Germany's collapse. The time had come for the German spirit to return home, with all its richness and depth, from both the inner and the outer emigration,* and also to break out of the ghetto of a narrow, national provincialism.**

The cultural history of the postwar years clearly illustrates the meaning of the "end of something bad and the beginning of something better;" namely, the possibility of escaping a totalitarian group identity and of finding one's way back to a cultural self–respect, realizing one's potential as a thinking, feeling, creative individual. Of course, the cultural development and advancement, the cultural transformation and consciousness, key words of the epoch, would not have been possible had not the Western Allies, with all the limitations and often also narrow-mindedness of their own political and economic ideas, striven for and actively promoted Germany's "spiritual rebirth."

This cultural history of the "rubble years" will attempt to investigate and describe the various lines of intellectual development of the period. Moreover, since the sources for much of the material are accessible only with difficulty or not at all, this work will not be so much concerned with presenting the entirety of data, but with shedding light on the meaning and interrelatedness of the facts. By focusing on pivotal junctures, it will attempt to unravel the various cultural phenomena of the "rubble years."

On the one hand, such junctures bring together the phenomena of individual cultural spheres in an interdisciplinary way. Art, which transcends aesthetic categories, is legitimately treated in such a manner. On the other hand, artistic works and cultural phenomena must also be considered within the context of their own respective genres, thus allowing an estimation of their relative value.

One could speak of cultural–historical or cultural–phenomenological "synapses," a synapse being the place of contact or communication between adjacent "nerve parts" where "impulses" are transmitted from one "cultural neuron" to another. An example is in order. The situation in "bleakest Germany," the profound physical and mental misery which is of great cultural significance, can be discussed in the context of medicine not only by underscoring the role of penicillin as the concrete "principle of hope," but by relating it to the film *The Third Man.* That this work of art made such a strong impression is a cultural fact whose significance far transcends the history of film.

Another example can be found by considering Jean-Paul Sartre's drama, *The Flies.* This play was a major event in the development of postwar German theater. At the same time, it touched a nerve far beyond the immediate context of dramatic art, for it evidenced, in the philosophical dimension, the contemporary crisis of consciousness. After bitter experiences with a traditional, often absolutized system of values, the crisis was expressed in a longing for the possibility of creating essense from existence. The leap into boundless freedom opened up a vast and frightening perspective, i.e., the ability to leave the role of object and become an historical subject, precisely by departing from history.

Finally, as a third example, consider the significance of the small, undestroyed university city that so typically characterizes the mood of the time immediately following the war, i.e. "Pan's Idyll." However important such a psychotopographical aspect is, the role of this type of university is larger, and must thus be understood in relation to the history of science and the humanities. The "genius loci" of Tübingen is one side of the picture. The other side is the significance of Tübingen's university in terms of education.

The aim of this volume is therefore twofold. The chapters of the first part are organized according to overlapping points of view, while those of the second part treat the specific cultural spheres separately. There will thus be overlappings and repetition. A true picture of reality, however, is not grasped in linear progression, but necessitates various converging descriptions. The time table and the index can therefore assist in tying up any loose ends that may result from this approach to the multi–dimensionality of phenomena.

A cultural history of the rubble years cannot, of course, claim encyclopedic comprehensiveness, especially if it is not a collection of works by several experts, but instead a synoptic presentation by one single author. This book tells the cultural history by presenting selective examples. To avoid misunderstandings, the reader should be aware that the book does not attempt to be a history of economics, ideology, society, politics, or of art, literature, or music. The concern is rather to focus on developmental *tendencies.* We will be looking at "land formations, landslides and faults" and not at the individual "mountains, forests, and valleys."

This work owes its existence to the reliable foundation laid by numerous individual studies, the quantity and quality of secondary literature, for which the author is extremely grateful. In addition, the *Neue Zeitung,* published by the American military government in

Germany, provided a well–founded and indispensible description of the postwar years. It featured the most important personalities of intellectual and cultural life. Its American and German journalists' extensive experience in the media, as well as the plentiful resources, most crucial for the flow of information and communication during the barren years, made this newspaper a rich source of the cultural consciousness of the time.

Since many of the significant sources, newspapers, magazines, etc., are not readily available for the reader, important passages are thoroughly reported or quoted. As a result, this volume can also serve as an anthology.

Though the author has been building up his own extensive private archive since 1946, his research was greatly facilitated thanks to the private collector Willy Proelss, who made available all the copies of the *Neue Zeitung* from 1945 to 1948. As an apprentice in a pencil factory, one of Proelss' daily tasks was to bring a newspaper to his boss. He always bought one copy for himself as well, which, considering his difficult economic situation at the time, was not easy. He represents an example of the thirst for information that marked these years. It was part of a "demand for culture," as well as of a longing for culture which was one of the greatest achievements of the rubble years, those years of glorious affliction on the verge of the abyss.

The beginning is marked by "Pan's Idyll," the concurrent opposites of anxiety and guilt, depression and hope, destruction and awakening. Those who were ready and competent, and, more importantly, who had the moral credentials to participate in the creation of "another Germany," "waited for a jeep" in order to be transported to responsible positions by the victors who were, for the most part, fairly well–informed culturally. This was prior to the cautious attempts at German self–determination and co–responsibility. The euphoria of the zero hour, which was frequently also a repression of guilt, cannot obscure the fact that a search for the "new Adam," for a democratic human ideal, proved very difficult in light of the intellectual–psychological depletion and cultural devastation left behind by National Socialism. The journeys into "bleakest Germany" showed that "peace" was still a utopia, even though firing had ceased and the unconditional surrender had been signed. "Guilt and atonement" was the most troublesome question to receive cultural reflection. The unfolding of artistic life in all areas, theater, cabaret, music, fine arts, and literature, clearly indicates that the expectation of a cultural spring time was justified. "It will not come again!" Will it come again?

After forty years it has become obvious that the roots of the Federal Republic are mostly buried. However, for the sake of the identity of the Federal Republic they must be uncovered. A clear examination of things requires that one take leave of them for awhile. The meaning of this phrase by Günther Grass has both individual and collective, historical and anthropological validity. Through the years, the rubble era has become an historically fixed and relativized phase. At the same time, when tracing the roots of the existence and appearance of the Federal Republic with empathy and critical reflection, it becomes clear that we may not bid farewell to this time and its world. Rather, we must ascertain its cultural accomplishments, errors, achievements, unfortunate developments, progress, omissions, successes and set-backs in order to reflect historically and thus think ahead in the current crisis of orientation.

Research into postwar literature offers an opportunity for fascinating experiences. It helps one find present-day answers to yesterday's questions. Whence do we come? Who are we? Where are we going?

PART ONE

PAN'S IDYLL

When the World Ended, It Also Began Again

He lay so carefree at the edge
of the road. His eyelids heavy and
content beneath the shade of his brow.
One might have thought him asleep.

But his back (we carried him a ways,
this heavy man, for he blocked the troops
that milled about), his back
was but a tattered, red rag, nothing else. . . .[1]

This common war experience was captured by Walter Höllerer in his first book of poetry, *Der andere Gast* (1952). Höllerer, born in 1922, was a soldier and prisoner of war in World War II, then a student and from 1959 on a professor of German literature at the Technical University of West Berlin. He became one of the most significant and influential figures of the fifties and sixties.

Countless human lives were lost in the World War II. Statistics, which are never more than approximations, show that in Europe, 19.6 million soldiers either died or were reported missing in action. Of these, 3.7 million were German. Civilians killed numbered 14.7 million; of the 3,640,000 Germans, 540,000 were victims of bombing, and about 2 million died during deportation. Approximately 6 million Jews of various nationalities were murdered; a total of 9 million human beings were killed in concentration camps. People who had earlier been forced into Germany totaling 9.6 million tried to return home, while 12 million fled from former German territories. From 6 to 7 million German soldiers were prisoners of war. Nearly 3 million German soldiers and civilians were wounded due to the war. Three million were left homeless; 2.25 million homes were completely destroyed; 2.5 were damaged. The war left 400 million cubic meters of debris in its wake.[2]

The Third Reich kills itself and the corpse is Germany. So notes Erich Kästner in his journal entry of February 27, 1945 in Berlin. Dresden sends dreadful news, the city has been erased. Possibly 35,000 people were killed in the last horrendous bomb attack on this refugee-packed city. "We've picked the first snowdrops. Noisy squadrons of returning starlings have flown overhead. Spring time and decay, in the heavens as on the earth. Nature and history are at odds with each other, warring before our very eyes. How beautiful it would be to experience the spring time of history! Yet it is nowhere on our calendar. The historical seasons last centuries, and our generation lives and dies in 'November of the new age.'"[3] This entry anticipates the mood of that historical day in May, 1945.

The weapons fell silent. After Hitler's suicide on April 30, 1945, came the unconditional surrender of the German forces on May 7 and 8 in Reims and Berlin-Karlshorst. A marvelous May. The zero hour appeared as Pan's idyll. That hour we held our breath, surrounded by horrors. A certain asymmetry marked the destiny of individuals and of the nation as a whole. Alongside peaceful, secluded rural areas stood patches of scorched earth. Small towns which had been left undisturbed by the war seemed irritated by the influx of refugees. The concentration camps, now open to the public, revealed the abysmal terror of National Socialism. Large cities were reduced to ruins, leaving the remaining population to live for the most part in basements. Alongside those who had survived were those who awaited the flood. Buchenwald next to Weimar. The scarecrow alongside the smug bourgeoisie. "A man comes to Germany. He has been away a long time, that man. Very long. Maybe too long. And he returns a different person from the one who left. Externally, he resembles the figure that stands in the fields to scare the birds and at night, sometimes, humans as well. Internally he is the same. He has waited a thousand days outside in the cold. His entrance fee cost him a knee-cap. And now, after waiting a thousand nights outside in the cold, he finally comes home. A man comes to Germany."[4]

Yet the survivors were also marked by a cultural euphoria. Hartmut von Hentig returned to Germany after the war, a young officer who had emigrated into the army at the advice of his father. Like so many of his generation, he experienced the zero hour as the most liberating event of his life. "Chaos and freedom, from that time on, will always be inseparable for me; in my mind they will remain associated with an overwhelmingly radiant summer, in which I crossed the countryside on foot like a hundred thousand others, sleeping behind bushes and barns, begging bread and gathering fruit from the side of the road, no one bothering anyone. The year 1945, now recorded in history books as the year of misery, of the last senseless act of destruction, of national humiliation and a feeling of having been personally violated or, more abstractly, as the year of the end of Nazi rule, the Thousand Year Reich, 1945 marks one of the most precious years of my life."[5]

Despite the profound humiliation, this great hour could signify Germany's return to humanity. This was the message that Thomas Mann, then living in exile in America, relayed over the BBC to his German listeners on May 10, 1945. The BBC had been broadcasting the author's words since October 10, 1940. This hour may be difficult and painful, for Germany could not bring it about on its own. It may well be that monstrous and inexpiable damage has been done to the German name, and that Germany has gambled away its power. "But power isn't everything. It isn't even the main thing and Germany's value has never come simply from its power. There was once, and there may come again, a time when to be German meant to be esteemed for the ability to relate power to dignity through the humane contribution of the freedom of spirit."[6]

This was the voice of a great soul, an ironic preserver of a myth, a poet and philosopher who in the end remained untouched by the blow dealt by the "unspirit" of National Socialism. Cushioned by his worldwide reputation, he held fast to the world of ideas despite their continual need for catharsis. Those, however, whose lives had been reduced to the bare minimum, who had perhaps vegetated in war prisons, had a different story to tell.

This is my hat,
this is my coat,
in this linen pouch
is my shaving equipment.

Emergency supplies:
my plate, my cup,

I've scratched my name
in the tin.

Scratched it here with this
precious nail,
which I keep hidden
from greedy eyes . . .[7]

Günter Eich was one of the first poets of the postwar generation to reveal the "other story." He wrote with directness, describing the situation in a lyrically reductionist, stark and unadorned, bold and non–defensive style. An unbridgeable gulf separated the traditional idealism from the degrading historical reality, the ground had been taken from under the cultural heritage.

Above the stinking hole,
paper smeared with blood and urine,
swarming with buzzing flies,
I squat down low.

With an eye on wooded shores,
gardens, a stranded boat.
The hardening feces
splash into the decaying slime.

Insane with Hölderlin's verse
resounding in my ears.
Clouds reflect their snow white purity
in the urine.

'But go and greet the
beautiful Garonne—'
The clouds swim away
from beneath the hobbling feet.[8]

While this poem entitled *Latrine* does indeed evidence a distance from the constellation of "beauty, truth, and goodness," the message proclaimed by Hölderlin, the "pure poet," could also be heard by those thrown into barbarism. Creative energy had been dissipated, not extinguished. The lead pencil became a most beloved instrument of hope for the solitary poet in prison. "By day it transcribed for me the poetry I composed by night."

When the world ended, it also began again. It later became clear that zero hour was not a genuine new beginning. From the point of view of the total collapse, however, it appeared to be a formula for hope, a synonym of expectation.

After the period of the suppression of spirit, a longing for the goods of civilization appeared. This longing, rather than being dampened by material need, was moved to seek maximum compensation. In the final years of the war, one often heard the cynical phrase "Let us enjoy the war, for peace will be awful." These words did not come true. "When the war ended, and people really did survive, when they were able to speak their minds much more freely than before, and to continue living, beacons of hope began to flicker on the horizon. For the majority of the younger people who lived through it, not everything broke down in that unredeemable and redemptive year of 1945. Rather, everything broke open."[9] Like the phoenix rising from the ashes, such metaphors remained popular alongside the disillusioned and reductionist speech of the times, a cultural consciousness arose that needed to find its place between yesterday and tomorrow, tradition and new beginning, provincialism and urbanity. In Munich, for example, in a lecture in 1947, Wilhelm Hausenstein spoke of the need to combine a provincial charm, not provincialism, with the renewing energies of cosmopolitanism.

Granted, the cultural undertakings of the first phase of the rubble years were more often expressions of provincialism than of provincial charm. They depicted more the spirit of the nineteenth century which was still deeply ingrained in the bourgeoisie of the Weimar Republic than that of modern urban life. Time and again there appeared well–meaning, uplifting prose, tributes to the classical writers, who were glorified in their heavenly kingdom of ideas—mediators of timeless, eternally relevant values, sustainers of life. Light, reflective literature, which had long since vanished, began to reappear in literary cafes. There stirred an eagerness to reestablish culture after a period of barbarity, a need to catch up that produced little that was new, but rather rediscovered the old, severed from ideology. Here we have the concurrence of opposites, the juxtaposition of the devastated internal and external worlds with an enthusiastic faith in the power of classical literature.

From the point of view of social psychology, many processes were interconnected. The return from the land of "judges and executioners" to that of "poets and philosophers" went quickly and smoothly. The affirmative culture did not feel disowned in the process of dealing aesthetically with the recent barbarities, rather, it maintained its confidence in its ability to mediate the cultural self–

understanding of a broken nation. The melancholy that could have brought about a period of mourning was both banished and repressed thereby. Culture, which could again be "served," revealed an eternally better and more valuable world, one commanding universal allegiance and unconditional agreement. It could be realized by every individual from within, rendering the total collapse, the lost reputation, the ruined civilization, and the corrupted disposition of relatively little importance. In the ordinary, daily routine of the postwar years, the aims and activities of culture were again accorded a position high above the more mundane concerns of daily life. Its reinstatement was an act of celebration and exaltation. The need of the solitary individual was answered by a call to universal humaneness *(Menschlichkeit)*, thus alleviating the misery of the flesh by recognizing the beauty of the soul.[10]

The re-emergence of Goethe's *Iphigenie* was significant. Many theaters opened their first postwar season with this play, others conceived it as the central work of their repertory for the rubble years. With the dead, the debris, and the misery all around them, people were uplifted by the play's all-reconciling feeling of humaneness.

THOAS: Do you believe that the
coarse Sythian, the barbarian, hears
the voice of truth and humanity that
Atreus, the Greek, did not hear?

IPHIGENIE: It is heard by all those,
from every land, through whose breast
the source of life
flows pure and unchecked.

It was precisely this idea, that everyone could hear the voice of truth and humanity, that was disproved in the most hideous manner by the Third Reich. yet no one wished to recognize this as a part of "culture." That people returned, with a certain forthrightness and naivete, to humaneness, cannot be omitted from a description of the cultural life of this time. Even the majority of those who emigrated from Germany managed to create a heaven of ideas about the German soul and spirit to overarch the desolate clearing wrought by the war. Wolfgang Langhoff, who before the Nazi takeover had emigrated to Switzerland, where he worked as an actor in Zurich, was one of the first to return after the German occupation. He became General Director of the Municipal Theater of Dusseldorf, and in

1946 moved to East Berlin to undertake the directorship of the German Theater there. On February 18, 1946, he worte a "Letter from Germany" *(Deutschlandbrief)* to friends and colleagues who remained in Zurich:

"When I look out the window, the empty holes and broken-down facades of the burnt houses stare at me from across the street. It is a sight that stops the heart of the returning traveler for the first two weeks, but that soon becomes so familiar that one's eyes pass lightly over it, as if everything were in perfect order. What can one do, when devastation seems normal, and anything in good condition looks out of place? This picture conveys the external decay which has become commonplace in the spiritual and moral life of the majority of the population. You have, then, a rough idea of the work implied by words such as "rebuilding," "renewal," and "spiritual recovery." Habit is a most dreadful force and fetter . . ."

Despite such a pessimistic, realistic estimation of the spirtual state of society after the zero hour, Langhoff ended his letter by immersing himself in the superstructure of affirmative culture that he had criticized for its suppression of guilt. "It is wonderful to be back home. What is it that I love? The countryside? The language? The literature? The Rhine? A dream? Once in Switzerland I recited poetry at a boarding school for girls. Young ladies from many nations were present. After the recitation, we stayed together for some recreation. The girls sang songs in every language, not so beautifully, but briskly and loudly. They kept time with their heads. Then a few sang solos, pop music, humorous pieces, even revolutionary songs. Finally a fifteen–year–old girl sang in a clear, thin, bell-like voice, free of sentimentality and affectation *'Sah ein Knab' ein Roslein stehn . . .'* That, I believe, is what I love and what preserves my faith in Germany's resurrection."[11]

Germany resurrects its spirit which was once buried alive and now rises up again from the depths! The fields are devastated. The first signs of hope. Doubt about what has remained. "Listen to the raging within you. Are you afraid? Do you hear the chorus of chaos in Mozart's melodies and Herm's Niel-Cantatas? Do you still hear Hölderlin? Do you recognize him, intoxicated with blood, dressed up and walking arm in arm with Baldur von Schirach (Hitler Youth leader)? Do you hear the soldiers' songs? Do you hear the jazz and Luther's hymns?"[12]

When Thornton Wilder's *Wir sind noch einmal davongekommen* written during the war became known in December of 1945, it was considered quite unusual and difficult to understand. This was because the ironic speech, constantly vacillating between optimism and pessimism in its contemplation of the end of the world, was not easily understood by the serious German idealist. The basic philosophy of the piece was that the same catastrophe afflicts the world over and over again, that good and evil are essential to life, and that life's purpose lies merely in being alive. This did not coincide with the prevailing idea that a moral turning point in history was just occurring. It bothered some that Sabina (Lilith) discouraged Mr. Antrobus (the eternal Adam) in the midst of all the catastrophes. "How do we know if it will ever get better? One day the world will just freeze over, and until then things will happen as they always have. There will be more wars, more walls of ice, more floods and earthquakes." Antrobus said she should keep quiet. She shouldn't reason, but work. Good, said Sabina, "I'll just keep on working, out of habit, but it has no meaning for me."[13] The consciousness of the rubble years made much of rebuilding and renewal. Indeed, the flood had not caused irreparable damage. However, the new beginning was to be undertaken because of an inner drive, and not simply from habit.

The cultural idyll progressively lost its Pan-like dimension, slowly shrinking to the size of a cozy garden bower which later degenerated into the sweaty idyll of the economic miracle, or *Wirtschaftswunder,* and nestling into the rubble-strewn landscape of the cities. It attained special significance in the provinces which, while they did suffer the general privation of the war years, remained relatively untouched by the actual fighting.

News from the Provinces

A small village in upper Bavaria, December, 1946 has a population of 1177 people, of whom 510 are immigrants. It used to be a village of farmers à la Ludwig Thoma, who daily tilled their fields, went to church on Sunday, and to the inn in the evenings for beer and cards. Then it was transformed into a colorful community of all types of people, from every class and occupation by the previous Reich. There are stranded soldiers, Berlin intellectuals, artisans from Switzerland, Hungarian aristocrats, Silesian farmers, the wife of a general undergoing trial in Nuremberg, people with no specific homeland, poor and rich, intelligent and stupid, energetic and lazy. To be sure, the political constitution of the village is only superficially affected by all this, for the people have not changed. As everywhere else, many flags have waved over this village, and the youths have marched around in uniform. No one knows where the flags have gone. People grumble and swear as they did before 1933. Why do we have democracy? Sometimes there's a dance on Sunday. The young people gather in their colorful attire to dance, yodelling. The beer is lousy but they dance anyway. The strangers shyly join in. Many have been living there more than a year, yet still they have little in common with the villagers. In the summer the cows graze in the fields, one hears the melodic tinkling of their bells. Harmonica music fills the night air, and in the distance the peak of the Zugspitze mountains glimmers in the setting sun. On Sundays people dress up for church in their local dress, the farmers spend the evening playing cards in the inn. It appears as though nothing has happened. The rich aristocrat sits in his castle, awaiting permission to hunt. The farmers sit secure in their farmhouses. A Silesian woman lives with her three children in one tiny room. Between three beds there is just enough room to stand. An oven smokes in the corner. The room is permeated with the smell of food and diapers.[14]

HEIDELBERG, AUGUST, 1947. A lawyer's ball is held in the castle, with special lighting and fireworks. Admission on the black market is 70 reichsmark. Country girls and female students from Elbing, Breslau, Hamburg or Berlin put finishing touches on their makeup. For many of them, even the older ones, this is their first ball. The male students prepare their coat tails and tuxedos. From eleven o'clock onwards, crowds walk up to the castle grounds. It has been some time since the curfew was lifted, and once again they're free to enjoy the moonlight, the romantic ruins, and the song of the nightingale. Floodlights reveal lines of people and police before the main gate. The clock strikes twelve, and red and green wheels of fire roll between cascades of vivid magnesium light, covering the castle's facade with shimmering fountains. With the last spark of light, voices hesitatingly rise to "Gaudeamus igitur . . . ," but die down after two lines. People disperse, shrugging their shoulders and smiling. The dust is kicked up. They dance the Swing Alongside the Waltz. Girls step out confidently in their unfamiliar evening gowns. Some return to reposition themselves on the sidelines. The young men are eager. They gaze intently, always somewhat beyond their female companions. Below, by the cool pond, many drink or quietly nibble on the rather meagerly filled sandwiches. "Vivant omnes virgines", sing the fraternity fellows, earnestly. And the serenaded beauties listen earnestly.[15]

NEWS FROM THE PROVINCE. News of the concurrence of opposites. Spiritual concern has been flattened, and the German feels quite well on completely flat land.

PROVINCE. This also denotes indomitable vitality, a warm, invigorating stream that renews the culture of cities devastated by the war, particularly if the stream has its source in Bavaria. Amidst all the material poverty, and the greed, scandalmongering and nagging, the Bavarian farmers have managed to stay quite sane. So wrote the Social Democrat Wilhelm Hoegner, appointed Minister-President of Bavaria by the Americans in September, 1945 to the poet Oskar Maria Graf, who had emigrated to New York during the Third Reich.[16]

The ideology of blood and soil was little able to influence this cultural originality. The caesura of 1945 did not interrupt the artistic development of either Georg Britting or Carl Orff. Georg Britting's novel, *Lebenslauf eines dicken Mannes, der Hamlet hiess,* first published in 1932, caused no big sensation when it reappeared in 1948. Yet it did touch a nerve, an inner striving, which could not be put off with sweet words. The Danish-Bavarian prince, who in his melancholy eats and drinks too much, his fat cushioning him against the world, is a positive hero inasmuch as he serenely "awaits a last day. With this attitude, he stands in contrast to those who stumble blindly toward their last day with sabre in hand, or a roll of bills in hand, or whose hands clutch the long hair of a woman." Germany was Hamlet again. "Why did they run about, screaming, still gazing silently and attentively up at the blue sky? And when they were no longer able to run or scream, or to sit mute in an armchair, gazing, gazing, then they became that which is called 'dead.'"[17]

Carl Orff's work derives its power from a consistent reduction of musical effects. Orff's creations, *Carmina Burana,* 1937, *Der Mond,* 1939, *Die Kluge,* 1943, *Die Bernauerin,* 1946, strongly emphasize rhythm, and subordinate the musical to the theatrical. His fundamentally national characteristics were, for ideological reasons, sometimes rejected and sometimes used by the National Socialists. This did not, however, affect his reputation abroad. He was recognized as the one interesting representative of young German music who still managed to continue working under the Nazi regime. Orff perceived, in the rubble years, a clue to the underlying spiritual basis of life, a ground that could offer support. When, under the direction of Hans Schweikart, *Die Bernauerin* opened at Munich's Prinzregenten Theater in July, 1947, following a premiere in Stuttgart, it was a "splendid success, especially for the Bavarian theatrical arts, friends of the theater, fanatics of the theater, and the spirit of the theater."[18]

Waiting for the Jeep

"Unfortunately, we weren't picked up yesterday. We sat for hours in front of the house, all bundled up, waiting for the jeep to round the bend. Hopefully it will come today." Erich Kästner entered these words in his journal on June 22, 1945. He had returned from Mayrhofen (Tirol) to Bavaria, where he had found shelter in a pleasant farm house.

Kästner had already been to Munich several times. The cultural life was beginning to stir there. Those members of American occupation forces responsible for theaters, movies and the press did not need to complain for lack of personnel. Their offices swarmed with German actors, stage managers, journalists, and filmmakers. "They want information. They want to make connections. They have plans. People hug each other with the joy of seeing one another again. They still live in the countryside. They want to move to Munich. Who grants permission? Will Falkenberg keep the Kammerspiele (one of the theaters in Munich)? What will he open with? With Thornton Wilder's *Our Town?* When? September?" Kästner met Wolfgang Koeppen and later, in the courtyard of the Kammerspiele, Rudi Schündler and Arthur Maria Rabenalt. Both wanted to start a cabaret at the theater with the city's permission. They were already experimenting, excited. They considered the works of Villon, Ringelnatz and Baudelaire, as well as blackouts, dancers, and pretty girls who were less rare than good plays. "Heaven has sent me. I must participate in this. So what if I haven't written anything new. It's a problem, yes, but I can make up for it. Give me a couple of days." This conversation was continued in the ruins of the National Theater. The canteen was still intact and run in a makeshift way. Robert A. Stemmle joined the conversation. He was preparing a colorful evening for the amusement of the American troops, a kind of "tour through the army." "A sound idea, arias in exchange for cigarettes, dances for canned food, humor for liquor, magic shows for gasoline. At the moment, of course, he is forbidden his little experiment. Why? He doesn't know. Is there a political problem with one or another of the members of his group? Or with several of them? In any case, he had to interrupt his experiment."

On June 25, 1945, Kästner was still sitting in Bavaria. "This burns me up. The jeep is not coming. We were to have been picked up on Thursday, and it is now Monday." Finally it came. After a brief stopover in Munich, Kästner returned to Mayrhofen, before taking over, after another stopover in Schliersee, the management of a section of the *Neue Zeitung*, published by the Americans.[19]

WAITING FOR THE JEEP. These were scenes of both real and symbolic meaning. Throughout the spring and summer of 1945, the representatives of cultural life were picked up, mostly by Americans, and driven from their places of inner exile or at least hibernation to their new jobs. Jeeps also transported important people from foreign countries back into war–ravaged Germany. In his memoirs, entitled *Ein Deutscher auf Wiederruf* (A German Waiting to be Recalled), Hans Mayer described how he was taken from Basel to Frankfurt. In a chapter entitled "The Jeep" he wrote, "In came two tall Americans in uniform. They greeted us summarily in their own style, and told us to get going. I think I remember them mumbling something about the difficulties we would have with the French if we crossed the French border too late. In any case, we would have to cross French territory to get to Frankfurt. The talk was about Frankfurt, even though it was in the American occupation zone.

"Due to our peculiar circumstances, none of us had the right papers for crossing the border, no matter whose zone it was in. Furthermore, we had no right either to leave Switzerland the way we did, or later to return to it in the same manner. It was a delicate undertaking, and the only way to get to Germany. Apply for entry? To whom, and why? It was a joke. In May the war was still going on. It was now October.

"None of us minded that much. We knew, or had come to understand, that the French would not let us in. On the other hand, they had no right to control American transports and passages. So. An American jeep waited outside. We, a woman and three men, climbed in. A relatively large trunk, and a coat, for it was autumn. Did we say good-bye in Basel? I don't remember any longer. Everything went so quickly and according to plan."[20]

The Western Allies thought carefully about the reconstruction of the intellectual and political life of Germany. For example, the Anglo-American occupation forces drew up a "white list" of over 1500 Germans who could function as the elite of the new society.[21] With the advice of the most well-informed emigrants, who often held leading posts in the army, the clearing of the grounds for Germany's new cultural life was inaugurated. Confidence was placed in the competency and democratic commitment of individuals. The attempt to trust this new republican individualism and idealism, however, soon got stuck in the bureaucracy of the de-nazification efforts. The hope for moral change was turning into a process of sifting through files and records. Furthermore, it was thought that it could not come about without the help of those high officials who had come over from the NS government. Thus the groundwork was laid for a bureaucracy which initially, because of its many small rooms and spheres of influence, hardly hindered the cultural willfulness and creative spontaneity.

The new reality in which culture began to flourish was determined by the unconditional surrender, the seal of total defeat. This new reality was desired, especially by those who had been spiritually and artistically suppressed during the Third Reich, the "Reich of the lower demons." Hans Rothfels spoke of the "profound paradox" of such a situation. "They were German patriots who must have prayed for the day when Germany would surrender, with few illusions about what would follow."[22]

The division of Germany into four occupied zones also left its mark on the cultural development of the country. The American zone was comprised of the province Hesse-Nassau, as well as the regions of Hesse (excluding the territories left of the Rhine), Bavaria (without the Palatinate) and the areas of the provinces of Württemberg and Baden that lay north of the highway connecting Karlsruhe-Stuttgart-Ulm, and finally the city of Bremen (which was given the attribute of a *Land*).

The British took the provinces of Schleswig-Holstein, Hannover and Westphalia, as well as the northern part of the Rhine province with the counties of Aachen, Düsseldorf and Cologne, the regions of Oldenburg, Braunschweig, Lippe and Schaumburg-Lippe, and Hamburg.

The French zone consisted of the southern section of the Rhine province with the jurisdictions of Koblenz and Trier, the area of Hesse left of the Rhine, the four districts of the province of Hesse-Nassau that lay between Westerwald and Taunus, the southern part of the regions of Baden and Württemberg with the Prussian enclave Hohenzollern, the Bavarian Palatinate, the Saar region, and also the Bavarian district of Lindau on Lake Constance.

To the Soviets went the Prussian provinces of East Prussia, Grenzmark, Posen-Westprussia, Lower and Upper Silesia, Pomerania, Brandenburg and Saxony, as well as the states of Saxony-Anhalt, Thuringia, and Mecklenburg.

A special government was created for greater Berlin. It was made into a fifth zone, to be governed by the four occupying forces.

The dismemberment of Germany was prepared for by the "Big Three" Roosevelt, Churchill, and Stalin in Tehera, November 1943, and Yalta, February 1945. In the Berlin Declaration of June 5, 1945, the victors implied that the Germans would have to submit to all demands imposed on them either then or later. In the closing statement of the Potsdam Conference, July 17 to August 3, 1945, it was declared that the German people "have begun to atone for the terrible crimes committed under the leadership of those whom, in the hour of their success, they openly avowed and blindly obeyed." German militarism and Nazism would be exterminated and means would be taken to ensure that Germany would never again threaten its neighbors or the peace of the world. It was not, however, the intention of the Allies to destroy or enslave the German people, rather, they wished to offer them the opportunity to rebuild their lives on a free and democratic foundation. Then, "in due time," the German people would again be able to "take their place among the free and peaceful peoples of the world."

The political guidelines which were agreed upon by the Allies in Potsdam were of great significance for cultural life. Among these were:

> The National Socialist Party, with all its affiliated organizations, shall be eliminated.
>
> All Nazi laws which provided the basis of the Hitler regime or established discrimination on the basis of race, religion, or political opinion, shall be abolished.
>
> Nazi party leaders, influential Nazi followers, and all other persons considered dangerous to the occupation or its goals, are to be arrested and interned.
>
> All members of the Nazi party who have been more than nominal participants in its activities, and all other persons hostile to the goals of the Allies, shall be removed from public and semipublic office and from responsible positions in important private undertakings. These persons shall be replaced by others whose political and moral qualities render them capable of assisting in developing genuine democratic institutions in Germany.
>
> The educational system in Germany must be supervised to ensure that Nazi and militarist doctrines are completely eliminated and that the successful development of democratic ideas is made possible.
>
> The administration of affairs in Germany should be directed toward the decentralization of the political structure and the development of local self-administration. All democratic and political parties under guarantee of assembly and of public discussions shall be permitted and encouraged throughout Germany.

The principle of representation shall be introduced into regional, provinicial, and state *(Land)* administration as quickly as can be justified by the successful application of these laws in local self-government.

Subject to the necessity of maintaining military security, freedom of speech, press and religion shall be guaranteed. Religious establishments shall be respected. The formation of free trade unions, likewise subject to the necessity of maintaining military security, shall be permitted.

The Intellectual Elite

The breakthrough to a new external and internal order, to the creation of a democracy founded on humane principles, which in unprecedented hypocrisy were also professed by the Soviet Union, was accomplished with assistance of those who had been transported to new jobs and decisively supported by the Allies. These people fell mainly into three groups:

There were those who underwent a type of inner emigration, whose personal integrity did not allow them to succumb to the spiritual seduction and corruption of National Socialism. It was often difficult to determine who these people were. Many had lived somewhat of a double life, making certain concessions to the "unspirit" while at the same time maintaining their distance from the essential features of National Socialism. To this group belonged a number of young Germans who, upon their return from prison or combat, quickly discarded the fanaticism which had been drilled into them in their years as Hitler Youth and as soldiers. Because of their youth, hardly any action was taken against them during the denazification proceedings. In short, they were ready and able to work on behalf of a democratic society.

Second, there were persons who had been persecuted by the Third Reich. Most of them had just been freed by the Allies from prisons and concentration camps.

Finally, there were those emigrants who had returned from other countries. They were affected on the one hand by the bitter experiences of deportation, escape, and exile, and on the other hand by the longing for a new Germany, a Germany characterized by their projections of an ideal democracy.

From the group of those who "remained at home," Theodor Heuss, Carlo Schmid, Hellmut Becker, Alexander Mitscherlich, Thorwald Risler, Wilhelm Hausenstein, and Marion Gräfin Dönhoff amply illustrate how much individual potential for culture was still present after 1945, and under what different constellations and conditions it unfolded.

In 1934, Heuss was numbered among the politicians of the "first hour." He was located in his shelter in Heidelberg and given a license to publish the *Neuen Rhein-Neckar-Zeitung* in that city. Later he became the first secretary of culture *(Kultusminister)* of the new state of Württemberg-Baden. He was among the co-founders of the Liberal Democratic Party, which elected him national party chairman in 1948. He was also professor of modern history and comparative government at the Technical University of Stuttgart. Heuss came from a family with a long democratic tradition. His father, Louis, was head of the municipal construction department *(Regierungsbaumeister)* in Brackenheim in lower Würtemberg, a rural town without industry or even access to railroad transportation. There Theodor, the youngest of three brothers, spent his childhood years. During the Nazi era, since he could no longer publish under his own name, he chose the pseudonym "Thomas Brackenheim." He was later raised in Heilbronn by a well-to-do family of civil servants. During the Weimar period he achieved a certain literary reputation. His social and political opinions were strongly influenced by Friedrich Naumann, who first entered social politics as pastor of the Inner Mission. As founder of the National-Social Union, Naumann had the goal of democratizing the *Kaiserreich* and nationalizing the Marxist working class. Heuss edited Naumann's journal, *Die Hilfe,* and from 1912 to 1917 he was chief editor of the *Neckar Zeitung* in Heilbronn. He always considered politics as an aspect of culture. In his book, *Hitlers Weg* (1932), he analyzed the phenomenon of National Socialism, describing it far too lightly as a collection of spruced-up shopkeepers from Kaiser Wilhelm's era. In March, 1933, along with four other representatives of the German *Staatspartei,* he voted for the Enabling Bill, an act which later caused him much suffering. His book on Hitler was publicly burned. With his wife, Elly Heuss-Knapp, he was able to survive the Third Reich economically through his work as a journalist and hers as a copy writer.

"Feast of the Epiphany, 1946. Stuttgart was in ruins. In the midst of the debris scattered between burned down New Castle and the shattered Little House of Württemberg's City Theater, the *'Demokratische Volkspartei'* organized the first Three Kings Party Meeting since 1933. Prime Minister Reinhold Maier spoke of the rebuilding of Germany, and of the necessity and possibility of a new beginning. Then a pleasant, attractive, elderly gentleman strolled toward the speakers's platform . . . Theodor Heuss. He was the Secretary of

Culture for the newly created government of Baden-Würtemmberg. He spoke an educated Swabian dialect familiar to everyone from Württemberg. But only externally did the professorial tone with its humanistic tradition sound familiar. The content was completely new, or long buried. The 'particles' of education, which had been dirtied with brown paint by National Socialist teachers and sprinkled on the young, began again to shine in pure colors full of promise. In the course of his talk, he spoke of Schiller's fragmentary poem, 'Deutsche Grosse' (German Greatness), a piece which even as a student, but especially as a soldier, I had always found arrogant and boastful. 'Would the Kaiser Reich go up in flames, German greatness would still remain.' How could anyone, even a politician, dare to speak such drivel about German greatness in 1946? Theodor Heuss did not, in fact, drivel on about it. Rather, he spoke of it with a mixture of the pathos of the great borugeois tradition and the 'sacred sobriety' praised by Reinhold Maier. Then he spoke of the Nazi's misuse of historical and intellectual tradition. He complained that Hölderlin, on the 100th anniversary of his death in 1943, was celebrated as if he were an old party comrade, precisely by those who would probably have gassed him in Grafeneck like thousands of other 'mentally ill' people."[23]

How was it possible for a people with this history, with these accomplishments, to live for twelve years in the Third Reich? This was the question asked by Theodor Heuss in one of his first great speeches of the postwar years, delivered in Berlin on March 18, 1946 at the invitation of the Cultural Federation for Democratic Renewal of Germany. "Guilt . . . Guilt of all Germans? Passive guilt? During these years, and because of these years, we have all become dirty. When you are born into a people, grow up with its spirit, understand its history, know and love its countryside, then you love those people to whom you belong. Thus we have loved our fatherland. And so, without having had to pat Beethoven or Kant on the shoulder, it happened that we became conscious of our pride as Germans. National Socialism has most dreadfully and frightfully forced us to be ashamed to be German, humbled us before our own feelings with coercion and shame, and made us long for the day when we can again freely be proud to be German. Difficult is the path we must take to purify ourselves."[24]

Carlo Schmid began his political and cultural-political career after 1945, when he became Privy Councillor *(Staatsrat)* of Württemberg-Hohenzollern. This state *(Land)* was created from the line of demarcation drawn by occupation officers through the French and American zones south of the *autobahn* Karlsruhe-Ulm. The former states of Baden and Württemberg became three states. Württemberg-Baden in the north, in the south, Baden with the capitol city of Freiburg and Württemberg-Hohenzollern with Tübingen as capitol.

The economy deteriorated. Industries were dismantled, and food provisions reached a daily low of 600 calories per person. There was a scarcity of raw materials, a rationing of food, and rampant unemployment. Despite all this, a tremendous spiritual transformation was occurring. There was a surprising amount of activity in the spheres of art, theater, and publishing, particularly at the University of Tübingen. By October 15, 1945, Carlo Schmid had already restored the university to its full teaching capacity. The son of a French woman, Schmid spoke fluent French. He had been an unsalaried lecturer of law for seventeen years, having been prevented by the National Socialists from becoming a full professor. He convinced the French to give appointments to some well-known academics, among them Eduard Spranger, Romano Guardini, Helmut Thielicke, and a number of famous scientists. Schmid brought together a number of exceptional colleagues, many of whom he personally recruited from other zones; for example, Theodor Eschenburg, who served first as Commissioner of Refugees and then became a senior civil servant, *(Ministerialrat)* and some of his prior students, known as 'Carlists.' With one grand move he organized this lively group of young officials and produced a state government.

Schmid served as Secretary of Justice *(Justizminister)* of Würtemmburg-Hohenzollern until 1950. In 1949, he entered the *Bundestag*. He joined the Social Democratic Party first as a member and later as its vice-president *(Bundestagsvizepräsident).* In 1952, Württemberg-Hohenzollern became part of the new *Bundesland,* Baden-Württemberg. When, in that year, the French *Land* commissioner, General Widmer, took leave of his post, he declared in his farewell speech that he would take with him from Würtemmberg-Hohenzollern something that couldn't be expressed in his mother tongue: *une pièce de 'Heimat.'*[25]

Hellmut Becker, an attorney, moved to Lake Constance when the war was over. He became interested in education when his friend, Georg Picht, assumed the directorship of the Birklehof education center after the war. Becker represented the free schools during disputes, improving their legal status. He felt that if private schools were given new rights, they would provide a genuine pedagogical alternative to state schools. With Alexander Kluge, then his assistant in the Bureau of Justice, he wrote his first major publication, entitled *Kulturpolitik und Ausgabenkontrolle.* Becker, who worked unceasingly for the "change of consciousness through institutions" and the "change of institutions through consciousness," was characterized by Hartmut von Hentig as one of the "last great Renaissance men." Educated in law, he was introduced into psychosomatic studies by Victor von Weizsäcker. He had an interest in and facility for psychoanalysis, taught sociology of education, and spoke French and English fluently. This cosmopolitan, gregarious man always realized, through his person and his deeds, his faith in the power of clear, enlightening, discursive processes.[26]

According to Hellmut Becker, he met Alexander Mitscherlich in the fall of 1945, at one of those unique events which took place in a somewhat poorly maintained, secluded place, barely accessible by bike or wood-combustion car. The group was hosted on Lake Constance by the Count of Baden. It included a variety of people, ranging from Friedrich Georg Jünger and Thorwald Risler, who later became General Secretary of the Foundation for German Studies *(Stifterverbandes für die deutsche Wissenschaft)*, to the Catholic psychologist Victor-Emil von Gebsattel, and finally to Alexander Mitscherlich.

Mitscherlich was the Secretary of Health and Nutrition in the small state of Mittelrhein-Saar, founded by the Americans with the capitol of Neustadt an der Weinstrasse. This government lasted only a few months in the early summer of 1945. In 1946 he published, with Alfred Weber, the book *Freier Sozialismus*, in which he authored a section entitled "Foundations for the Development of Free Socialism." In this piece, he wrote: "We are deeply mistrustful of the government. It is supposed to be the expression of the best of our public life. It is difficult to remember when, in our history, it stopped functioning this way. We have lost contact with it, for it has failed to represent or further us either within our own country or to others. Instead, it has coerced and misused us, and thus there is no longer anyone who wishes to be identified with this government . . ."[27]

Already in this work, Mitscherlich deals with so-called progress. He anticipated the dialectic of enlightenment, the dialectic of technology, and the dialectic of reform. The optimism of progress had passed away. As a psychoanalyst, he also questioned the scientific orientation of the medical profession. In 1946, he attended the Nuremberg trials of physicians both as an expert and as a reporter. In a book that he published with Fred Mielke, entitled *Medizin ohne Menschlichkeit* (Medicine without Humanity), he demonstrated that the medical crimes had their basis not only in the criminal spirit of National Socialism, but in the nature of the tradition of scientific medicine. The response was immediate. "The accusations against us have ultimately grown to such grotesque proportions that one would think we invented everything for the sole purpose of degrading the honorable profession of medicine. It is not easy to be the focus of the animosity of one's colleagues, even when one understands the basis for this hatred. The unveiling of such an immense horror before the eyes of the entire world, a world which perceived it not simply as a 'big criminal story' but as the most incriminating evidence against a profession and an entire nation, was too heavy to bear. It became necessary to find new persons to blame, in order to be freed of the incomprehensible yet perceptible share in the guilt. These persons were Mielke and I. With the meager hope of improving our lot through our publications, we finally submitted them. We sent 10,000 copies to the *Arbeitsgemeinschaft der Westdeutschen Arztekammern* (Syndicate of West German Medical Associations) to be distributed to its doctors. Unlike the 'decree of contempt for humanity,' this work elicited no response. The book was hardly read. There were no reviews, no letters from readers, of those people that we met in the next ten years, no one had heard of this book. It was and remains a mystery, as though it had never appeared. We do know, however, that it reached the International Medical Association which, relying largely on our documentation, found in it proof that members of the German medical profession had moved away from the criminal dictatorship and could again be accepted as members."[28]

Thorwald Risler taught history and ancient languages at the Schloss Salem school from 1945 through 1947. In Freiburg and Rome he studied both history and archaeology, In Baden where he was born in 1913 he was among those who, in 1945, founded the CDU and the *Jungen Union.* He was a representative of the first national meeting in 1949, and was therefore actively involved in the establishment of the Federal Republic of Germany. Since the rubble years, he has worked to build a foundation that would enable a democratic society to develop an intellectual elite.

Risler was affected by the cultural pioneer spirit of the postwar years, when the general situation was discussed in every circle, and the creation of a democratic culture was inaugurated. Ever since he attended his first conference of intellectuals at Lake Constance (described above by Helmut Becker), Risler became involved in efforts to bring together the political, scientific, economic and pedagogical spheres. There was hardly one major postwar cultural event in which Risler did not in some way participate. He was General Secretary of the Foundation for German Studies from 1965–1978).

Wilhelm Hausenstein was a central force in the cultural life of Munich. He began working with the *Frankfurter Zeitung* in 1917, serving as co-editor from 1934–43. He and his French-Jewish wife lived in the town of Tutzing since 1932. Their daughter was still able to emigrate in 1942. In 1950 he was asked to become the first German *charge' d'affaires,* first as consul–general, and then as ambassador to Paris, where he was to restore diplomatic relations with France. In an address entitled "Munich: Yesterday, Today, and Tomorrow," he delivered July 27, 1947 in the Brunnenhof Theater, he claimed that "the personality of Munich," for all its provincialism, had the capacity to assimilate whatever might come its way, and to turn even the most cosmopolitan influences into a part of itself without surrendering its own characteristic personality.

Many intellectuals, artists, publishers and poets awaited the end of the war in homes and villas surrounding Lake Starnberger and Ammer Lake. Thus they were quite anxious to see that Munich, which has almost been reduced to ashes and ruins, would again achieve cultural prominence. In 1948, Hausenstein, along with the Secretary of State Dieter Sattler and Emil Preetorius, was instrumental in influencing the state government to establish the Bavarian Academy of Fine Arts. It was Hausenstein's goal to reconstruct Munich in such a way as to make it a major center of western–Christian and Bavarian–liberal culture. Emigrants were encouraged to return so that the city could again take its place alongside the cosmopolitan cities of Paris and Florence. He wished to rid the city of the self–serving, sheltered, petit–bourgeois tendencies it had been manifesting since 1918. His method was to bring together several complementary forces: the past and the future, caution and daring, the indigenous and the cosmopolitan, youth and old age. In agreement with Karl Wolfskehl, a German Jew and citizen of Munich by choice, Hausenstein thought that hospitality toward the intellect was the mainspring of Munich, the locus of all essential interests of the city, including the economic ones.[29]

Marion Gräfin Dönhoff was born in 1909 on the estate of Friedrichstein in East Prussia. After studying political economy in Frankfurt and Basel, earning her doctorate in Basel in 1935, she became director of the Dönhoffschen Estates. She left East Prussia on horseback in 1945, escaping the advancing Soviet troops. " . . . 'Arrival' was apparently a word to be stricken from our vocabulary. We pressed further and further into the frontier, through Mecklenburg, Lower Saxony and on toward Westphalia. By then I had crossed the three great rivers that once characterized eastern Germany: Weichsel, Oder, and the Elbe. I departed with the full moon, traveled with the new moon, another full moon, and still another new moon. I had left home in the dead of winter, and by the time I finally arrived at Metternich's in Vinsebeck in Westphalia, it was spring time. The birds were singing. The ridge-drills raised clouds of dust from the dry soil. Everything prepared for the new beginning. Should life really go on as if nothing had happened?"[30]

In 1946, Marion Dönhoff joined the staff of the weekly newspaper, *Die Zeit,* becoming the editor-in-chief in 1968 and publisher in 1972. She is largely responsible for its liberal profile, and the paper has her to thank for much of its success and influence.

JOURNEYS THROUGH BLEAKEST AND INNERMOST GERMANY

The Joy of Endless Futility

Author and architect Max Frisch traveled throughout a war–ravaged Europe in an attempt to produce an unprejudiced survey of its conditions. In May, 1946, he arrived in Frankfurt by way of Munich. "A signpost marks where the Goethe House once stood. The fact that one no longer walks on street level influences perceptions. The ruins don't stand upright, but sink deeper into their own debris, reminding me often of the mountains at home where narrow goat paths cross the mounds of rubble, and only the bizarre towers of a weathered roof still stand. A sewage pipe soars upward into the blue sky, three joints showing where the floors used to be. Now people walk around, hands in their pockets, not knowing where to look. It is all as they had expected from the pictures. And yet still it is shocking that there is nothing more to be had than what lies before them. The grass pushes up through the houses, dandelions grow in the churches. Suddenly one imagines how it might be if it continued growing: a primeval forest covering the city, slowly, steadily, without the help of human hands, a silence of moss and thistles, an earth without history, only chirping birds, and spring, summer and fall, the year's breathing with no one to count the pulse.

Travels through bleakest Germany lead from ravaged city to ravaged city. Along the way, however, in the midst of all this, there emerges the "beautiful German countryside" with the splendor of Pan's Idyll. "Nothing but waves of fertile plains, hills with white clouds above, churches, trees, villages, the outline of approaching mountains; here and there an airfield, the glitter of silver bombers lined up in long rows, in one spot a shelled tank slanting downwards into a ditch, its cannons pointing to the sky, elsewhere a twisted propeller in the field. . . ."

Such topographies of large city rubble and the cheerful countryside surrounding them brought several contradictions into focus. The burden of ideological debris did not stifle intellectual activity. The new life that bloomed in the midst of the ruins was defined by cultural hope. People pinned their hopes on change, on self-recollection and reflection. At the same time, they closed themselves off, suppressed feelings of guilt and escaped into illusions and longings. Despite the rubble, misery and hunger, there stirred the feeling that the spiritual Germany, so long in hibernation, was now set free. Never before was there so much "beginning." Zero hour passed over into hour one. The clearings were again "reforested." One often gets the feeling, wrote Max Frisch in the postscript to the account of his travels through Germany, that the only possible future lies in the hands of the despairing ones. To what extent can self-disgust, as shocking to listen to as it is embarrassing, ever be fruitful? Could it be an indication of that genuine knowledge already attained by the despairing ones? Frisch also found, however, that misery itself makes change more and more difficult. "If I were dying of pneumonia and someone told me that my neighbor had died through some fault of mine, I would hear what was said, I would see pictures held up before me, but I would not be able to take it in. My own distress would narrow my consciousness to one single point."[31]

In bleakest Germany it was still possible to find the light of clarification and illumination. The predominant mood, however, was what Mitscherlich referred to as the Kasper-Hauser-complex. In social-psychological terms, it is characterized by a loss of historical orientation, with a corresponding flight inward.[32] According to the educator Herman Nohl, the spiritual situation of contemporary Germany, especially that of young people, was marked by a very secure feeling of "simple morality." The fundamental virtues of honesty, righteousness and loyalty were combined with a deep respect for spirit and beauty, an undogmatic piety, and a search for the eternal.[33] In bleakest Germany, the vertical axis of sensitive reflection crossed the horizontal explosion of a will to life. Was the transformation genuine, or merely auto-suggestion? Was it possible for a new, spiritual Germany to rise up from the ashes, from so many ashes? In her essay, *Von der Verwandlung* (Concerning Change), written in 1946, Marie Luise Kaschnitz discussed the fact that only since the war's end could the full extent of German poverty and homelessness be brought to light. Those who took stock of these days were like a ship's captain keeping his log, faithfully recording the course, the weather, the condition of the ship and its crew; in stressful situations, his handwriting becomes more and more uncertain, and when he has reason for hope, his words gush forth with an aching longing for life. "But what is essential is that he doesn't lay down his pen, that he doesn't close his book for good. As long as the ship remains afloat, he will continue to write his testimony. His experiences form but a tiny piece of the history of all the ships that sail upon the oceans, just as the experiences of those explorers lost in the wilderness represent only a small contribution to the infinitely complex, infinitely confused history of the world."[34]

". . . And then I traveled to Dresden." In September, 1946, Erich Kästner returned to the home he had not seen since Christmas of 1944. What used to be understood as Dresden no longer exists. One goes through the city as if running through Sodom and Gomorrha in a dream. Tinkling trolleys occasionally drive by in the dream. Nobody should be here in this wilderness of stone. At most one should simply cross through it. From one shore of life to the other. There is not a house to be seen from Nurnberger Platz far behind the train depot to Albertplatz in Neustadt, a forty-minute walk. Kästner's parents had survived, a happy reunion. He realizes that most things are insignificant. The two fires of guilt and suffering should have burned all the inessentials to ashes. Then all that happened would not have been so meaningless. Those who possess nothing in the world know for the first time what they really need. When one's view is no longer obstructed, one sees further than others, one sees the essentials. "So it is! Is it so?" In bleakest Germany it becomes clear that humanity is essential. In bleakest Germany one senses that essense constitutes existence.[35]

The total war had led to total defeat. What did a country look like after plummeting from unimaginable *hubris* to unimaginable misery?

Alfred Kerr was doubtless the most influential critic of the Weimar Republic. He wrote for the *Neue Rundschau,* and worked with the *Berliner Tageblatt* from 1919 to 1933. In 1933, he was able to emigrate through Switzerland and France to England. Having, since that time, become the London literary correspondent for the *Neuen Zeitung,* he spent five days in Germany in 1947. He finally returned home and died in Hamburg in 1948. "Today I am, for the first time in fourteen years, again in the land of my love, my torment, my youth. And of my language . . . I am not growing sad. . . . But how should I feel, with all that has transpired? Not like a vengeful enemy. Certainly not. Rather like a shocked companion. Shocked . . . but mistrustful." Kerr saw three German cities of Munich, Nuremberg, and, Frankfurt. The effect was overwhelming. With Munich it is not at all hopeless. Munich will rise again. But Nuremberg . . . We will only be able to talk of Nuremberg as a beautiful dream. And as a heap of rubble. It was once comfortably civil. Now it is ghastly. "A horror without tragedy, just something unpleasant. A shabbiness. An ugliness. A desolation . . . A waste–heap. In the 'Meistersingern von Nurmberg' they sang pleasantly, peacefully, 'How fragrant are the lilacs!' . . . The fragrance has disappeared." Though the Lorenzkirche is still standing, and opposite it the wonderful grave of Sebaldus, the road between them remains a mental torture. Hardly anything but rubble. The word "ruins" is misleading. It conjures up thoughts of buildings of the past. Here, however, things are much closer to the dust than are those crumbling walls that still bear traces of their initial state. The thought enters my mind that we must construct a new Nuremberg and leave the old one as it is. The old Nuremberg would then be a place of interest just like Pompeii, like Rothenburg, or like the shocking Timgad in North Africa. It would be a pilgrimage for foreigners. Frankfurt will be the first city ready to receive visitors. it will be the first to have a sociable and political future. "I don't know if I have rightly seen everything in five days, but I know that everything I have seen I have rightly described."[36]

Comforting Localities

Peter de Mendellsohn left London, where he had emigrated and worked as an author, political journalist, and translator, to begin a long "tour of Germany." The tour lasted four years. It began in the north in 1945, when the last puffs of smoke still hovered above the cannon mouths, and ended in 1949 on the peaceful, undisturbed, and southernmost tip of Germany, Lake Constance. In the land of his fathers, which was no longer the land of his children, he saw, in the person of Ernst Jünger, the stirring ambiguity of the German situation. This man dared to cross the rivers of the times and land on other shores, covering his own questionable character with elitism. He cultivated a coolness of heart, distancing himself from the mob of National Socialists. Yet at the same time, as a member of the German army, he was only an observer of the inhumanity. He took no counteraction, for he was more fascinated by the depravity of the barbarians than he was engaged in realizing a humane ideal. In response to Jünger's war diary, *Strahlungen* (Radiations) written in 1949, Peter de Mendelssohn wrote his journal, *Gegenstrahlungen* (Counter Radiations), bringing together his impressions of the piece of Jünger and his own experiences of Germany. Jünger was unquestionably one of the genuine, great shipwrecked people of his times.

"What can we advise people, especially the simple folk, in order to save them from a standardization, one in which technology also plays an important role? Only prayer," wrote Jünger. And in another place, he stated "Of all the cathedrals only those remain that are formed when two hands clasp together in prayer. In these alone can security be found." Peter de Mendelssohn found such comments especially irritating. "Does this take him to God? One should mention, by the way, the remarkable fact that throughout this devastated country the cathedrals have remained undestroyed. But since when is a cathedral a place of security? And who is this God? God is—and I'm almost reconciled by this, for it shows me that no matter how much one wishes to slip out of one's skin, the skin won't permit it—none other than the God of 'steel storms.' God is military power. And this comforts me with regard to prayer."[37]

The inner path that Jünger in his own exaggerated way suggested to the simple folk, anticipated the misery of the lost war and represented a significant tendency of the collective consciousness and unconsciousness of this time. People had been warriors long enough, they now wanted to pray. Disappointed by a world to whose corruption they had all too willingly contributed, they hoped for salvation, an end to moral scruples, through a retreat into the enclaves of inwardness. Such escapism was especially present and much more convincing with those who had been led out of guilt, who, while in bleakest Germany, had ascended towards an inner light. In the midst of Western darkness, after the frustration of the "experimentum medietatis," the attempt to take God's central place in the world, they undertook a trip to the East, "ex oriente lux." In addition, they stylized the Third Reich, which Ernst Niekisch, a surviving representative of the national Bolshevik resistance, aptly characterized as the "Reich of the Lower Demons." They transformed it into a "higher demonry," thus giving an apocalyptic dimension to an otherwise worldly event. "Hitler within us," the title of the Swiss Max Picard's philosophical attempt to settle accounts with National Socialism (1945), seemed much easier to overcome the less it was characterized by the banality of evil.

In Hermann Hesse's *Glasperlenspiel (The Glass Bead Game)* "he has, in the portrait of the hierarchically–organized province of Castalia, fulfilled that longing which has existed since the human spirit first achieved consciousness, the longing for a pure and higher Being. The words of Hermann Hesse are, however, meant for our times. 'There may come other times of horrors and profound distress. However, if any good is to come from this misery, it can only be a spiritual one, one which looks backward for salvation to teachings of former times, and forward to the patient and cheerful expression of the spirit of a time which would otherwise completely succumb to the material.' Hesse has still more to say, especially to us, the young students: 'You must not long for the perfect teaching, but for the perfection of yourselves. This striving for perfection, and the knowledge that truth is not taught but lived, is the goal of Hesse and of Knecht, and should be ours as well.'' These were the final words of Siegfried Unseld's review of Hermann Hesse's *The Glass Bead Game,* which appeared in October, 1948 in Tübingen's *Studentischen Blättern.*[38] In December, 1946, three years after its appearance in Switzerland, the novel was made available to the German public through S. Fischer Verlag, a Berlin publishing company run by Peter Suhr Kamp. The conferral of the Goethe prize on Hermann Hesse fortunately gave him the opportunity to prepare this version for publication.[39]

This distinction, claimed Unseld, signified more than just the gratitude felt toward this author and his persistent warnings. It was also the symbol of an inner bond which united Hesse and Goethe. *The Glass Bead Game* has been rightfully compared with Goethe's *Wilhelm Meister.* ''Goethe's pedagogical province has become a reality in the district of Castalia. Indeed, one can rightly say that *The Glass Bead Game,* with its depth of thought, its almost magical concentration on subtle, psychological studies, and its musical, reverently meditative tone, has indeed reached the stature of Goethe's mature work.'' In his review, Unseld also recalled Hesse's early poem, *Stufen.* It was received by young people who considered themselves the remainder of a generation that had been used and burned on the battle fields of World War II, and that now sought safety in a distant, poetic world. ''The heart must be ever ready to go/ from every walk of life to uproot and start again/ bravely and without sadness/ to enter into new relationships.'' Bravery, though a very different one, was taught, and indeed, people did, ''without sadness,'' enter into new relationships. ''And there is a magic within each new beginning, a magic that protects us and helps us to go on living.'' Romanticism, always the German fate, promoted that suppression of reality which made a ''magical new beginning'' even out of bleakest Germany. And thus Herman Hesse could be greeted enthusiastically as a promoter of life, indeed, his works expressed a serene, clear, unearthly wisdom, learned through many mistakes and difficulties, and victories over temptation.

> "On the remains of a bench,
> next to the remains of a fair,
> sit the remains of a generation
> smoking the remains of a cigarette butt,
> and together we enjoy
> what remains of our feelings
> without hope for the remainder of our lives!"[40]

So runs the last strophe of the song, "The German Lovers," from the "Revue of the Zero Hour" staged by Günter Neumann in Berlin, 1947. It was a cabaret-like extravaganza. The "remaining generation" had long since been engaged in the superstructure of new sensuality. In bleakest Germany, there were enough comforting little places where one could go, as in Hesse's Castalia, leaving behind the old, sombre, evil and deceitful times and recuperating with the help of cheerful strolls through intellectual spaces.

One such "genius loci" prevailed in Tübingen. Of course, the "bleakness" of Germany also cast its shadow on this city. Sensitive souls could smell the odor of decay which everywhere seeped through the cracks of Pan's Idyll. As a sheltered cultural niche, however, it did reveal something of an inner glow. Linked with the tradition of Hölderlin, Hegel, Schelling, Schiller, Mörike, and Uhland, the liberal humanity of "Württemburg" had a special opportunity to develop, especially "Weimar," except for the fact that it lay in the Soviet zone, which put an end to the Weimar Republic, and was overpowered by "Potsdam." South German republicanism, supported by a host of prominent philosophers, theologians, and scholars from the arts and sciences, was instrumental in the democratization of Germany.[41] Thaddäus Troll whose real name was Hans Bayer, was born in 1914 and came to Tübingen in 1932 at a time when it was thoroughly infused with the German-national, reactionary spirit. National Socialism had loudly proclaimed itself there. "Once I had a German teacher who told me: 'Don't read so much Tucholsky, don't read so much Remarque, don't read so much Döblin. There are two books which you must read. One is Hitler's *Mein Kampf,* and the other is Rosenberg's *Myth of the 20th Century.* I read these useless books, written in terrible German. Thus I knew what was coming, and was immune. The associations were for the most part nationalistic *(völkisch).* Many of their members trained with the

Black Army, where everything was prepared. In contrast to these were those associations opposed to the NS Student League and wishing to preserve their own traditions." After 1945, Tübingen had become a focal point for the "other Germany." Under these circumstances, Troll, who in 1938 had been called into the army and in 1945, after a short time in an English prison, was set free, wrote: "In April, 1946, I wrote my first report on Tübingen. There I wrote that the prudence of the army physician previously stationed there had saved Tübingen. With his weapon in hand, he challenged those who had wanted the worst for Tübingen after their departure. The French occupied Sout Württemberg and looked gently at the marks left from cutting a few strips from the facing. They gave out less aid than the Americans, but were more generous when it came to denazification activities. The streets of Tübingen smelled of cheap tobacco, Chanel No. 5 and non–rationed, white cabbage. The students were thankful to have escaped the war and political terrorism. They were industrious, looking rather like punctual bookkeepers who hoped to win the good graces of the boss . . . Over their heads hung the sword of damocles of the devaluation of their property. In my report I called them 'skeptics, who grasp the crutch of belief so as to be able to move about in the misery of our spiritual world.'"

Tübingen had at that time one of the best German theaters. Among the cast were Anna Dammann and Elisabeth Flickenschildt, Hanne Wiederand and Theodor Loos, Otto Wernicke, Angela Salocker, and Werner Kraus who was boycotted for his part in *Jud Süss.* Carlo Schmid translated Calderon's *Morgen kommt ein neuer Tag,* and wrote excellent cabaret music for Hanne Wieder. Heuss said to the students "Flight into the romanticism of illusion is cowardice."

Hans Bausch, later manager of the *Süddeutscher Rundfunk* (South German Broadcasting Station), made his way to Tübingen in 1945 with cunning and spite. When the French invaded in early April, 1945, Bausch, who had been married only three days before, lay in the local military infirmary. From there he was able to get a release and to become a regular student. He wrote "I was then only a student, although very active in the AStA (German federal student organization). I soon carried a *'carte rouge,'* which allowed me to meet with the French university official René Chevall at any time. With his help, I also obtained a license for a *'Revue Mensuelle'* with the title *'Studentische Blätter.'* . . . The newspaper appeared monthly in an edition of 20,000 copies, for which we were given a ton of paper each time. In search of a publisher, I happened upon an old, well–known, academic publishing company, J. C. B. Mohr (Paul Siebeck). Though the student paper did not fit into the publishing program, when I told them about our paper allowance they soon found a place for us."

Tübingen was at that time a stronghold of German philology, with Hugo Moser, Paul Kluckhohn, Herman Schneider, Wolfgang Binder, and Friedrich Sengle. Theodor Eschenburg and Carlo Schmid gave lectures on law. Schmid discussed intensely with the younger people who had been seduced by the Nazis, hoping to awaken in them a new democratic understanding. Every week the philosopher Wilhelm Weischedel invited doctoral candidates and friends to discuss a particular theme that had arisen among the students. His special private seminars, which extended over a period of ten days, were well attended and highly celebrated. Martin Heidegger's *Holzwegen,* for example, was among the topics discussed.

Martin Walser came to Tübingen from Regensburg in the summer semester of 1948. "I, for one, was not at that time aware of any contemporary literature in Tübingen. At most, the contemporary scene was observable in Tübingen through the movies. At that time, two films were showing in Tübingen *Die Kinder des Olymp* (The Children of Olympus) and Kautner's *Der Apfel ist ab* (The Apple has Fallen). Those were the two film experiences I had in Tübingen. Otherwise things were, in comparison with today's university, grotesque. I imagine myself in class, with the German philologist Hermann Schneider proclaiming triumphantly from his podium to the overflowing classroom, 'I go only as far as 1832.' But that 'only' was, so to speak, ironic. He was lucky to have only reached that far . . . When Professor Beissner looked for a second examiner for my dissertation, he found no one who wanted to examine a work on Kafka. If I was told rightly, Prof. Kluckhohn said he would serve as second examiner if he didn't have to read Kafka. That's at least what I heard. People in Tübingen wanted little to do with something so new. Of course, by that time Kafka had already been dead almost 30 years.[42]

On the Move

The enclaves of the tiny university cities, for example, Tübingen, Erlangen, Göttingen, Marburg, and Heidelberg, seemingly undisturbed by the war, belonged to the fortunate superstructure. Underneath, however, it was dreadful. From the tremendous amount of debris that cluttered the nation, it appeared that reconstruction would take half a century. Supplies of energy, electricity, gas and water were at best deficient, and it was hardly possible to live on the rationed food. There were millions of transients, refugees, exiles, prisoners of war, fugitives, people who left cities and people who wanted to return to cities, people who lost their homelands and people who returned to their homelands. Some drowned in the troubled streams of the time, others could barely keep their heads above water, and still others managed to bob up and down like corks on the surface of the water. A wide path branched off from the road toward inwardness that was built on a spiritual foundation. It led in the opposite direction, towards a new understanding of reality. Born from necessity, it a made virtue of this necessity, ultimately accomplishing an economic miracle *(Wirtschaftswunder).* Soon the substructure of bleakest Germany was also illuminated with a flash of light that gradually cleared away the clouds. From the point of view of a phenomonology of culture, certain characteristics of the times can be recognized. There occured a radical re–shuffling of social groups, classes, ranks and positions, of regional and racial mentalities and peculiarities. This resulted in the formation of a "Federal Republic type" molded by a materialistic orientation.

The rubble years were a transitional time. There occured a move from totalitarian non-culture to democratic culture, from one-dimensional, spiritual–psychological existence to the openness of pluralistic society, from totalitarian puritanism to civilizing abundance. The postwar world was a world "on the move, first from necessity, and then because mobility paid off. Flexibility was imposed by historical fate. From wandering the streets and riding the rails, the country has developed a culture of migration, promoting the quality of improvisation, and overcoming the uncertainty of traveling with a vagabond's lack of anxiety. This movement between zones and situations, regions and ways of being, was mirrored in a pronounced journalistic literature whose impressionistic realism captured the migrations of the times.

Isaac Deutscher, a Polish–English author and journalist, was a member of leftist Polish organizations in Warsaw and head of the anti–Stalin opposition. He emigrated to England in 1939. In the June 23, 1945 issue of the *Economist,* he published a report on the streets of Bavaria. He thought that if it were possible to express what he had seen in the last months and weeks, he "would tell a story as broad, simple and stirring as Tolstoy's *War and Peace,* more fearful than Dante's *Hell* or the phantoms of Edgar Allen Poe, and at times, as tragi–comic as Hashek's *Brave Soldier Shveik."*

Every major highway presented a chaotic and unique picture of the great problem of Germany and Europe: a stream of emigrants flows from a totally destroyed city, through a lovely countryside showing hardly a hint of destruction. Large convoys, crammed with German soldiers and led by officers in their official cars, travel to gathering points and prison barracks. The soldiers are disarmed, some officers still have their side arms and bellow their last instructions in the manner of field sergeants. Troops of the defeated *Wehrmacht* meet troops of Americans, traveling in opposite directions. There is momentary confusion. Embarrassed German officers salute the victors. The soldiers of both armies regard each other with curiosity or indifference, or they ignore each other, according to their individual moods. Somewhere on the side of the road a man wearing the striped garb of a concentration camp prisoner trudges slowly homeward. A short time before, he was approached by an SS officer who was driving by with his orderly. They had exchanged harsh words and threats, accompanied by the appropriate gestures. An American jeep approached, the fight broke up, and the SS officers' car continued on its way. The former concentration camp prisoner explains, with a certain pride, that he was an official in the Social Democratic Party in Breslau. The farmers are friendly and obliging. They take the concentration camp man in for the night and stuff his knapsack full of food, before he starts his long day's journey. He hasn't heard from his family for years. Freed prisoners of war, hunched over from the burden of their heavy knapsacks, heads bowed, move towards their hometowns, alone or in pairs. They are liberated farmers, miners, or transportation workers. Very few of the surviviors of the German *Wehrmacht* believe that the Führer is really dead.[43]

Hans Werner Richter referred to the railroad that ran in all directions throughout the country as the "lifeline of a people." "The railroad itself and the passengers on it mirror the spirit of a people, their mentality, their internal and external cares, their hopes and fears. Thousands of conversations have been carried on there, between people who have never seen each other before and will never see each other again. The conversations flair up and die out, come and go, day in, day out, and all contain a bit of the truth of everday life. When a people undertakes a journey, one can discern the times. And today a people is on the move. They wander from north to south, from east to west, and from west to east. Many are homeless, populating the railroad stations and trains. They live on the railways. In thousands of discussions they try to demonstrate their right to live, in thousands of conversations they go astray on the path of the past, looking for hope from the future. The themes that stir them are always the same: the lost war, the boundaries of the zones, the German girl, the denazification, the alleged democracy and the hopeless future."[44]

The word "democracy" is treated like a shriveled orange peel, it is associated with defeat, hunger, misery, corruption, and bureaucracy. When the train compartment has no windows, when the toilet is constantly occupied, when the train arrives late, then they say, this is democracy! A new order of the military government, a decrease in rations of lard, the registration card, the identification card, the standing in line are for them signs of democracy. The German girls' lack of national feeling is objected to. Have you seen what's going on in Hamburg? an old man with a pince-nez and unshaved, sunken cheeks asks a younger man who elegantly lights an American cigarette. All these Tommies with German girls. That's going too far, definitely too far. To which the younger man says: You should come to Frankfurt. There you'll experience something. An old woman, looking very well-traveled, interrupts, what are you talking about? Hunger hurts. And finally, there are still respectable girls around!

The bureaucracy. Nothing has brought the German administration of our time so much discredit as the questionnaires and the continually growing paper war. Again and again the comparison with the National Socialist bureaucracy, and the conclusion that it has grown even worse. Three hundred grams of lard and ten questionnaires and 20 registration cards and 30 identification cards and 100 civil employees to administer everything.

Little was said of the lost war, and thus all the more of the coming war. The Russians will come, and then it will be all over with the new German democrats, say some. Others say that the Americans will hunt down the Russians as far as the Ural, and then there will be peace. Think of the atom bomb, says a fat, nervous man to another, who looks like a liberated official. Ridiculous, answers the latter, the Russians have too many tanks. The decision lies with them, even today. A woman asks why are you always talking of the war? There is no war. There must be no war.

Dolf Sternberger, born in 1907, edited the *Frankfurter Zeitung* until he was fired in 1943 due to political unreliability. In a magazine entitled *Die Wandlung,* which he co–published with Karl Jaspers, Werner Krauss, and Alfred Weber since 1945, he noted that when people bought tickets at the railway ticket counter, it was never clear that they would ever reach their destination. There were so many names, so many risks. The idea of "connections" eventually became a fantasy. The traveler might have to cross the borderline between zones, lines which, while invisible, were quite tangible walls crossing the country. One could never be certain of permission to pass through these walls.

"This small opening in the window of the ticket counter must be perceived as the crossing point for unsuspected and unsuspecting fates. The civil servant, behind whom a young lad industriously filled out tickets, appeared to be some kind of magician who fulfilled every wish, every single one. And every wish was, of course, the same 'to go home.' It was written down on every note presented by the travelers, who hoped to buy tickets to happiness. Who would have thought that this tiny black door and these steep back steps to the railroad station would lead to such a magical place? Those who had no note bearing the touching inscription 'to go home,' were sent by the young man in the open collar to get such a note from the manager. Thus, no one would miss the goal of all goals. Or was it simply an exchange of papers? A useless shuffling of papers back and forth? In any case, they were all filed away in a hundred coats, in pockets glued shut with sweat, always there where it seemed most secure, against the breast and the pounding heart. One hundred attempts to go home."[45]

Klaus R. Scherpe pointed out that the journalistic literature of postwar years represented a distinct counterpart to the literature of inwardness which manifested such a fatal inclination for the "essential," the psychical and metaphysical verification of the external universe. This countermovement of the "realism of the immediate" gave rise to thousands of stories of daily life, reports of experiences, descriptions of reality, travel notes and reflections, letters from Germany, and interviews. There appeared a "reported reality" that was highly significant as a descriptive and effective moment of genuine postwar development. It was above all intended to be informative and communicative. "There was much to tell in this time of personal division and political and social upheaval in divided Germany. The journey extended from zone to zone, city to city, compensating for the information shortage resulting from the destruction of communication lines and the political divisions. The constant need to scrounge gave rise to a certain compulsion for mobility. People ventured into realms of life which would otherwise have remained unknown to them, a freight depot, a stubble field, a food line. Stories of these places circulated, fostering feelings of familiarity and security with respect to this unknown terrain. People were able, through this documentary literature, to salvage some humor, adventure, or protest from the bitter experiences. There was an element of adventure even in stealing coal and hoarding food, for such activities were part of the story of life."[46]

The train depot was located at the junction of misery. Its tumultuous atmosphere encompassed the chaos of Germany, flight, the return home, hunger, and the black market. All of Germany was one huge waiting room. Talk of "quarantines," "no man's land," "vacuum," and "interregnum" could be heard everywhere. Such metaphors corresponded to a specific mentality shared by every stratum of society; namely, the sense that "society" no longer existed. At the same time, one sensed that this loss of society could be a transitional phase leading toward a totally new society. The objective facts of "social disorganization" were experienced by everyone, producing a real loss of social identity. Among these "facts" were the breakdown of production and of lines of transportation, the shortage of supplies, the separation of families, the fate of the refugees, the changing of sex roles and professions in the course of extensive unemployment, the process of decentralization and regionalization, and, last but not least, the foreign and inexperienced political authorities. However, in the midst of this vacuum of social achievement there arose the spirit of the "self-made man." People appreciated the Robinson Crusoe image. There were signs of joint undertakings. Individual struggle and endurance not only manifested itself aggressively and destructively, it also brought about a sense of co–humanity. Reared under authoritarian personalities, people first reacted with fear and insecurity when confronted with opportunities for new identities. These were, however, accepted more and more. People increasingly saw, in the weakness of class structures and the loss of the institutional hierarchy in government and society, opportunities to create new structures. With the overall disintegration, the rules and values that upheld the old order were also destroyed. Social type–casting according to class, occupation, education and religion was less significant than categorization according to destinies such as returnee, refugee, prisoner of war, war widow, displaced person, and concentration camp inmate. The "cultural liberation" occasioned by the zero hour was both a burden *and* a joy.

According to Klaus F. Scherpe, the following points are central to a definition of postwar reporting:

There was a need to concretize and fill in the gaps of those years of life perceived as a "vacuum," a "no man's land," and a tendency to express every detail in the smallest possible space, no doubt influenced by the forms of publications available. These conditions, and the priority given to quick but meaningful observations, rendered the texts somewhat "empty," or at least modest and hesitant, with respect to historical discussions of Fascism and the possibilities for a socially relevant prognosis of the future.

The observed social emptiness and uncertainty should in no way detract, however, from the need for concrete action and personal responsibility. Various factors contributed to the loose reporting style. Among them were the disintegration of up–to–date information, historical knowledge, and accounts of people's lives, as well as the striking tendency to give a personal perspective on day–to–day life. These factors strengthened illusions of both personal activity and the potential for creating social relationships.

Before re–politicization and re–socialization occured, postwar commentaries had dealt almost exclusively with reports of human relationships. This was also true for those topics normally covered under the "classical style" of reporting practiced also in the twenties and thirties, topics such as work–relations, and legal and political life, eg. the Nuremberg Trials, or reconstruction attempts of the Krupp industry.

Significantly, the structure of these reports has often been identified with a "mosaic" or a "kaleidoscope." While it is possible to characterize the historical practice of postwar reporting as "open," lacking historical contours, and as "empty," referring to the historically conditioned "vacuum" of the postwar years, it is not possible to define it any more concretely.

The transition to short stories is easily made. In the context of the waiting room, the railroad, the ruins and the refugee camps, there is, according to the spirit of the times, a green border between substantial, life–content and its human or historical significance.

Nobody has more movingly demonstrated the skill of poetic commentary, of a condensed observation of day–to–day existence, than Wolfgang Borchert. Seen from the perspective of today's leftist literary cirticism, he belongs to the pseudo–concrete authors, for with all his pathos, his outcry against the evils of humanity did not take into consideration the conditionedness of the misery. He transposed and sublimated the migrating culture into poetry, witnessing to the transitional generation that, out of its despair, dared to hope with all its might. In bleakest Germany, people were not only on the move but they also anticipated an arrival.

"We meet one another on this earth, human being to human being. Then we slink away, for we have no ties, we do not stay or bid farewell. We are a generation without farewells, slinking away like thieves, for we are afraid of our crying hearts. We are a generation without a homecoming, for there is nothing to return home to, no one to whom we can entrust our hearts. Thus, we have become a generation without farewells and without homecomings.

"But we are a generation of arrivals. Perhaps we are a generation full of arrivals on a new planet, into a new life, full of arrivals under a new sun, to new hearts. Perhaps we are full of arrivals to a new loving, a new laughing, a new God.

"We are a generation without farewells, but we know that every arrival belongs to us."[47]

A DIFFICULT SEARCH FOR THE NEW ADAM

Werewolves Become Innocent Lambs

"A world catastrophe can serve many purposes. It can, for example, provide one with an alibi before God. Where were you, Adam? 'I was in the World War.'" This thought, penned by Theodor Haecker on March 31, 1940 in his *Tag und Nachtbüchern,* was taken up by Heinrich Böll in his novel, *Wo Warst du Adam?* (1951). By recounting the lives of several people, Böll depicted the war and its insidious effects.

Which Adam came forth in the zero hour? Was an alibi possible, even a weak one, in light of the terrible crimes committed by the National Socialists with almost full consent of the people? Could one place one's hopes in a new human being, someone who, purged through guilt and shame, would actively bring about Germany's return to basic human values? Observers of the German psychograph were uncertain, especially those western non-Germans, many of them emigrants, who traveled through bleakest Germany. After intensive investigation of German history and the German national character, they confronted a mystery. By the end of the war almost all the National Socialists had disappeared. Fanaticism was expected; wolves and werewolves were anticipated. Yet one met innocent lambs. The people seemed changed. Was it a change? Could one trust this mutation?

The "blonde beast" was domesticated. That beast which, with a delusion of racial superiority, subjugated other people, exterminated European Judaism, destroyed the German spirit, provoked a total war, and left behind a vast rubble. They attended the nursery school of democracy with zeal. Even the highest ranking officers indicated and condemned in the Nuremberg Trials claimed to have had almost no knowledge of the crimes. Through individual and collective autosuggestion, people were convinced that Hitler and Himmler, together with a few henchmen, were the only ones responsible for the crimes. "Hitler within us?" Certainly not. Thus there was no need for feats of exorcism to free Germany from the ideology of National Socialism. The new environment created the new type of democratic citizen in an unbelievably short time. A nation of "quick change artists," the Germans internalized, as if possessed, Russian, English, French and especially American thinking and feeling, according to their occupation zone. Zealous youths, who had for so long embodied the myth of the invincible German soldier, became civilians overnight. Originally educated in unconditional obedience, they were instantly prepared to reorient themselves. The pain of separation did not last long. Someone from this generation reported, "And then came the day on which I renounced my Führer. A drunken Polish corporal fetched my mother and me from our beds one night. He threatened us with a pistol, knocked our heads together and shouted, 'Me Polish SS! You love Hitler!.' In my mortal terror my words gushed forth like a waterfall, 'Hitler is a criminal, Hitler is crazy. We don't love Hitler, we hate him, etc.' The chickens were awakened by the noise from the house. The cock crowed in the middle of the night. I felt like Simon Peter."[48] Though the edifice of ideology was destroyed, the newly budding self-consciousness quickly found, in the soul's debris, soil in which to send its roots.

Alexander and Margarete Mitscherlich later analyzed the phenomenon of the non-observance of mourning. They pointed to the defense mechanisms that had been developed in relation to the entire period of the Third Reich: renunciation, isolation, changing the details, feigning attention and affection. In short, de-realization. Had these not been developed, a great many people in postwar Germany would inevitably have been overcome by an oppressive melancholy as a result of their narcissistic love for the Führer and the crimes committed in his service. "In narcissistic identification with the Führer, his failure became the failure of the 'I.' Although de-realization and the other defensive techniques hindered the outbreak of melancholy, they were not completely able to prevent a 'tremendous impoverishment of the I.'"[49]

What appears in retrospect as a fatal deficiency in the geneology of the Federal Republic types, i.e. the non-observance of mourning, was in fact the very presupposition of the birth of this type. Repression made adaptation possible, and adaptation enabled one to open up. In the occupation zones of the Western Allies one adapted to a multi-dimensional, humane and democratic image of the human. What Friedrich Nietzsche satirized about the "contemporaries" in *Zarathustra,* i.e. that they sat around with filthy freckles painted on their faces and limbs, that the ages and people looked colorful through their veils, but in reality were only scarecrows, this eclecticism proved to be the great opportunity for a new cultural orientation after 1945. The as yet unformed features of the former compatriot made it possible to shape his profile anew. Furthermore, the change of consciousness literally had something to do with clothing.

Evidence of this new openness could be seen in the "rubble fashions" created in response to everyday needs. Head scarves of every shade, coats with angular, padded shoulders, long pants, pedal pushers, outfits put together from theatrical garb, warm-up suits, pleated skirts, thick knee-highs, ski boots, dancing slippers, fur coats from the pelts of every animal, punched-in hats, berets, safety helmets which had been demilitarized, frayed shirt collars of every width, mostly too wide, ties of all colors, gray, leather, and narrow shouldered military coats minus the epaulets, double breasted lounge jackets, knickerbockers. People left behind the monotonous brown and appeared gaudily creative. Josef Müller-Marein provided an autobiographical report of such a change. In Lübeck, one day before the English arrived, he found shelter in a town theater. He took off his military uniform and searched for something funny, something peaceful. "Everything fell into place. One thing left, another took its place. War disappeared, peace approached. War exchanged for peace. . . . Beige pants, light brown jacket, both elegantly tailored, with very impressive buttons. Under the collar is sewn a note wrapped in cellophane, 'Wedding Night in Paradise. Buffo Walter Müller.' Thus I stepped out that morning, and I saw what the English would have done to me had I not managed to switch costume. They herded my comrades together. 'Quickly, quickly!' They pushed them, kicked them with their boots, fenced them in for the night in parks or on some patch of grass, and the next day ordered them to begin, without provisions, the long march to Schleswig-Holstein. I was still wearing the 'Wedding Night' outfit when we founded the *Zeit.* I had no other civilian clothing and continued to wear it for years. When it finally fell apart and I threw it out, Marion Dönhoff said I never should have done so. It could well be that I was mistaken in my conduct. When the spotlight was pointed on that jacket, its buttons would shine with an awesome, astonishing power and splendor. Even the sun could work this effect."[50]

One should not read too much into such scenes, yet they are still significant. The change of clothing, of conviction, and the new cultural consciousness all belong together. One of the first industries to flourish was that of the tailor who produced dusters out of bedsheets, thereby communicating an air of springtime urbanity. Throw in a pair of sunglasses and stick an American cigarette in his mouth, and your average consumer breathed in a bit of the great, wide world. Good clothing lightened the burdens of every day life. In the midst of the rubble, there stirred a people who were neatly, and soon also stylishly, attired. The "rubble look."

According to an article on the revival of the clothing industry (*Neue Zeitung* May 31, 1956), it would be unjust to associate fashion automatically with luxury. Fashion is as much a part of life as the sun, the flowers, and everything else that offers levity, joy, and color to an otherwise gray life. It brings life and movement to the dreary streets. Those involved in production should make an effort to pull us out of our lethargy, so that we may learn to see and feel again. Our art, our culture, our entire way of life has just come out of a serious state of shock. Now people are searching for new modes of self-expression. In every sphere they strive to express their personalities, and every goal is but a milestone on the path of development. If opponents to the fashion industry soberly protest, "Why do we need this fashion? With our poverty, our misery, we can hardly afford this or that," one should answer that everything that creates value is necessary, especially now. And besides having cultural significance, fashion provides numerous consumer goods. As a key industry, it keeps other industries going, and will soon become an indispensible economic factor.[51]

After All the Menacing Deaths, Alive under the Sun

According to Joachim Fest, all those 15 to 25 years old by the war's end had been politicized in some way by the Third Reich. Granted, its defeat also signified the victory of a freedom that included the right to be non-political. Yet this generation became much more rooted in democratic principles whose underlying presupposition was that it was no longer possible to find happiness in private pursuits, in the satisfaction of personal inclinations and whims, in short, in political indolence. Rather, it became important to be integrally involved in social relationships and their demands.[52] An individual growing up in the Hitler Youth, the civil service, and the army, was condemned to be a permanent cog in the wheel of the state's machinery. Indeed, the freedom of privacy provided great satisfaction. Yet in order to maintain it, it was necessary to secure the political and social presuppositions of this freedom. In this way, privatism created democrats by conviction. The forerunners of the skeptical generation who rejected all totalitarian ideologies wanted as little government as possible, or just enough to protect the desired individualism and eudaemonism.

Writing on the fate of thirty-year-olds in 1948, Walther von Hollander claimed that the main point was to move away from the destiny of a lost and abused generation and into the individual form which, transcending every generation, has always been loved and will exist forever. "The total solitude of the rest of our generation." an acquaintance once told him, "condemns us to sterility. Our words find no echo, for our peers have been almost totally wiped out, and the others come from such different situations that they simply can't understand our manner of speaking or living." That may be the impression of an unwarranted pessimist, said Hollander, for this lost generation has also been favored by fortune. Indeed, they belong to the survivors. They have come through so much misery that they possess the distinct ability to succeed, if only they can discover and use it. "At the very least, those now living are exceptional in that they have endured such frightful dangers that to them it has been permitted to remain alive under the sun and the changing constellations even after all the menacing deaths. Since they had the power to endure all those dangers, why shouldn't they also have the power to build a full and complete life?"[53]

Today, when those who escaped are now 50 years old, one might well wish to ask whether they themselves did enough to build a better Germany. Winfried Maas posed this question, in the form of individual biographies, in his attempt to "draw the portrait of a betrayed generation."(1980)

"The generation of 'burned children' understood the value of democracy more quickly than others. But they fought too little for its creation.

"Many remained outside of politics for a long time, for they required all their energy just to secure a naked existence. Almost all of them had a difficult start. They were hindered by gaps in their education. Only a small portion of former air raid assistants *(Luftwaffenhelfer)* picked up their *Abitur* after the war. Hundreds of thousands had to look for a new homeland. Some returned from the war and from prisons with serious psychological or physical injuries.

The universities were overcrowded, apprenticeships rare. Big businesses in Germany, for example the *Wolfsburger Volkswagenwerk,* got permission from the military government to procure workers, thus commanding the returning child-soldiers to work on the assembly lines rather than giving them an education in some proper occupation. Hitler's last heroes were West Germany's first "foreign workers" *(Gastarbeiter),* a spare herd of workers who could easily be ordered here and there. Emaciated boys and girls, still marked by the war, helped build that which would later belong to those through whose guilt everything had been destroyed.

"It was not before the students stormed the barricades at the end of the sixties, and the extra–parliamentary opposition resisted the Great Coalition under the fomer NSDAP (National Social Democratic Worker's Party) member Kurt Georg Kiesinger, that some of those who had by then turned 40 awoke from their political lethargy. As journalists or authors they publicized their support of those who rebelled against authoritarian governmental structures. Reinhard Lettau, by then almost 50, formulated the slogan: 'No more writing, just action!' The older people felt a solidarity with the younger ones, but they no longer had the power to bring about great changes. Shuddering, they withdrew into their own homes as the riots turned into senseless terrorism.

"Now in their 50s, the generation that was born between the mid-1920s and the early 1930s is as divided as is our world, between West Germany and East Germany, social democrats, liberals, christian democrats and communists, conformists and nonconformists. Yet whatever they may be, these once-betrayed people must now ask themselves if in the meantime they have not also committed treason against their children. Is it the case that in those years for which they can be held responsible, democracy has progressed and life in Germany has become freer and more humane?"[54]

From NS-Maid to Woman of the Rubble

Women played the most decisive role in the development of the Federal Republic "type." The German woman: truly a dismal chapter in the history of patriarchal oppression! For the first time the opportunity had been present for true emancipation. Of those women involved in the women's movements of the Second Reich and the Weimar Republic, there were admittedly only a few who, immediately after 1945, consciously worked for equal rights and for the strengthening of women's positions in the family, the business world, and in public office. There were only four women among the 65 voting members of the parliamentary council set up in 1948 (three years after the military defeat of National Socialism) to formulate the constitution. After vehement disputes, the equal rights of men and women were guaranteed in Article 3,II.

The legacy of the Third Reich was atrocious. The ideology of National Socialism completely subordinated women to masculine superiority. The racist delusion of masculinity, bound up with a purely utilitarian cult of motherhood, turned women into 'breeding machines' who were to supply suitable human products for the imperialistic goals of the National Socialists. It was possible for the denigration and oppression of women to continue unchecked for so long because the frustrations which it caused were compensated for in part by the hysterical Führer-cult. The physical and mental use which the National Socialists made of such organizations as the BDM (League of Young German Women), the *Arbeitsdienst* (Civil Service), and the NS women's leagues was propagandistically concealed beneath a slick exterior. The denigration of women was "aesthetically giftwrapped." The NS-Maid depicted a lofty idealism with the pathos of *"volkish"* pride, manifested most commonly in tasteless, sentimental songs. They were characterized by athletic, womanly muscularity and the cultivation of fertility, a hearty comradery and sentimental, submissive behavior toward the hero, a longing for the beautiful, the willingness to serve and the readiness to fill in wherever needed. With this, the NS-Maid filled the spiritual and mental emptiness that resulted from her lesser status. The Füherin of young maidens was a super-Gretchen with Amazonian allure. "Faith and Beauty" was her motto.

Behind an aesthetic facade, the subjugation of women was accomplished according to the tenets of the ideal of racial breeding. Adolf Hitler's position, which he openly expressed in *Mein Kampf*, was that of an imperious, bourgeois patriarch for whom marriage served only to propagate and preserve the culture and race. Beyond this, it had no meaning or purpose. The man was to marry early because of his reproductive potential, the woman was simply the passive partner.

National Socialism, so totally antagonistic to the spirit, could only conceive of love in terms of lust or reproduction. Consequently, its solution to the problem of replenishing the population after the war was to project a kind of national "fertility bordello." "The survival and life of a people depends on its ability to reproduce itself . . . Now women, who by the end of this great war have neither married nor plan to marry a man, cannot conceive children by the Holy

Ghost . . . We must hope that these women, who lost their husbands in the war and/or have no future marriage prospects, will have something like a marital relationship with preferably one man, thereby producing and raising as many children as possible . . . For the sake of the future of our race, we must promote a veritable cult of motherhood . . . In special circumstances, a man should be allowed to enter into a permanent married relationship with a woman other than his spouse. This woman would thereupon take the man's name and the children would then take the name of their father."[55]

Since the devaluation of women reached its nadir in the Third Reich, the total defeat offered an opportunity for a comprehensive new beginning. In the language of depth psychology, it could be said that the energy of frustrated desire for liberation, pent up through subjugation and exploitation, was now ready to be released. It fueled the capacity and readiness of women to take their own fates, as well as that of their families and communities, into their own hands. The patriarchal–authoritarian model of ideology and organization had been smashed to pieces. A good number of men were away from home, either dead, missing, imprisoned, in hiding, or on the road. If they were at home, they were unemployed, disoriented, and morally confused. And so the "women of the rubble" began to rebuild. Their optimism and courage, together with their resourcefulness and knack for improvising, enabled them to overcome the lethargy and resignation that threatened to spread like the plague throughout the rubble of the lost war.

By the end of the war, "there was hardly a family that was not in some way affected by Nazi persecution, the war, the downfall of the regime, or denazification. Hardly a body or a psyche survived the gruesome and terrifying events unscathed."[56] Helmut Schelsky, in his *Wandlungen der deutschen Familie der Gegenwart,* writes of 1.5 to 2.5 million war widows, 2.5 million seriously wounded, 4.5 to 6 million injured by bombing, and 1.5 to 2.5 million who lost their former stations due to the war. He estimates the number of people affected by typical social disasters in the postwar years as about one third of the West German population.[57] There is, in fact, no statistical information regarding income and unemployment in the years before 1949. However, the unemployment ratio was still 11 percent after 1950. The average gross wage was approximately 304 DM for men and 165 DM for women. The black market was of course quite significant until the currency reform. In 1946, there were 7,283,000 more women than men, and of these women 6 to 7 million were of marriageable age. Until 1947, employable war widows received no stipends. In 1946, Berlin alone reported 25,000 divorces, which meant that of 724,625 married men 3.5 percent petitioned for a divorce. At that time 140,793 Berliners were still in prisons. In 1948, which was a census year and the high point of the postwar wave of divorces, there were 186 divorces for every 100,000 inhabitants of the western zones. In these years, 80,000 children became "divorce-orphans." Even by 1950 only about 60 percent of the total West German population lived in "complete families."

This statistical background conveys the terrible and tremendous individual dismay. A woman recalls the summer of 1945, "I needed a job. Gradually those of us who were to be evacuated began our journeys back to our bombed home towns. I joined a acquaintance and her three children. We received a permit to cross the next zone, and crawled into a truck that took us as far as Immenstadt. There we boarded a train. The French zone was the first to re-open the railroads. Of course, this pleasure lasted only until Lindau. There, we had to get another permit, but were not able to do so until the next morning.

"Frau R., with her three children, found lodging in a hayloft belonging to the German police precinct. I recalled a sister of a friend, who lived in a little chateau near Lindau. I set out, found the chateau and also the friend, who with spouse and three children had fled from Riga as far as Lake Constance. The couple, completely emaciated, was about to go out to beg some milk from a farmer who lived two hours away by foot. It was a joyful reunion. We felt joy for each person who had come through everything alive. I was even given a bed.

"Even a bed . . . In my memory, that seems to have been the most important thing. Finding a bed was in those days a stroke of good luck. The next day, then, I had to stand in line for the permit for the next leg of the journey. We found a truck, and hitched a ride. In the evening, we looked around for a sleeping space in a large hall with broken windows. I woke up during the night, crying from the cold. Frau R's thirteen-year-old daughter crept up to me and tried to warm me.

"One trip in many stages, as were all the journeys in this country at that time. By the next afternoon, we arrived in Ulm. There were benches around a table, and hot soup with noodles—free, requiring no foodstamps. The woman who had organized this food for the returning Germans was the wife of the new mayor of Ulm, the mother of the assassinated Scholl children (assassinated in 1943 by the Nazis for resistance activities) . . ."[58]

Inge Stolten, in an autobiographical report, summed up the situation of women after 1945 as "hunger for experience."[59] The women carted the debris, directed businesses, raised their children, revived cities and communities in their capacities as mayors, worked in so-called male occupations, and in effect accomplished, under the most adverse conditions, the major portion of the reconstruction of Germany, until the men returned from war prisons and sons and daughters were fully grown. Thus they achieved emancipation through praxis. Consciousness lagged somewhat behind the actual reality. The opportunities to make these advances permanent were ultimately missed. It was not so much the children that kept these women from living their own lives, as it was the striving for family happiness, which more than anything served the convenience of the men. They let all that the men had relinquished to them during and immediately after the war again be taken from their hands.

One of the first investigations of the family to appear after the war was Hilde Thurnwald's *Gegenwartsprobleme Berliner Familien* (1948).[60] This work showed just how great was the distance between the liberating thirst for experience and the regressive patriarchal structure. One sees this not only as a result of her data, but also in the social morality of the author herself. In the first decades after the war, this conflict was played out on different levels, in political parties, through publications and other media. The necessity for full equality, brought to the fore by the difficult circumstances of the war and supported by liberal and feminist positions, was debated and attacked.

This great range of opinion was also apparent in the films of the time. For example, the critical-satirical, erotic-irreverent and sacrilegious film *Der Apfel is ab* (1948) by Helmut Käutner stands in marked contrast to the bourgeois family happiness that the *Berliner Ballade,* (1948), by Buch Gunter Neumann and Regie R. A. Stemmle portray as constituting the meaning of life. Already during filming, major protests from the Archbishopric of Munich opposed handling original sin in cabaret fashion. The Bavarian military government intervened and achieved a truce in the form of a communiqué, in which Käutner explained that he had never intended to injure any religious or moral sensitivities with the production of this film. He promised that his future work on this film would be carried out in this spirit. The church, which included representatives of both Catholic and Evangelical-Lutheran persuasions, declared that it would refrain from influencing public opinion until the film was finished.

For Hilde Thurnwald, everything hinged on the renewed attempts to strengthen traditional values. Inter-family conflicts could be dealt with if families returned to the morality of the bourgeois-Christian work ethic. Conflicts were a result of individual failures, namely, the failure to adapt to one's surroundings or to respect authentic morality. Unstable families produced "inferior characters," unfit for family life, lacking in appreciation of the bourgeois virtues that define and organize private lives. Among those virtues were thriftiness, the ability to organize time and space, propensity for repetitive tasks in women and the lower classes, physical and psychological endurance (the greatest goal of which was self mastery, the ability to compromise, sacrifice, and suffer), domesticity, an understanding of budgeting and rationing, the capacity for renunciation and deferred gratification, stability, obedience, discipline, hard work, conscientiousness, taking pleasure in one's work, moderation, respect for private property . . . Everything else was considered and labeled harmful: laziness, slovenliness, depression, despair, extravagance, selfishness and egoism, promiscuity, and fraudulence. Black market dealings were denounced as moral failures. The ability of each family member to repress desires was deemed the most important positive value. Throughout, Thurnwald showed understanding for those returning from war who could accustom themselves once again to monogamy only with difficulty. At the same time, however, the violation of marriage was said to lead to the demoralization of women. It was understandable that frequently the men who returned from the war opposed the considerable independence won by the women during their separation. "Even though the man acknowledged the need for his wife to make independent decisions and take on serious responsibilities during the years of separation, he generally hoped to return to the same woman he had left." This desire increased when the man, returning demoralized from the war, was confronted with that sense of superiority characterizing the independence of the younger women. The harsh reality caught up with them through unemployment, loss of status, unsatisfying new jobs, war disabilities, defeatism, loss of home and possessions, the "faded beauty" of the wife who, "after years of shouldering heavy burdens and generally exhausting her strength, often developed a hard-hearted and rationalistic personality." According to Thurnwald, men needed to overcome their feelings of inferiority and loss of authority. Since their wives showed little understanding for the "special and difficult state of mind suffered by their returning husbands," these men fled home to their parents. With father and mother they sought, "like children, the consolation that their wives, as companions were unable to give them." Hilde Thurnwald does not deal with the fact that wives frequently cited their husbands' violence and brutality as grounds for divorce.

Hilde Thurnwald's study was intended to offer ideology-laden advice, and thus it serves as a paradigm for understanding the family in postwar Germany. Critical of the advances made during the zero hour, it went backward in time, reinstated the traditional division of labor and the internalizaiton of sex roles. "The housewife as guardian of the home and loving, nurturing, healing center of the family should undertake without gratification, the reproductive labor of giving birth to the new generation, socializing them into the acceptable morality. The man, however, should be physically, psychologically, and morally freed to concern himself with the public world away from the home. As head of the household, however, he should receive compensation for all the authority that society had either taken away from him or denied him through industrialization, technology, destruction of property, power and influence, and at that time also through Fascism, war, defeat, and the division of the German Reich . . . The strict sexual hierarchy, particularly characteristic of the bourgeois family, was presented according to the accepted perceptions and discourse of the time as 'equality in difference' . . . The ideology and structure of the family was thereby determined for many years. Opportunities to discuss the form and structure of the private lives of adults and children in terms of freedom and self-realization passed by unheeded."

WHEN WILL THERE BE PEACE?

When One Has Meat, and Asks Friends In

The power of longing, which was to become an outstanding phenomenon of cultural anthropology in bleakest Germany, concerned mainly flight from material misery. At the same time, however, such a "principle of hope" had a rekindling effect, and might one day serve to "bring back" dreams. When will that happen? Karl Schnog supplied an answer in a poem published in the *Ulenspiegel*, No. 5 (1948):

When the world is filled with laughing children,
when corn piles up and kites soar high,
when doctors have to search for patients,
when houses sparkle with "fresh paint,"
when fraying hats are thrown away,
when "excuse me" is heard on subway cars.
Then, finally then, will there be peace.

When folk build silos and storage bins,
when a young girl asks
"what are troops?"
When a pulled tooth gives the worst pain known,
and newspapers report obesity,
when the major heroes come from sports.
Then, finally, then, will there be peace.

When joyful mothers rock their babes,
and uncles send their nephews watches,
when one can freely change address,
or drive a car that one has bought,
when worn out furniture gets replaced,
when one has meat and asks friends in.
But when, dear grandchild, will that be?[61]

The *Ulenspiegel*, a magazine for literature, art, and satire, was founded by Herbert Sandberg together with Paul Rilla, Horst Lommer and Güenther Weisenborn. Sandberg, while in prison and the concentration camp, planned that if he got out he would recreate something like the *Simplicissimus.* In 1945, in Berlin, he received an American license.

At about the same time that Karl Schnog's poem appeared in the *Ulenspiegel*, the *Neue Zeitung* analyzed the pipe dreams of children and youths who participated in an essay contest for students from the elementary grades through senior high school. The main theme of the majority of the essays was food. "I could go to the bakery and get me some danishes, pretzels, and other sweets. And then I could go to the butcher and have some sausages." . . . "I see mountains of chocolate, boiled sweets, dried fruits and pudding." . . . "I run to the baker's and fetch a sack of rolls. Then I run quickly to the dairy and pick up three pounds of butter. Then I sit down in front of the shop and eat my snack." In addition to fantasies of liberation, children dreamed of freeing their fathers and other relatives from prison and other emergency situations, another dominant motif involved fantasies of departure, interlocked with food fantasies. "If I were invisible I would never go to school. Then if I got hungry I could go into farmers' pantries and get something to eat. On Sundays I would always go to the movies. I would never have to stand in line. I could go to Africa in search of adventure. I could enter every circus and cimena."[62]

The later *Wirtschaftswunder* (economic miracle) grew out of severest privation and profound existential threat, though the children and grandchildren of the war generation were hardly able to understand this. The cultural ideal of the "Americanization of reality" thus became part of an aesthetics that, after a phase of totalitarian darkness, understood human dignity as a "more beautiful life," with all its bodily and spiritual needs. This ideal, however, gradually degenerated into a fetish of consumerism.

During the time of growing East-West tensions, extensive Americanization was undertaken in order to improve living conditions. From 1947 on, Americanization was accomplished largely through the Marshall Plan, named after the American Foreign Secretary George Catlett Marshall. Early signs of this process were the food support for schools, and the care package. Individuals, groups and organizations in the United States, as well as American citizens among the occupation forces, were given the opportunity to send food to specific German recipients. Because of its content and its perfect, aesthetically pleasing wrapping, the care package fostered the mythos of the "beautiful new world." It also inspired authors and artists to "materialistic" praises. The package contained samples of earthly paradise: about 8.8 lbs. of meat, 5.8 lbs. of biscuits, 3.5 lbs. sugar and chocolate, 3.2 lbs. marmalade and pudding, 2 lbs. of vegetables, 1 lb. cacao, coffee and instant drink mixes, 350 grams of milk, 200 grams of butter, 200 grams of cheese, totaling about 40,000 calories. Within two months after the establishment of the *"Deutschen Zentralausschusses für die Verteilung ausländischer Liebesgaben"* in Stuggart on June 20, 1946, 32,000 parcels had been delivered to 27,000 recipients in the American zone. Another 68,000 orders had come in and 113,000 were on their way by ship. It was estimated that, in the future, 600,000 parcels would arrive per month for all of Germany.[63]

The 1946 census registered 46.8 million inhabitants in the four occupation zones. There were 43 million in 1939. One could be quite certain that most of them were starving. The daily ration was at first 800 to 900 calories, rising later to 1000 to 1200 calories. The minimum requirement was thought to be 2200 calories. Those living in the city without relatives or friends in the countryside suffered the most. Those depending on coupons had too little to live and too much to die. The average weight for an adult male was 51 kilograms in 1946. Only 12 percent of all children in Cologne attained the normal weight for their age at the end of 1945. In Hamburg, even one and a half years after the war, more than 100,000 people were diagnosed as having edema due to starvation. Hunger was a psychological, political and cultural phenomenon. In 1946 F. H. Rein, a nutritional scientist, wrote that no moral or material reconstruction could take place without the possibility of a natural, free choice in diet. This actually meant the abrogation of food rationing. The "search for food," he maintained, would deprive those involved in reconstruction of much of their capacity for thought and action, already weakened by chronic starvation. Attempts at currency reform would also fail because of the absence of honest means for attaining supplementary provisions. Morally upright people would undoubtedly choose the "black market" as a last resort in emergency situations. All moral education for democratic consensus through school, church and law would remain illusory so long as psychological legitimacy could be found for dishonest and self-centered action. Even law enforcing institutions would be dishonest inasmuch as they tacitly assumed that individuals would find a way to care for themselves.[64]

The activities of the English publisher and author Victor Gollancz were encouraging. As the founder of the committee "Save Europe Now" and a "brave champion of humanity and Western culture," he demanded humane living conditions for the Germans. In November 1946, while on a trip through Germany that included the Ruhr Valley and Berlin, Gollancz strongly criticized the fact that the British people were being allotted additional rations, admittedly only a slight increase, for Christmas. In light of the situation in the Ruhr Valley, he thought this abominable, explaining that such acts not only brought despair to the people in the British occupation zone, but hurt British prestige in Germany as well. In his book *Unsere Bedrohten Werte,* Gollancz offered some practical suggestions for a British policy in Germany. He advised, for example, that the zone confusion be done away with. "Give the population enough to eat to keep them healthy. Do not confiscate the good buildings for our army and for English wives, letting the natives live between ruins. Have respect for civil rights. Support the democratic parties. Give democracy a chance!" Gollancz discussed the breakdown of European morality and the dangers that would result from its disintegration. The endangered values were those values typical of Western culture. Despite the record of European cruelties, violence and greed, and despite constant relapses, these values have haltingly and painfully perservered. Gollancz suspected, however, the danger of a retrogressive development.

Victor Gollancz fulfilled a "prediction" made by Thomas Mann, "After the breakdown of the German people and the Hitler regime, the first voice raised on behalf of Germany will be that of a Jew." Many Germans considered him a protagonist of a practical, western culture, one that did not take flight into a sphere of ideas, but rather worked for the elimination of concrete problems, and encouraged humane activity. "If we do not bring the Germans at least up to the pitiful level of 1500 calories, whether through monitoring our consumption, or surrendering part of our own provisions, we will lose for Western culture that aspect of Germany that could be saved. What is even worse, we will inevitably call upon our souls something that will not be a blessing. We are confronted with a moral crisis that is perhaps more severe than the physical one we faced during the war. If humanity chooses greed, hatred and national selfishness, then it will end up, with or without the atom bomb, on a subhuman level."[65]

Most people were starving, but not all. Those who lived it up were the profiteers and black market swindlers, war profiteers and peace profiteers, people with influence and connections. People eagerly awaited a well–functioning economy, one in which they could not only live, but live well, without having to rely on "connections" and "coupons," ration cards, permits. When will there be peace? When one can freely change address, or drive a car that one has bought, when worn out furniture gets replaced.

The every day ethics had generally broken down. The "big ones" openly exhibited this fact: dismembering Germany, dismantling, unemployment. The small ones had no choice but to cheat their way through the misery. It is significant that the word "stealing" was so central in the essay contest for the "rubble children." "I would go into a shop and steal some goods." . . . "Then I would steal a car.". . . "Then I would steal gold and silver from the king's treasury." . . . "I could go to the post office and steal a few parcels." . . . "If I got hungry I could enter a shop and steal a cake." . . . "I could break in without being seen or getting caught." . . . "I would steal everything from the grocery store." . . . "I could steal an air plane." The word "stealing" took on the meaning of "organizing." It was a form of appropriation which, in the fight for survival, was legitimated, so to speak, by natural law. There is a "morality of stealing," said Margret Boveri in a commentary written during the winter of 1946–47:

"One may not steal from another person, even during those times when it is not possible to stay alive on institutional provisions. But it is acceptable to take from public funds when the general public suffers no harm. I would let the park benches stand. Fences enclosing a subway whose function has been taken over by growing hedges I would cart off without scruples. They would have rotted away anyway in one or two years. Moreover, it is no longer necessary to try to prevent people from falling down subway embankments when they have experienced several years of air–raids and even city battles. With this report, it is not my intention to encourage others to steal wood, rather, I wish that everyone, myself included, would be allotted a ration of wood or coal. I would merely like to describe the situation in Berlin today. For I am not the only one. Early today I caught a woman, I moved closer to her and told her, reassuringly, 'Don't be afraid, I'm also involved.' Responding in a hard and mean-sounding East Prussian dialect, she said, 'We're being forced into it!'"[66]

The Black Market

The black market came about because the Reichsmark became almost worthless as legal tender. Due to the high cost of armaments, too much money was circulating in Germany. In light of the small quantity of goods available for trade, people exchanged goods for goods, or cigarettes were substituted for money. The workings of this operation were described in the *Telegraf* in June, 1947, "A hungry friend was offered a pound of butter for 320 Reichsmark. He took it on credit, for he did not have that much money. He wanted to pay for it the next day. He gave half a pound to his wife. With the rest we went 'compensating.' In a tobacco shop the half pound was worth 50 cigarettes. We kept ten of them for ourselves. The remainder we took to a pub. We smoked one cigarette, and we were able to get a bottle of wine and a bottle of liquor for the 40 cigarettes. We took the wine home and the liquor to the countryside. Soon I found a farmer who exchanged two pounds of butter for the liquor. On the next morning my friend gave the first butter supplier his pound back. Our compensation had brought one and a half pounds of butter, one bottle of wine, ten cigarettes and the pleasure of conducting a tax free business."[67]

The skill of wheeling and dealing, the totally unheroic cleverness with which official regulations were violated because the black market was, of course, strictly prohibited, fostered the agility of the person who no longer felt bound to "great heroic deeds." "You are nothing, your people is everything." These people learned not to pursue their desires in a straight line, but to take a meandering route. Here on the black market, free enterprise was already practiced, in contrast to the bureaucratized, controlled economy which, with its ration–card thinking, attempted fair distribution of scarce provisions, but succeeded only in creating frustrating lines.

It must also be said, however, that the black market followed the structure of social Darwinism, especially with respect to the activities of the big profiteers. The weak grew more and more exploited, and the strong were able to accumulate more goods. In a 1947 report, Thaddäeus Troll referred to the "black market as Janus-faced." On the one hand, its consequences were economically destructive and humanly demoralizing. On the other hand, the severity of the conditions of life made the black market indispensible for the survival of many, saving hundreds of thousands from demoralization and starvation.[68] The crude commercial thinking, the fierce concentration on material goods, the elevation of ecomony to the level of ideology all resulted from the black market. It provided the incubation period for the *Wirtschaftswunder* and the apprenticeship of the later captains of economy; in short, it was the precursor of the ensuing free market. "This is not only true in the figurative sense, for the bases for most of the big fortunes that were made in a matter of a few years with the new German mark were laid by hoarding goods in the days of the black market. No one who experienced it will ever forget the astonishment with which people stared into the shopwindows the day after the currency reform. They had been empty for years, and suddenly overnight they exhibited such wonders as watches and nylon shirts."[69]

When the Swiss publisher Adolf Guggenbühl summed up, in *Die deutsche Tragödie,* his impressions from his first trip through Germany after the war, he understood the black market as a consequence especially of the disastrous nutritional conditions that resulted not only from a scarcity of goods, but from the organized chaos of a controlled economy. Only a free market economy could make the enervating, absorbing, and illegal bustling unnecessary. Among other things, he expressed the decline of cultural morality in Germany with the example of the 65 year-old-wife of a rector who, while once very distinguished, had to sustain her family by going on "hamster trips."

"Since in Bochum there had not as yet been any potato distribution for the winter, she decides, as does everyone else, to go to the countryside to acquire this important food. By giving up a pair of old boots that had belonged to one of her sons, she is able to get an old potato sack and a primitive cart, a board on four small wheels. Frau Pasedag then travels 200 kilometers into the region of Hannover, to a farmer whose daughter used to work as her maid. She travels the whole night through. It is two hours from the railway station to the farm. She finally reaches her destination, only to find that the farmer died in the war. Other people now live on the farm. They refuse to part with anything. Thus she begins to knock at random on strangers' doors, as other 'hamsters' do. Often no one opens the door, or she is too afraid to approach the house because of a big, snarling dog. Finally, she finds a farmer who is willing to give her 50 kilograms of potatoes. 'Money, out of the question. What else do you have?' Like thousands of German women in similar situations before her, she pulls her gold wedding ring from her finger. The farmer already has dozens of such rings in his possession. One the way back to the station the makeshift cart breaks down. The old lady has no alternative but to carry the potatoes on her back, resting every ten minutes. When she finally reaches the station, the train she planned to take is long gone. She is forced to spend the night in the waiting room. She does not dare to fall asleep for fear that the potatoes will be stolen. The next morning, as she goes to board the train, she discovers that all the cars are already overcrowded and that hundreds more are waiting to board with their sacks, bales, and suitcases. The old lady is unable to push her way in. She has no choice but to take another train, and then to transfer. She sits totally exhausted atop her potato sacks. Suddenly the train stops. Everybody out, inspection! A wave of despair rushes through the crowd of hamsterers. But nobody revolts. The traded goods are confiscated by police without compensation. Frau Pasedag arrives more dead than alive in Bochum, without potatoes, without wedding ring. Unfortunately, her only shoes were damaged on her adventurous journey. She must undertake another trip, sacrifice the other wedding ring, and then perhaps she will succeed in getting the urgently needed potatoes."[70]

In October 1947, the *Frankfurter Hefte* reported a farm search in some counties in Lower Bavaria. Sums of cash averaging 150,000 marks were found, as well as supply stores that would last for more than a decade. An investigation in Hesse produced similar results. On one farm, enough sheets of leather had been accumlated to cover the shoe requirement for the farmer's family and servants for the next forty years or more. Chests were filled with horseshoes and nails; closets with linen; mouldy bacon. Granted, there were many upright and decent farmers. It is certain, though, that the starving people from the big cities no longer believed in the upright and decent majority. "One farm house has already been set on fire; near the big cities, whole fields are being robbed, it looks like an organized, mass raid. Semi–legal 'direct action' is being taken by unions. There are already rumors that people are determined to get back what they dragged to the countryside. In other words, an active opposition is beginning to form against what is felt to be a direct class struggle on the part of farmers. The fact that the occupation forces will be able to prevent the worst from happening does nothing to change the situation itself."[71]

Also in the *Frankfurter Hefte,* Clemens Münster noted that the farming population, apart from some honorable exceptions, had failed to master the two tasks facing it that year. First, it failed to deliver all its goods, keeping in mind the generous allowance it took for itself, and to make use of all available means for the increase of production. Second, it failed in its task of receiving refugees from the eastern regions. It was recognized, however, that while the farmers were largely responsible for the difficulties in this regard, they were not the only ones to blame. Those aware of the typical relationships between large and small farmers of a village, and between farmers of a village and other people living there but working in other capacities, would not be surprised about this failure, nor about the fact that the average productivity of small farmers and cottagers was greater by far than that of the large farmers. "This failure to meet the two tasks under the current circumstances reveals also the erosion of Christian life in the village. For it is tantamount to a failure of justice and of love, the highest and first commandment. Thus, it comes as no surprise that no major differences could be observed between Catholic and Protestant, and Christian and non Christian villages."[72]

The little tragedies of the black market years, which contributed to the great guilt of the time, received almost legendary expression in the film *The Third Man,* based on a book by Graham Greene and directed by Carol Reed. It treats of a penicillin profiteer, Harry Lime (Orson Welles) who feigns death to escape police investigations. Calloway (Trevor Howard), the chief of the British military police, takes Limes's friend, the American author Holly Martins (Joseph Cotten), on a hospital tour, drastically illustrating the many who vegetated and died because profiteers diluted the medicine. Martins helps search for Lime, who, after a suspenseful pursuit through the Vienna canals, is finally killed. The film ends as it began, only with the real funeral of Lime. That the film with its "nervous" zither music by Anton Karas, moved the people of the rubble years so deeply, almost mystically, was largely due to the fact that the medication that had been made the object of criminal manipulation was also very much in demand at the time. Americanization of life promised liberation from illness and epidemics, to which the suffering Germans were no strangers.

When will there be peace? "When doctors have to search for patients!" With the aid of penicillin, streptomycin, and paludrin, to which later antibiotics, especially sulfonamides and streptomycine were added, grown, in the truest sense, on American "fertile soil," sicknesses previously considered deadly could now be healed, often quickly. It was considered a great blessing that there was a 99 percent success rate in the use of penicillin against pneumonia, a prevailing sickness due to malnutrition. In 1946, the United States alone produced 800 billion units of penicillin per month, shipping it to almost every country.[73]

Cities Plan Rebuilding

When will there be peace? "When houses sparkle with 'fresh paint.'" The people of the rubble years, a migrating culture, longed to settle down. What existentialist philosophy referred to as "being thrown" was part of daily experience. The unsettled wanted to rediscover their homes and native lands. Children searched for their parents, and parents for their children. Those who had been evacuated strove to return to their cities, even though they were a desert of ruins. Those expelled searched for a place to settle. Those coming home from war hoped to find security in family and profession. Emigrants were tired of foreign countries. In March 1946, on the occasion of a conference of former prisoners of war, the Bavarian Minister-President Wilhelm Hoegner said, "Now that you have come home, many of you find your birthplace destroyed. Do not despair, for you are young. Your homeland invites you to work unceasingly, with a faith in the future that can move mountains, and with a will that can accomplish the impossible. If you are inspired, you will work your way out of this disconsolate present into a better future." One of the conference participants quoted Friedrich Hebbel, "The German people are not cautious, and lose again and again their political and economic freedom. When they recognize what they have missed, they will work to the bone until they again possess this freedom." He continued, "Thus we will work ourselves to the bone at this time, during these days, weeks, and years, until we again possess a decent life and a genuinely positive political and economic freedom."[74]

To be at home means to live in a dignified manner. In 1947, author Rudolf Krämer-Badoni, at that time the editor of the newspaper, *Die Wandlung,* analyzed the life of the rubble city Frankfurt. He estimated that it would take 18 years to rebuild the city with the available skilled workers, assuming the smooth delivery of the necessary materials. Through the effects of the war, 44.4 percent of the apartments were destroyed. The average number of persons per room was 1.37; in 1939 it was 0.8. This data doesn't perfectly portray the situation, since the quality of the rooms had degenerated. Now each makeshift room, eg. the cellar, attic, and even the kitchen, was included in the reckoning. Krämer-Badoni reported on a number of visits through apartments in cellars of very different qualities.

They were mirrors of a society that, despite its radical intermingling, still manifested clear class differentiation. Take, for example, Herr L. He is lucky. Because of his former job with a major firm, he has connections. Thus he can live comfortably, even build a wooden floor. Though his walls are wet, they are covered by an extensive library. The front room, which gives the impression of a grandiose hall from the wild west, leads directly to the garden where there is an arbor under large, old trees. Herr L. and his wife are not hurting for food, and they still have enough possessions left over to peddle at the black market. "Hmm, the next sacrifice will be one of our Persian rugs."

Another cellar is cold and damp. The only utility is electric lighting. One of the children has rheumatism of the joints, and had to lie across chairs for three months because the beds had become too wet. A small stove, an army locker, and a chest. "Where and how did they live before? On Obermainstrasse in two rooms and a kitchen. In 1937, her husband died of tuberculosis. She goes to work. Her husband didn't pay enough in, so she receives no pension. She has no fuel as yet; in May, her fuel rations and various other belongings were stolen. She showed me the police report. As of yet, despite much running around, she still has not been able to find someone to issue a duplicate. In winter, after the thaw, there were 30 cm of water in the cellar. She has been living this way for two years. 'There they build churches,' says the cave dweller, bitterly. 'When the *Paulskirche* is finished, I will move into the sacristy.'"[75]

These were the apartments in which the will to rebuild developed, advancing slowly from improvement to improvement, frequently immobilized by obstacles or ending in despair.

In light of the devastation of the war, it was estimated that 6.5 million apartments were needed. "Rebuilding? Technologically, financially impossible, I tell you. What do I say? Psychologically impossible! However, it is possible to build simple rooms on the present foundations and out of salvageable debris . . . bright rooms in which a simple law, equal and understandable for all, is discussed and decided upon . . . no small print . . . no embellishment. Rise, up, lawyers and architects! Plan and design models, rooms of pure, simple clarity and power . . . rooms in which our children and grandchildren can follow honorably and freely the universally accepted law!" This passage comes from Otto Bartning's *Ketzerische Gedanken am Rande der Trümmerhaufen* (Heretical Thoughts at the Edge of the Rubble Heaps),[76] which characterizes the mood of the survivors who experienced, after a total war, total defeat. The dominant mood was one of despair, pessimism, and resignation. In almost every city, however, people began to work on restoration plans based on more optimistic premises.

The new layout of Berlin *("Kollektivplan")* was to become extremely important for the architectural history of postwar Germany. It incited, for the first time, intensive discussion of city planning. Developed under the direction of Hans Scharoun, the first planning officer after the war, this layout did not preserve much of historical Berlin. Freeways were the focal point, only the city center and the area around the museum were spared, as memorials to old Berlin. Scharoun wrote, "What remains after everything has been torn apart by bomb attacks and the final phase of the war, enables us to rebuild a real city." Furthermore, "In our opinion, the large city is not outmoded. It has not, however, been given its true form as yet. When we think of Prague as a picturesque city, Paris as the salon of the world, New York as the expression of technological power, Rome as the Eternal City, or London as the culmination of spiritual traditions, we understand them to be expressions of specific motifs. One thing is certain, the large cities are cultural, political, and economic centers that cannot simply be wished away." Applied to Berlin, this meant for Scharoun a whole new street plan. He considered the previous radial and circular roads antiquated. The spacious and equally important residential and business districts of the modern large city necessitated a system of roads that could serve them both. Efficient use of modern transportation demanded a distinction between pedestrian and vehicular traffic, creating footpaths, bicycle paths, motorways and tramways. "We don't need any race tracks through Berlin, but rather a system of parallel and perpendicular highways." It was calculated that even with the expense of this road development, considerable savings would be made in the long run. Already by 1927, 32,000 accidents with 15,000 deaths and injuries had caused expenditures reaching 1.2 billion marks, while the cost of building roads and bridges came to only a half billion marks. Through such a system of roads, business and residential districts could be coordinated so that business traffic would not congest the roads. The residential areas would then be more attractive, thereby curbing the flight of highly qualified workers to the suburbs. The intention was to organize basic units of about the size of the center of Siemensstadt so that they would reflect the unity of life. These would be comprised of apartment buildings, single family homes, dwellings for single people, and visitor accomodations. There should also be a cultural and social center, with clinic, kindergarten, nursery school, movie house, theater, library and so on. For every group of eight units, there should be a hospital and an outpatient unit, and for every group of 16, a swimming pool. The school system, too, should be organized according to the city structure. Each basic unit should have an elementary school, and perhaps a high school. With this plan, it would be possible to take systematic advantage of the open spaces brought about by the war's devastation. Residential areas could be opened up to the sun and fresh air. The city center would become the window of Berlin in the most comprehensive sense. An exhibition center and theater for world premieres, a meeting place and conference hall in one. Furthermore, newspapers, magazines, book publishers, paper wholesalers, the export industry, clothing manufacturers, insurance companies, banks, businesses, and the film industry were all to be included. They would stand along side the administrative buildings of governmental and other public institutions. Lastly, malls, theaters and museums.[77]

Big city of the future. The Charter of Athens, Le Corbusier's program for city planning from 1928, sends its greetings. The devastation wrought by war seemed to offer the chance for architects, who had renounced organic growth in favor of geometric spaces and planetarian abstractions, to realize their visions. The exhibition "*Planungen zum Wiederaufbau Berlins*" in 1946 was happy to accept alternative ideas of historical worth. This exhibition became the focus of the rebuilding of the city of Nuremberg. For example, it was determined that the network of medieval streets and lanes should be preserved. The houses should have Franconian gables and should never be so high as to block the view of the castle.

Thus we have various viewpoints on the rebuilding of Germany. The one orientation, influenced by the functionalist architecture of Mies van der Rohe, Gropius, and Scharoun, opted for a radical, modern, and comprehensive solution in light of the magnitude of destruction. With the most progressive architectural minds, new "city organisms" were to be created. In 1947, the same year that the Marshall Plan, part of the anti-communistic Truman Doctrine, was decided upon, thus guaranteeing comprehensive foreign aid to Germany, the American military adminstration sponsored a lecture tour to Germany by Walter Gropius. In his lectures he re-instated the idea of the "*Bauhaus*" and praised Scharoun as the best planner and architect for the country. This socially conscious architecture, once expelled from Germany, was brought back to a bewildered Germany as a symbol of freedom and individuality by one of its most prominent representatives. The modern architecture was supposed to represent and mirror the honesty, transparency, and openness of the young country. Its light, eager, liberal, and international style was completely focused on the progress of technology and civilization, and expressed the social and utopian ideal of equal housing. It was opposed to provincialism, folkishness, monumentalism, and historism, especially since National Socialism favored these forms of architecture.[78]

The other orientation emphasized the need to guard and preserve the past, and was committed to the restoration of old city centers. In 1947, Heinrich Tessenow, referring to four proposals for the rebuilding of the inner city of Lüebeck, said that the "most hygenic demand" that everyone should have light, sun and a garden cannot always be applied to old residences, and likewise, historical city centers may not be redesigned to suit the modern demands of traffic. He criticized those solutions conceived almost exclusively in the interests of automobile traffic, suggesting the preservation of the houses that still remained standing, and rejecting the expansion of roads. He argued that some of the destroyed buildings should be restored in their previous locations, and some new open areas created.

Whichever camp won then determined the restoration of the respective city. In Munich, Nurenberg, Freiberg, Mainz, and Wüerzburg, a careful, historical restoration was undertaken in line with the principle of preserving the historical layout. In Berlin, Hannover, Frankfurt, and Cologne, the "new style" succeeded, thus completely changing the street structure in accordance with the demands of traffic.

The architect Alfons Leitl wrote an article in support of the modernists in the *Frankfurter Heften* of July 1946. He argued that most city planners showed a compromising half–heartedness that was downright shocking. Except for Hannover, he said, almost no city had presented a fundamentally new idea, only preservation, restoration, or at most cautious correction. Apparently, this was what the city officials and citizens believed in. The basic issue was not one of the street and city design, building locations or what to do with spaces, but of new spiritual and material changes. "For fifty years, city planners and social reformers have led a sacrifical crusade against the architectural inheritance of the nineteenth century, against the excesses and distortions of our cities. Today we have the ominously unique opportunity not only to make small improvements, but to make fundamental revisions. In all this talk about historical preservation, doesn't the tremendous responsibility toward present and future life force us to discover ideas and solutions that are comprehensive and logically consistent? Today, should we not design anew a well structured, livable and life-fulfilling city capable of answering our spiritual, physical, social and artistic needs? It could happen, however, that a conscientious city architect, an experienced and wise teacher of city planning, is confronted by a wave of rebellion because of his logical suggestion that the old, totally destroyed city center not be rebuilt, but that a completely new city be constructed at a more suitable location."[79]

Time and again, the modernists and traditionalists were able to find a common denominator. The *Aufruf zum Neuaufbau* (Call to Reconstruction) of 1947, bears the signature of such different personalities as Willi Baumeister, Richard Doecker, Egon Eirmann, Hans Schmidt, Hans Schwippert, Max Taut, Wilhelm Wagenfeld, Heinrich Tessenow and Otto Bartning. In "almost biblical language, this publication speaks of 'the visible collapse' as an 'expression of a spiritual derangement,' demanding simplicity and authenticity."[80]

The quarrel over the Goethe House in Frankfurt am Main (Goethe's birthplace on the Hirschgraben) became a point of convergence for the opposing ideas of the modernists and traditionalists. Ernst Beutler, director of the Goethe Museum and of the "*Freien Deutschen Hochstifts,*" wanted to restore the Goethe House to its original condition, a task which would involve imitating destroyed parts. Karl Jaspers, Ernst Robert Curtins, and Max Planck immediately agreed with the plan. Others, such as Reinhold Schneider, Leopold Ziegler and Karl Scheffler opposed such restoration. Schneider wrote, "Are we not creating a lie to help us bear our losses, our pain, and the disaster of our history? . . . The Goethe House would hardly have been destroyed if we had preserved the poet's dignity and commitment to humanity . . . We cannot avoid the question, Would such a deceptive imitation of the Goethe House really honor his spirit?" Admirers of Goethe from home and abroad gave generous donations for the restoration of his house. The architect Otto Bartning said, "This discussion allows for a both/and; however, for architects and construction workers, there is only an either/or." For example: should the new Goethe House be completely plumb and level, or give the appearance of being settled? Should the stucco ceiling, once made by hand, remain white as in the days of Goethe's father, somewhat dirty as in 1832, or quite dirty as in 1932? An undestroyed door is to be put in its place, shall the doorstep have sharp edges or should it be somewhat worn? Should the other doors be copied with all their carvings? Can the wizard be found who can simulate the originals? In the antique business, this is called forgery. . . . The result, thinks Bartning, would be a pseudo-Goethe

House, in which one would no longer be able to differentiate between the original and the imitation. The way to the Goethe House should not be through stylistic architectural forms transmitted from past to present, but in the solemn feelings one experiences when crossing the threshold that Goethe's own foot once touched. Bartning suggested the construction of simple rooms upon the foundation of the original house. They could then reflect the former proportions and conditions of light in order to receive, in a dignified and neutral manner, the salvaged furniture, pictures and household articles. All other rooms needed by the *Hochstift* should be simple additions to this central part.

With the Goethe House, a discussion that pertained to almost all the destroyed or badly damaged historical monuments of Germany was settled. The question was: romanticism or reality? In his *Gedanken über den Wiederaufbau* of July, 1947, Bruno E. Werner framed the question as follows, "Will the day come when imitations and wax replicas of cities will take the place of the real thing? Or will we have the courage to leave behind that which has been destroyed, creating in its stead a new and living architectural achievement that reflects the spirit of the present, the new building materials, and the new tasks?"[81] What Bruno E. Werner did not understand was that no matter how rigorous and "honest" his functionalist ideas of architecture might appear, they could easily be usurped by economic thinking. More than anything, the "clarity" of the concrete was inexpensive. The question was less one of metropolis than of profitopolis.

Immediately following the war, discussions of the respective conceptions of reconstruction involved mainly disputes over designs and blueprints. First of all, the cities had to be cleaned up, the dwellings passably repaired, and bombed out areas filled with cheap and simple buildings. Improvised and provisional constructions characterized the building activity. Special attention was always given to cleaning away the debris. The strength of the will to rebuild could be determined by the "cleanliness" of the removal. Due to the lack of materials and expertise, the removal of rubble was followed by very few deeds of reconstruction, at least until the currency reform. In contrast, however, illegal employment flourished. Thus the word "reconstruction," which had initially aroused the nation, lost its effectiveness. Especially demoralizing was the fact that building materials were peddled on the black market, so that only those with connections and items to trade were able to restore and improve their places of residence and business.

Swinging Tavern Life

The place where people felt more at home than in their scantily repaired rooms in deserted corners of the city was an "ethereal one." The sound and ether waves played no small part in the development of a more light hearted dimension of life.

"The whole world seems to be preparing for a super spring of art. To live like a gypsy, behind broken windows, without a book or a second shirt, undernourished and without coal in the winter was not a problem. One had life. Nothing more was needed to begin anew." So wrote Erich Kästner in September, 1945.[82] Such a lofty mood had musical undertones from the beginning. The transition from Wagnerian music to American jazz was a clear sign of the cheery, "swinging times." Although jazz was condemned during the Third Reich as "nigger art," it survived in private places, especially among youth critical of the regime. Walter Kempowski relates that his brother Robert, a jazz fan, owned so many shellac records during the war that he filled 10 tightly written sheets of typewriter paper wtih around 250 titles ranging from Ambrose and Armstrong to Fats Waller and Benny de Weille.[83] Such youths were called "Swing-Heinis." Swing was the music by civilians for civilians. It was specially broadcast in World War II by Allied military stations, branches of the BBC on the French coast. The music of Benny Goodman, Tommy Dorsey, Artie Shaw and especially Glenn Miller inspired the common soldiers, who then as POW's were inspired by these melodies that testified to a new feeling for life. Many German professional and amateur musicians played in American clubs after their return.

"After the lethal drug of snappy, cynical marches, the music of the oppressed brought many people together again. We have experienced this with jazz. Originating with the songs sung by slaves on the cotton fields of the southern states, jazz articulates the rising of the oppressed of all the world, strumming away boundaries between races, and prohibitions of fraternization.

"Musically understood, it is only a small step from oppression to freedom. With the 2/4 rhythm of the march, state authorities command obedience; with the 4/4 rhythm into which one slides almost imperceptibly from the 2/4 rhythm, the fighting spirit disappears, people loosen up, and swing with each other in fellowship.

"We experienced it. We listened around and slipped in unnoticed when jazz musicians, both Americans and Germans, met at night at the end of their formal entertainment in order to make music together. Not for dancing, not for the public, just for their own private enjoyment, freely improvising, without sheet music, without pay, without time limits.

"Such journeys into the realm of sound were called 'jam sessions.' Here jazz advanced as a living language; new syntaxes, new forms of expression, and new harmonies developed naturally.

"Variations on known pieces occasionally led to new ones. One person began with a theme, someone else took it over or responded, a third played a contrast. They entered into captivating instrumental dialogues, ultimately uniting in one final, bold and harmonic movement, relishing their unity despite their differences of color and nationality. They did this over and over again, for it was so beautiful . . ."[84]

From a cultural perspective, zero hour was the hour of the radio. Theaters and movie houses were often either destroyed or confiscated by the victors. The curfew kept people tied to their houses, so the radio provided welcome relief.

"Those of us who were making up for our lost youth sat nightly in front of the radio to listen to what was no longer forbidden, Swing from AFN, the Allied military network. So when Mark White, the small, slight disc jockey for the program *Midnight in Munich,* announced the records in his deep, sonorous voice, we indulged ourselves in a feeling for life. At midday we were fueled with the Swing from *Luncheon in Munich,* a daily program broadcast from the fomer palace of the painter, Friedrich August Kaulbach."[85]

Radio Munich, a station the military government began in 1945, attempted re-education not only with lectures, but especially with snappy music. Together with Werner Gotze, Jimmy Jungermann took over *Midnight in Munich* from the Americans and changed it into *Mitternacht in Munchen,* one of the hottest jazz programs in Europe. The program aired for two years. Sixty thousand listener requests poured in, one third asking for "Don't Fence Me In."

"A sigh of relief could be heard through this music, and through that of the following years. A breath of freedom and optimism came from the new titles, as well as from the old ones that could now be listened to without fear of reprisal. The light shined again as Harry James played 'I'm Beginning to See the Light' on his trumpet. Doris Day painted the 'Sentimental Journey' on a slowly dawning horizon. Peggy Lee pointed to 'Mañana,' and all the worries faded away when Louis Armstrong comforted us in 'Blueberry Hill' with 'I'll Bring My Horn With Me.' At the same time, the Andrew Sisters brought American symbols into German postwar life with 'Rum and Coca Cola.'

The Destroyed Fountain of Hercules at the Lütowplatz in Berlin, 1946. PHOTO: FRIEDRICH SEIDENSTÜCKER.

Bombed Street in Hamburg, 1945.

Franz Radziwill, *Die Welt ohne Verhältnisse* The World Without Relations, 1947.

Berlin Ruins, 1945.

Evacuees Return to Berlin, 1945.

The "Hamsters," 1947. PHOTO: FRIEDRICH SEIDENSTÜCKER.

Munich Dwelling, 1947.

Women of the Rubble Years in Berlin, 1945.

Lunch Break, Berlin, 1948. PHOTO: FRIEDRICH SEIDENSTÜCKER.

Friseur
Damen

Overlooking Demolished Dresden, 1945.

"The first German jazz record after the zero hour appeared in East Berlin. Rex Stewart, the trumpet player of Duke Ellington's band, played with German musicians. It was a time of encounter. Freddie Brocksieper had never dared to dream that he would even see Lionel Hampton, that master from across the ocean, let alone play music with him.

"Margot Hielscher said, 'A time in which there is too little to eat and no place to sleep becomes fantastic only through music.'"[86]

The tavern, and not only the jazz tavern, was central to the entertainment of the rubble years. Because these rooms were more easily able to withstand bomb attacks, they could be restored with relatively little work. The tavern-cabaret, the taverny-variety show, the tavern-restaurant with music and entertainment mushroomed, their cosmopolitan aims far overreaching their means. Dancing schools experienced a renaissance. Graduating from dance school, people formed dance clubs, privately sponsoring balls. Since the big city dance halls were destroyed, country inns and restaurants had to be used.

Jazz was popular, but only with the minority, the majority still did not want to get involved with "black art." Thus, the common dance music was moderately modern to conservative. The newly developing dance and entertainment orchestras set a tone of refinement that corresponded to a regressive longing, the desire for the five-o'clock tea culture of the Weimar Republic. This culture continued to exist in certain metropolitan areas of the Third Reich, combining with the Viennese race romanticism promoted by the state authorities. Symptomatically, in 1947 Radio Munich limited its jazz programs in favor of "*Volksmusik*," and already by 1948 produced the record "Capri-Fischer" by Polydor "under permit No. B 510 of the media control organ of the military government." It had already been copyrighted in 1943. The fact that people soon gave up Boogie-Woogie and Swing, taking up instead the waltz, tango, and polka, was associated with an improved lifestyle. Long skirts became fashionable, indicative of the new social prestige that began to supplant the fundamental and spontaneous joy of living that had characterized the rubble years.

In any case, whether people were swinging or doing the polka, peace was in the air. The desire for life avoided contact with a gloomy and inwardly directed Germany. The warning voices were unsettling, but they did make themselves heard.

GUILT AND ATONEMENT

A Shaken Conscience Awakens the Conscience

"Everywhere the tolling of bells announces victory and peace; there is abundant toasting, embracing, and well wishing throughout the land. The Germans, however, who once lost their nationality at the hands of those least fit to pronounce such judgments, and others who were forced to avoid their country because of its gruesome behavior and begin anew in friendlier territory, these Germans bowed their heads while the world rejoiced. It was heart wrenching to ponder the significance of this joy for Germany. The country would have to endure dark times, years of degradation in expiation for its deeds. It would be a long time before people would again have the strength for self-reflection."[87]

Thomas Mann, in his fifty-fifth and final radio broadcast from America to Germany, urged his compatriots to undergo radical changes. The British Broadcasting Corporation, BBC, had carried his talks since 1940. In the beginning, written texts were cabled to London, where they were then read aloud, later, records of the poet's talks were made in Los Angeles, sent by air to New York, and from there carried by telephone to London, where a new recording was made and played before a microphone. Mann spoke with all the pathos of a *"Praeceptor Germaniae,"* of an exile who had been proven right, who was filled with understanding of his profoundly degraded nation. Now this nation must atone for its wrongs, including those committed against him, eg. revoking his German citizenship. It was precisely those people who were persecuted, exiled, or driven into inner or outer emigration, who felt obliged to come to terms with German guilt and to bring about a "purification" (catharsis) through atonement.

Among the first books to be published after the war was Reinhold Schneider's *Das Unzerstörbare* (The Indestructible). Schneider, born in Baden-Baden in 1903, dealt primarily with historical topics from an unorthodox point of view. "The secret of the crucifixion is undeniably the answer to history." He carried out his campaign against the Nazi unspirit on two levels. For those generally unfamiliar with literature and history, he wrote a number of reflections, meditations, sermons and sonnets. Others were presented with extremely fastidious historical treatises which, in the tradition of Friedrich Schlegel's notion of "prophetic hindsight," were able to speak to the immediate present when dealing with the past. Schneider was deeply saddened by the failure of the Catholic Church and the Christian bourgeoisie to respond to the Third Reich. "At the very least, the Church should have stood beside the Synagogue on the day it was destroyed. It is of decisive significance that this did not occur. But what did I do? When I heard of the burning, plundering, and other abominations, I locked myself up in my study, too cowardly to take a stand and proclaim it."[88]

The young people, he wrote in *Das Unzerstörbare,* now enter a rubble upon which they must build their lives. They must be affected by pain and shame, and perhaps also by resentment against their ancestors for leaving them, so unprepared, to inherit this devastated world. They can never hope to fulfill more than a small fraction of their dreams, for that range of possibilities which one expects to be entitled to by virtue of one's humanity was now closed to them. They must accept the fact that contemplative life has become bitterly impoverished. It was no longer necessary to shake these youths out of their dreams; they were wide awake in the middle of a horrifying world covered with graves, debris, and guilt. A power had been let loose which despised humanity, perhaps as never before. Behind the atrocities and the suffering lay hidden a demonic passion to degrade human beings, to wrench from them the nobility of their freedom and their chosenness, and to subject them to a destiny conceived under the power of demons and to which no one anywhere should ever bow again. "It is also our pride to confine the blame first of all to ourselves, thus not speaking of the guilt of others. This 'also' is naive. Indeed, there is never any crime committed which does not have broader ramifications in the world. Yet no attitudes are implied by this 'also,' and everything hinges on this. The principle underlying atonement is that one's value is inherent, that although it may be impaired it can always be restored. The guilty person who refuses to atone loses his or her dignity completely." There may come a time in the history of a people when atonement is the only possible principle by which to live. This then becomes the historical task of that people. A truly shaken conscience awakens the conscience. "The honest acknowledgement of guilt or complicity and the firm desire to atone and purify oneself will not go unheeded as long as there are people of good will upon this earth. Truly we can never in our lives hear a confession of guilt without at the same time recognizing and admitting our own guilt. Responsible atoning patience is the power which is able to overcome any suffering. Consequently, those who take guilt upon themselves may speak with a voice that reaches further into the future, that is of greater historical value, than the voice of the accuser. Only those who change themselves can hope to bring about change in the world. Those who change carry the power for change. There is no longer any question that this world, which now stands under unparalleled judgment, must change from its very core." May it be the great privilege and act of grace of the young people to serve as the "voice of change."[89]

Immediately after the war, many outstanding poets and philosophers were inspired, whether for religious or for humanitarian reasons, to engage in an intense and far reaching dispute with National Socialism. With a contrite heart *(contritio cordis)* they intended, through public confession *(confession oris),* to show the world that zero hour signified a turning away from error, offense, and crime. They were prepared to render whatever works were necessary for atonement *(satisfactio operis).* Can one then really speak of the collective guilt of Germany? Did the National Socialists "simply" seduce the German spirit? Did they conceal their evil intentions behind the facade of bourgeois propriety, or was the bourgeoisie actually an accessory to the crimes? Did National Socialism grow out of the German essence and culture, or was it merely an historical accident?

Sigrid Undset, the Norwegian novelist and Nobel prize winner who fled to the United States during the war, expressed her pessimism regarding Germany's re-education in an article written for the *Neue Zeitung,* October 25, 1945. In a nation of 70 million people, she wrote, it is only natural to expect to find both the good and the evil, the intelligent and the stupid. There exists, however, something like a national character that is clearly discernible. "There must be millions of German children whose fathers took part in the atrocities against civilians, women and children in Russia, Poland, Yugoslavia, Greece, France or Norway! Countless German children have parents who experienced a fleeting prosperity as a result of the plunder of

Europe, or who took part in the murder of 4 million Jews, pocketing some of the booty which had been taken from the dead! There must be millions of children whose mothers have made the German woman almost more loathesome than the German man, as they gleefully took over the homes and property of people in occupied territories, even keeping family portraits which they occasionally offered to sell back to their owners at a high price! . . . The greatest hindrance to German re-education is not German thinking, but rather the actual deeds which have been committed as a result of this thinking."[90]

Karl Jaspers responded to her article, agreeing that Sigrid Undset's indignation was completely justifiable in light of Germany's collective guilt. He added, however, that "those who are hopelessly condemned will never be able to respond. Inasmuch as they still have the will to live, they will only be capable of powerless obedience and suffering. This is not our present situation. The victors, who respect human rights, including those of the guilty, have declared that the German people will not be destroyed. This means that we have been given the chance to live. And the German people shall be educated, indicating that we must rebuild and further develop that which is good in our own way of life."

Karl Jaspers, who during the Third Reich was ostracized and removed from his teaching position, was reinstated as professor of philosophy at the University of Heidelberg. He called for a comprehensive revolution of the German consciousness, arguing for a re-education which would include the following:

FIRST. Unreserved comprehension of the activities of the previous 12 years and of the present situation. It is difficult, he admitted to look the truth in the eye. Yet one must recognize the roots and interconnections of the activities of the National Socialists, and understand that these deeds could not have been accomplished without a certain readiness in every segment of the population.

SECOND. We must learn to speak with each other, discarding forever the dogmatic proclamations, bellowing, stubborn indignation, and the type of honor that feels offended at every opportunity and thus refuses communication.

THIRD. With historical self-consciousness, we must discern the underlying basis of the millennium in which we stand. A new historical image can only emerge as a result of thorough investigation. The road from Frederick the Great to Hitler was a long one, but it is now closed. In our great misery, we are now more aware than ever that the exalted spirits of our forebears wish again to speak to us, exposing the seductive and inhumane idols. Hitler's Germany is not the true Germany. However, Germany did bring this regime into power, and, whether due to fear or active participation, allowed it to stay in power.[91]

In 1947, Jaspers won the Frankfurt Goethe Prize, and also published *Die Schuldfrage, ein Beitrag zur Deutschen Frage (The Question of German Guilt),* which deals intensively with National Socialism. One year later, he accepted a call to teach at the University of Basel. Despite his insistance that no confession was implicit in either his staying or his leaving, a certain resignation was apparent. He was drawn into the lovely world of Swiss freedom and humanity. With the allure of all of Europe and the literature of the entire globe at his disposal, he was newly motivated to develop his thought.[92] As a moral authority he always commented, as he proved in the following years on the political, cultural and social life of the Federal Republic. He did so, however, from without. He left Germany at the point when intellectual willingness for discussion with the past had already decreased.

Renunciation of Germany

There was another great moralist who did not even return to Germany. To the disappointment of many literary colleagues and his ever growing public, Thomas Mann refused to take up residence in his native land. Walter von Molo, author of historical novels and president of the Prussian Academy of Poets before 1933, tried to persuade Mann to return in August, 1945. He wrote:

"Please come back soon and give to these crushed souls consolation through humaneness; revive their faith that justice does exist, that it is indeed wrong to split humanity so cruelly, as has been done here in our recent, gruesome past. This dreadful lesson must not be lost on any human being who endeavors to live with faith and understanding in this demonic and most imperfect world, who prays to end the blood feud of our epoch and achieve a new order with the words: 'Forgive us our trespasses, as we forgive those who trespass against us, and deliver us from evil!'

"We call this humanity.

"Please, come soon and demonstrate that we have the duty to believe in co–humanity, over and over again to believe in it, for otherwise humanity must disappear from the face of the earth. There were so many slogans, so many pangs of conscience. So many have lost everything either before or during this war, absolutely everything, except for one thing: they have remained reasonable people, neither excessive nor pretentious, German human beings who have longed and continue to long for the return to that which once made us respectable in the council of all peoples."[93]

The publication of Molo's letter caused quite a sensation in Germany. His ideas were picked up in an article written by Frank Thiess, which called for the unity of the inner with the outer emigrants:

"I also have often been asked why I didn't emigrate, and I could only repeat the following answer. Should I succeed in surviving this dreadful epoch, the duration of which we completely misjudged, I will have thereby gained much for my spriritual and human development. I will have emerged richer in understanding and experience than if I had observed the German tragedy from the box seats of foreign lands. It makes a big difference whether I live through the burning of my own home or merely watch it on a weekly news program, whether I actually experience hunger or read about it in the newspapers, or whether I survive the bombing attacks or hear about them. To recognize the singular, violent downfall of a lost people through direct knowledge of a hundred individual cases is far different from registering it on one's mind as an historical fact.

"We expect no reward for not having left Germany. It was natural for us to remain here. Yet it would appear to us quite unnatural for those native sons such as Thomas Mann, who have so earnestly and deeply suffered for Germany, to fail to return today, preferring instead to wait and see if its misery will lead to death or new life. I can think of nothing worse than that they might return too late, perhaps no longer understanding their mother tongue."[94]

Thomas Mann finally responded in October 1945. With a certain irony, he stated that he was pleased that Germany wanted to have back, not only his books, but his person. And yet, "Can the events of the past 12 years simply be wiped from the slate as if nothing had happened? The year 1933 was bad enough, with the shock of the loss of my normal life, my home and country, books, memorabilia, and possessions, accompanied by petty political action at home, dismissals, and refusals. . . . The ensuing time was likewise grim, a life of wandering from country to country, worrying about visas and hotels, while my ears were daily bombarded with abominable accounts of a lost land which had grown wild and strange. You, who pledged allegiance to this 'charismatic Führer' (terrible, terrible, such base education!) and made culture under Goebbels, did not go through any of that. I am not forgetting that you experienced even more horrors which I avoided. Yet there is something you haven't known, the heartache of exile, of being uprooted, of undergoing the unnerving experiences of homelessness." Thomas Mann settled his accounts with the "denial of solidarity" that he had experienced.

"Today I am an American citizen, and long before Germany's shocking defeat I publicly and privately declared that I had no intention of ever leaving America. Of my children, I have two sons serving in the American army. They all have roots in this country, and English–speaking grandchildren are growing up around me. I, too, am in many ways already tied to this land, with relationships I must honor. In Washington, near the major universities which have given me honorary degrees, I have built my house. Here, on this beautiful, futuristic coast, in this atmosphere of power, reason, abundance and peace, I hope to complete my life's work. Frankly, I see no reason why I should not enjoy the advantages of my unusual destiny, given that I have also drunk its disadvantages to the dregs. Furthermore, it seems particularly unnecessary to forego my present life when there is nothing I can do for the German people that I can't also do from California.

"I did not plan for things to happen the way they did. Absolutely not! What occurred was a consequence of the character and destiny of the German *Volk,* a nation which is noteworthy and tragically interesting enough so that many people put up with it, suffer under it. But then the results of this should also be acknowledged, and not simply dismissed with one banal 'Return home, all is forgiven.'"[95]

Thomas Mann remained true to his role in the grandiose but questionable manner of a "comfortable martyrdom." Inwardly a sensitive, torn, and, with respect to his bourgeois life, difficult man, he was engaged in the constant and successful effort to screen his anxious and tormented life from every fatality. He was helped in this by his relativizing reflections, his distancing irony, and his undaunted stability. When he did in fact, after much hesitation, settle down in 1952 in German-speaking Switzerland, from 1954 in Kilchberg on Lake Zurich, young authors such as Ulrich Sonnemann, Walter Boehlich and Hans Egon Holthusen, were disappointed in this 'poet without transcendence.' They turned away from him. The enthusiasts of change and those ready to turn around found no mentor in this man, for whom everything had turned out to be a "civilized adventure."

Hermann Hesse, another great German author who had already been living for decades in Switzerland, having settled in Montagnola in Tessin in 1919, declined the invitation to come to Germany to help with the re-education process. "I have grown old and tired, and the destruction of my work has made my last years ones of disappointment and sorrow." Hesse decried the opportunism that was growing in Germany and that was evident in the many letters sent to him. Of the hundreds of letters he received, there were several discernable types. There were, for example, all those old acquaintances who stopped writing the moment they realized that an exchange of letters could be dangerous for them. "Now they tell me they're still alive, that they've always thought fondly of me, and envied my good fortune of living in the Swiss Paradise and that, as I suspected them to say, they had never been sympathizers of those cursed Nazis. And yet many of these confessors had been party members for years. They explain at length that during all those years they constantly lived with one foot in the concentration camp. I am compelled to answer that I could only take that opponent of Hitler seriously who had both feet in the concentration camp, not one in the camp and the other in the party."

Then there would be those letter writers who went into lengthy discussions of their contempt for Thomas Mann, expressing as well their regret or indignation that he, Hesse, could be friends with such a man. Finally, there was the group of those who publicly and unequivocally rode on Hitler's bandwagon all those years. "They give all the details of their daily lives, describing the losses incurred by the bombing, their domestic worries, their children and grandchildren, as though nothing had happened, as though there were nothing wrong between us, as if they hadn't cooperated in murdering the friends and relatives of my Jewish wife and in discrediting and ultimately destroying my life's work. None of them said they were sorry, or that they saw things differently now, that they had been deluded. Yet neither did they write that they were Nazis and would always remain so, without regrets, loyal to the cause. Would a Nazi ever remain loyal to the cause if the cause failed?"[96]

Together with Thomas Mann and Hermann Hesse, many observers and visitors to Germany stated that one could not trust the alleged inner change. Indeed, one could find everywhere those quick change artists dressed in penitential garb, yet one had to doubt the sincerity of their repentance. People were especially mistrustful of those who seemed to play an ambiguous part in the Third Reich. Among these were Ernst Jünger, Martin Heidegger, and Gottfried Benn.

People were irritated that Heidegger, who in 1933 had been elected rector of the University of Freiburg, had spoken four months after Hitler's appointment to the chancellorship of the "greatness and beauty" of this new starting point, and yet later kept his silence without any sign of humility. His spiritual existence seemed unaffected by the anxiety that prevailed around him.

Gottfried Benn had originally been fascinated with the sweeping irrationalism of the Third Reich. He was now considered dangerous for his expressive, artificial, mystical and rhapsodic lyrics that once made him the idol of those terribly misguided, academically oriented youth. He was a man who had already lived through the nihilism which many were now just beginning to experience. The tone of his language, oscillating between cynicism and melancholy, penetrated to the marrow. He gave a stylistic veneer to the yearnings and anxieties of his time.

"The German youth of 1945, forsaken and demoralized as perhaps no youth before them, were lured by the opiate of Benn's verse, confusing the nihilism of the poetry with their own despair. Truly they deserved better comfort than that. Meanwhile, throughout the world, there occurred a great turning of art towards religious and ethical themes. Germany alone remained unaware of the change. Instead of listening to the words of those who had been sacrificed, the Germans let themselves be sedated by the master of lyrical anesthesia at the very time when clear thought and a pure conscience was most important."[97] This was the judgment of Walter Muschg, who spoke with an enlightening, missionary zeal.

Leaving the Past Behind

For the moralists who pushed for re-education, Gottfried Benn's conviction that history was meaningless, that it was but "one great case history of mental illness," was a thorn in the flesh. They drew a sharp contrast between true and false history, true and false consciousness, and a true and false world of ideas.

"Will the German people, these great lovers of order, undeniably brave, talented, and yet for the most part self estranged today, possibly be able to comprehend what actually happened to them? Not externally. Soon even the blind will be able to understand the frightening logic of the entire process once they are apprised of the true facts which have been, for the part, withheld or distorted up to now. But spiritually! Will they have the capacity, the greatness of soul, in their misery and affliction to come to terms with themselves while under foreign pressure and dominion? Will they be able to humble themselves, to rediscover the depths of their humanity, finding therein a new source of liberation? Or will they instead become consumed with bigger reaction, or worse yet, with hatred against the stern executors of the fate for which they themselves had asked, and either distort or forget the horrible events for which they are responsible? Will this nation be able to undergo the most difficult task ever imposed on a great people in history, and still emerge victorious? Can it jump over its own shadow? Will it rediscover, while fighting against itself, its inner richness? If so, it will again become the equal of any other nation in the world."[98]

Alfred Weber asked these questions in the preface of his book *Abschied von der bisherigen Geschichte,* written prior to Germany's final collapse. He hoped not simply to conjure up apocalyptic visions of the decline of the West, but to suggest ways of overcoming nihilism. The zero point would never have been reached had not forces begun to emerge around 1880 which were opposed to the spirit of the West, forces which rejected the former depth of the West, which were intended to overcome nihilism but in actuality constituted its most refined climax in later, popularized versions of Nietzsche. These forces were in fact anti-spiritual, exhausting not only a refined libertinism of spirit and a brutal libertinism of power, but also in the upsurging naturalisms, imperialisms, and nationalisms. The racial theories, the eugenic calculations, which with blood and vulgarity were thrust into history, were only the demagogically leveled, flat and dreary massif that was reached with relief by a West that had rejected all depth. Only evil specters now danced a final dance on this massif, which was once unfathomable but incalculably rich. Since Germany lacked the indomitable will to exercise its own judgment and the strength to act contrary to its own advantage, the first signs of freedom disappeared, and what remained was a subjected race, today's lamb-like animals of order. The former educators, the select ones, had for the most part failed.

"Let us go forth with the formation of a new kind of education and a differently inspired selection process. Both are intimately connected. We will be a beggarly people; we will at first have but a few useful educators for the new and great task of re-educating the nation; and we will have only an old, deep-rooted routine of education and selection. If we wish to establish an educational system which transforms character and broadens judgment, we must keep in mind that Russia, alleged to be culturally backward, established a norm of twenty elementary students per teacher, and achieved something thereby. The urge to go to the people and to re-educate their ability to judge must permeate our former educators and the developing elite. Is there anything more beautiful and precious than the still unformed young person, one in whom a new ideal can be brought to fruition? The desire to create the superman, that ghastly, useless extravagance, was presumptuous folly. First and foremost, let us create the person by bringing out recessive inclinations and by driving back those which have dominated until now. . . .

Then the person will be able to make decisions freely, to say yes or no, to have a clear, unequivocal sense of his or her potential, no matter how complicated he or she may be. Then the person can live with dignity as a free citizen, even if burdened by poverty. That is what we need. Therein lies our future."[99]

The darkness was light enough. One simply had to emerge from the historical thicket and take the right road, then salvation was in sight. The "Observations and Memories" from Friedrich Meinecke's *Die deutsche Katastrophe* (1946) were similar to those historiographies that combined a pessimistic, generalizing, inventory approach with an immanent, exuberant optimism. With the justifiable painting of past German history in gray on gray, with the exposition of all its mistaken paths and dead ends, it became possible to begin a "new, humbled, yet spiritually pure existence, and to strengthen the decision to utilize one's remaining power for the salvation of the enduring substance of a people and its culture." The world spirit was contained, yet released whenever necessary. The German catastrophe was described in metaphoric and experiential language. What again and again proved to be the "final" solution was the ever reliable, "internal Germany," the Germany that never demanded change. Friedrich Meinicke concluded his monumental work in a truly moving manner, stirring the historical consciousness of the postwar years by painting a "wish image conceived in the terrible weeks after the collapse." The final passage of the book, quoted below, makes clear how little the zero hour actually lived up to its name. One experiences instead a reflowering of the affirmative culture stemming from the nineteenth century and finding security in the educated bourgeoisie that was leveled (but not exterminated) by the mass movement of National Socialism. With the help of the "true" (Goethean) Germany, prostrated Germany would again recover. Concern for the cultural heritage was an uplifting motto, enabling the transcendence of guilt and shame. Now then take from the little treasure box of Germany:

"Among the good experiences we can use, there are even some that come from the Third Reich. The clever Goebbels actually knew quite well how to catch harmless souls by placing worthwhile articles into the party shopwindows. Every Sunday morning, to detract from the church services, a 'little German treasure box' was offered on the radio. Listeners were provided with the most beautiful German music and exquisite poetic pieces. At that time I heard how the old Friedrich Kayssler, shortly before the collapse, held a Goethe afternoon in the Harnack home in Dahlem, reciting Goethe's poetry in front of a small and unusually receptive audience. My thoughts turned ultimately to the Greeks, and I realized that Homer had been infused into their hearts much more through the rhapsodists than through any readings . . .

"In every German city and larger village, we hope, in the future, to establish a society of similarly inclined cultural friends, which I would like to call 'Goethe Societies.' Might it not, however, be objected that these would provide unfair competition with Weimar's long established 'Goethe Association' and its numerous local branches? I hope not, since the tasks would be different, and there should be no monopoly on Goethe. I could even imagine and wish for a non-institutional, human and nurturing relationship between the Goethe Association and the 'Goethe Societies.'

"The 'Goethe Societies' would have the task of carrying the most lively testimonies of the great German spirit, through recitation, into the hearts of the listeners. The noblest German music and poetry would be offered at the same time. The book shortage, to which we have all been subjected due to the burning of many libraries, book stores, and publishing houses, further legitimates this suggestion. Who today is still in full possession of even his favorite books, of his complete works of Goethe, Schiller, and so on? Perhaps in the future, many young people can be introduced to the external poetry of Hölderlin, Mörike, C. F. Meyer, and Rilke through one of the regular musical-poetic celebrations of the 'Goethe Societies' which we now wish to establish permanently. Perhaps weekly we can have a late Sunday afternoon hour, and, wherever possible, even in a church! For the religious dimension underlying our great poetry justifies, yes even demands, that it be made concrete through such symbolism. The beginning and end of such celebrations should then always be elevated through great German music, through Bach, Mozart, Beethoven, Schubert, Brahms, etc.

"Lyric poetry and reflective pieces should constitute the inner core of these celebrations. Those wonderful lyrics that reached their height with Goethe and Mörike, where soul becomes nature and nature becomes soul, and those profound reflections in the style of Goethe and Schiller are perhaps 'the most German of the German' in the whole of our literature. Whoever immerses him- or herself entirely in these works, will experience, amidst all the misfortunes and the destruction of our fatherland, something indestructible, a German *character indelebilis.*"[100]

PERIOD PIECES OF HISTORICAL SIGNIFICANCE

One of the most impressive history lessons of the time was provided by Carl Zuckmayer's play, *Des Teufels General* (The Devil's General). In it he achieved a balance between empathy and condemnation, prosecution and defense, guilt and atonement. After a short delay because the Allies were somewhat slow to release it, the play appeared on nearly every German stage. In 1945, the author returned to Germany from his exile in the United States, and became a civilian cultural advisor for the American government. He hoped, through the example of the sympathetically drawn charcter of Airforce General Harras, to show how a specialist with a love for flying could succumb to the National Socialists despite his actual rejection of the party. Central to the play was the fate of Ernst Udet, airforce engineer of the German army, who in 1941 was killed, possibly murdered, while testing a new weapon. He received a state burial. The General's self-knowledge and sense of guilt had brought him to the point of deliberately entering a defective machine in order to kill himself. The juxtaposition of characters, opposite Harras stood the Gestapo man Dr. Schmidt-Lausitz, an icy, dangerous functionary, the refusal to paint a black and white picture, and the discussions of guilt and expiation that pervaded the work, rendered it, according to the *Neue Zürcher Zeitung, the* German tragedy. Does one have the moral responsibility to revolt against a criminal government, or must one always maintain one's allegiances? Should one utilize one's talents in ways that run counter to one's own beliefs, or would that make one guilty before oneself, one's country, and one's people? These were questions that especially affected those returning from the war, confronting them, at least later, with the question of their own guilt.

Great historical novels also appeared at this time, taking their place alongside the great dramatic works. Thomas Mann's *Doktor Faustus: Das Leben des deutschen Tonsetzers Adrian Leverkühn erzählt von einem Freunde,* appeared in 1947. The book stimulated considerable interest, for it dealt with the metaphysical significance of National Socialism, indirectly offering those who had succumbed to Hitler some explanation of their situation. The dangerous position of the artist, characterised by the portrayal of Leverkühn, symbolized the peril of the German soul, its oppression and ultimate annihilation at the hands of the National Socialists.

The life of the modern Faust is narrated by his friend, a schoolteacher by the name of Doctor Serenus Zeitblom. The composer, who comes from one of the best German families, attended high school in a little, somewhat medieval town, went on to study theology, and later music. An infection contracted in a bordello results, in later years, in a progressively advancing madness. Adrian moves to Munich, where the decaying bourgeois society is depicted through an extensive panorama of characters and events. While on a trip though Italy, Leverkühn meets the devil. It becomes apparent that the prostitute Esmeralda, had also been one of Satan's tools. Leverkühn would now achieve great things with the help of the devil. After an 18-year absence from his own country, during which time he wrote his musical compositions, he finally succumbs to his madness. Just as he hopes to play his last composition the symphonic cantata, "The Lamentations of Dr. Faust," for a couple of friends, he falls dead. It is 1930. The narrator, however, carries the story to the end of World War II. The correspondence between Leverkühn's death and the collapse of Hitler's Reich is typical of the parallelism Mann employs in this work. "The Germans always come too late. They arrive late, just like music, which is always the last of the arts to give expression to a world situation, if in fact it even manages to capture it before it disappears. And, like this beloved art, they are abstract and mystical to the point of criminality." So wrote Thomas Mann in an essay entitled *Germany and the Germans.* In Germany, one either seeks solutions and salvation in a highly cultural aestheticism, or turns to a kind of instinctual primitivism. "The proud spirit, threatened with sterility, thirsts for freedom from inhibitions at any price." In a discussion of his novel, Mann drew the parallel between this "proud spirit" and the "depraved German euphoria with the fascistic nationalist frenzy that ends in collapse."[101]

Doktor Faustus, as a book of the end, written from the perspective of the end, is an attempt to conjure up the "feeling of the end in every possible sense," the end of the bourgeois artist, of the bourgeoisie, of all previous art, of all previous philosophy; the end of traditional humanism, the end of rational and scientific notions, of the liberal state, the capitalist society. The Germany that existed up to now is perishing. Those who have represented our cultural life up to this point are now beginning their descent into hell.[102] Serenus Zeitblom's "epilogue" to the biography of Leverkühn ends with words that indeed offer hope, but only insofar as one is able to see, from the bottom of the abyss, the light of hope.

"Germany, with feverishly red cheeks, reeled from the heights of its depraved triumph, cherishing notions of conquering the world by contracting agreements signed in blood. Today Germany hurls downward, clasped by demons, a hand covering one eye and the other eye staring into the horror, further and further downward into ever greater despair. When will the bottom of the abyss be reached? When will that miracle surpassing all belief bring the dawning light of hope into this hopeless gloom? A solitary man folds his hands and speaks, 'May God show mercy to your poor soul, my friend, my fatherland.'"[103]

Besides those by Carl Zuckmayer and Thomas Mann, a number of other important works dealing with guilt and atonement appeared. They were written by authors who had suffered greatly under the Third Reich, some of them even unto death.

In 1945, there appeared Günther Weisenborn's play, *Die Illegalen.* Incorporating songs in the style of Brecht, this work portrayed the opposition movements. It ran in over 350 theaters. The author had been condemned to prison in 1942.

Also appearing in 1945 were Albrecht Hausofer's *Moabiter Sonette,* reflections on the great gloom that had settled over Germany. The author, who wrote these sonnets in prison, was murdered by the Gestapo shortly before the fall of Berlin.

Auf dem Weg zur Freiheit. Gedichte aus Tegel, was written by theologian Diedrich Bonhoeffer, who was murdered by the National Socialists. It came out posthumously in 1946. This year also saw the publication of anti-Fascist poem, *Dies irae,* composed by one of those who underwent an "inner emigration," Werner Bergengruen.

Publications of 1947 included Theodor Haecker's *Tag und Nachtbücher 1939–1945,* descriptions of his inner suffering during the regime of National Socialism, the play, *Draussen vor der Tur* by Wolfgang Borchert, who was twice court-martialed for subversive activities in the army, *In den Wohnungen des Todes* by Nelly Sachs, a Jewish woman who in 1940 was helped by Swedish author Selma Lagerlöf to emigrate from Germany to Sweden.

All those who through good will and the demands of conscience were convinced of collective guilt and shame, were deeply touched by the literary treatment of the unhappy events. In general, however, there were few with whom the works resonated. The "onlookers" looked further on:

> " . . . you onlookers,
>
> who never lifted a hand to kill,
> but who never shook off
> the dust of your longing;
> it stayed with you, there, and
> was transformed into light."

Settling Accounts and Beginning Anew Politically

The majority of cases brought by the Allies against the war criminals, their organizers, those who carried out their orders, and especially those in charge of concentration camps exposed the tremendous evil of the National Socialists. These cases also demonstrated that those who carried out the extermination of the "subhumans" in the name of the "Arian" race belonged to the "lesser demons." "Police agents, cheats, liars, swindlers, con-men, thieves, hoods, adventurers, quacks, cultists, tacky sentimentalists, actors, babblers, torturers: these were the people of the Third Reich."[105]

Equally pitiful was the picture presented by the leading figures of the Third Reich when, on November 20, 1945, the proceedings were opened against the principal defendants. In the eyes of the world, this "reckoning" was also a "cultural" event. One hoped to discover how a people of poets and philosophers *(Dichter und Denker)* could degenerate into a people of judges and executioners *(Richter und Henker).* This expression, though debatable, was coined by Karl Kraus, and continuously came up in reports. Questions were asked about the development of the German spirit and the reasons for its destruction in the nineteenth and twentieth centuries, as well as about the ideological precursors and pathbreakers of National Socialism. Among others, John Dos Passos reported for *Life,* Erica Mann for London's *Evening Standard,* and Peter de Mendelssohn for the *New Statesman.* When the special reporter of the *Neuen Zeitung,*

Erich Kästner, returned to Munich on the second day of the proceedings, he noted, "The war, the pogrom, the kidnapping, the mass murders and the torture all sit on the bench along with the accused. They sit enormous and invisible next to the accused. Those responsible will be made responsible. Will it really happen? If it does, it should not only happen this time, but in every future case! Then war would be no more. Like the plague and cholera. And the worshippers and friends of war would die out. Like bacillus. And later generations could one day wonder how people could be killed by the millions. If it could only be true! If only they would one day really wonder."[106]

Upon the conclusion of the proceedings, Hans Mayer, then employed with Radio Frankfurt, wrote a most significant commentary, "There is a frightening gospel verse. It is the passage which foretells of great calamities, crying woe to the persons through whom these calamities enter the world. In the worldly sphere, we have all witnessed something like this with the trials of Nuremberg. Beneath the surface of German life, everything was ready to foster the development of this diseased seed. Those generals who survived the Kaiser's downfall after the last war, assisted in this process, as did the judges of the Reich courts who took part in the secret rearmament. Help came, too, from the business leaders, who with their money organized civil war gangs. And it came from the leaders of the *Stahlhelm,* from the nationalistic spokespersons of the veteran associations, and from the German educators and intellectuals. When we consider the civilian occupations of the 21 men of Nuremberg, we know that there are still many among us who are like them, even though they may not have gone as far as these Toms, Dicks, and Harrys. Every politician, from Brüning, to Papen and Schleicher, who worked to undermine the German republic, rendering it incapable of opposition and susceptible to this terror, also aided in the development of this diseased seed.

A calamity was bound to come. Every man from Nuremberg, and his helper's helper, presented the world with the drama of this recognition. Either they received their penance, or they were going to receive it. It is for us, however, to learn from this, to turn away from the cult of blood and steel, from the scorn of freedom, humanity, human rights and the rights of peoples. We must learn to return to simple, human decency. The judgment of Nuremberg affects us all. It is up to us to make real the words of Kant, "The end of the world will not come to pass through a decrease in the number of evil people. Moral evil is such that it works against itself or destroys itself, thus leaving room for the moral principle of the Good to progress, albeit slowly."[107]

What will the future development of Germany be like? Adolf Guggenbühl, the Swiss publisher, asked this question while writing, during a trip through Germany in 1948, a recapitulation of the attempts made by Germany to deal with its past over the last two and a half years. "There are two possibilities. The first, in which we place our hopes, would be that the feelings of guilt would suddenly burst forth with elemental force. Then the way would be cleared for rebuilding. Then the collapse would no longer signify the senseless malice of blind fate. Rather, it would be meaningful, a penance which one could undergo with dignity. A new Germany could then arise from the blood and tears, ready for great feats. . . . If, however, the change in Germany is not real, or if it is only partially real, then surely there will be a different outcome, namely, the emergence of false prophets offering pseudo-religions of salvation." Deep inside, the Germans know of their guilt. Yet because they don't acknowledge it, the road to atonement and spiritual liberation is blocked. Consequently, the unconscious sense of guilt gives rise to an expectation of punishment. This unacknowledged guilt will haunt the Germans with nightmares, with destructive fantasies which they may then rationalize and seek to prove in reality. Perhaps, however, suggests Guggenbühl, the turnabout has already begun. Unobserved, maybe even despised, the bearers of the new attitude may already be among us.[108]

They were, in fact, present and perfectly capable of making themselves noticed. For the most part, they were those who had in some way been affected by Nazi persecutions. Many had just been liberated from concentration camps and prisons by the Allies. They were ready to engage in democratic and humanitarian activities, and determined to make the rooting out of Fascism one of the major points on the agendas of the new political parties.

The basic democratic consensus of 1945 was characterized by a passionate and uncompromising profession of a free, republican form of government. It was unanimously agreed that not only the political and ideological, but also the social and economic bases of National Socialism should once and for all be destroyed. The "elite" of the Third Reich were to be removed from their positions of power in government and business, and the social structures were to be so fundamentally changed that Fascist tendencies could never again be produced.

Already on April 19, 1945, even before the end of the war, social democratic officials met in Hannover at the initiative of Kurt Schumacher. Schumacher had spent 10 years from July 1933 to March 1943 in the concentration camp of Dachau, preparing for the founding of this party, which eventually took place in Hannover. In his founder's address, he maintained that the people understood the Social Democratic Party (SPD) as the polar opposite of Nazism. The SPD was the only party in Germany to uphold democracy and peace without making concessions. While the liberal parties were unable to recognize the political necessity of democracy with respect to governmental forms, the communists failed to see its class-political relevance. It must be made clear to the German people that they are now experiencing the unavoidable consequences of what were for the most part their own actions. Because many people had wanted and put up with a regime that disallowed any checks and balances, the Germans today are being controlled by foreign powers. Schumacher expressed absolute confidence in the English and French revolutions and the American declaration of independence. Freedom and social progress are realized in the clashing of ideas, in the political disputes of the great parties and classes. The bitter experiences of the Weimar Republic have taught us that, due to the special German situation, a functioning democracy and thus the maintenance of freedom are only possible under special socialist conditions.

The proclamation of the Social Democratic Party of June 15, 1945 in Berlin demanded, among other things:

Complete eradication of all traces of the Hitler regime from legislation, jurisdiction, and administration.

Assurance of adequate food, man power, and of the transformation of agriculture into cooperatives. Assurance of the minimum requirements of housing, clothing and heating, with the assistance of the local, self-governing communities.

Rebuilding of the economy with the cooperation of the local, self-governing communities and the unions.

Revival of popular culture. Education of youth in the spirit of democracy and socialism. A fostering of art and science.

Re-organization of social law. Establishment of worker's rights according to the principles of freedom and democracy. Inclusion of workers' councils in businesses.

Fostering of housing assistance and the building of housing developments. Local administration of housing.

Nationalization of banks, insurance companies, mineral resources, mines, and energy production. Limitation of rights of inheritance to the immediate family.

Adaptation of laws to the anti-fascistic, democratic idea of the state. Government protection of the individual. Freedom of expression in speech, art and writing to the extent that it does not interfere with state interests or the rights of others. Freedom of conscience and of religion.

According to the protocol of the 1946 SPD convention in Hannover, the class politics of the principal landowners were responsible for all of Germany's misfortunes. Nazism appeared as the final consequence of class conflict, as the most dangerous manifestation of the later capitalistic system.

The SPD did not, however, stand alone in its rigorous anti-capitalism and profession of socialism. There were many men and women instrumental to the founding of the Christian Democratic Union (CDU) who recognized, due to persecution and opposition in the Third Reich, the necessity for peace between confessions and the solidarity of all democrats. They strove for far-reaching social reforms. The program of Cologne's CDU from 1945 on called for an end to the predominance of big businesses, of private monopolies and industries. The following comes from a CDU declaration of June 26, 1945:

"The extreme misery of our people obliges us to enforce stern measures for the building up of our economic life and for the securing of work, food, clothing and housing, without any regard for personal interests or economic theories. Before all else, we must provide for bread, shelter, and work. Therefore, in order to protect the government, for all time, from the illegitimate influences of powerful economic groups, it is paramount that mineral resources become the property of the state. Mining and other monopolistic key industries of our economic life must clearly be controlled by the state.

We affirm private property that ensures the development of personality, but which at the same time is tied responsibly to the whole."[109]

The Frankfurt Program of the same party proclaimed, "We stand bound to an economic socialism based on democratic principles." The Hesse constitution of December 1946 contained, in agreement with the CDU, articles providing for state ownership of basic industries. Those forces in the individual cities and communities which actively participated in the formation of a Christian-social people's party were often more radical in tone. The proclamation of Berlin's CDU (1946), for example, stated, "Workers of the mind and hand! We are standing at the beginning of a new era! The bourgeois-capitalist age is over! The future belongs to socialism! True socialism, however, is not collectivism, and responsible socialism does not imply mob mentality! Worker! Are you for a sensibly controlled economy! Are you for a just compensation of burdens incurred by the war? Are you for socially just prices and incomes? If so, then fight with us for a socialism based on Christian responsibility, for the full freedom of personality, for true democratic self-administration. Workers! Enter, therefore, the Christian Democratic Union of Germany, enter the great German socialist people's party."

Clearly, it was also the intention of the CDU to fight against all the consequences of the dictatorship of Hitler.

Opportunities for Christian Renewal

The question of guilt and atonement was also the focal point of the Evangelical Lutheran church's struggle for renewal. The Third Reich had caused a profound schism. There were the "intact churches," as in Württemberg, Bavaria and Hannover, whose leaders were able to fight off the attack of the German Christians in 1933. And there were the "destroyed churches," whose Brotherhood Councils, institutions of the Confessing Church, were only with difficulty and under persecution able to agitate against the German Christian opposition.[110] Bishop Theophil Wurm was one of those brave leaders able to withstand National Socialism. It was largely due to such leaders as Wurm that it was possible after 1945 to form despite their great differences, a confederation of the *Land* churches, that is, the German Evangelical Church (EKD). Similar influences were also at work in issuing the "declaration of guilt" on the occasion of the second meeting of the EKD council in Stuttgart on October 18–19, 1945. Admittedly, this declaration was vehemently debated within the church. "With great pain we say that unending suffering has been brought by us to many peoples and countries. That which we have often witnessed through our congregations we now proclaim in the name of the whole church. We have in fact fought for long years in the name of Jesus Christ against a spirit which found its terrible expression in National Socialist government by force; but we accuse ourselves that we didn't witness more courageously, pray more faithfully, believe more joyously, love more ardently."[111]

A new beginning was now to be made in the Evangelical Church. This was not easy, of course, for the camp of those who attempted to minimize, to excuse, and to justify, was quite large. This was a consequence, too, of the questionable Lutheran tradition, which with its uncritical relationship to authority made it easier for National Socialism to become acceptable. The call to "be faithful to the church" helped deaden or do away with the moral scruples now surfacing.

The theologian Karl Barth was a crucial force in the opposition against Hitler and was removed from his teaching post at the University of Bonn in 1935. His *Offenen Briefe (Open Letters),* sent from Switzerland in 1935, were in no small measure directed against the hypocrisy behind the attempts to cover all guilt with the decorative pastoral garb of brotherly love.[112] Barth blamed in particular the German intellectuals and their theological colleagues for having allowed the state to vegetate. The German problem did not lie with Bismark or Hitler, but in the weakness that the intellectuals felt for these men. Barth saw that Germany was for the first time in the situation to begin completely anew. The total defeat makes possible the total turnabout. "God's mercy is always directed to the afflicted, and the Germans are the afflicted of today," wrote Barth on July 1945 to those German theologians who were prisoners of war.

Karl Barth saw the "good pastor and confessor" Martin Niemöller as a believable witness to Jesus Christ. As the most important protagonist of the Confessing Church, he fought like no other the spirit of ethical indecisiveness and theological appeasement.[113] When Bishop Otto Dibelius, already in the Second Reich representative of the alliance of throne and altar, suggested that the church should pick up in 1945 where it left off in 1933, Niemöller was outraged. He acknowledged collective guilt. Moreover, he felt personally guilty for having been a patriot and U-boat commander in World War I and for having trusted Hitler until 1933, and not participating in attempts to stop the "brown" fanaticism on its way to power. Representing the chairman of the EKD council and serving as director of the church's department of foreign affairs, he was significantly involved in the formulation of the Stuttgart confession of guilt. Niemöller entered the concentration camp of Sachsenhausen in 1937 and later that of Dachau, and was freed by the Americans in 1945. He felt drawn to Kurt Schumacher, who like him refused to bow to National Socialism. In 1946, one year after the war, they met in Detmold and had a long conversation. Soon, Niemöller had to recognize that the newly formed churches were mainly interested in accommodation, succumbing to the temptation of "entering a realm of consolation and peace, without passing through the gate of penance." This was for Niemöller unacceptable, "Gospel is attack," appeared in one of his letters from the concentration camp.

On January 22, 1946, Martin Niemöller gave a talk to about 1200 mostly Protestant students at Erlangen University, in which he emphasized that Germany's confession of guilt for the misdeeds of the past 12 years was an essential condition for the spiritual renewal of Germany. His talk incited vigorous opposition, which was evident by the many interruptions. On the university bulletin board, the students posted a flier which heavily attacked Niemöller. The Bavarian cabinet council dealt with these events, and put the rector of the university in charge of immediate action against the militarist and National Socialist circles. They were to discern the ringleaders and relentlessly expel all those who participated in such meetings. Student complaints against political views of professors and lecturers increased during this time. In Göttingen, a critical remark about Hitler led a student to exclaim, "It's time we had another Vehmic court!"

Martin Niemöller's Erlangen speech represented both a moral and a cultural climax in the efforts of the anti-fascist circles to undergo a mourning period and to bring about an inner change in people. He was speaking, said Niemöller, as a man who had experienced the collapse of his people and fatherland with a passionate heart, a collapse that shook not only the political, economic and social aspects of life, but also their religious foundations. The Christians of Germany were guilty because of their blindness, coldness, and lack of love; they were guilty before themselves, before the world. There is much crying and lamenting, but there is little talk of this tremendous German guilt. "Certainly, our eyes must first be opened! There is much lamenting about our hunger and affliction, but I have not yet heard one man in Germany, whether from the pulpit or anywhere else, express his regret for the terrible suffering that we, we Germans, have brought upon others. There is no talk about what happened in Poland, about the eradication of millions in Russia, about the 5.6 million dead Jews. This is written down on our people's guilt-account, and no one can take this away. There is only one power that could expiate this guilt which has poisoned the world and thus purify the air. That is the forgiving love of God, which, were it to become real, would be such an unbelievable miracle, that we could never fathom it with our reason. Without the Holy Spirit, it is impossible to believe in this love. Only the love of God can restore the peace of our own people and of our nation with others! We have confessed this guilt before the representatives of foreign churches. At the same time, however, we have confessed it as Christians. We said 'Dear Brothers! We feel guilty!'"[114] The protocol of the speech indicated that precisely at those places where Niemöller spoke of crimes against the Poles and Russians, as well as about the Stuttgart confession of guilt, there was much shouting and heckling from the audience. The pastor of students reminded them of the sacredness of the place, (the *Neustädter Kirche*) and called for order.

With the signing of the Reich Concordat on July 20, 1933, the Catholic Church recognized the government of National Socialism. A number of church representatives alligned themselves with the Third Reich, while others, such as Munich's Cardinal Michael von Faulhaber, vigorously opposed it. On the whole, however, the Catholic Church was characterized by accommodation. Its most serious failure was its silence in the face of the persecution and extermination of the European Jewry. On August 23, 1945, the German bishops together published a pastoral letter concerning the events of the Third Reich, "Terrible things happened already in Germany before the war and much suffering was inflicted by Germans in occupied lands during the war. We most deeply deplore that many Germans, also from among our ranks, have let themselves be deluded by the false teachings of the National Socialists, remaining indifferent to the crimes against human freedom and human value, that many supported the crimes by their attitude, and others even became criminals themselves. All those bear a heavy responsibility who were in a position to know what was going on, who could have used their influence to prevent these crimes, but failed to do so. Yes, they made these crimes possible and thereby proclaimed their solidarity with the criminals."[115]

The church's responsibility and the relationship between Catholics and Jews was cleverly avoided. The results of National Socialism were mainly expressed theologically as "defection from the church," whereas the church, in actuality, through its indifference, encouraged the growth of National Socialism. Demons rose in legions from the depths of hell, lamented Cardinal Faulhaber, he should have turned his critical eye more to the Vatican and to the residences of bishops and other members of the church hierarchy.

Like Niemöller among the Protestants, Eugen Kogon together with Walter Dirks tried to make Catholicism sensitive to the new moral tasks which lay ahead. The Austrian Kogon, who with the annexation of Austria in March 1938 was arrested as an opponent of the Nazi regime, entered the hell of Buchenwald concentration camp. His intended transfer to Auschwitz was blocked three times; a telegram from the Reich's security office postponed his liquidation until the end of the war. He was eventually scheduled to be shot, shortly before the Allies' liberation, along with 46 other comrades. The massacre did not take place.

Kogon, along with various groups of fellow prisoners, was asked by the Psychology War Division, set up when the first Panzer units were formed, to write an extensive account of the role of concentration camps in the National Socialist state. At the suggestion of an American general, this text was made into a book and distributed under the title, *Der SS-Staat. Das System der deutschen Konzentrationslager.*

Eugen Kogon's book, according to Walter Jens, is the testimony of a man who, all the while he is writing and setting down his accounts, is already able to adopt the other perspective. He writes in the light of regained reason as a Nathan, who tries to help reason to another breakthrough, speaking despite all his terrible experiences, from a Christian standpoint.[116] Together with Walter Dirks, Kogon founded the *Frankfurter Hefte* as a "journal of culture and politics," publishing the first volume in April 1946. The intention was to approach the renewal of Germany from a pacifist, anti-Fascist, leftist-Catholic point of view. Thus the journal was aimed at reflective, involved readers, with hopes that they could be drawn from their "reflectiveness" into making the necessary breaks and decisions, into the courageous assertion of either yes! or no! "We repeat this, for it is important. Have the courage to say 'no' and even more to say 'yes.' We hope to nourish with insight that power of the heart and spirit which underlies this courage. The clarifying and nourishing ideas which this journal will offer will be defined by a Christian conscience. It is not, however, simply concerned with the religious world, but with the whole, multifaceted, rich and poor reality."[117] In the first issue, Eugen Kogon dealt extensively with the theme of "law and conscience." The article opened with the citation of Walter Bergengruen's poem *Die letzte Epiphanie* (The Last Epiphany), from *Dies irae.* " . . . I came as a prisoner . . . Now I come as a judge . . ." Seduced by Hitler, the German people have not recognized the manifold warning appearances of the Lord. Deadened by the voices of accusation, they are also unable to recognize him as judge today. The Germans must exercize that objectivity for which they were once famous, and read the truth which has been investigated and disclosed through the proceedings, and then ask themselves, how did we get there? How was it possible? What can we do so that we can face ourselves and the world?

As a people, the Germans did not react to the injustice. That is a bitter truth, but a truth just the same. Millions of individual Germans accommodated to the system of dictatorship. When one is cognizant of their high qualities, their diligence, cleanliness, love of order, dutifulness, sense of honor, objectivity and sense of justice, then one can only say that it was an unparalleled tragedy. "Germany must recognize itself with hindsight, its noble and terrible traits, in order that its deformed and deranged face may regain its harmony again. Thus it will not have to be afraid of the judge anymore, since it will honestly have passed judgment on itself. And when the judge again asks Germany, 'Do you know me now?,' then Germany will recognize in him the redeemer from error, crime, blood guilt, shame and misery, the redeemer for freedom and human dignity. Germany will then leave the concentration camps far behind, a reminder from the times of the gloom of this Third Reich."[118]

In light of his terrible experiences during the Third Reich, Eugen Kogon is a prime example of what constitutes the cultural "miracle" of the rubble years, that the persecuted, the tormented, the tortured, and surviving found the power for the practice of humanity and for tireless democratic involvement. The National Socialists had not been able to break the spirit of freedom and love for humanity that these people had. The warm current of idealism flowed through the country. The period of mourning set faith free for a better, and also one day, a happier Germany.

In retrospect, from the vantage point of the year 1964, Walter Dirks claimed that the immediate postwar period brought with it weeks and months of elation:

"Never before in our life did the opportunities for the Christian renewal of society appear as great. Only the Allied forces held us back, but that, we assumed, would not last forever. Some Catholics at that time even dreamed of a Christian society, of a renewal of the Christian West . . . Furthermore, most of us had either overtly or covertly come to appreciate the inner power of non-Christian positions, especially that of communists and Social Democrats. They did not intend a Christian, but a worldly society, a society nevertheless, in which the power of the Christian tradition and the Christian faith could become effective, possibly even the leading force. Solidarity with the secular world, a profound solidarity especially with the needy of any imaginable kind, had been branded on our souls. It affected not only the sphere of religion, but was a dimension of faith itself, a task not of some ecclesiastical office, but of the Christian person of the world, the laity."

The Catholic socialists saw the chance to be able to manage key industries and banks as public property. Furthermore, they preferred collectivist solutions, without essentially rejecting private ownership of the means of production. This phase received concrete expression in documents such as the Dusseldorf or the Frankfurt Programs, and later the Ahlen Program of the CDU, a 1947 proposal inspired by Karl Arnold, the prime minister of North Rhine-Westphalia, and leftist-Catholic sympathizers. They did not confuse the intended model of society with the Kingdom of God. However, they believed that a people purified through suffering, emerging from the desert of destruction, would both want to and be able to reorder and renew the social structures according to the basic principles of social justice. Even the neo-liberals agreed to reforms.

The old structures of power and ownership were, however, much more persistent than was thought in 1945. Owners of capital recovered from the shock and established the status quo even before the currency reform. What applies to them, applies also to all imaginable interest groups and ideologies; they proved themselves to be stable. Walter Dirks commented, "The Christian impulse to reform dwindled in the first years. It used all its powers for charity, for the revitalization of the administration, for the continuous dispute with the occupying forces, and eventually also with the two socialist parties. From very early on it was the painful experience that first the communist party, and then the social democratic party, came forth unchanged from camps and bunkers . . . The Christian Union party was basically a new conception, but because of the restoration of the two leftist parties it became the heir of former bourgeois interests and parties, against the wills of a number of its founders. Through this the reform impulse of Catholic renewal was soon slowed down."[119]

The Split Consciousness

In his later years, Konrad Adenauer was so successful because he responded to the will of the people, who did not want to bear the burden of a mourning period. Immediately after 1945, the later chancellor was, however, convinced of the need for a party based on an ethical foundation. "The National Socialist state opened our eyes to the power possessed by a state ruled by a dictatorship. I learned to experience the cruelties of National Socialism, the consequences of dictatorship. I lost my job, which was extremely important to me. My wife, due to her time in the Gestapo prison of Brauweiler, fell hopelessly ill. I experienced the consequences of war. Three of my sons fought on the front, and I had to worry about them daily, one was seriously wounded. I heard of the crimes, which were perpetrated on the Jews, which were committed against Germans by Germans. I saw what could become of a human being through an atheistic dictatorship. I experienced the fall of the German people into chaos."[120]

Rather than radically thinking through the basic questions, i.e., investigating them to their roots, Adenauer let himself be more and more determined by that pragmatism which, on the whole, corresponded to his character. This genial realist and concretist was little inclined or prepared to orient his politics on ideas. To cite some examples. When his Mercedes was poorly repaired, he began to ask questions about the political background of this situation. "I'm convinced that Dr. Kurt Schumacher from the SPD would have been treated quite differently." He was concerned about the treatment of plants before a frost. He criticized the wrong use of color in some pictures of the Rhine which had been sent to him. ". . . Since there are no red roofs in all the villages on the Rhine, but only slate roofs. . ." In the presence of Cardinal Frings, he criticized the behavior of the Catholic church in the first campaign for national elections. With the secretary of the department of food, he was adamant that eggs not be delivered in the case where the number of chickens was fewer than that of persons. "I own five chickens, my household consists of eight persons. . . ."[121]

A platform of "overcoming the past" would never win a clear majority, so he tried to finish with the trials of the NS criminals as soon as possible, to secure pardons for the condemned, and generally to let things slide so as to effect a beneficent "barring" under the statute of limitations. The intended integration of the young Federal Republic into the Western Alliance could not succeed unless it were able to defend itself, thus requiring a revival of the German armed forces. The "not I" attitude which had become widespread in Germany as a result of wartime experiences could only be overcome with a denial of German collective guilt. The German soldier had fought gallantly. Such "pride" could not be maintained, however, if it was constantly stressed that precisely this gallantry shielded a million crimes, thereby enabling them to take place.

The anti-Fascist consensus did not last long. The road went from socialist anti-Fascism to a conservative anti-socialism. Freedom, when it included the trial of individual and national consciousness, was especially burdensome. Fear of such freedom was grounded in the dread of falling into a collective melancholy. And yet there did exist the desire to progress and rebuild. The longing to be free from external misery was greater than the willingness to undergo an internal misery.

For those who counted themselves among the inner emigrants, there existed a twofold relationship to judgment and confession, shame and repentance, guilt and atonement. On the one hand, they could claim a clear conscience, for they had done nothing to promote National Socialism. On the contrary, they preserved, often quite cautiously, their distance. And yet this distance, which was often merely indifference, was enough to take them to task, if they were serious about getting to the bottom of the truth. They had not burdened themselves with guilt, so they supressed their shame for the fact that they had done nothing against those who were called criminals in the name of the people. To compensate for their questionable status, they dramatized the isolated and anxiety-ridden situation in which they had found themselves during the Third Reich, over-emphasizing the moral stance of their engagement during the rubble years. The debate over Thomas Mann's unwillingness to return spotlighted the hypocritical attitude of those who had remained at home. Of course, only *one* segment of the broad psychic spectrum of inner emigrants was thereby characterized, the morally arrogant, ignobly compensatory, self-pitying, self-evasive, conceited type. The spectrum ranged from those just described to those who mercilessly accused and punished themselves. Christoph Meckel, using the example of his father, Eberhard Meckel, 1909–1969, successful writer of the 1930s, described with critical empathy the situation of the "retiring lyricists," of those who created a sentimental realm of inwardness in the face of the brutality of the National Socialists:

"I have often asked my father what the 1930s meant to him, how he lived and, most importantly, what he and his friends were thinking. I received no particularly enlightening answers. While Brecht, Döblin, and Thomas Mann emigrated, and Loerke and Barlach suffocated to death in Germany; while Dix and Schlemmer disappeared in South German villages, and musicians, scientists and stage managers also vanished; as colleagues were slandered, persecuted, and banned, and books were burned and pictures confiscated, he wrote peaceful verse in the traditional style, and built a house in which he waited to grow old. He hardly seemed to notice the exodus of Jews, communists, and intellectuals, the sudden and the gradual disappearance of the entire avant garde. While the SA marched, the *Reichstag* burned, and he himself witnessed deportations, a squad also interrogated him and went through his books, he proceeded to write stories and poems which gave no hint of their historical setting. He was not alone in this. Various literati of his generation, an entire phalanx of the youngest intelligentsia continued to live amazingly unaware of the times. They isolated themselves in nature poetry, hid themselves in the seasons, in the eternal, ever-valid, and non-temporal, in the beauty of nature and the beauty of art, in consoling images and in a faith in the transience of historical miseries.

My father was ambitious, sporty, healthy and inexperienced, and he had a name to make. Günter Eich had studied sinology in Paris, and Huchel had traveled through Europe for years, but my father had only lived in Germany, experiencing nothing but German intellectual life. With neither a thought nor a word, he abandoned the stable, idea-oriented, literary German middle class. He was not thinking about fleeing or changing countries. There was probably no talk about emigrating between himself and his friends. There seemed to be no necessity. They could live, they had family and a house, their business was seldom questioned, and they were not persecuted because of their past or their opinions. They had just begun to work, just begun to establish their success in writing, in occupational and private self-assurance. Outside of Germany they had no chance; they were mostly too young and had no name that carried weight in other languages. My father lived unmolested in the Third Reich. He lived blindly in the ever-waning future, emphasized dislike, scorn and pride, and he trusted powerlessly in the power of the spirit. He left everything else up to fate. *Fate*, the concept was free for the taking, and was taught him from the cradle. The conceptual world of idealism was intrusive, hollow and inescapable in the 1930s; it was polished up with government propaganda, concealing quite different worldviews. It allowed itself to be fitted with blinders of astounding thickness, according to personal need. He, like Martin Raschke, was not impervious to the *atmosphere* of the progress of National Socialism, and yet he was and remained on the outside, unable to understand actual politics. *I live for the moment, I live for the day*. His nature lyrics were placed in the arbor, but the arbor stood on steel ground and was surrounded by barbed wire."[122]

What is here captured in an impressionistic biographical form, was called, in the course of a systematic study by Hans Dieter Schäfer, a "split consciousness."[123] The reality of life in Germany from 1933 to 1945 was for the most part described as a thoroughly organized and perfectly orchestrated system of control. However, this system allowed for various interim solutions utilized by the intellectuals and artists, solutions which they then suppressed after the collapse, even though the fact that they remained in the country and needed to make a living rendered their stance toward the regime perfectly understandable. Yet, their behavior then was not that of the high moral quality they pretended to have after the zero hour. "Just as, after the breakdown, the Germans demonized Hitler as the overwhelming power in order to avoid the question of personal guilt, many authors and publishers exaggerated the penetration of the reactionary cultural politics of the National Socialists, covering up their own work and unrealistically describing the cultural life of the Third Reich. Again and again the authors of zero hour focused on the regime's attempts to control everything through book burning and expulsion. Due to the need for self-justification and legitimization, it has been little known that under Hitler's rule, as under every dictatorship, arose spontaneous relationships, some of which were even able to succeed in public. It was doubtless true that the Führer's government was relentless in its desire to destroy the individual freedom that is bound up with a living culture. At the same time, however, in order to win the majority of the population in the long run, it had to foster a sphere free from politics. Because of these goals, which were difficult to keep separate, it was possible for a number of young, relatively unknown authors to publish, despite the fact that their ideas were in part considerably distinct from the aesthetic norms of National Socialism."

Thus, in publishing houses such as C. H. Beck, Goverts, Rausch, and S. Fisher/Suhrkamp; in magazines such as the *Neue Rundschau, Europäische Revue, Deutsche Rundschau, Literatur, Hochland,* and *Eckart;* and in the serials of the *Berliner Tageblatt,* the *Frankfurter Zeitung,* the *Kölnischen Zeitung,* and even in the weekly paper *Das Reich,* closer to "vokish"-nationalistic propaganda, authors such as Emil Barth, Johannes Brobowski, Günter Eich, Peter Huchel, Karl Krolow, Horst Lange, Wolf von Niebelschütz and Eugene Gottlieb Winkler began their careers. Max Frisch already made a name for himself in Germany under Hitler's dictatorship, more than a third of Günter Eich's postwar volume of poetry, entitled *Abgelegene Gehöfte* (1948), was written during the Third Reich, and had in part been printed in newspapers and magazines. Similar things can be said about Peter Huchel, who is known for at least 14 radio plays written before 1939. Eich broadcast 22 radio programs by 1940. Wolfgang Koeppen's novel *Die Mauer schwankt* appeared in 1935. Similarly, many of those writers who determined the intellectual life of postwar years were already engaged in significant work before 1945. The writings of the inner emigrants were characterized by the "mediating" style of one willing to compromise. They were especially well suited, after World War II, to continue developing under the influence of modern classics from abroad. For the most part, they consisted of attempts to escape both the enslavement of future technology and the deception of parties and propaganda. "In some cases, they went so far as to broach the subject of their own existential doubts, others calmed their anxiety with plants and stones, encapsulated themselves in old forms, or designed pretty scrolls, for consolation, like embroidered pillows. Inasmuch as the young authors did take note of the loss of perspective and the petrification around them they bore witness, as powerless observers, to the decline of the future."

When Oscar Loerke spoke of "underlying forces," he was not referring to world- or history-transforming powers. "Nature" provided the background for a program of escapism:

> It matters not to you that I suffer in pain.
> The willow is calm
> when folk cut and whittle the flute
> yet that I suffer without mutiny,
> and that I purify myself by talking with you,
> that does matter."[124]

The success of the first artistic postwar films is largely due to their guilt and atonement themes. Occupied for some time with the production of those illusory diversions promoted by National Socialist propaganda up to the last days of the war, the movie industry soon made significant attempts to offer a balanced judgment of the previous 12 years. Of note in this regard are Helmut Käutner's *In jenen Tagen,* Harold Braun's *Zwischen gestern und morgen,* and Kurt Maetzig's *Ehe im Schatten,* all from 1947; and from 1948 Erich Engel's *Affäre Blum* and Eugen York's *Morituri.* With *Die Mörder sind unter uns,* (1946), produced by Defa, licensed in East Berlin, as the first movie following the collapse, Wolfgang Staudte began his career as the great moralist of postwar movie houses. The film portrays a physician, Dr. Mertens (Ernse Wilhelm Borchert), who, while in Poland, witnesses the killing of innocent hostages under the orders of an officer. Back home, he again meets this officer, who is now a respected, prosperous factory owner (Brueckner), unplagued by pangs of conscience. Mertens meets a former inmate of the concentration camp (Hildegard Knef), through whose love he is freed from his guilt complex, she also keeps him from killing Brueckner. In the original draft of the script, Mertens actually does kill the manufacturer, the end, however, was changed due to the protest of the Soviet officer of culture, who did not wish to encourage vigilantes.

Staudte, who with his masterpiece *Der Untertan* (1951) investigated the genesis of National Socialism, "wished to comprehend, and through his films render comprehensible, how these horrors could have come about. With this goal, he categorically rejected any kind of film that functioned to offer alibis for Germany's collective guilt, leaving everything else pretty much untouched."[125]

Staudte's film portrayed a humanity trapped in the machine of totalitarianism, a mechanism of command and performance. The film also illustrated the collective guilt, making it clear that the system would never have been able to function without its many individual parts, even those that inwardly protested the evil. He showed the profound traumatic effects of such surrender, and yet also opened the way for catharsis, the love of one once persecuted, her understanding humanity, allowed the wounds to heal.

It was the opinion of the great Austrian painter, Oskar Kokoschka, that the thesis of collective guilt let the individual off the hook. Kokoschka fled to Prague in 1934, and then in 1938 to London. The individual, he maintained, cannot and should not hide in a group, but rather must take responsibility for his or her part in bringing the world to ruin. "The seeds Hitler planted began to sprout," he wrote to Alfred Neumeyer in 1948. "His diseased brain contrived the idea of collective guilt, and the postwar world, inasmuch as it judges according to this notion, remains unfortunately tied to the insane idea of a crazyman. In such a world I cannot live! I feel personally responsible for the crimes of the society of which I am a member."[126]

On May 5, 1945, three days after the surrender of the German troops in Italy, the well-known son of a famous father traveled to Munich from Rome, through Florence, Bologna and Verona, working as special reporter for the US army newspaper, *Stars and Stripes.* In Munich, he visited the house in which his family had once lived. On May 16, 1945, Klaus Mann wrote to his father, Thomas Mann, then living in New York, "In Germany . . . one now hears many contrite speeches. The defeat is too obvious, this much is recognized. What is still denied is one's personal guilt." Klaus Mann also visited Richard Strauss in Garmisch. With a soft and sonorous voice, the composer discussed how he, too, had in certain respects been burdened by the Nazi dictatorship. There was, for example, that most irritating incident where a group of people whose homes had been bombed wanted to make his home into their temporary quarters. "Imagine that! Strangers here, in my home! Some of those Nazi chiefs,' said Richard Strauss, 'were splendid human beings.' Hans Frank, for example, Poland's head of compulsory labor 'Very fine! Very Cultivated! He admires my operas!' and Baldur von Schirach, who governed 'Ostmark' (otherwise known as Austria [Oesterreich].) Thanks to his protection, the Strauss family enjoyed an excellent position in Vienna, and this, despite the fact that the composer's son was married to a woman of not entirely unobjectionable racial background! 'I might well say that my daughter-in-law was the only free Jew in Greater Germany.'

'Free? Not really, dad! Or not completely!' This coy and wistful protest came from Frau Strauss 'junior,' nee Grab: 'My freedom leaves much to be desired. You forget what was denied me. Could I ever go hunting? No! Even riding was forbidden me at times . . .' I swear, these were her words! The Nuremberg laws existed. Auschwitz happened. An unparalleled massacre has taken place. The most infamous system of government history has ever known has degraded the Jews to the point of making them fair game. All this is well known. And the daughter-in-law of the composer Richard Strauss complains because she is not allowed to *hunt* . . ."

The meeting of two cultures, a German who emigrated out of the country meets a German who remained at home. Scornful of the nationalism which destroyed the German spirit, he nevertheless hoped that this spirit would still be found somewhere. Take, for example, this world-renowned musician. "Shame and tact aren't his thing. The naivete with which he admits to a totally spineless, completely amoral egoism could be disarming, perhaps even amusing, were it not, as the symptom of a moral-spiritual nadir, so terribly shocking. *Shocking* is the word. An artist of such sensitivity, more apathetic than anyone else when it comes to questions of conviction and conscience. A talent with such originality and power, practically a genius, and he doesn't know how to take responsibility for his gifts! A great man so completely devoid of greatness! I cannot help but find this phenomenon shocking and even somewhat disgusting."[127]

Re-education

The Allied occupation was quite rigorous in its first phase, particularly with regard to the re-education policies carried out by the United States and Great Britain. The Germans were expected to find the way back, through punishment, to a political and cultural morality. With the changes taking place in world politics and the onset of the cold war, sanctions were increasingly replaced by benefits. When the Allied forces first marched in, they upheld the prohibition against fraternization. The chief commanding officers forbade the soldiers to have private contact with the German population. This prohibition demonstrates the views held regarding both the strength of the National Socialist influence, and the devastating effects of its ideological venom.

"The officers and enlisted men of the 21st division must steer clear of German men, women and children while on the street, in their homes, in cafes, movie houses, etc. Contact with the population is allowed only on official business. Every form of personal interaction must be discontinued. I expect no visits with the enemy, no participation in their social events, no handshaking. Mere capitulation does not yet signify peace. Nazi influence has extended to every facet of life, including the church and the schools. The occupation of Germany is an act of war whose ultimate aim is the eradication of the Nazi system. For you soldiers, it is still too early to distinguish between good and bad Germans. Non-fraternization does not mean revenge. We do not recognize the theory of a master race, but we wish to ensure not only that the guilty are judged, but that they understand the full extent of their guilt. Only when that is achieved will the first step toward German re-education be taken, a step which will make possible Germany's return to human decency. Previously, we won the war, but we let peace slip through our hands. This time we must not be lax. We must win both war and peace."[128]

Although the treatment of the German people was meant to be harsh, the primary purpose of re-education was to some day be able to include a purified Germany again among the community of nations. Thus the purpose of the Morgenthau Plan, conceived by Henry Morgenthau, then Secretary of the US Treasury and trusted advisor to the American President, was overruled.[129] This plan was drawn up in September, 1944, against the background of the "solution" of the Jewish question put forth by the National Socialists. Germany was to be turned into an agrarian state . . . the fate of the population was not the point; we didn't ask for this war, we didn't send millions of human beings into the gas chambers . . . They, the Germans, would have it no other way . . . Roosevelt, who at first accepted the plan, quickly withdrew his support due to the storm of criticism it received from the American public. Those politicians prevailed who wanted America's German policy to remain uninfluenced by petty economic vengeance. On May 16, 1945, at the request of Roosevelt's successor, President Truman, Henry L. Stimson wrote a memorandum declaring that the previous suggestions for dealing with Germany, keeping it on the verge of starvation in punishment for its crimes, were gravely mistaken. Stimson, who served as Secretary of State from 1929 to 1933, and later as Roosevelt's Secretary of War, possessed a more thorough understanding of the European problem than all the other leading politicians in Washington. He recalled the unhealthy economic effects of the Versailles Treaty, and pleaded for an economic policy that would guarantee a lasting peace.

Dwight D. Eisenhower, Commander-in-Chief of the British and American invading forces in Europe from 1943 to 1945, and the first American military governor, wrote in his memoirs that both he and General Lucius Clay, first his representative, and then, from 1947–1949, his successor, were convinced that a speedy restoration of the Ruhr area, which Morgenthau had wished to turn into a ghostland, would also be in line with American interests. Germany would otherwise suffer greatly from hunger. Americans, he maintained, must not permit their former enemies to starve, and must freely undertake the costly task of feeding them.

It was also possible that hunger and poverty would encourage revolutionary endeavors, and this was by no means desired. The Western Allies were skeptical about socializing intentions. The unions were only allowed to rebuild slowly, in this way offsetting the danger that they would fall into false hands. On similar grounds, the permissions to form parties were restricted. The democratic buildup was to take place from below, through local and regional establishments. The middle class was thereby given a greater chance to again become the ruling force.

Cultural politics was the most important instrument for re-education, for here the focus was less on institutions and more on persons. In October 1945, the American Office of Information Control made public that it had a list of 1440 Germans, stipulating the possibility of their participation in the various sectors of cultural life in the American occupation zone. The list was of special significance, for all the activities in news and cultural events which the occupying powers had carried out during the previous six months were to be gradually returned to trusted civilians. On the "white list" were 441 Germans, of which 207 were found to be politically reliable for leadership positions. The remaining 234 persons could hold key positions only on approval. The 389 Germans named on the "gray list" could participate in cultural events, but could not, however, take leading or initiating roles in politics or in business. On the "black list" were 327 persons who were basically denied any employment, and another 283 who "if possible" were not to be employed.

Among the prominent people on the "black list" were pianist Walter Gieseking, Bavarian music director Hans Knappertsbusch, movie actor Emil Jannings, authors Ernst Jünger and Friedrich Sieburg. Many of those affected by this prohibition gave long explanations in hopes of exculpating themselves.[130]

An open letter signed by a number of prominent Berlin personalities supported the re-instatement of Wilhelm Furtwängler, who was also among those incriminated, to his position as a director of the Berlin Philharmonic Orchestra. The American authorities explained that the director must stay on the "black list" because by remaining in a prominent position during the Third Reich, he had identified himself with National Socialism. The worldwide interest in Furtwängler's case, wrote Alexander Mitschlerich in an "Analysis of the Star" (July, 1946), proved it to be not simply a German matter, rather, it concerned the solution of a major problem, a test of strength. The idea that art had nothing to do with politics, conceding to the artist a *sacro egoismo* could now, in light of the crimes of National Socialism, have no credibility. People like Furtwängler wished that everything could be forgotten, that the instruments could be retuned and that the play could go on. "It will definitely go on. Should it continue with the old players? Shall what Furtwängler said about Hindemith before he forgot about him hold true for himself as well, that one should not easily disclaim a person of his quality? Yes, if one falls into an insoluble conflict with the clear conscience. If everything were to go on with the old players, then nothing will have been gained, and every sacrifice will have been in vain."[131]

The denazification proceedings which took place against Furtwängler in December 1946 offered a richly informative insight into the artistic psychogram of this outstanding "culture producer" of the Third Reich. In some sense, his case was typical of many. The chair of the denazification commission explained that Furtwängler had in fact never belonged to the party or any of its organizations, but that the main trial must ascertain the extent to which the director, as privy councillor *(Staatrat)*, as vice-president, as one of the main presiding members of the Reich Music Chamber and as head of the Philharmonic Orchestra, participated in the spread of National Socialist ideology. Furtwängler emphasized during his interrogation that it was necessary for him to work with the government in order to be able to work against it. He could not reject the title of Prussian privy councillor which had been conferred on him in 1933, and he considered it at the time to be the duty of every German to hope for the best from the new government. He had often appealed to Goebbels to discontinue the terrorizing of the musical world. The prosecutor responded, presenting a letter from Furtwängler to Goebbels, in which he had indeed spoken on behalf of directors Bruno Walter and Otto Klemperer. He had also, however, approved of the "fighting against subversive elements." As to Furtwängler's numerous concerts abroad, he noted that he constantly placed art above politics. It had certainly always been clear to him that the ministry of propoganda had, for cultural-political reasons, an interest in his activities abroad. In protest of the prohibition against presenting Hindemith's work, he resigned from his positions, keeping only the title of privy councillor. A formal reconciliation with the Führer of the Third Reich later came about through a "declaration of loyalty," made known to the public when he again directed the Berlin Philharmonic Orchestra for the benefit of compulsory relief work. At the end of the concert, Hitler greeted him with a handshake.[132]

Gustaf Gründgens, as manager of the Berlin National Theater, also received the title of privy councillor from the National Socialists, and was arrested several times after 1945. In a 1946 essay on the "Sociology of the German Actor," he wrote that the actor was in general uninterested in politics. "The most important thing for the actor is art or, better yet, the good role, the interesting dramatic challenge. The German actor shares this defect in political education with the entire German people . . . National Socialism, which was an external teaching that only worked with mass psychosis, did not really penetrate the depths at least not consciously for most people. And so foreign observers get the astonishing picture that actors who have performed in the past 12 years have never felt themselves affected by National Socialism, and never identified themselves with their disgraceful activities. These actors, as a result, do indeed acknowledge German collective guilt, resign themselves to it, and remain unaware of any personal guilt."[133] One could assume, countered a weekly bulletin of the US military government at the end of January 1946, that no artist of note had been forced to become a member of the Nazi party. The Ministry of Propaganda handled them with kid gloves. Theater people had to pay lip service to National Socialism either because of their careers or because they were vulnerable to accusations of having Jewish ancestry or engaging in communist activities. Many, however, whose papers were in order, had distinguished themselves as Nazis.[134]

Such ambivalence with respect to the activities of artists in the Third Reich led to correspondingly ambivalent reactions on the part of the Allied forces. In a 1943 study of the leading personalities of German cultural life, researched on behalf of the US government, Carl Zuckmayer wrote that actors enjoyed the Third Reich as a theater production in which they played some role.[135] This assertion did not, however, conform to the moral requirements with which life was to be reordered, that is purified of National Socialism. Quasi-anecdotal events, however, documented the uncertainty of the Allies concerning this "pretending." Gründgens, said Zuckmayer, should in no way be considered an inscrutable villain, but as an actor-type, one who engages in the *"grand jeu"* both on stage as well as in real life.

Helge Rosvaenge was able to give a concert in October 1945 in Stockholm. However, shortly thereafter he was outlawed as a sympathizer of National Socialism. He, along with some other emigrants, took off for Venezuela in a rickety cutter, became stuck, however, in Fascist Spain, and sang there. The Luxemburg actor, René Deltgen, was unsuspectingly playing Macduff in Munich when he discovered that he was considered a war criminal in his own land and that his possessions had been confiscated. In the midst of a rehearsal in Stuttgart, Rudolf Fernau was called to a district-court hearing. Shortly thereafter he was condemned to nine months in prison and was forbidden to act for the rest of his life. Already by the beginning of January, 1946, the sentence was changed to a small fine. Victor de Kowa had a similar experience in Berlin. He was arrested in the middle of a song, the audience, thinking that it was a smart theatrical idea, applauded. Heinrich George, once the manager of the Schiller Theater in Berlin, earlier a communist, ended up in an internment camp. Willy Birgel, however, accused on account of Goebbel's much beloved film *(Reitet fur Deutschland),* was able to survive on Lake Woerther. Film producer Arthur Maria Rabenalt produced films in Heidelberg despite the fact that he was forbidden to work. When the Americans protested, he moved to Baden-Baden, where the French authorities declared him a desirable factor in the building up of German cultural life. Swiss-born Emil Janning's efforts toward rehabilitation were miscarried. Karl Böhm and Clemens Krauss sat unemployed in Austria. Herbert von Karajan, who in 1942 was expelled from the NSDAP, gave an enthusiastically received performance in the British zone. He was then denounced and forbidden to give appearances. The married couple Attila Hörbiger and Paula Wessely were at first allowed to play only in Innsbruck, but not in Vienna. Also "banned" was Hans Moser, who was married to a Jewish woman. And so on . . .

The Allies were strongly criticized for the fact that denazification took so many popular favorites away from the theater business. Admittedly, most of those affected were soon on the stage again, for it was claimed that anyone who wanted to succeed as an artist had to make a distinction between art and politics.

On the other hand, some artists rightfully rebelled. They had been forbidden to work during the Third Reich, and they now saw that those well trained in opportunism could quickly switch from one regime to the other, from one influential position to the other. Georg Meistermann, whose works were banned during the Third Reich, criticized the mistaken paths of the past from the standpoint of fine art. The reality of spiritual decay had in no way disappeared by 1945.[136] When, for example, Theodor Heuss founded an emergency association for art in 1949, the list of invited artists was at first comprised exclusively of names of painters and sculptors who were prominent in Hitler's Germany. Georg Meistermann, however, with the help of an alternative list of names of people who had been outlawed or had been named "degenerate," was able to reintroduce many artists to the public, people whose artistic endeavors had been hindered by police action, whose paints and canvases had been seized, whose work had been taken by the thousands from German museums during the thirties, and then either burned or sold abroad. Unfortunately, it happened that often the cultural reviews were written from an overly conservative point of view, thereby leading, for aesthetic, not political reasons, to restorational or downright reactionary consequences. Thus there existed a paradoxical situation. And so one of the "culture hounds," Hermann Kaspar, who furnished Hitler's chancellery and designed and organized the torchlight parade for the dedication of the "House of German Art," was able to present himself to the Allies as the banished Carl Caspar, whose reputation was to be restored.

The contradictions resulted for the most part from the situation itself. Very few of the culture creators had been able consistently to avoid the embrace of the total regime. Already before 1933, for example, Emil Nolde had written in his memoirs of the German national art, which was later called "blood-and-soil-art," in a propagandist fashion, polemicizing against Cezanne and the whole of French art. He joined the NSDAP in 1928. "That he was later thrown into the same group as the 'degenerates' occurred in order to avoid a discussion that might have caused a controversy which the Nazis were not anxious to be part of. The German governor in Vienna actually had the idea in 1941 to rehabilitate Nolde with a great exhibit of this 'pure' national artist, this National Socialist pioneer of German art. Goebbels prevented this exhibition, ostensibly with the argument that it was first necessary to win the war before entering into details."[137]

The *Neue Zeitung*, published by the American occupation government, had its own incident of cultural-political ambivalence, one which caused quite a sensation. The author and journalist Erich Ebermayer worked for the literary section of the paper. His contributions seemed not only to have literary significance, they were also expressions of a writer who had been under pressure in the Third Reich. There appeared in the paper one of Ebermeyer's letters of May, 1942, in which he claimed to have received the benevolence of one of the highest ranks of the Third Reich. The editor's reaction to this reflected the moral rigorism with which those who had been able to maintain their ideological purity judged those with a "double life." "The author, Dr. Erich Ebermayer, presently a citizen and notary of Kaibitz, is the son of the late democratic high court judge *(Oberreichsanwalt)* who was dismissed by the National Socialists. He is also the cousin of the National Socialist Reich leader Philipp Bouhler, who wrote a biography of Napoleon to demonstrate that Napoleon was essentially a precursor of Hitler. Although Erich Ebermayer was a cousin of a Reich leader, he had occasional difficulties publishing his books during the Third Reich. Despite these difficulties, he was one of the most respected film writers. Although he was one of the most respected film writers, he employed for years, at times with some risk, a Jewish secretary. Although he employed a Jewish secretary, he wrote to a colleague, who happened to have criticized one of Ebermayer's books, that letter which later appeared in the *Neue Zeitung*. Although he was capable of writing such a letter, shortly after the National Socialists had been eliminated he described the abysmal horror of the book burning by Goebbels and other brown shirts in an advance copy of his three volume diary 'Night Over Germany.' And although the same human being was capable both of writing such a letter and of exposing the horrors of the Third Reich, he had a highly respected, democratic, high judicial official for a father. It is no wonder that foreign observers shook their heads over such two-faced characters, and that many Germans were embarrassed by such realities. One can imagine countless human beings who were disgusted by the book-burning, and unfortunately also others who were in the position to write a letter similar to the one we have reproduced. But to find someone who accomplishes both, that is quite a feat. Such inconsistency not only offends our moral sense, it is also an attack on good taste! And that is perhaps even worse!"[138]

It was not only the mismanagement of the past that continuously threw the cultural life of the rubble times into turbulence. Partisanship and the sympathies which this involved were also capable of causing scandal. The case of Jürgen Fehling can well illustrate this aspect of the cultural guilt-and-atonement complex.

In Berlin of 1946, it was enthusiastically agreed that Wolfgang Langhoff, who had just come from Düsseldorf to take over the management of the German Theater, would be able to find the best stage-manager for the theater. A new epoch was anticipated. When Heinrich George died on September 25, 1946, Fehling wrote, in an obituary published by the *Kurier*, licenced by the Americans, on January 12, 1947: " . . . I loved him like no other living actor of the German tongue . . . Like a powerful dog he fetched every role for me . . . Compared to his colleagues, he was like an old golden eagle amongst chickens." Langhoff, who had never seen George in his major roles, published a reply, charging Fehling with "disrespect for the contemporary German actors." For Langhoff, in these early hours of the new communistic, humanistic, and simplistic theatrical culture, the entire cast was more significant than even the most genial individual. Fehling submitted a description of his interview with Langhoff to the *Kurier*. "What happened in that room, where once Max Reinhardt, and before him, Brahms, had sat, was horrifying. I could not help but remind him of Brutus, who with his perhaps noble, but historically speaking most despicable, 'idealism,' did the most stupid and irresponsible deed. For the sake of mediocrity, the common horde, the ones without judgment, he sacrificed the one person who was able to rule, and who should have ruled, if the endangered Roman empire was not to fall into decay and into the hands of stupid and egocentric notables, excuse me, I mean Diadoches."[139] Already before this publication, the German Theater let it be known that its dealings with Fehling would be terminated in light of his excessive claims. His obituary of Heinrich George indicated that he was not capable of drawing a line between the cultural epoch of the Third Reich and that of the future. There were "boundaries to the worship of a genius which could not be crossed without either destroying or bursting open the entire structure."

Tearing Down the Intellectual Ghetto

The Allies also had difficulties with the insubordination of those media enterprises that interfered with their attempts at re-education. The most spectacular incident concerned the ban on *Der Ruf*, a magazine published by Alfred Andersch. Its editor was Hans Werner Richter, who, while in an American war prison in 1945, had worked on a newspaper of the same name, intended for the Germans imprisoned in the United States. "The editorial office consists of one single room, located in a house in Krailling, twenty kilometers from

Munich. The office includes two tables, three chairs, an old typewriter, an editing secretary, a Bavarian bookstore owner whose dialect I don't always understand, and one editor, myself. Alfred Andersch, the publisher, comes by only occasionally. He works on the *'Neue Zeitung'* under Erich Kästner. A critical friendship arose from our first meeting in Munich, I did not know him from the war prison. This friendship makes our work together easier. There are disagreements. Andersch more or less wishes to support the American re-education program, with reservations, of course. I hope to be strongly critical, to keep a clear distance from the occupying forces, and to take advantage of every democratic right."[140]

The first volume of the *Ruf* (August 15, 1946) already made it clear that collective guilt was not acknowledged, that the measures taken by the American military government were critically opposed, and that a conscious distinction was made between the politics of the newspaper and that of the victors. These people felt tied as "Young Germany" to the youth of Europe. Europe's youth was humanistic in its inexhaustible hunger for freedom. Humanism meant for them the recognition of the dignity and freedom of humanity, no more and no less. They were prepared to abandon socialism when they saw it forfeiting human freedom in favor of some old, orthodox Marxism which postulated economic determinism and denied freedom of will. Fanaticism for the right to human freedom was not in itself contradictory, but the great lesson gleaned by European youth from their experience with dictatorship. They would fanatically lead the struggle against all enemies of freedom. "This dual search for freedom and social justice had strong roots in the religious experience which the younger generation took with them from the war. True religion cannot be had wherever rigid race or class distinctions are upheld. There is no greater proof of human freedom than the freedom to choose for or against God." One should not fall prey to that common cliché, the "lost generation." If one refuses education, let it be because one seeks that experience of freedom because one wishes to accomplish the radical new beginning with one's own powers. The new spirit of the German youth is expressed also in its infinite desire to make good the spiritual development of recent years. "It will not be long before the younger generation of Germany will have closed the gap. Their solution can already be heard, we must surpass our educators. Under no condition would Young Germany let itself be cut off from Young Europe. Neither will it trudge sluggishly and reluctantly behind, especially because, without Young Germany, Young Europe cannot exist."[141]

According to Peter de Mendelssohn, an officer for the English press, everyone was talking very big at the time. They were aggressive, overbearing, and arrogant, said Hans Werner Richter, even in reference to himself. Yet they were effective. With the fourth volume, *Der Ruf* achieved its goal of one hundred thousand sales, it was read everywhere, especially by those who returned to Germany after the war. Andersch and Richter, both functioning also as publishers, wrote the lead articles, criticisms, reports and commentaries almost completely alone up through the fifth volume. Thereafter they were accompanied by a number of co-workers, among them Walter Maria Guggenheimer, Hildegard Brücher, Walter Mannzen, Heinz Dietrich Ortlieb, Wolfdietrich Schnurre, Nicolaus Sombart, and Wolfgang Bächler.

The first attacks against the *Ruf* were made by Karl Hermann Ebbinghaus in the *Neue Zeitung* and by Erich Kuby in the *Süddeutschen Zeitung*. "The reproach, unwarranted criticism of the occupying powers, and nationalism. The accusation of nationalism especially irritates me. I feel German, I am a German, and I cannot jump out of my skin. Yet I am not responsible for Hitler's crime and for the chauvinism of past ages. Nor are those young soldiers returning home responsible, whether they believed in National Socialism or not. I am also not prepared to accept uncritically the imperialistic claims of the victors. We will continue to write. We demand a reform of the universities and a university for workers. We consider denazification a farce and will say as much, and we will continuously oppose the humiliation of an entire people. This humiliation cannot be justified with the claim that Hitler acted much worse. We counter the attacks, not in lead articles, but in the commentaries. We hope to render the argumentation of our opponents laughable."[142]

The tone of the *Ruf* was too insubordinate for the Americans. They expected more humility, more conformity. Instead they found illicit criticism of Allied politics in Germany, unwarranted attacks on international personalities, and false reports of the activities of Allied soliders. Volume 17 (April 1947), was no longer acceptable. It was marked by a strong, independent, leftist tendency, on the one hand distinguishing itself from a dogmatic, outdated Marxism, and on the other hand demanding a united, socialist Europe, despairing over the ever-expanding opportunism. Andersch and Richter lost their license, and it was passed on to Erich Kuby, who worked in the publication division of the American military government.

Such crass poor judgment as that exercised in the *Ruf* incident was admittedly an exception to the rule of the cultural politics of the Western Allies. Those officers appointed to work on the re-organization of the newspaper and publishing businesses, education and theater, were for the most part cultured personalities, inclined toward freedom and well-versed in Germany's history and character. Of special significance for the assessment of the German situation were reports written by emigrants, such as those of the "Frankfurt School," among them Herbert Marcuse, for the American Secret Service between 1943 and 1945.[143]

The long German-American symbiosis frequently molded the education of the American officers appointed to cultural re-organization. These were often people who had been introduced to Germany's intellectual life in the Weimar Republic, like Shephard Stone, who worked first as Major in the Information Division in Wiesbaden, where he licensed, among others, Theodor Heuss in 1945. With competence and commitment, these people endeavored to tear down the walls of the ghetto in which Germany had been enclosed.

In Spring 1946, Ernst Rowohlt, who had organized a makeshift office in the attic of the bombed out publishing house of Broschek, was given the opportunity to rebuild, in Hamburg, his publishing business that had been destroyed by the Hitler regime. He showed himself anew to be the most significant German agent of modern, for the most part American, literature. In a speech given in December of 1946, he said, "Do you know that we have in Germany an entirely new generation of young people that is completely unaware of that which to us comes under the name of literature? Sinclair Lewis, Joseph Conrad, André Gide, they hardly know the names. Already by 1938 no English or American author was allowed to be published, and with the outbreak of the war all foreign works disappeared from the libraries as well. Today's thirty-year-olds were 17 at that time. This and this alone is what interests me at present, this intellectual vacuum in the generation that is to pull the coach out of the muck. This is what I see my task to be." . . ."How could such an extensive program even be thinkable under the present circumstances? We are lacking the most basic technical prerequisites for the production of books, quality paper and all those materials required for book binding. It will only be possible to print a few copies, and these at a correspondingly high price. A bound book costs between six and ten marks today. In a short time, that will prove to be a prohibitive price, especially for those readers that are important to us." Rowohlt then came up with the plan of distributing modern literature by doing away with the book form, implementing instead the rotary printing machines and paper used for newspaper. The reading material would be 23 by 30 cm, with no special cover and no special machine-folding characteristic of the bookbinding process. Thirty-two pages printed in three columns would offer the equivalent of 350 book pages. With a circulation of 100,000 copies it would be possible to fix the price at 50 pfenning per booklet. In mid-December, the first *Rowohlt-Rotations-Romane* (rororo) were distributed. "This plan breaks with a tradition, the German inclination towards 'mummification' of libraries. But will we be leading them astray by asking hard-earned money for a poorly bound book made of perishable newsprint? And where will they find room for large shelves in their current housing arrangements? Our emergency product will accomodate present circumstances very well. It will not, however, compete with the book form. On the contrary. If I am able, from 100,000 readers of one booklet, to get even 10,000 who have a true and enduring interest in one author, that will serve as an advertisement for a later date, when books will again be available in unlimited quantities."[144] The first issue (" . . . a happy miscellany") included titles such as Ernest Hemingway's *In Another Country,* Kurt Tucholsky's *Schloss Gripsholm,* Alain Fournier's *The Wanderer,* and Joseph Conrad's *Typhoon;* there followed Erich Kästner's *Drei Manner im Schnee,* Jörgen Frantz Jacobsen's *Barbara und die Manner,* Joseph Hergesheimer's *The Party Dress,* William Faulkner's *Light in August,* Sinclair Lewis' *Dodsworth,* and Richard Hughes' *A High Wind in Jamaica.*

Shortly after the end of the war, the publisher Peter Suhrkamp followed his pedagogical leanings and attempted to provide new direction in life for those coming home from the war by writing a *Handbook for Young People.* In an unpublished postscript, he wrote, "Up until 1939 the young people knew only of a life within walls, the rest of the world was closed to them. After that they were allowed to take all of Europe by storm, but they then met Europe under abnormal circumstances. Everywhere they encountered disintegrating, old, or imperiled circumstances. They had to govern, to train, and, under certain circumstances, play the hangman's assistant, before they could teach themselves. The world, however, had lain unbounded before them. And then in one blow the walls again appeared, only more real and more isolating than before the war. The endless possibilities were dissolved into a denial of possibilities."[145]

The *Neue Zeitung,* published by the American military government and brilliantly edited by Hans Habe and Hans Wallenberg, proved to be the most important and exemplary vehicle for the transport of spiritual goods over the walls of the cultural ghetto. In fact, as General Dwight D. Eisenhower expressed in his guiding remarks of the first issue, printed October 8, 1945, the new German press and the cultural life that flows from it can serve as an example with its "objective reporting, unconditional love for truth, and its high journalistic standard."[146] Hans Habe embodied the spirit of an elegant, sarcastic, slightly snobbish, somewhat affected, cosmopolitan urbanity, which for the dull and basically provincial Germany appeared to be an energizing influence.

Isolated Germany had its advocates from the "other Germany," whose representatives, despite their bitter experiences under persecution and emigration, frequently returned, at least for some time.

Otto Zoff, the German author who fled to New York via France, wrote the following in his diary on December 28, 1942, "The more certain the victorious outcome of the war becomes for the Allies, the more frequently is heard this conversation among the emigrants, will one go back, will one stay here? The discussion never ends without mutual disdain and spite. The politically-inclined people may all intend to go back, even those of the younger generation. For the pure Jews who did not immediately settle here, an almost insoluble problem presents itself. It is simplest for them if close relatives or even their parents have been murdered over there. The personal, terrifying experience makes them shudder at the thought of ever running into the murderers. Yet, for others the question emerges, is the personal experience more important than the lasting, the eternal, the spiritual ties to centuries of a strong and invincible culture?"[147] Despite everything, these ties were so strong that the exodus was followed by a strong movement of returning men and women. As Zoff predicted, the Jewish representatives of German culture, with few exceptions, did not venture a lasting return.

On the whole, it was not simple for the exiles to enter Germany. While, on the one hand they had made a clear denunciation of National Socialism, which gave them moral legitimacy, on the other hand they often refused to perform the political tasks requested of them by the occupying authorities, thus undermining their desirability. The leaders of the Social Democratic Party living in London had to wait until February before they could again tread upon German soil. Ernst Reuter, later the Governing Burgomaster of West Berlin, had to wait until October 1946. In early June, Wilhelm Hoegner managed to make an illegal entry from Switzerland into Munich, where he later became the Bavarian Minister-President.[148] In Zurich, U.S. officers picked him up in a jeep like Hans Mayer and passed him off as an American while crossing the French zone. In this way they hoped to avoid rejection by the border authorities. By the end of April 1946, there were still 1200 exiles waiting in Great Britian for their visas to be approved. The *Aufbau* commented on this situation with the words, "It is highly unlikely that they will be able to return within a short period of time. Difficulties with transportation have been insurmountable up to now. The problem of entrance permits is still more complicated. There is temporarily no possibility of gaining entry into the British occupation zone of Germany. Only in a few exceptional cases have the British authorities themselves requested the return of a few politicians and journalists. The Russians . . . have promised from 300 to 400 visas, but reserve the right to investigate the political 'reliability' of every applicant."[149] The story was pretty much the same with the French and American military governments. Exiles had to wait no matter how urgently they were needed.

While the exiles were able to follow German events and their developments from abroad, those who remained in Germany were hardly able to ascertain the quantity and quality of their cultural loss. Richard Drews, along with Alfred Kantorowicz, who returned to Germany from the United States, published the anthology *Verboten und verbrannt* in 1947. With this book they sought to give a rough idea of that which had been repressed in the intellectual spheres for 12 years. The task which they set up for themselves was nearly impossible. "To collect, classify and work through the hundreds of German authors who have appeared abroad in the last 15 years, some of whom are out of print, some of whose publications are difficult to find, and then to describe the contribution to literature of the completed works of each author, this is a work requiring long planning and investigation by qualified literary critics. And yet we have not even discussed the immensely difficult task of making the as yet unpublished works of exiled German authors available. Yet precisely in these works which remain in manuscript form, perhaps lost somewhere abroad or at home, one will find timeless masterpieces, which, while not aimed at the general public, will some day prove to be enduring works from among the great literature of our times. Therefore, it is necessary for us to say and for the reader to understand, that this publication pretends to be no more than a general outline, a first, rough, non-classified, and not yet fully comprehensive overview, a type of reference booklet that lays out the perimeters of the burned and banned literature, no more and no less. This is not an excuse, but a statement of that task which is at present possible and necessary."[150]

For the writing of his proposed history of German literature from naturalism to the immediate present, Paul E. Lüth received advice from, among others, Alfred Döblin, returning to Baden-Baden from

Los Angeles, F. C. Weiskopf, New York, and Werner Bock, Buenos Aires. Authors and publishers from home and abroad submitted material, enabling him to give an overview of the main currents and developments from 1933 onward. This overview, and herein lay Lüth's special service, covered the literature of the Third Reich as well as that written in exile. The publisher clearly described the positions of the authors, indicating whether they opened the way for National Socialism, actively promoted it, or at least accommodated themselves to it. The situation of the year 1945 was so characterized, that after the euphoria connected with the liberation from Fascist terrorism, there came the "inevitable depression."

The German spirit must, after this period of forced simplification, again be made aware of the tremendous depths of its literature. The youth have special significance in this regard. In that one moment, when everything topples down into a great waste heap, writing takes on a new role. Lüth closed his work with a quote from Alfred Döblin, "When the divine approaches, with its sincerity, its outpourings, its truth and its beauty, the songs take on a different melody. The harps are returned. It is no time for a class, individual, or national epoch, when once again, and not for the last time, the question of humanity again comes up after a test."[151]

While Lüth undertook the intensive, if inadequate task of working with the literary precursors and protagonists of National Socialism, the Allied authorities relied more on "cleaning up." According to them, the German people should no longer come into contact with dangerous intellectual material. Asepsis appeared more reliable than immunization. Undoubtedly driven by a guilty conscience, the German authorities zealously promoted this activity of separation. In Berlin, with the help of a state board of examiners, not only National Socialist and Fascist literature was removed from libraries, also eliminated were around 350 authors of aesthetic works, 370 publishers of works for young people, and 1500 political and scientific authors. Individual works of some authors were banned, such as Hans Carossa's *Rumänische Kriegstagebuch*. Only a few works of Knut Hamsun, held in Norway at the time as a war criminal, could be borrowed from libraries. Also named in the Index were, among others, Werner Beumelburg, Arnolt Bronnen, Edwin Erich Dwinger, Walter Flex, Gorch Fock, Hermann Löns, Walter von Molo, Luis Trenker, Georg von der Vring, Hans Zöberlein, Ernst von Wolzogen, Adolf Bartels, Houston Steward Chamberlain, Sven Hedin, Paul von Lettow-Vorbeck, Erwin G. Kolbenheyer, and Heinrich von Treitschke.[152] Only those writings of Ernst Jünger were burned which supported war and conflict, not, however, his volumes of essays and aphorisms such as *Das abenteuerliche Herz, Blätter und Steine,* and *Auf den Marmorklippen.* The complete works of Wilhelm von Scholz, Erwin Guido Kolbenheyer, except for four speeches, Walter von Molo and Hans Fallada remained untouched. Not included on the list were various representative authors who, while submitting to National Socialism, were not completely taken in. This group included Rudolf Herzog, Wilhelm Schaefer, Rudolf G. Binding, Paul Alverdes, and Joseph Weinheber. Those who wrote historical or documentary literature were treated "generously." The works of Friedrich the Great, Clausewitz, Bismark, Moltke, and even Hindenburg were not prohibited, except those the National Socialists had worked on and re-published. Treitschke and Nietszche were treated similarly. Unaffected by the prohibition were Paul de Lagarde, Karl Eugen Dühring and Oswald Spengler.

The German library in Leipzig played a definite normative role in the prohibition politics of each occupation zone. This library, working in conjunction with Leipzig's bureau for popular education, published a comprehensive inventory of the literature that was to be singled out. It included 15,000 book titles and 150 journals. The point of departure, for all such measures, was the elimination of all literature with Fascist and militaristic content, as well as those writings containing evidence of the expansionist thinking of power politics, National Socialist racial theories, or ideas that ran contrary to the politics of the Allied forces.

The Paper Revolution

Denazification represented the central aspect of the Allied re-education strategy. The "questionnaire" served as the instrument of examination. While the proceedings against the major criminals of war took place before an international military tribunal in Nuremberg, 11 of them were sent there on October 16, 1946, the day after Hermann Goering poisoned himself, the general population initiated an "ideological stock-taking," a "paper revolution." With the help of 131 questions, the Germans were to be examined in their inmost depths. "By March 15, 1946, approximately 1.4 million questionnaires had been distributed, of which nearly 742,000 were filled out. Because incontestable evidence was required before a certificate of good character could be presented to denazification board, a flood of papers constituting so-called *'persilscheinen'* poured in. These were filled out by Germans with clear records on behalf of their countryfolk, often out of sympathy or courtesy. Personal relationships, and corruption in the form of bribery were often involved. Of those interviewed, 19 percent were dismissed from their positions, and dismissal was suggested for another 7 percent. For 25 percent, dismissal was left to individual discretion; 49 percent were found to show no evidence of National Socialist activities; and another 4 percent could show proof of resistance activities, which qualified them for a job recommendation. The overwhelming majority of those detained in the US zone were 'regional functionaries, minor civil employees,' and people associated with middle class businesses. One could not really speak of 'concentrated measures taken against the German elite.'"[153]

Due to numerous obvious defects and blatant mistakes in management, the task of denazification was soon turned over to the Germans. The intention behind this unpopular process was to encourage German self-government in the hope that "cooperation" would train the Germans in democratic praxis. The political parties likewise encouraged this transfer, for they were interested in going about the process in a different way. The CDU/CSU and the FDP aimed only at the prosecution of the major political and economic leaders of National Socialism and the actual criminals of the regime. The general mass of people who were cited to be tried were instead expected to be reintegrated into society through rehabilitation, thereby regaining the inner peace of the country. Viewing things slightly differently, the Social Democrats wanted a thoroughgoing purification, with the goal of achieving a comprehensive structural reform of society, thereby completing and safeguarding the intended socialization process.

On March 5, 1946, the "Law for Liberation from National Socialism and Militarism" was signed by the chief administrator in the upper house. The "Law for Liberation" was based on American law, with additions conditioned by German contributions. It was more or less a dictate of the military government. Five classes of persons were defined, major offenders, offenders, minor offenders, followers, and pardoned. Of the 13 million questionnaires in the US zone, 3 million required further attention. There were 545 denazification boards with 22,000 employees. Due to the lack of personnel, furniture, office machines and material and ultimately even paper for the mounds of questionaires, the tribunals often could not begin on time. Those sitting on the tribunals often had little preparatory training for the task. Corruption could not be avoided. Mistakes, especially those of the witnesses for defense and prosecution, often led to illegalities. In addition, the Americans were much stricter than the English and the French in their denazification efforts, although by proclaiming two amnesties they "cleared" approximately 3 million people. The amnesties affected those who were born after January 1, 1919, those who had been physically wounded, and those whose taxable income did not exceed 3630 Reichsmarks.

In August 1947, the American Military Governor, General Clay, ordered that the denazification process be completed by March 31, 1948, since West Germany was to be included in the anti-Soviet alliance. The criticism came that denazification had thus far been concerned with the minor cases, leaving the more serious offenders untouched. "The little ones are hung, the big ones are set free." In a letter to Walter Dorn, American historian and civilian officer of the military government, the Bavarian Minister-President Hoegner wrote that the "Law for Liberation" supported a change in the denazification policies such that "the little people were the first to be hit with the full weight of the law, while the real offenders are only now coming forth, benefitting from the greater leniency of the present proceedings. Time heals all wounds . . . In a few years erstwhile National Socialists will predominate in the German government, and that is no exaggeration." The possibility of passively electing former "followers" has already resulted in the shocking fact that in many places, former Nazi Burgomasters have been reelected with a large majority of votes.[154]

From the American occupation zone, close to one fourth of the 13 million people required to fill out questionnaires were charged; 950,000 cases were handled, 600,000 persons received fines, of which 500,000 were to be paid in money. There were 1549 major offenders in Group I, and 21,600 offenders in Group II.

The purpose of the questionnaires used in the denazificaiton proceedings was a moral one. They were intended to force the individual into an examination of his or her identity. It was hoped that a puritanically motivated introspection would not only further bureaucratic punishments, but also further some internal insight. Instead, however, claimed Lutz Niethammer in his comprehensive study entitled *Die Mitläuferfabrik*, denazification nipped German anti-Fascist organizations in the bud. He saw the elimination of German anti-Fascists and the use made of conservative circles for the rebuilding of a functional and non-political administration to have its genesis in the "Law for Liberation." In its final formulation, the "Law for Liberation" was depoliticized, fashioned solely for the administrative transmission of denazification, and, as Hoegner suspected, used as a decisive instrument for mass rehabiliation of former NS followers.

"Immediately following the Third Reich, denazification pushed many people, especially those of the middle classes and the civil servants, into a defensive position. It thereby buried the motives of the active political reorientation of former NS adherents, making these people much more inclined to adapt themselves to the present ruling order so long as it ensured private success without public conflict. As last ditch efforts of the liberal occupation dictatorship, it actually paralyzed the autochthonous alternatives to Fascism, undermining on the right the onset of an authoritarian constitutional state, and on the left taking the wind out of the sail of anti-Fascist structural reforms, whose goal was a complete reordering of society. Even before the cold war reached its dramatic climax, the American type of denazification, under the banner of radical measures against National Socialism, laid the foundation for integration into the West. This helped overcome the profound social crisis that followed the collapse of Fascism, providing a stabilizing intervention in the form of general continuity in the social order, and the unimpeded establishment of liberal political institutions. At the same time, however, denazification required a modification of liberal goals. In the course of restraining both authoritarian and socialistic alternatives to Fascism, the restoration of a basic legal system had to be deferred, since it was not possible to awaken the political interest of large groups of people."[155]

The manner in which denazificaiton was handled augmented the quandary in which those who were prepared to work with the occupying powers in the interest of a democratization of Germany found themselves. One thinks especially of those emigrants and persecuted people, and also of those who had overcome the failure of the Third Reich and now wished to engage in the building of a new government and society. This difficulty caused Eugen Kogon to pose the question of collaboration. On the one hand, people were convinced that the deep roots that National Socialism had in the majority of the population could only be pulled out with stern measures. On the other hand, the formalism and the frequent arbitrary actions contradicted the ideal image of a pure Germany for which they were striving. The distinction between justified cooperation and despicable collaboration was that between matter-of-factness and servility, insight and deadly obedience, true partnership and a purely subordinate relationship.

One can almost speak of a culture-shock experienced by all those who, for whatever reason, began to have doubts about an honest partnership between the Allies and the Germans for the "overcoming of National Socialism." Those returning to Germany, in particular, were aware of the loneliness that increasingly surrounded them in their role as "moral admonishers."

The "prescribed democracy," with its purgatory of denazification, was questionable. However, there was also lacking the inner readiness of the Germans to re-think and to separate from the past. The inability to mourn was compensated for by arrogance. When Ludwig Marcus came back for the first time to Germany, relatively late, in 1949, he experienced a "return to something foreign." He had left Germany in 1933, and six years later flew from France to America, where he held a chair in German and philosophy at the University of Southern California. He visited Dolf Sternberger in Heidelberg, and described this experience in a letter to his university collegues, Harold von Hofe and Stanley R. Townsend:

"Ilschen, his Jewish wife, he is Protestant, is an old friend of ours. Wild with joy at seeing us again. We went out in her volkswagon. Up the Neckar. On the other side. Dining in a small village. Famous for raspberry brandy. Talk, talk, talk. Complaining about the Belzners. Complaining about Dombrowski. They are isolated and lonely, like all my acquaintances in Germany. They say, in Hitler's day we still had friends. A federation of Anti's. Now everyone is against everyone. No, Germany is out of the question for me. Johst is classified as 'follower,' Sieburg is a great man 'today.' I sent Belzner the title for an article about myself, *Ruckkehr in die Fremde.* Even Novalis can't make Sieburg palatable for me. Germany had a past, and has no future that will concern us in our life-time."[156]

When the deputy Keetenheuve, while enroute to Bonn on the Nibelungenexpress, in Wolfgang Koeppen's novel *Das Treibhaus,* recalled the postwar years, he described with melancholy the loss of high expectations. He had returned to a demolished Germany after 11 years in emigration.

"Keetenheuve's activities, his cooperation in the rebuilding of Germany, his eagerness to create new political foundations for the nation and to work for the freedom of democracy, resulted in his election to the *Bundestag.* He was given a privileged position, receiving his seat without having had to put out much effort in campaigning for it. The end of the war had filled him with hope, which he kept for a time. He believed he must not give himself to some task, after having stood apart for so long. He wanted to realize the dreams of his youth. He had believed in a transformation, but soon saw how insane this faith was. For people naturally remained the same. They had no intention of becoming something other than what they were, not because the forms of government had changed, or because instead of brown, black, and field-gray, there were now olive-colored uniforms walking through the streets, making babies with girls. Everything was ruined again because of small things, because of the viscous mud that blocked the streams of fresh water, leaving everything stuck where it was, in a transmitted form of life that everyone knew to be a lie."[157]

PART TWO

TO THE LIVING SPIRIT

Internal Reform and Pedagogical Renewal

While denazification was rigidly dominated by the Americans, educational reform, aimed at realizing liberal principles, included the efforts of German institutions. The number of teachers who survived the Third Reich "untainted," maintaining a distance from National Socialism, was quite small. However, by distinguishing themselves through democratic involvement, many were soon able to take leading positions as school principals or head administrators on regional or federal boards of education. In an article written in October, 1945, Hans von Eckardt of the Bavarian government declared that it was time to turn to other matters besides the hitherto prevailing issue of the guilt or innocence of party members. In his view, education was the most pressing concern of spiritual renewal:

"We need teachers. We lack young, fresh, enthusiastic personnel who can inspire children to leave the streets, educate them, and teach them that to become a good person one must study hard instead of beating up the neighbor boy or picking on the weak. We believed people should be noble, helpful and good, and we thought everyone would understand. Goethe once said he hated nothing more than careless work, which he thought the most unpardonable sin. After 12 years of boastful stupidity and a disgraceful lack of education, we thought that every responsible teacher, parent, politician, government administrator and civil servant, pastor and bishop would have the most burning desire to respond to Goethe's challenge. But no. Far from it! Wherever we went we heard only of our duty to understand the great injustice party members would experience if they were asked to step aside for the sake of those who had not been allowed to work for the past 12 years. These latter had to keep their mouths shut, although they did have something to say about their sense of responsibility, about how they loved their people and believed in effort as the measure of the individual." With the help of education, democracy was to develop on the foundation of a "pure attitude, manly decisiveness, and honest self-reflection." For this aim pure and righteous people died, people like professor Huber and the tender Sophie Scholl, who feared God more than human beings. It was time for the wretched to recognize who they were, and with humility, begin to learn.[158] The idealistic passion that tried to bridge the abyss of National Socialism combined with a hardy pedagogics molded by conservative values to form the mentality of those who saw it as their "honorable duty to begin work immediately." They spoke continuously of "internal reform," and yet in their efforts to purify themselves from Fascist evil, they relied mainly on a tradition that was rarely reflected upon. Whenever public institutions or private life proved themselves in danger or in shambles, people sought security in tradition. "What else could they latch onto?"[159]

The CDU was the first party to formulate its pedagogical interests. It did so in the *Berliner Aufruf* (Berlin Declaration) of June, 1946: 1) Guaranteed parental rights; 2) Religious education in public schools under the direction of the churches; 3) Moral reconstitution of the German people through "true humanitarian teachings;" 4) More stringent requirements for entry into higher education.

During the Third Reich, the government had restricted parental rights, eliminated ecclesiastical influence, and leveled the advanced schools in favor of a racist ideology. This experience did not lead to a future-oriented educational policy, but to the restoration of conservatism.[160]

In contrast, the policies of the Social Democrats were traditionally more reformist. They had long since pleaded for a standard school system, and were able to establish a common elementary school during the Weimar Republic. Among their most important demands were the separation of church and state and the democratization of education. The latter included the elimination of tuition for classes and cost for teaching materials, the involvement of parents, and uniform education for all teachers. After 1945, the SPD remained vague about their educational aims. They wanted to develop from a "poor people's party" to a "people's party," and at first their goals converged with American ideas. The direction given to the American educational officers encouraged and supported democratic reforms aimed at achieving a comprehensive educational system. Instead of different types of schools, two sequential schools, an elementary and a secondary school, were to be developed. Differentiation within the secondary school was to facilitate easy transition. All teachers were to attend university. In addition, demands were made for the elimination of tuition and fees for teaching materials, and scholarship aid for the needy was promoted.

Even as late as February, 1948, Oskar Vogelhuber of the Bavarian Ministry of Culture *(Kultusministerium),* later a focal point of educational restoration, interpreted the comprehensive school as the realization of both the American model of democracy and the Christian ideal of the equality of all before God, regardless of ancestry, class, or property. The comprehensive school *(Einheitsschule)* at the time of Humboldt was an expression of the widely emerging German national consciousness. It was hoped that "unity, rights and freedom" would overcome the narrowness of the territorial principalities, with their authoritarianism and submissiveness. "This national ideal of a comprehensive school then entered a new era beginning with the world wars. The new task conceived at this time of confusion was to realize world peace through cooperation and social democracy. This aim corresponded to the American plan for a social and democratic comprehensive school. The ideal was grounded in the course of history, and thus the command of the military government to make a comprehensive school system out of the separated system was in accord with the demands of an educationally matured situation."[161]

The rapid pace of the progressive American educational policy was problematic, however, for the gradually emerging secret alliance between the CDU and conservative American circles. Resistance came from those groups working for the restoration of a neohumanistic ideal of education, emphasizing the elitist character of school systems, and for the renewed influence of churches. The politicians of reform were not able to withstand the *Realpolitiker.*

All discussions about structure were eclipsed by problems of material need. The practical problems served as alibis for those who avoided thorough reflection on the educational system. The many totally demolished or only partially useable school buildings had to be reconstructed. For the larger cities especially, this task lasted decades. Moreover, many of the school buildings were used for military hospitals, camps for refugees and people whose homes had been bombed, and for the purposes of the occupying forces. In Hamburg, of the 400 schools, only 60 were still useable. In Kiel, before the outbreak of World War II, there were 1134 class rooms. By September of 1945, only 100 of them were still useable. In 1952, despite seven years of school reconstruction, a quarter of the class rooms in use in 1939 were still lacking. This meant for Cologne, 64 percent; for Dusseldorf and Bremen, 32 percent; for Bonn, 33 percent; Munich, 35 percent; and Mannheim, 57 percent.

Immediately prior to the war, there was a high birthrate in Germany. These children, as well as the many children of refugees, were ready for school by the end of the war. There were very few teachers to be found. In Bavaria, for example, the total number of students at the *Volksschule*, (A German type of primary school comprised of *Grundschule* and *Hauptschule*.) increased by 59.4 percent in the years from 1939 to 1947. In Schleswig-Holstein, the increase was 136 percent. In 1947, a teacher in Bavaria averaged 65 students, compared with 44 in 1939. In Schleswig-Holstein in 1947, there was one teacher per 78 students, compared with one per 39 before the war. In Lower Saxony in 1946, the *Oberprasident* of Hanover was forced to increase the intended ratio of students per teacher to 70.[162]

There was also a shortage of space, school benches, supplies, and teaching materials. Almost everything hitherto considered necessary for teaching and studying was missing in the "pedagogically primitive state" of the postwar years. Such was the verdict of *Die Schule* (1948), a journal edited since 1946 by Adolf Grimme. In its first years, this journal carried the subtitle, *Monatsschrift fur geistige Ordnung* (Monthly Journal for Intellectual Order). Everything seemed to be lacking, even windows, doors, tables, benches, blackboards, and notepads. "The work was begun anyway, and one obstacle after another was overcome. What the anonymous efforts of German educators have created says more for the spiritual situation of the schools than does any noisy or quiet, but mostly unpedagogical, quarrel about school reform."[163]

The quality of school books posed a special problem. Although millions of textbooks were needed, the propagandistic and ideologically influenced books of the Third Reich could hardly be used. Thus texts from before 1933 had to suffice. The textbook misery was reflected on the inside covers of the books, where statements such as the following emphasized the transitional character of the teaching materials: "This book is among the many textbooks published under the order of the Supreme Commander of the Allied Forces . . . This book was selected after a thorough review of many texts used before Hitler seized power. It is an abridged version of a book written by Germans, and the exerpts here printed contain no changes. The fact that this book is being reprinted does not mean that it without problems regarding education and other points of view. However, in the present circumstances, it is the best there is." Efforts were quickly undertaken to commission "untainted" authors to write textbooks. Already in 1946, a competition was held in Bavaria, and many were encouraged to participate.[164] Even before that, from June to December, 1945, the military government had evaluated 318 books for secondary schools. Of these, 174 were approved, 30 were recommended on the condition that they be edited, and 113 were rejected.[165]

The greatest difficulty of all was the lack of teachers. The teachers or potential teachers lost in the war, and the dismissal of many others due to denazification, 50 percent in the American zone, had fatal consequences. The average age of the teachers was relatively high. In 1945, 53 percent were over 38 years old, indicating that a large number of these had already taught during the Third Reich. Since most of them belonged to the category of nominal party members, they did not become active representatives of the new government system.

To hasten the availability of new teachers, training classes for *Volkschule* teachers were established. Of importance in the selection of trainees was not only their educational preparation, but their political and social circumstances, as well as their human potential. Admission was determined by both a comprehensive test and a psychological examination. In one report on such an examination, the following was noted, "The preliminary results showed that 4 percent were especially suitable, 48 percent suitable, 33 percent less suitable, and 15 percent were not suitable. The examiners emphasized good intentions and intellectual aspiration. At the same time, however, they stressed the 'often shocking discrepancies between attained education and possibilities for education.' It is a bitter fact that not even the 52 percent of the first two categories can be admitted for training. Moreover, there exists the difficulty that some of the perhaps highly qualified refugees speak such difficult dialects that they cannot even teach the required, and very necessary, first years at a village school. How would a West Prussian, a Pomeranian, or a Silesian teach the ABCs to beginning school children in a remote village, or win the trust of the often mistrustful and closed-minded farming parents? The severity of the selection process was only justified by the loftiness of its aims. They would have very much preferred to avoid this harshness, which again struck undeservedly at the young people to whom destiny had already dealt so cruel a blow."[166]

In addition to these emergency measures, the various educational practices in use during the Weimar Republic were resumed. In Hamburg, teachers were educated at the university. In other parts of the British zone, pedagogical colleges were established. Southern Germany had educational institutions resembling a cross between a college and a seminary. Admission to each of these types of institution, including also those bound to a specific confession, was dependent on completion of the graduation exam *(Abitur)*. This is the standard exam for graduation from *Gymnasium*.

In the *Gymnasium* (a secondary school that prepares the student for university), the shortage of teachers was solved in part by the hiring of pensioners, even those quite advanced in years, and by enticing experts from other fields like natural sciences, to come and teach.

By the fall of 1945, Berlin already had 96 secondary schools with a total of 27,863 students, compared with 58,000 students in 1938. In the British zone, 330 secondary schools with 110,000 students were re-opened; in North-Wurttemberg, 90 schools with 30,000 students; in Wurtemberg-Baden and Greater Hesse, 213 schools; and in Bavaria, 123 with 30,575 students. However, because heating was not yet available, only one to two hours of classes were held each day.[167]

Gerhard Storz, Secretary of Culture in Baden-Wurttemberg from 1958 through 1964, described the faculty of a secondary school shortly after zero hour, using a school in Schwabisch-Hall as his example:

"When the faculty assembled on the first day of school, I noticed a change in the familiar circle of teachers. Those colleagues who had once hesitantly worn the swastika, the 'anxiety button,' were for the most part missing. Only one or two had been classified as 'nominal party members' by the trial court of the new German bureau for the 'denazification' of public services, thus allowing them to teach. Others still awaited their turn at the trial court. One did not need to wait longer, for he had been recruited into the *Volksturm* (a territorially-based army established toward the end of the war consisting of boys and men unfit for the war), and only shortly before the war's end had been killed in the Black Forest by a shell fragment. New colleagues, who had once lived and taught in Stuttgart, were now a part of our secondary school. There were also others, some coming from the middle of Germany, from the East, and from the Banat. There was even one colleague who had taught in a secondary school in Dorpat before the deportation of the Germans. He still looked strained from the flight and its attendant privation. Two of the new teachers had not only moved, but had temporarily changed vocation as well. One had been an engineer in the Baltic provinces, and the other was an industrial chemist in the Rhineland. Both waited in Hall to return to their vocations, serving as teachers in the meantime. The school was temporarily directed by the teacher who had taught the longest. Though he returned from the war as a major of the reserves, the Americans fortunately did not see this as politically incriminating.[168]

Belief in the Eternity of the World of the Mind

Pragmatic and political discussions about school constituted one aspect of postwar educational concern. Should the schools follow the example of democraticization through Americanization as in the American zone, or the general reserve and early German involvement as in the British and French zones? An intense debate over values was also occurring. In October, 1945, Herman Nohl set the tone for *Die Sammlung,* a journal with a reputation well beyond the immediate circle of educators. "Our compass is simple morality, a steadfast belief in the eternity of the world of the mind . . . We have spoken quite loudly until now, and thus we must again become silent and objective. We have directed our people's thoughts and fantasies outward for too long, so let us lead them inward again, allowing them to collect themselves." The educator Adolf Reichwien, executed on October 20, 1944, provided an example of moral resistance against Hitler.

Adolf Grimme, the Prussian Social Democratic Secretary of Education during the Weimar years, "explained to the teachers of Hamburg the 'meaning of education' in light of the idealistic polarity of spirit and matter. He did not touch the social-political problem of school structures, although this issue was not foreign to him. His work as Cultural Secretary of Lower Saxony from 1946 to 1947, clearly showed him to belong to the circle of determined school reformers. Like many others, however, he gave internal reform priority over external reform. Grimme and the Social Democratic educator Erich Weniger held similar ideas concerning the restoration of the Prussian pedagogical academies under the name of pedagogical colleges *(Padagogische Hochschulen).* Regarding teacher education, both wished to lay the accent on a 'radical consideration of the foundations of morality.' Weniger understood the *Volkschule* teacher to be an 'advocate of farmers and the proletariat.' At the same time, in the tradition of the German idea of education, this teacher had the socially integrative function of 'bridging the gulf' . . . giving centrality to the common German cultural tradition."[169]

The educational policies developed for secondary schools after Germany's collapse were essentially a flight of idealistic fancy, one which left facts and reality far behind.[170]

The northwestern German policy, developed largely by Josef Schippenkötter, aims at a Christian humanism as the answer to the crisis that rendered everything human questionable. The downright "passionate contemplation of humanism" proves to be a necessary reaction. For the knowledgeable, the word "humanism" conjures up a world rich in content, spiritual values, the finest human behavior, profound expressions, great ideals and purposeful relationships. Antiquity refers to "a contemplative commitment to eternal values, proven knowledge, sound spirituality," "developed form," "sacred cheerfulness," "clear insight and the sunny warmth of noble humaneness." It is the place of "profound progress in human seeking and investigation, perception and comprehension, so profound that we are grasped by eternity and at the same time made aware of living novelty and creative fertility, both for the present and the future." In the Western view, the standpoint of universal depth, width, and height embraces the whole of reality as well as an "affirmation of the transcendence of a personal God." "We are of the conviction that without this creative polarity, a true humanism is not possible. Indeed, the actual process of becoming human can only begin with the acceptance of humanity as being in the image of God." Christianity is seen as closely related to the whole of Western culture, especially that of Germany. Included in this relationship is the "ecclesiasticism founded, shaped and developed through Christ the Lord and God."

The so-called *"Marienauer Pläne,"* published without a signature by Adolf Grimme in *Die Schule,* focus on three key concepts: antiquity, Christianity, and mathematics. The new German education was to mold a German person "who is able to produce high-quality work, who has the will to create a democratic and social constitutional state and to integrate it into a community of peace-loving people, who is inspired by the faith that people can only be saved through intellectual and religious ethical power." The main reasons for the intellectual and moral decay were the undervaluing of the mind and the diseased sense of values. Therefore, German youth were to be protected from the cult of force and material prosperity. "Without the awakening of religious powers within the German people, the recovery of the nation is unthinkable." The religious feeling was also to be maintained outside the bounds of religious education by teaching that all subjects approach "a border between that which can be researched and that which cannot," and that the realm beyond may be understood as religious life. "The transmission of the necessary knowledge and skills for survival of the child and of society must be subordinated to the central aim of education, which is guidance to a clearer recognition of reality, to the experience and affirmation of absolute values, and to moral action."

The *Fendt Plan* was drawn up in 1946 by Franz Fendt, the Bavarian Secretary of Culture. It was based on the assumption that the shaping of society depends on a revitalization of the appreciation of cultural values, that is, that a return to humanity would generate the energy to overcome a value-free naturalism. The idea of true humanity, already portrayed by Humboldt, was to be translated into politics through social democracy. "The aim of education is the harmony of social humanity" . . . "a synthesis of individual, social and moral values through the conscience." Quite untypical for Bavaria, the principal parts of this proposal do not mention the words "Christianity" and "religion." Democracy takes the place of the absolute value, in closest agreement with American ideas. Since formal education was only oriented around value-related phenomena, Fendt rejected encyclopedic aspirations. He hoped that an examination of the content of values would lead to a wise limitation of the many objects of the cultural tradition. The later dispute over the meaning of the exemplary and the essential was already indicated here. Not only individual abilities, but also the manifold expressions of human inclinations, skills and preparedness were considered, thereby justifying diverse avenues of education. Fendt countered the argument that the secondary school was a school for the upper classes, demanding that it be expanded to include recruits from among farmers, the middle class and the working class.

In 1947, Franz Schramm introduced his proposal "as a contribution to the formation of a new people's education." Based on the knowledge of many proposals and programs, including American ideas, he attempted to develop a comprehensive concept of education. His images are summarized in Pestalozzi's epitaph. "A human being, a Christian, a citizen; everything for others, nothing for himself" and in Goethe's three attitudes of reverence, proclaimed in *Wilhelm Meister* as reverence for "that which is above us," "for that which is below us" and "for that which is equal to us." "The downfall of the Christian West took place on German soil with such intensity that the individual and even whole groups of people were powerless in the face of it. The only possible recourse was prayer and the hope that a heavenly storm, the *Pneuma Theou,* would blast away the storm which had been permitted. That has now taken place." While his interpretation of the times and of humanity was equally profound and Christian, Schramm differed from Schnippenkötter in that he lacked specifically humanistic theses. He did in fact integrate the social and democratic aims of Grimme and Fendt, yet he interpreted them more in terms of Christian and philosophical anthropology and history. Despite his world-historical and salvation-historical perspectives, Schramm related concretely to the contemporary problems that needed solving. He advocated a system of choices that would do juctice to the abilities of the individual student. He maintained that "every native ability is connected with a right and a responsibility, the right of the individual to develop his or her talents, and the right of the community to all the intellectual riches that have been developed in the individual."

Almost all reform proposals gave priority to three basic principles: humanism, Christianity, and democracy. Other epistemological concepts, such as antiquity, culture, western studies, religiosity, morality, eternal values, freedom, social thinking, and independences, were used more as interpretative tools than as supplementary notions. Scientific-mathematical thinking and skills received less attention.

Nurseries of the Intellect

A value-oriented approach was also predominant in the reconstruction of universities. National Socialism had not been able to cloud the heaven of ideas. The stars of beauty, truth and goodness began to shine anew with eternal purity.

On November 6, 1945, the University of Hamburg was again turned over to the youth. Senator Landahl gave a speech, appealing to "the best of this heavily afflicted nation" and to "glory of the eternally youthful Hanse city of Hamburg" to again place emphasis on "the German share in Western culture, to the honor of the immortal German spirit." "On this occasion of the solemn reopening of the University of Hamburg, which was once and will be again no more and no less than a rebirth out of a new spirit, our first thoughts must of the students of every university and college from the old world and the new who, during the six-year struggle of the peoples of this earth, found their deaths on battlefields and oceans around the world. Their life was still beginning, irradiated with the power of idealism that inspires every young man. It ended early. Their mothers, young wives, and fiancees have shed and will continue to shed tears for some time to come . . . We Germans want to face the bitter truth courageously, avoiding the lure of self-delusion.

Only in this way will we be able to find and preserve our bearing and our dignity in the face of collapse. Defeated in two wars due to the dilettante and irresponsible nature of our political leadership, we stand here not only in the midst of the rubble of our cities, but also of our Reich and of our spirit."[171]

In September, 1946, Alfred Döblin reported on the inauguration rituals of the Univeristy of Mainz in the magazine, *Das Goldene Tor,* published by him, "At about ten o'clock, we hear from the anteroom the beginnings of gentle, wonderful music from Mozart's *Magic Flute,* accompanied by movement in the hall. Footsteps approached. It was the university procession. These solemn processions are familiar: learned men, dressed in wide, mostly black robes, step slowly, two by two, wearing black mortarboards inherited from a past century on their often white or bald healds . . .

"The procession is followed by a number of citizens, dignitaries, civil servants, and, finally, by people in uniform. We recognize the Director of Public Education, General Schmittlein; the head of the civil admistration of the zone, Mr. Laffon; and finally, the head of the military government, General König. Intermittently, we hear the sweet sounds of the *Magic Flute,* but the rustling, shuffling and whispering swallowed up the music.

"The first to speak was the Burgomaster. His voice was transmitted by loudspeakers to hunderds of people in the anteroom, the stairway, and in the yard. He admitted that when he was asked to establish a study group for the re-establishment of the university, he did not believe that it would bring forth tangible results. The destruction of the city and the depression of the citizens had been too severe, and concern over food, clothing and shelter so urgent, that everything else, he thought, would remain in the background for a long time. With great pleasure, he announced that he had been wrong. After less than nine months, people were gathering to inaugurate the university . . .

"The president of the government of Hesse-Rhineland then took the stand, stating that he saw in the Gutenberg University the key to the material and cultural reconstruction of this area. Then the Bishop of Mainz put his congratulations into a nice picture. Just as the cathedral of Mainz unites all styles in its architecture, so this intellectual center should embrace and assimilate all things intellectual, and then crown them with eternal truth. The Protestant communities donated an organ for the main hall. The President, Dr. Boden, exhorted the university to grow, blossom, and become successful, and Professor Geiler recalled the words of the English amateur historian Wells, who understood history as a race between education and catastrophe; 'May the university contribute to the victory of education.'"[172]

Despite its deep entanglement with National Socialism, the university considered itself a place apart. It cultivated a defiant tone of "nevertheless." The German spirit was misused and dishonored, nevertheless, it survived. The clearings have become quite extensive, nevertheless, as nurseries of the intellect, the universities make reforestation possible.

Most univeristy students were returning soldiers who enjoyed their withdrawal from the vastness of conquered countries into the domain of the intellect. They had had enough of the great years, whose pathos, however, now turned toward democracy, was still welcome. However, it helped carry them through the years in which the reality of the "new university" differed markedly from the metaphors suggested by the official speakers.[173]

In November 1945, a report from Heidelberg provided the following information: The faculty of the medical school was only able to take 1,000 out of 5,000 applicants, while the school of theology still had openings available. The problem increased to such proportions that it was expected that the rejected students would study "illegally." In the opinion of the rector, Professor Bauer, the only solution was to open more faculties. Heidelberg developed criteria for acceptance and rejection. It rejected outright National Socialist activists, students who held positions in the Hitler Youth or in the Federation of German Girls, volunteers of the former SS students or members of the *Ordensburgen.* It favored accepting those who had suffered politically, were disabled due to the war, students who had to interrupt their studies over a long period of time, non-party members, citizens of Heidelberg, and Eastern refugees.

The University of Göttingen was inaugurated on September 3, 1945. Only 4,830 out of 10,000 candidates had been admitted. The university sought to improve its standing through strict selection according to ability and previous education. At the end of the first semester, the students were required to pass an examination in order to correct any possible misjudgment that may have occurred during the selection process. "Max Planck, 87 years old, Nobel Laureate, recipient of this year's Goethe Prize, and inventor of quantum theory, is physically broken due to the loss of his son, who had been hanged by the Nazis in relation to the events of July 20. Yet he has retained his mental alertness, and is now considered the 'Nestor' of the leading university in natural sciences."

At this time also, Giessen was preparing its academic courses. Three thousand students were expected, compared with a previous enrollment of 12,000. Ultimately, it was able to use a barrack for teaching purposes.

The University of Marburg opened its medical school on November 6, 1945, closely followed by the opening of the school of theology. Supplementary classes had to be arranged for some students, among them the young physicians who had to pass their examinations prematurely before the Americans came in, students with emergency certificates who had not properly passed their graduation examinations *(Abitur)*, and those who had dropped out for more than one year.

The turbulence following the collapse of the Third Reich continued to surge into the collective unconscious of the young students. The excess pressure, however, rarely found an outlet. This became evident in September, 1946 in Marburg, on the occassion of the first large international meeting to take place on German soil since the end of World War II. This international training seminar drew twenty university teachers from America, Britain, France, and Switzerland. The discussions were primarily concerned with Germany, past and present. An observer noted the psychological state of the German students: "What is striking is the difficulty that most of them have articulating their views verbally, the flightiness with which they jump from theme to theme, the intensity, even sometimes uncontrolled passion, with which they respond to an unexpected answer, the frequent use of slogans, the urge to patronize others, the shocking lack of knowledge, and exaggerated, almost nervous, national sensitivity. Their thinking is neither flexible nor consistent, but over-hasty, internally agitated, or stiff. The feeling of preconceived opinions, encountered everywhere, may well be the result of the unscrupulously controlled freedom of action during the war."[174]

At the end of 1947, Karl Barth provided a comprehensive analysis of the situation of the German students.[175] First, he developed a catalogue of demands posed by the future to the German academician. He noted that those about to leave the university and take leadership responsibilities in German life, would find themselves situated in the midst of a materially impoverished and spiritually confused people, and in most cases would be impoverished themselves. They were, however, to take part as little as possible in the spiritual confusion of their people, transcending it whenever feasible. As participants in the external suffering that would last years and decades in Germany, they were to learn to discern and judge the spiritually, morally, socially and politically sound or sick thoughts and tendencies. They "will have to think on the basis of an interpretation of

German history that is objective, as much positive as critical, freed of certain old myths, and hopefully unburdened by new myths. Only in this way will it be possible to do justice to the Germany of the present, which will in any case stand under the sign of a radical new beginning. They will have to participate fully and joyfully in the great traditions of this history in ways not even possible, much less actual, for previous generations. It will, however, be necessary for them to distance themselves, decisively and consistently, from certain small and misleading traditions which have been lived through especially by the last generation of Germans." Tomorrow, continued Barth, the German academicians would be the first to spread to the German people the more difficult but fertile enthusiasm for common sense, rather than the enthusiasm for dangerous illusions and ideologies that had been nurtured and spread by German universities. It would be up to them to replace the apathy that followed the exitement of the Hitler years due to the collapse with the courageous will to undertake detailed tasks. It would again be up to them, the academicians, to make the German people familiar with the real world surrounding them, with the peoples of Europe, as well as those of America and Russia, but as they are, and not as they are pictured according to some German construction, and to lead them into a new, realistic interaction with these surroundings.

In the second part of his investigation, Barth responsed to the question of whether the German students of his day were aware of these problems, and studied accordingly. Were they aware of the situations and demands that must be met in order to get a job? On the whole, Barth's conclusion was positive. Most of the German students were more open and more earnest than he had expected. Even the fact that these German students had to pass through Hitler Youth, the National Socialist Labor Service, the army, and Hitler's war, was not necessarily an obstacle to the formation of new characters and new manners. Of course, there were also considerable dangers:

The harsh and often bleak external circumstances of almost all of these students and their families made it necessary for them to finish their studies quickly in order to earn a living. "It is clear that students of this type will not become the salt of the earth that they will need to be tomorrow."

Those Germans not previously convinced that the Allies represented the better side *vis à vis* Germany would also not be convinced by the occupation, by the Allied presence in Germany. "Obviously it is not easy to be the victor, and at the same time, the police, judge, recoverer of debts, educator, and wherever possible even the practical example for the defeated nation."

Barth further noted that the fact that Germany was still hermetically sealed from other countries did not contribute to a better generation of academicians. It was not good for German students to live in the ghetto forced on their nation at that time. As long as the foreign universities remained closed to German students, except for a few fortunate ones who managed to enter with great difficulty, they would miss those inspirations most important for their future. "Furthermore, it is highly possible that the isolation in which the German student is forced to study will further the recurrence of intellectual self-sufficiency, that is, the German introversion, which never served the best interests either of Germany or of the rest of the world."

The majority of those professors who with some title had managed to escape denazification, were unsuited to help the academic youth with the clarification, so urgently needed for the future, of the relationship between the German past and present, or with the development of a real receptivity toward new questions. "It is fatal that so many German students are exposed to the teaching, education, and example of this type of professor. In this school they will never become free."

Nevertheless, Barth went on, the intellectual disposition of the German students gave reason for hope regarding their future. They could, if necessary, survive the external pressures of their situation with good humor. They could if necessary, remain calm despite the sins of omission and commission attributable to the Allies. They could, if necessary, become earnest and open people even in the midst of the German ghetto. If need be, they could transcend the direct and indirect prophesies of the older generation. If need be, they could, as German students, become already today what they should be in the future. "It is hardly possible, but still it is possible. If I am right in this opinion, with which I intend to do honor to a certain type of German student, then there are hidden possibilities which are more powerful than the most visible dangers."

Karl Barth's critique of the old spirit of the new universities proved to be correct even in the sciences, which sought to pioneer new ground and thereby question the accustomed process of research with its affirmative image of humanity. This was true for psychoanalysis and psychosomatic medicine. One of their outstanding representatives, Alexander Mitscherlich, was thus "academically" negated and defamed. Even as late as 1956, when on the occasion of the hundredth birthday of Sigmund Freud the Hessian state government established a chair for psychoanalysis and psychosomatic medicine, the University of Frankfurt showed no interest. It did not want to be under the same roof with psychoanalysis and psychosomatics. Americans achieved little success in their efforts to re-establish psychoanalysis in Germany after its prohibition and persecution by National Socialism. Commenting on the University of Heidelberg, where he began his work, Mitscherlich noted that the situation "looked bleak, for it was highly unlikely that we could get any funding for psychosomatic research, whether from the government or from private sources. It is quite certain that we would never have received any money had Alan Gregg not been willing to make available a half million dollars from the Rockefeller Foundation. This generous donation carried with it the stipulation that an equal amount would have to be raised in Germany. It is probable that neither the donation mediated by Alan Gregg nor the successful collection of the complementary German funding would have been possible were it not for the fortunate circumstance that I, as a politically 'unaffected' and 'persecuted' man, made the application. This classification was used during denazification for those who were not involved in any of the activities of the Hitler Reich or who had also suffered under the regime. Thus, after the successful collection of funds, we could begin to build up, step by step, the department of psychoanalysis. This happened in the years from 1949 to 1950, despite the intentions of the trend-setting leaders of the big hospitals. It would be a grave exaggeration to say that the university was proud of the appearance of this new clinical and theoretical field of research. We were kept on as low a low flame as possible. Still today, I am ready to burst with indignation over the University of Heidelberg, which with its liberal humanist tradition was still unable to accept the humanism of Freud."[176]

Karl Jaspers, then full professor of philosophy at the University of Heidelberg, described the responsibility of the universities at a conference of university rectors in the American zone held in the spring of 1947. His speech wandered far into the realm of "fiction" when he began to describe the ideal of what the German university of the postwar years neither could, nor intended, to carry out.

According to Jaspers, the task of the university was to rekindle the spirit, the idea, the spark in the heap of ashes. This could only take place through the collective efforts of productively researching, spiritual people who, on the whole, despite unavoidable failures, would radiate an intellectual aura. This restoration, he continued, is inseparable from the revolution of thought springing from a catastrophe which, after a long preparation, broke surprisingly in 1939.

"We cannot live as if nothing had happened, as if we could begin again where we stopped in 1933, as if we only needed to restore what used to be. We must find ourselves in a new world, thus contributing our share on the way to a world order. It is not yet determined what we are and what we shall be. Morally and spiritually, it remains decisively a matter of our freedom. The university is to be the intellectual wellspring of democracy as a way of life in the future, not through political activity, but through preparation. Either the university will educate itself and its youth in the full freedom of the truth which emerges through radical discussion, thereby allowing truth to show its unifying nature even through the modulations of speech, or, the university will disappear in the leveling process of a mere school with only finite, utilitarian purposes and no power to mold people."[177]

Exactly the latter occurred. The university was neither able to legitimate itself as a "people's university," through the selection of the best of the population, nor was it able to operate out of a spirit of social and political responsibility. It disappeared "in the leveling process of a mere school with only finite, utilitarian purposes and no power to mold people." If Karl Jasper's call to responsibility would have been taken seriously by the universities, the materialism of the fifties would not have become so rampant, paralyzing the awakening of the postwar years. Likewise, the later uprising against the universities with a thousand years of mustiness in their gowns would not have been necessary.

Adult Education

Adult evening classes *(Volkshochschule)* experienced a boom shortly after the end of the war. They were unable, however, to build a bridge to the university which would have opened new avenues for both institutions. Rather, the idealistic, largely aesthetic tendencies of the movement for adult education in the Weimar Republic were continued and augmented in light of the general retreat into introspection. As in the schools and universities, the exhortations to "change" and "reflection" dominated, at least in theory, and were expressed with the pathos of "radical humanity." The temporal downfall of German culture did not affect the "immortality of the German spirit." In both small and large cities, evening classes and plans for adult education were developed. They abided by the principle that all spheres, classes, vocations and age groups should meet, thus anticipating the pluralistic society in practice before it was conceptualized constitutionally. Granted, the attempt to find a common denominator for the different interests and expectations coming from the most diverse educational backgrounds, often led to watered-down jargon, later characterized by Theodor Adorno as "jargon of authenticity" *(Jargon der Eigentlichkeit)*. However, this attempt represented not only the "wrapping" of a conservative model of thinking, but democratic progress as well.

In his novel, *The Glass Bead Game,* Hermann Hesse spoke of an approaching "Age of the Feuilleton" (Age of the Serial), characterized by superficiality. Those loyal to the spirit lived in Castalia, a province of the spirit in the midst of a chaotic world. "Adult evening classes" were a combination of both feuilletonism and Castalain contemplation. They showed an eclecticism that retreated into the cloister, contemplating the world from within, but as a dilettante "lover" of the spirit.

Also imbued with a Castalian mentality were many of the regionally developing Protestant and Catholic academies, which were often closely connected with the movements of adult education. These places were characteristic of the contemplative spirit of the postwar years, exemplifying the willingness to tackle problems in the spirit of openness. They were expressions of the euphoria of encounter that climaxed in the fifties. Teachers, pastors, artistically inclined housewives, and hesitantly skeptical students felt inspired by images of adulthood coming from former adolescents. They met together in solitary, country places for discussions of basic principles. In an article written for the *Hochland* (1947), Heinz Flugel reported that Protestant churches had created places of encounter *(Akademian)* where continuous systematic *"Dialogus christianus"* took place between the Protestant Church and the world. These encounters were intended to provide an open dialogue with the world, to whose criticism the church would expose itself with the same openness with which it expected the lay person to respond to God's question, "Adam, where are you?"[178]

In April, 1946, a survey was made of the reconstruction of the adult education classes which, as free education for adults, had been destroyed in 1933. The survey showed that despite regional differences, the institutions in the various zones had the following characteristics in common:[179]

For a minimal fee, they were open to all adult persons, regardless of sex, heritage or creed.

They encompassed all areas of knowledge, but concentrated on the political and social education of those in attendance.

Their goal was not research, but the formation of persons. The focus was not expertise, but a free interchange of ideas.

Interest was very high because the classes met the demands of the population. At that time, the greater Berlin area alone opened 25 adult education centers. The charge for a two-hour class was 1.50 Reichsmarks. Apprentices and people disabled by Fascism paid half that amount. The total number of students per trimester was 40,000. Women constituted 60 percent of this total; 20 percent came from the working class, 40 percent were office workers, 10 percent were civil servants, and the remainder consisted of youth and the self-employed. Of the students, 40 percent were under 25 years old, and 35 percent were between 25 and 40. Approximately 800 instructors taught 945 courses.

At this time, Munich offered 50 courses and seminars in its adult education program. Under the directorship of Max Ludwig Held, it cooperated with the libraries and art museums of Munich. Among its staff were professors and instructors of the University of Munich, "important private scholars and famous people from the business and cultural spheres." Special emphasis was placed on seminars. "Their task lay in the clarification of scientific concepts and in the education toward independent judgment through free dialogue on a nonpartisan and interconfessional basis patterned after the English and American debating clubs."

In the British zone, 35 adult education centers were established. At a seminar in Hannover which brought together important representatives of adult education theories, Adolf Grimme described the pedagogics of the adult evening classes as work in the German person. If Germany was to have any future at all, he maintained, its citizens should be as good Germans as they are good Europeans.

A report from 1946[180] recognized the further growth of the adult evening classes, and a strong intellectual upsurge in the large as well as the small cities. The astonishing fact was that the degree of destruction in a city had little significant influence in this regard. The decisive factor was the inner spiritual vitality of the city and the supportive participation of the city government. Berlin reported 38,000 students, Hamburg 15,000, and Dusseldorf 12,000. However, these attractive totals included no fewer than 16,000 language students. As to the age of the students, in Stuttgart 80 percent were between 18 and 35; in Hamburg, 75 percent were between 16 and 25. The number of male students increased substantially, and in Berlin male students had already outnumbered the female students.

In contrast to the popularity of courses in practical and directly job-related fields, and to lectures on cultural-historical and philosophical subjects, there was little interest in youth-related subjects. Courses such as "Talks with Youth about Youth" and "Forum for Youth" were fiascoes. This indicated that the older generation was unable to approach the young people on subjects directly related to them. Political subjects fared similarly, and courses such as "People, Government, and Democracy," "The Rebuilding of the Reich," "The Struggle for Economic Democracy," and "Socialist Principles" were poorly attended. This general rejection of subjects critical of contemporary issues gives reason to think.

Adult evening classes were quite influential in Ulm. They were headed by Inge Scholl, the daughter of the presiding Burgomaster and sister of Hans and Sophie Scholl, who were killed by the National Socialists. At 28 years of age, she founded the adult evening classes in the summer of 1946. After one year, they attained a membership of 3,000 students, or 5 percent of the population. Every member was allowed to attend as many performances, courses, and seminars as he or she wished for a monthly fee of two marks. Each month was given a certain theme. Furthermore, there were exhibitions of modern art, readings by authors, and guided tours through technological industries. There were also "competitions" during the first year. The theme for one of these was "which do you think is better: a reconstruction of Germany that would take 50 years because it respects the freedom, inviolability and dignity of each person, thereby respecting differences of opinion, or a dictatorial reconstruction wielding power over individuals and therefore only taking five years? Why?" Another subject was "Ulm in the year 2000." The center also established a studio theater managed mainly by amateurs.[181]

Inge Scholl brought a new aesthetic dimension to the adult evening classes. It was a continuation of the Bauhaus ideas in that it brought about the founding of a "College of Design" *(Hochschule für Gestaltung).* The "'Geschwister Scholl Hochschule' intends to educate its students in independent political thinking. It hopes to participate in the establishment of a democratic elite. As heir to the resistance movement of the Scholl brother and sister, it intends to support progressive political forces . . . It especially seeks to influence the design of social products, and will help industry bring form and quality into harmony. Through the rise in exports which will possibly follow, it seeks to increase the living standard."[182] The Swiss architect and sculptor Max Bill, himself a student of Bauhaus, designed the college buildings, becoming its first rector in 1951. In

1955, Walter Gropius gave the address at the official opening. Inge Scholl's husband, the architect Otl Aicher, influenced the design of products in the Federal Republic of Germany. He worked above all in cooperation with the electrical company "Max Braun" in Frankfurt. There emerged the style of "beautiful practicality" *(schöne Sachlichkeit).*

Youth in the Rubble Years

The situation of young people was, on the whole, quite dismal after the war. There were some who had not been recruited into the army, or who had at most entered the *Volkssturm* or become flak assistants at the last minute. Some had been sent to the countryside and had avoided the bomb showers. The return from this rather idyllic atmosphere to the demolished cities at zero hour was a schocking experience. Other children of this generation, inhabiting basements and emergency shelters or fleeing from east to west, lived through this odyssey only through repression and isolation. This shielding mentality, which both registered and repressed the disaster, and scarcely recognized either injury or recovery, was reflected in the thousands of essays written shortly after 1945 on the theme of "war experience." The mediation of this insight into life courses provides a look at the collective "stuff of experience" that fermented the postwar will to live. The following excerpt is from one of the 7,000 essays initiated by the Nuremberg Bureau of Education in 1946:

"I was born in Nuremberg on July 10, 1932. I was seven when the war broke out. There followed hunger, privation, anxiety, misery, tears and frightful bomb attacks. We spent weeks in the bunkers until the Americans arrived. There was a lot of heavy fighting in and around the city. We feared the coming winter. Some weeks ago, I received the news that my father was killed shortly before the end of the war. This affected us deeply, especially since I have more brothers and sisters. But it is better to know that he is dead than to think he is starving or freezing to death somewhere in Russia or Siberia. I am now 14 years old and must think of getting employment. I want to become a correspondent, and still have much to learn before I can fulfill all the demands of my job. But somehow things will work out, and with time the wounds of the war will heal."[183]

Paradisaic memories of the times before the war emerged. There was candy, whipped cream, and chocolate. People looked enviously at the Yankees, who indeed had everything, and yet lived in their civilized ghettoes while the surrounding population lived in want. The school meals, however, offered a glimmer of hope. Children remembered how it was when the message arrived that their father had been killed in war. People experienced the war in their immediate surroundings, and also on their own bodies. The most brutal experiences were the nights of bomb attacks and the fire from low-flying aircraft. "The green grass was red from blood." The dramatic events were described in a stilted, precocious, essay-style German, with borrowed metaphors and phrases and pre-established patterns of feeling. What was shocking was the talkative speechlessness, and the discrepancy between the actual event and the way it was described.

"I rushed into the basement right away. After a short time, everything was quiet again. But as I was leaving, half the city was already in flames. I went home to see what was happening there. Luckily, our house was not on fire. But there had been an accident. My mother lost her life because she stayed at home. My father was at work. I ran to see him. When I told him that mother was dead, tears rolled down his face. He went home. The next day, my mother was buried."

A report of an entrapment due to bomb explosions concludes with this remark, "Flak soldiers came in and dug us out, first my grandfather, then me, then my grandmother, then my uncle. The people who died were my mother and our landlord."

One wrote, "It was almost as if I had been dreaming the whole time, for everything happened so mechanically."[187]

In the October, 1949 issue of *Die Sammlung,* Rosemarie Winter wrote an article about these essays, referring to the 10,000 that had been collected in Northrhine Westphalia in 1948:

"Stacks and stacks of full pages, notebooks were still rare that first year, open dialogues, much more open than the students had ever been allowed to be during those 12 years. Those who did indeed experience it, have forgotten it. Some who recently came over from the Soviet zone sometimes mention gratefully that now they can write freely.

"And the teachers? In many cases, they felt controlled. Some asked, 'Should we permit our enemies this look into the souls of our youth? There were also some who saw the results of this collection as a cry for help, which indeed it was. 'We are dealing with young people whose minds are burdened by experiences and memories which they frequently cannot digest. They search also for internal paths in the midst of material misery. This ambiguity demands our assistance!' Will today's school be able to live up to this task?"[185]

In what is today the Federal Republic, about 1,220,000 children had lost their fathers in World War II. Of these, 250,000 had also lost their mothers and were orphans. There are exact statistics for the state of Bavaria in 1949: 244,462 children and young people were without fathers, and 3,445 had also lost their mothers. A condensed, well-researched statistical overview of the emergency situation was made by Ulrich Chaussy. "The situation of the 1.25 million half-orphans was characterized by the mother needing to find work. The children and youth were mostly by themselves during the day. From early on, the older ones had housework and babysitting responsibilities in addition to their school work or apprenticeships.

At least as severe was the fate of another group. In early 1949, in the area of what is now the Federal Republic, there were a total of 1,555,000 youth between the ages of 14 and 24 who had been expelled from former East German and Sudetan territories. The living space decimated through bomb attacks was already too small for those who had traditionally been living in the Federal Republic. Therefore, 730,000 of these young refugees were housed in provisional camps and emergency shelters in the countryside. In Bavaria alone, at the end of 1949 there were 27,000 youth living in so-called 'mass camps.' The scarcity of space was even greater in Schleswig-Holstein, where 61,034 youth were crammed into 491 large camps.

Even in those cases where the refugees were alloted some living space by the authorities, they were still at a disadvantage with respect to the natives. Reporting in January, 1950, on the situation of the young refugees, the *'Jugendaufbauwerk'* took as its example an anonymous Hessian town. On the average, three natives lived in two rooms, while nine refugees had to be satisfied with two rooms of similar size. A significant number of young refugees between 14 and 24 went without shelter. In 1950, the newspaper *Die Zeit* estimated their number to be 100,000.

Despite all efforts at reconstruction, the material insecurity of large segments of young people continued over the years. In April, 1952, the 'Committee for Regional Politics ' of the SPD published the following data: Nine million children and young people live unsatisfactorily, often in inhumane conditions. About half of the 300,000 living in camps are children and adolescents.' In 1956 in the Federal Republic, there were still about 100,000 young people in institutions, or so-called 'youth villages.' Similarily, in Bavaria of that year (1956), there were still 216 camps due to the war, with a total of 48,000 residents, 2000 of whom were children under the age of 14."[186]

In October, 1949, the Bavarian Secretary of Labor and Social Welfare turned to the public with a well-distributed *Call for the Elimination of Youth Unemployment (Aufruf zur Behebung der Berufsnot der Jugend).* "More than 80,000 young people are without work or vocational training in Bavaria. Thousands of them are young refugees living in mass camps under socially inhumane conditions. Craftworkers, industrialists, and business people, establish apprenticeships for our youth! Only one out of ten young people is able to attain a position as an apprentice. The apprentice of today is the skilled worker of tomorrow. An orderly vocational training is the best education for citizenship. Idleness, however, even if not due to one's own fault, is a moral danger that can lead to a basic rejection of government and society . . . The provision of living space for apprentices is as important for the elimination of unemployment among young people as are the apprenticeships themselves! Therefore, take apprentices into your families and register accomodations at the employment office."[187] Still in May, 1950, 472 youth under 25 were registered as unemployed. When school dropouts were added to this figure, the number was estimated at 700,000 which constituted 20 to 25 percent of the unemployed.

Economic misery led to an increase of crime among the youth of the postwar period. "Degenerate youth" became a key term. With all the lamenting, indignation, and emergency measures, people were still powerless in the face of this problem, for its root lay in circumstances which would last a long time. At the end of 1947, a poll offered some insight into the milieu in which young people were forced to grow up.[188] In Fürth, for example, of 11,000 school children, 60 percent were without good shoes, 35 percent had to sleep two or three to a bed, and 40 percent had no winter clothing. In Kassel, 7.5 percent had no shoes at all. In Berlin, they counted 125,000 children without a single pair of functional shoes. In Munich, 20,000 children lived separated from their parents, 17,000 did not have their own bed, and 14,000 had no tooth brush. In Mannheim, 70 percent reported that their parents had no fuel for heat. Only half had a second set of clothes, and 12 percent suffered from edema due to hunger. In Frankfurt, up to one hundred youth slept nightly in the bunker of the central station. Of these, about 60 percent had as their only identification papers, a certificate of discharge from a correctional institution.

Case studies[189] show how broadly the concept of "degeneracy" was understood. Very often, it referred only to a special form of the art of survival.

A twelve-year-old girl writes that the best day in her life was the day her brother died, for then she was able to get his shoes and his pullover.

A thirteen-year-old girl becomes a mother, and a half-dozen boys of 15 argue over the honor of fatherhood.

A married student of twenty-two deals in the black market. His customers and his professors are equally satisfied with his efforts. He has to deal in the black market to finance his studies and to support his family. He studies in order to be able eventually to stop his dealings in the black market.

A refugee girl, once a competent secretary in Stettin with the best of references, is constantly placed by the employment office in positions calling for barn work. Finally, she runs off to take her chances in the big city. The same office permits a farmer's daughter who had been familiar with barn work since she was a child to work on a typewriter as the secretary in the office of the village magistrate. The runaway secretary does find a position in the big city without, however, attaining permission to take up residence. She is forced to stay in all kinds of accomodations until one day she must go to a specialist for skin and venereal diseases. She is now considered "degenerate," whereas the typing farmer's daughter still accepts cigarettes and fabric for blouses without falling into disrepute.

A fourteen-year-old boy from Berlin has been in custody in Bavaria for five months. His father was a transportation worker, and served on the front line during the war. His mother worked in a factory. There was one warm meal in the evening, and they eventually had to go into the air raid shelter. "My brother Willi is 18, a Hitler Youth, who entered the *Volkssturm* at 16. He was still fighting when the Russian tanks were already in Berlin. The Russians did nothing to him, but his neighbors did. He was fired everywhere, because his neighbors reported that he had fought to the very last moment. When I finished school, we skipped town. Illegally, across the demarcation line, a raid, no papers, one week in prison. There we got to know all sorts of people. I would like to become a precision mechanic, but most of all, I want to get out of the camp. People steal here, and the straw mattresses are dirty."

Those who were able and willing to express themselves, in letters to newspapers, to radio stations, and especially in discussions, showed the central component of their psychic profile to be the "psychic picture" of a loss and betrayed generation, an aversion toward their elders. They could not vote in 1933, nor were they entitled to do so later. The National Socialist's stock of military ideas has been preached at school and during their apprenticeship as the single truth, the only right way. A man of twenty-six wrote, "It degrades our fathers' generation that today they repudiate the former attitudes in which they educated us, and with which they threw us into tragic guilt. For we could draw no comparisons with former times, and thus we had nothing with which to criticize. Where are those fathers today who stood in the streets saying 'These happy youth?' when the Hitler Youth marched by? Today these fathers proclaim that they were never Nazis. At that time, however, most of the educators demanded membership in the Hitler Youth . . . What, in fact, did we know in our youth, which truly was no youth? Compulsion and commands! And what did we experience during the last six years, the years that were supposed to be the happiest and most delightful? Horror, death, and heartbreaking misery! Was it our task to break these chains, while the older generation who had launched the dictatorship, almost without exception, did nothing against the regime? Are we to blame?"

Besides disappointment, apathy, and outbreaks of despair, there were also the first signs of a will for reconstruction, a longing for "leadership and guidance." Heinz Piontek, who later became a lyricist and author, wrote a letter in 1946, giving a poetic description of the loneliness of youth. At the time, he was twenty one and studying Germanistics, philosophy and history of art in Munich. He wrote:

"With their eyes opened wide, having aged through the misery and dangers of war, boys and girls stagger into a new, unknown life. Without comprehension, they hear and read about the plots and intrigues of a shameless politics, about the bloodthirstiness, brutality, and megalomania of their leaders. They believe they are dreaming when it is proven to them step by step that all the ideals they once were taught sprang from an arrogant brain without conscience, and were not worth a penny . . . Independently, we clung to these ideals in order to repress the thought that we had sacrificed ourselves for nothing . . . Now we are standing in a new world. We have cast out the old idols. We want to work, to produce, in order to make up for all the things lost and missed, and to reduce our debt. However, the new poles that so powerfully pull us toward them are too different. We are still not ready to discern between good and evil, to perceive clearly our goal. Helplessly, we look at our elders, the more mature and experienced. We need leaders, and more importantly, educators who are able to nurture and secure that which is noble within us, until we are ready to stand on our own feet. And so, on behalf of many, one person asks for all those men and women who despite lies and slander did recognize, with a noble heart and clear reason, the way to a better humanity, to care for the youth."[190]

The Munich Kammerspiele, the Munich Youth Advisory Board, the magazine *Echo der Woche,* and the Bavarian *Jugendring* met together with Carl Zuckmayer for a discussion of his play, *The Devil's General.* Hundreds of young people were invited to take part in this event, which occurred in Munich's city hall in March 1948. The author's formulation, that democracy is to be a process of continuous self-criticism, drew spontaneous applause. A participant noted that "we young people see the actual tragic figure of the play to be second lieutenant Hartmann," a young soldier who initially believed in the ideals but later recognized their hollowness. Again, there was a roaring applause. There was more of the same when someone stated, "Herr Zuckmayer, you may believe us, we are not Nazis anymore, but not all of us met a Harras who was able to open our eyes in time." A girl lamented, "What appeared beautiful and ideal to us, what inspired us, how can all that, be suddenly criminal?" Critical remarks were made about the models of today's democracy and about the educational efforts of the occupying powers. Sadly, it was noted, much of the world was on a path that had already been overcome by this generation.

Bruno E. Werner, one of the leading cultural critics of that time, asked whether this was the picture of a hopeless, apathetic, nihilistic youth. "One could not stop wondering whether, because of their experience, the youth had not made a big step forward which, with all its ramifications, the elders had not yet understood. This became obvious when a fifty-year-old man rose and entered the discussion with pathos and a right of conviction. His words appeared like foreign particles in a purified atmosphere, leaving behind an awkward feeling. This youth, in comparison, is free of pathos. It has grown weary of big words. Those remembering their time as students after World War I would compare in their minds the pathetic, bombastic speeches in the meeting halls, filled with slogans, dominated by party doctrines, and constricted by ideological class prejudices, with the speeches of this youth of 1948. Clumsily or adroitly, they spoke moderately about their own experiences, hardly using slogans, and if they did, they were responded to with cheerful laughter. There was no trace of party lingo. Rather, it was with a questioning and self-critical tone that they asked permission to speak. What could not be overlooked was that behind their skepticism and sobriety there was a yearning for truth and the recognition that an entirely new way had to be found. While walking down the staircase, a person unknown to us said, 'the politicians can learn a thing or two from these young people.'"[191]

Those who began anew socially, politically, economically and culturally did not very often have the trust of the youth, who felt seduced and betrayed. According to an analysis published in the *Frankfurter Hefte* in July 1947, the mistrust was directed against the older generation as a whole, no matter whether this meant politicians, educators, pastors, artists, or parents. The conflict between generations became a key problem, and the mistrust of the young toward their elders threatened to make it impossible for the latter to influence the former.[192]

When the youth organizations started up again, they connected strongly with the organizational forms of those groups formally oppressed by the National Socialists. These included the traditional youth associations of the Protestant and Catholic churches, as well as the unafiliated, socialist, and union-related groups. They united locally to form *Kreisjugendringen*, regionally defined youth associations, by states to form *Landesjugendringen*, and later nationally to form the German *Bundesjugendring*. Because these youth associations were refounded and reconstructed mainly by older functionaries, they did not find much response.

At the beginning, the youth work of the American government enjoyed great popularity. Until the fall of 1950, the Americans had invested 60 million Deutsch Marks especailly for the GYA (German Youth Activities). Sympathy for these institutions was often, of course, very superficial. The program director of the GYA said in 1951, "At the beginning, today we refer to it as the chocolate candy era, our American soldiers treated the German children like American youth. They gave them candy bars and Coca Cola, let them form small Jazz bands, and played baseball and football with them. The officers who had just arrived in Germany simply did not understand the German way of life at this time."[193]

Youth newspapers and magazines were very popular then, covering a broad cultural spectrum and enjoying a large circulation. They addressed youths as individuals, as people like themselves from the younger generation, and not from the older, prejudiced one that had failed. Outstanding papers were the *Ende und Anfang*, a "Zeitung der jungen Generation" published by Franz Josef Bantz as of April, 1946; *Junge Welt, Pinguin, Horizont, Ziel, Ins Neue Leben, Die Zukunft, Jugend,* and *Wir*. Their titles signaled the new awareness of life.

The Allies were especially interested in the old genre of youth magazines. They wanted articles that would "move the youth," idealistic stories, impassioned poems, sports, suggestions for tours, puzzles, and columns for crafts and humor. Increasingly, however, the youth magazines became debating clubs, release valves for the pent up, critical displeasure of the younger generation.

Demythologization

The philosophical consciousness of the time, understood as the locus of intellectual democracy, was determined by demythologization. "Sacred sobriety" was to rule. One's own existence and freedom of decision became the focus of a new individualism. Although the theory behind plans for pedagogical reform was marked by a call to enthusiastic faithfulness, belief in Christianity, antiquity, humanism, democracy, and absolute ideas and ideals, the skepticism arising from the rubble world aspired to an ethic of action. The willingness to establish essence through existence increased when the younger generation received the opportunity to enter leadership positions.

Precisely while reflecting on belief and religion, the intellectually restless and disquieted dared to leap into the freedom of a new bond, but one based on their own decision, thus leaving behind the realm of a traditional, idealistic and affirmative introspection. Their guides or "instigators" were "Nestors" who had always rejected National Socialism.

Great philosophers and theologians, born in the 1880s and thus standing in 1945 on the threshold of their sixth decade, personified the historical experiences of this century. They played a significant, stimulating role through their postwar writings. These people were: Rudolf Bultmann (b. 1884); Romano Guardini (b. 1885); Karl Barth (b. 1886); and Paul Tillich (b. 1886). Protestantism, especially, evolved from a church oriented thought to one oriented on society. It went beyond exegesis and saw itself as an academic discipline directed towards action.

A part of the Catholic branch of the youth movement, Romano Guardini brought about a regeneration of lay Catholicism through his lectures at the University of Munich since 1948. His book *Das Ende der Neuzeit,* published in 1950, was based on his previous lectures in Tübingen, as well as those in Munich. In it he concludes that the modern ideas of "nature," "subjectivity," and "culture" are beginning to founder. Nature suffers from the loss of its saving and recovering powers, appearing unfamiliar and dangerous. The mass man takes the place of rich individuality. The promises of culture become unbelievable in the face of the shaking trust in the automatic process of progress. This, however, represents the very possibility for human beings to become "persons" at last, that is, people who are willing to accept the responsibility given them by God. "The meaning of the world is decided within every person." This confidence is based on the assumption that personality and individuality are related to one another in inverse proportion. People must first lose their natural and cultural riches, which have made possible their individual self-realization, in order to experience the essense of their poverty, of the personhood that is left to itself with the demand to become itself. With his theology, Guardini provided orientation for a spiritually confused generation living in a rubble. It was received with great eagerness.

"The attempts at orientation reflect the mood of awakening that predominated in Germany after 1945. No doubt, the motivation issued from the need to understand the century-long developments of Nazi rule, though this was never stated. However, the guiding aim was not the criticism of the past, but the understanding of the tendencies with which the new epoch proclaims itself. With greatest certainty, says Guardini, we can say that from now on a new phase in history began. For Guardini, the approaching new era is even more than an epoch. In his view, the moment has come for humanity to either lose itself or realize itself in accord with its eternal destiny."[194]

Karl Barth, as the leading representative of the Confessing Church, was a legitimate spokesperson for spiritual renewal. On the Protestant side, he represented a theology that saw National Socialism as a consequence of a "world without God." He radicalized the concept of religion with his criticism of religious saturation, petrified institutions, and the mistaken development of the churches. Believers were challenged to prove themselves existentially. Due to his refusal to deliver the pledge to Hitler while a professor in Bonn, he was forced to leave Germany. He was regarded as the actual head of the program of theological resistance in the Third Reich. One of his followers was Pastor Dietrich Bonhoeffer, who was later executed by the Nazis.

"We are permitted to be God's witnesses. He did not call us to be his advocates, engineers, managers, pollsters or directors of administration." The suffering desire and the suffering courage of the postwar generation closely correspond to Barth's exhortation to take the path through the abyss rather than sneaking around it. In his July 1945 letter to the theologians in war prisons he wrote, "Is it not as if all the angels in heaven are holding their breath in anticipation of what could and should happen among the Germans after their loss of splendor, honor, and pride? The Germans are in an enviable position because of the offer now presented them."[195] Barth thus demonstrated his great hope in the spiritual and moral renewal of a country which, because it was struck down, was offered "healing."

According to Rudolf Bultmann, humanity is given a finite knowledge about itself that lies before all reflection, all anthropological discoveries and epistemological problems. This original knowledge derives from the "original deed" of the faithful acknowledgment with which humanity submits to salvation. This frees humans from themselves in order that they may become free for the open future of God. The faith with which we acknowledge our own nothingness and learn to discover ourselves as potential being, as the possibility of becoming ourselves, is the liberation toward the future. It is already salvation. It is the answer to the revelatory word of God.[196]

"A person is not immediately available as such and cannot be regarded objectively as a thing or an animal. The person transcends him or herself, and is only a person in relation to a transcendental world. Persons are only comprehensible in relation to something beyond themselves.

"This idea is explained through the concept of historicity as coined by Heidegger. Persons are historical, that is, their presence is always marked by a decision between their past, with its inheritance or curse, and the future that approaches them. Thus, it may be said that a person is always that which she or he becomes. Personhood is approached; its true presence is still ahead, and can be grasped or lost, in life as in death. Even in death, God will come toward me and challenge me to enter into God's future, into my freedom. I do not yet know how God will meet me. Yet I know that God will meet me there to disclose for me this freedom . . ."[197]

When Bultmann criticized Biblical theology from the standpoint of modern science, asserting that it speaks of God incorrectly, he was not implying that science embraces all of reality. Myths, he argued, prove to be expressions of the insight that humanity is not lord of the world and of its life, and that the world is full of questions and secrets. Mythology is the expression of a certain understanding of human existence. It is a belief that the world and life are grounded in and limited by a power beyond all that which we can figure out and control. In this sense, myth approaches more closely than natural science the whole truth that embraces the world. However, mythology is an insufficient expression of this power, because it treats it as another worldly power. It objectifies the world beyond this world. Radical truth, however, is that of demythologization, myth is only the dress of religion. It is not possible to use electric light and the radio, to utilize modern medicine and clinical means for healing the sick, and to believe at the same time in the spirits and miracles of the New Testament. Faith in spirits and demons is finished. Finished, too, are miracles as miracles. We are done with the stories of Christ's ascent into heaven and descent into hell, and of the return of the son of man at the last judgment. That the words of the Bible are God's words cannot be proven. This is not, however, a sign of the weakness of faith, but of its true strength. For the one who surrenders all security will find true certainty. Humanity cannot attain objective knowledge from God. For Bultmann, radical demythologization parallels the Pauline-Lutheran teaching of justification by faith, without the law. Demythologization destroys all desire for security. There is no difference between the security based on good works and that based on objective knowledge. Those who believe in God must know that they have nothing in their hands which can make them believe. They are, so to speak, placed in the air without being able to ask for a certificate for the truth of the word which they speak. The foundation and object of faith are identical.[198]

Credo, quia absurdum. A generation that had no basis for its intentions experienced in the existential challenge of such a theology a new quality of hope. "Having been thrown" into an all-embracing insecurity, one could find ground in the decision to believe. This was true even with respect to the worldly present. One had nothing in one's hands, but one could be of "good faith" if one mistrusted the person of gullible faith with his or her "insuring" myths.

Existence Determines Essence

Alongside the theological radicalism, which in a world without transcendence made transcendence into the actual world, there existed an atheistic existentialism which discovered the transcendence of immanence. Both movements agreed that only existence determines essence, that existence precedes essence, and that tradition, faith, and customs are not trustworthy structures offering security. One is thrown into this world, even "condemned" to it, and is thus forced to find one's way by taking responsibility through decision. Increasingly, Jean-Paul Sarte influenced German intellectual life during the postwar years. According to him, we as acting beings are not determined in our decisions by specific necessities. What we are, we become through our actions. The only instruction for this action is the instruction that it rest entirely on our own decision. To be bound to any norms would only be a betrayal of freedom. For a free person, the only answer to the question of why this and not another decision had been made is because that was how I decided. Concerned German philosophers argued that freedom could suffocate in its own exuberance, that if it is no longer possible to ascertain a ground for deciding for or against something, there will soon be nothing more to decide. People will then have to be content to roll like a ball between the cliffs in their lives.

Knowledge of Sartre's philosophy remained vague at first. As late as July 1947, Julius Ebbinghaus, professor of philosophy in Marburg, claimed that he had been unable to find Sartre's novels. "But perhaps we will be able to convince the occupying officers to loosen up the ban on books by informing them of how much we would like to know what stirring literature the French had been able to produce by knocking off the overly profound head of a philosophy invented in Denmark and systematized in Germany."[199] He was referring to Kierkegaard, Jaspers and Heidegger.

In any case, later, the theater club "Möwe" produced Sartre's existentialist Oresteia, *The Flies,* written in 1942. Successful artists met at the Möwe, enjoying beer, Vodka, hot dogs and Borscht. The author came to the premiere with his life companion, Simone de Beauvoir.[200]

Orestes murdered his mother and step-father. While Electra was conscience-stricken, Orestes stood by his action, "I have done *my* deed, Electra, and that deed was good. I shall bear it on my shoulders as a carrier as a ferry carries the traveler to the farther bank. And when I have brought it to the farther bank, I shall take stock of it. The heavier it is to carry, the better pleased I shall be, for that burden is my freedom. Only yesterday I walked the earth haphazardly, thousands of roads I tramped brought me nowhere, for they were other men's roads. Yes, I tried them all, the haulers' tracks along the riverside, the mule-paths in the mountains, the broad, flagged highways of the charioteers. But none of these was mine. Today I have one path only, and heaven knows where it leads. But it is *my* path." Sartre portrays the Furies, once admonishers of divine justice, as a swarm of disgusting blowflies that cover the city and transform it into a repulsive place. The gods themselves look like a band of haggling gangsters. They perceive anxiety and bad conscience in people as a "scent pleasing to the nose." Orestes separates from them. He alone determines the laws of his actions. He is his own God. "Neither slave nor master. I *am* my freedom. No sooner had you created me than I ceased to be yours. . . . Suddenly, out of the blue, freedom crashed down on me and swept me off my feet.

Nature sprang back, my youth went with the wind, and I knew myself alone, utterly alone in the midst of this well-meaning little universe of yours. I was like a man who's lost his shadow. And there was nothing left in heaven, no right or wrong, nor anyone to give me orders . . . Foreign to myself, I know it. Outside nature, against nature, without excuse, beyond remedy, except what remedy I find within myself. But I shall not return under your law. I am doomed to have no other law but mine. Nor shall I come back to nature, the nature you found good. In it are a thousand beaten paths all leading to you, but I must blaze by own trail. For I, Zeus, am a man, and every man must find his own way."[201]

Sartre's *Flies* was prohibited at first in the western zones, due to its rebellious and amoral content. In 1947, Gustaf Gründgens produced it in Dusseldorf. In the same year, Friedlich Luft reported on a performance of the play in Berlin. He also depicted the "progressing" discussion of existentialism:

"Satre's *Flies* was performed. It has been staged so compactly that after the premiere, Berlin humor re-baptized the play 'The Meat-Flies of Fehling.' German staging placed more emphasis on ideas, on turning away from repentance while postulating the unlimited freedom of humanity. When Sartre arrived last week in Berlin, greeted by the magistrate of the city and by the interest group of German authors, he made himself available for a private discussion to clarify the concepts of his play. As a result, the former impressions had to be fully revised. Sartre, who was small of stature, completely unpretentious, appearing highly interested from behind his thick glasses, personable and skillful in dealing with his surroundings, portrayed nothing of the distorted image of a lustful writer who sat drinking absinthe while flirting with nihilism . . . He brought clarification to the round table discussion which took place in the overflowing Hebbel Theater Sunday morning. He thoughtfully limited his subject to a discussion based only on *The Flies.* Again, he impressed people with his manner by repeatedly leading the often heated discussion back to the realm of correct thinking . . . Satre showed how a piece, originally written as a disguised call for resistance during German occupation, obviously had the reverse effect today. The negation of the repentance against which he had fought because it had been suggested by the Nazis, would today render assistance to those same Nazis. In response to the argument gleefully put forth by the Marxists, that the piece would in this way be determined by the dialectical process denied by Sartre in his system, he countered that repentance had never led to action in history. Responsibility would, however, and he would relieve no one in his play of responsibility. His call for full freedom implied absolute responsibility. In this connection, he was challenged by arguments from the Christians at the table. In their view, freedom without direction was inadmissible. Freedom towards what? Sartre replied that the very question was already unfree. Indeed, Christians had clearly used their freedom by choosing God. He, Sartre, the atheist, had used it to negate God. In response to this argument, a Christian speaker pointed out the difference between their points of view, namely, that in the Christian world, essence preceeds being. He concluded on a conciliatory note, quoting Pascal's idea that the Christian lives in anxiety of losing God, while the atheist lives in fear of finding God. When again attacked by the Marxists, Sartre clarified his concept of freedom, defining it in a three-fold manner as metaphorical, artistic, and social-political."[202]

People began to trace the roots of existentialist thought. In contrast to the French philosophers, Karl Jaspers had been present in the rubble world from the beginning. That one might, in the midst of failure, attain true being, was for him balm on the wounds of those who by zero hour had lost hope. Jaspers pointed out that people continuously pretended to think and act in the name of supposed absolute demands, but that in fact they really stood in crass contrast to them. They spoke of morality and law, but these demands only hid immorality and violence. They mutually condemned their opinions in the name of some truth, yet with this unrealizable pretention to truth, they made everyone into liars. What was spreading under the veil of objectivity, was in reality unjust, pompous subjectivity itself, injuring the subjectivity of others and of itself. In contrast, the existential dialectician held onto the paradox that persons possess the norm for action and for self discovery and the discovery of others only in the renunciation of all normativity.

Martin Heidegger's philosophy was also rediscovered. It understood humanity's existence as concern. The person gets lost among the manifold cares and concerns. Anxiety appears as a basic condition, revealing the reality of our lostness in a "strange" *(unheimlichen)* world. In *Holzwege (Woodpaths),* published in 1949, Heidegger described the mood of decline which since Nietzsche had characterized the German spirit.

The optimism of planning which was opposed to self-ruin was in fact furthering the progress of doom with the growing perfection and independence of scientific and technological tools. As with Gottfried Benn, Heidegger possessed a fateful and mythical understanding of doom. It was linked with a strong antipathy to technology, expressed in a language that prevented "enlightenment," illumination through reason and "logical thought," with its mumbling mystification.[203]

The wrapping is the message! Theodor W. Adorno later called this talk the "jargon of authenticity" *(Jargon der Eigentlichkeit).* Hypocrisy became an *a priori,* an everyday language that is spoken here and now is thought of as sacred. "This could approach profane language by distancing itself from the tone of the sacred, not by imitating it. Blasphemously, the jargon trespasses against the sacred. By clothing empirical words with an aura, the jargon spreads general philosophical concepts and ideas so thickly that their conceptual essence, their mediation through the thinking subject, disappears beneath the covering. Then, as the most concrete concepts, they attract. Transcendence and concreteness glitter. Ambiguity is the medium of a linguistic attitude whose favorite philosophy is condemned by the former."[204]

Albert Camus' *Myth of Sisyphus* was felt to correspond most closely with the situation of the individual. Even when texts of his work were not yet available, his "absurd thinking" entered the postwar consciousness by osmosis. People were fascinated by the idea that action could be both sensible and nonsensical. The point was to roll the stone without even the chance of getting it up, and yet to experience happiness. Those who decided to act, gave a purpose to their existence that reality seemed to withhold. *The Myth of Sisyphus* became the breviary of a generation that sought to flee from the pressure of an anonymous destiny by accepting it as their "own." This constituted the entire secret joy of Sisyphus, his destiny belonged to him, his rock was his own. "The absurd man says yes and his effort will henceforth be unceasing."

If there is a personal fate, then there is no overriding destiny, or at least only one that he finds disastrous and disdainful. Furthermore, he knows himself to be master of his time. Precisely at that moment when he again turns toward his life, a Sisyphus returning to his stone, he looks, while turning, at the sequence of disconnected actions that have become his destiny, his original creation, united in memory and soon to be sealed by death. Convinced of the purely human origin of all humanness, he is always under way, a blind person who wants to see but knows that night is without end. The stone rolls again.

"I leave Sisyphus at the foot of the mountain! One always finds one's burden again. But Sisyphus teaches the higher fidelity that negates the gods and raises rocks. He too concludes that all is well. This universe henceforth without a master seems to him neither sterile nor futile. Each atom of that stone, each mineral flake of that night-filled mountain, in itself forms a world. The struggle itself toward the heights is enough to fill a man's heart. One must imagine Sisyphus happy."[205]

And then, suddenly, the stone was indeed up. The cold war had made it possible. The philosophical radicalism was pushed aside by German materialism set in motion by the Western Allies. The now successful "skeptical generation" paved the way into the country of the economic miracle. It was "skeptical" inasmuch as it distrusted the world of ideas.[206] Courage in absurdity was replaced by a sharpened sense of reality, one which decided for the practical and teachable. Existentialism was displaced by concreteness. Intellectual sobriety freed forces for the unfolding of a unique fitness for life. The vertical line of introspection turned into the horizontal line of an expansive striving for success, more concerned with prices than with values.

By the end of the 1940s, as West German society became more and more determined by the process of reconstruction, restoration, and consolidation, as well as by the increase in living standards, there emerged a youth motivated by a profound yearning for security. It considered its primary task to be the stablization of personal and private everyday life through material values and the improvement of the quality of life. When "skepticism" is considered the intellectual attitude of this youth, what is referred to is the rejection of romantic and naturalistic zealotry, of a vague idealism lacking in the possibilities for concretization, and also of the intellectual systems of planning and ordering that presumed to explain and clarify all things at once. What prevailed instead was a sharpened sense of truthfulness and a relentless desire for reality. Out of this basic attitude, there developed an almost masterly flexibility in the realm of practical life, a clear and sure sense of the possible and the necessary, a sharp and sober estimation of one's own capacity and that of others, and an astonishing sense for that which is useful.

Existentialism, which has stirringly determined the sensibilities of the postwar, rubble generation, degenerated into a fad. Essence, however, continued to be determined by existence as freedom towards the compulsion of consumption, which determined social prestige. The absurd, turned over on its head, learned to walk. It moved out of the realm of questions of purpose and into the arena of utility. The poor could find rest in concreteness.

CONSTANT INTERCHANGE OF IDEAS

The Glory and Misery of the Licensed Press

More than in any other area, claimed Norbert Frei, the structural and personal interventions in press and radio by the Allies were of greatest importance for the later development of the Federal Republic.[207] For a variety of reasons, the idea of reeducation found an especially fertile soil:

Because of their own history, the Western Allies understood the significance of the publishing world for a democratic society.

They were assisted by outstanding experts who not only had long experience with the freedom of the press in England and America, but who were also aware of the unfortunate developments of the Western press. The *tabula rasa* of zero hour offered them the chance to design their ideal model in the occupied country.

The German hunger for information grew more intense with the insight, which even spread among former National Socialists themselves, that they had been incredibly deceived by NS propaganda.

The Allied press officers had not only a good knowledge of the unincriminated journalists, but also a good sense for skilled young people who would soon come into their own, despite the domination of Weimar veterans. Much attention was devoted to the problem of junior staff members. Munich became the center of requisition efforts. Otto Groth, a journalist and former editor of the *Frankfurter Zeitung*, dismissed in 1933, began conducting classes for the press in 1946. Werner Friedmann, licensed to begin the *Suddeutscher Zeitung*, inaugurated a course in editing that resulted in the German School of Journalism *(Deutsche Journalistenschule e.v.)*

The majority was made up of those who had participated in the Third Reich and had now changed their positions. Their denazification was dealt with relatively quickly, for their experience was needed.

For its first phase, the Allied press considered a general news blackout. The population was to be cut off from all information until the total surrender. It was intended that such a "purification" be followed by a reorientation through a new press. But because the war continued so much longer on German soil, it was not possible to realize this concept. While the *Völkische Beobachter*, with its constant calls to hold out until victory was won, was being published in Berlin and Munich as the official organ of the NSDAP, the Allied armies were printing army papers in the German language throughout western Germany. The first of these appeared on January 24, 1945. The *Aachener Nachrichten* was founded by a team, headed by the leader of the press department of the Publicity and Psychological Warfare Division (PWD) in the Allied headquarters, Luther Conant. It was published by the Social Democrat Heinrich Holland. The front page headlines read as follows: "Russian Victory March Presses Onward;" "Bromberg Captured, East Prussia Overtaken 270 km from Berlin;" "Allied Airforce Batters Rundstedt's Retreating Coumns;" "Allied Bombers Attack Fuel Depot in Duisburg;" "Allied Army Generals Meet;" "American Troops Advance on Manila;" "Factory Owner Gets Prison Term for Hoarding;" and "Earlier Police Hour Tomorrow."

The *Aachener Nachrichten* represented a pilot project. The leader of the PWD of the 12th Army, Hans Habe, founded and managed eight of these German language army newspapers from Bad Nauheim. They reached a total circulation of almost four million. They were regionalized, with names such as *Kölner Kurier, Braunschweiger Bote, Augsburger Anzeiger,* and *Stuttgarter Stimme.* As Habe's press, these newspapers represented only a transitional solution. It was often the case, however, that because of them the licensing of German papers was delayed.

The replacement of Allied military newspapers by a German licensed press led to a real "Press Miracle" *(Pressewunder).* On June 27, 1945, the first license was given to the *Aachener Nachrichten,* thereby transferring it to a German publisher. The *Frankfurter Rundschau* followed on August 1, 1945. Between July 1945, and September 1949, the three Western Powers gave licenses to 155 new daily newspapers, 61 each in the American and British zones, and 33 in the French zone, in accord with the News Control Regulation No. 1, drawn up on May 12, 1945. Among the newspapers licensed from the American zone were: *Süddeutsche Zeitung* (Munich), the *Nürnberger Nachrichten;* the *Münchner Merkur;* the *Stuttgarter Zeitung;* the *Stuttgarter Nachrichten;* and the *Weser-Kurier* (Bremen). Licensed papers in the British zone included, among others: the *Rheinische Post* (Dusseldorf), the *Westfälische Rundschau* (Dortmund), the *Hannoversche Presse;* the *Hamburger Echo;* the *Kölnische Rundschau;* and the *Freie Presse* (Bielefeld). Permission was granted to the Berlin papers *Der Tagesspiegel, Telegraph, Der Kurier, Der Morgen, Nachtexpress,* and *Berlin am Mittag.*

Berlin provided an example of the rapid rise of a multi-tiered "newspaper landscape." Peter Weidenreich, Berlin's chief correspondent for the *Neue Zeitung,* spoke of a "Newspaper paradise of Berlin" only eight months after the end of the war.[208] Nearly 3 million newspapers were available for 3 million Berliners. In 1937 to 8, only 2.5 million newspapers were printed for over 4 million Berliners. "Beside the German readers' need for the information provided by a free press, the reason for the popularity of the new journalistic products is doubtless to be found in the fact that even more than before 1933, every Berlin paper gradually developed its own distinctive character. The average newspaper reader in Berlin bought at least two papers daily, usually one for news and a 'party paper.'"

Der Berliner, the newspaper of the British military authorites, was possibly Berlin's most popular paper. It was different from the others in that its articles appeared almost completely without commentary. *Der Tagesspiegel* was highly critical in a nonpartisan way. Its articles were meant to clarify for the German reader the interrelatedness of current world politics and the events of the previous twelve years. The *Nachtexpress* recalled Berlin's earlier *Nachtausgabe* not only in name, but also in layout and style. Its tabloid printed the evening news by using various news agencies, as well as a serlialized novel entitled *Mord in der Oper* and local commentaries with such headlines as "Knock Three Times and Get Caviar."

"A rather incisive polemics has been developing in the Berlin press in recent months. With a few unplesant exceptions, this polemics has generally remained objective and to the point. We have witnessed lively debates and critiques, covering such topics as the measures taken by magistrates and parties, the demands of adherents of Federalism, the handling of political cleanup jobs, the disconcerting social occurrences of postwar years, and the question of party unity. Stimulating controversies have also abounded in the spheres of art and culture. In Berlin, the rigid uniformity of the National Socialist Press has given way to an exciting and often fruitful plurality, and the argumentative discussions have helped to clarify many lingering problems."

A report given somewhat later on the former Ullstein House offers some insight into the conditions under which the rise of the new Berlin Press came about.[207] The printing establishment *Tempelhof* was occupied by Russian troops on April 25, 1945, and given over to the business attorney appointed by the magistrate of the city of Berlin. There were no longer any buildings that had not suffered considerable damage from the burnings and bombings. The newspaper rotary machines were still standing, but were not ready for business. Slightly more than a hundred people began working. First machine shops and then the plants were restored. The hydraulic Matern printing presses were uncovered from under many feet of debris. A workable typesetting machine was put together out of three damaged ones. At first, people worked without compensation. Burned paper and other half-charred scraps were sold in order to get funds. Since at the same time a number of branch presses in the city were opened for business, it was possible to undertake publication of the two newspapers of the newly formed political parties. Underneath the rubble was found a treasure chest of ready money.

In July 1945, the American army occupied the sector in Berlin where the two printing businesses of the Ullstein House were located. The restoration and production of the *Allgemeiner Zeitung* published by the US Army was transferred to them. This offered a powerful impetus for reconstruction. The newspaper appeared three times a week, first with a circulation of 200,000, and then 300,000. Soon, it was joined by *Der Berliner,* published by British military authorities, and *Der Kurier,* licensed by the French military government. Eventually the production and distribution of *Der Tagesspiegel,* licensed by the American military government, was ordered. It began to appear daily as of November. The *Deutsche Verlag,* affiliated with the Ullstein publishing house, was charged with the production and distribution of the following licensed newspapers and magazines: *Sie,* a weekly newspaper for women; *Horizont,* a biweekly magazine for young people; *Ulensplegel,* a bi-monthly magazine of literature, art, and satire; *Petrus-Blatt,* put out by the Catholic Church for the Berlin diocese, and *Kirche,* a paper for Protestant Christians. Books were also beginning to be produced by the publishing companies licensed by the Ameircan military government. As of January 1946, the business of the Neue Zeitung, the journal Heute, the *Amerikanischen Rundschau,* and the *Neue Auslese* was ultimately taken over by Ullstein.

The rise of journalism was closely connected with the beginning of the news agencies. The Allied Press Service (APS) of London, which former Ullstein journalist Peter de Mendelssohn helped found, was of decisive significance until the end of 1945. As of June 1945, there was a German News Service (GNS) for both the American and the English zones. The enterprise was then renamed. As the *Deutsche Allgemeine Nachrichtenagentur, Dana,* and from 1947, *Dena,* it served the papers licensed by the Americans. In October 1946, the *Allgemeine Deutsche Nachrichtendienst* (ADN) was started. As of December, 1945, the GNS, run by the English in Hamburg, became the Deutscher Presse Dienst (dpd). The French founded the *Rhenia* in Baden-Baden, later called the *Süddena.* The Allies maintained direct control of news agencies considerably longer than of newspapers and magazines. Until 1947, the possibilities for German contribution were limited to editorial collaboration.

The publishing license was transferred to *Dena* and *dpd* in July of 1947, and in 1949 these two merged to become the *Deutschen Presse-Agentur (dpa).* Editor-in-chief Fritz Sänger, an SPD party member whose appointment the newly elected Konrad Adenauer wished to obstruct, arranged to have the following text as the first announcement: "The news agency will be characterized by a concern for objective reporting, and independence from every interest group, be it of the state, political party, or business."

In Berlin, and in the Soviet, English, and French zones, the parties participated in publishing newspapers. The Americans, however, conferred licenses only on publishing staffs consisting of three or more persons of differing political orientations or world views. "Underlying this panel model was the idea that the entire spectrum of democratic opinion should be mirrored in the commentaries, first of every large city newspaper. The precepts of fairness, independence, and objectivity were upheld. The 'opinionless' general announcement press and the selectively reporting party organs were to be relegated to the Weimar past. This procedure demonstrated the efforts to learn of the structural shortcomings in the history of the German press, exposed by emigrants in knowledgeable studies, without attempting to clumsily impose native American ways.

"Naturally, some of these panels that were genuninely innovative came to quarrel a lot, almost regularly in those cases where KPD people (Communist Party of Germany) were licensed. The Americans revoked their licenses with the intensification of the 'Cold War' toward the end of 1947. Negative experiences with strangers to the field also caused the Information Control to revise their concepts. In the beginning, impressive political personalities and exemplary opponents of National Socialism frequently obtained licenses, and then never made any effort to move beyond their dilettante status. Therefore, the press officials decided to license at most only two persons per newspaper, giving them clearly defined tasks, like editor and publisher. They tried to fill these positions with people who had already worked with the press during the Weimar era, and/or had lost their editing licenses on political grounds during the Third Reich. These criteria did not immediately result in a younger force of licensed press, the average age in the U.S. zone was around fifty years."[210]

The selection process was quite thorough. In Bavaria, more than 2,000 applicants were examined for 49 licensed positions. Granted, the relationship of the journalist to the means of production was not redefined wtihin the new context of the licensed press. The new press was indeed independent of capital. The new publishers, however, became the "capitalists" upon whom the journalists again became dependent, determined from without just as before. They simply started where they had finished in 1933.[211] The licensed newspapers flourished, and thus no one saw the need to worry about co-determination and co-participation. The "Union of Bavarian Newspaper Publishers" even gave an ethical foundation to the accumulation of wealth. According to a resolution passed in October 1946, presses licensed by the American press regulations were called into being in order eventually to found trans-partisan newspapers. This move presupposed their intellectual and economic independence. "This can only be guaranteed if the license-holders on whom personal responsibility is conferred are able to make decisions freely and without the influence of external developments. For this to be possible, they must be the actual proprieters of their own firms. They cannot simply be the trustees of foreign property owners, taking on all the accompanying dangers, such as bureaucratization and the crippling of personal initiative in both the spiritual and the economic sense."[212] Helmut Cron (b. 1899), was editor-in-chief of the *Manheimer Tagenblatt* until 1933, and the chief editor and co-publisher of the *Wirtschafts-Zeitung* from 1946. He was also the chairman of the Association of German Journalists from 1949 to 1953. As one of the leading journalists of the reconstruction era, he declared: "We journalists will not be considered presumptuous if we lost confidence in a press whose licensed dilettantes accumulate great wealth over the years with the help of their political papers. This type of commercialization of our profession is the most unfortunate thing ever to happen to the German press."[213]

The licensed publishers took advantage of their monopoly in a commercially adept manner, creating major papers for the respective regions, controlling the advertising business, and, often at the expense of the quantity and quality of the editorial staff, bringing in modern technology. Granted, they were not backed by political morality as they had been in the beginning when, for example, the American handbook for the control of German information services required that anyone applying for and receiving a license must intend to act on behalf of the public with the goal of achieving democratic freedom. As custodians of German democracy in the present and the future, they would have to practice greater economic restraint. Geoffrey Parson, the editor-in-chief of the Paris edition of the New York Herald Tribune, spoke the following words to the licensed members of the German press at a meeting in Coburg in September 1947: "You gentlemen gathered here are the most significant men in Germany today. So much depends on you. If you faithfully fulfill your task, you will be making an enormous contribution not only to the future of Germany, but to that of the entire world."[214] Nearly one year later, in the *Frankfurter Hefte,* when Eugen Kogon claimed that the "most significant men" had not done their work well, he spoke of the "wretchedness of our press."

"The licensed press is an emergency measure. This cannot be said too clearly, concisely, or often. Whoever wishes to perpetuate it is a reactionary against the progress of intellectual and material freedom, a monopolistic class warrior of whatever color. The spirit does not need the security of a license, but is in fact corrupted by it. If it is genuine, it is as strong as ecrasite, a veritable atom smasher. No, what it really needs is a place from which to speak. It alone will choose that place. The objective preconditions of this choice shall be provided by the people, for we need it if we don't wish to lapse into idiocy.

"The introduction of press licensing by the Allies had a certain pedagogical usefulness, but nothing more. People developed in this classroom, and then outgrew it. This is equally true of the establishment of general democracy. The Germans are not a permanent class of retarded schoolchildren, requiring an entire life of remedial education."[215]

At about the same time, the head of the Bavarian FDP, Thomas Dehler, stated that "the fate of German democracy is largely dependent on the quality of the German press. It was founded on a system of licensing that was meaningful for months during the transitional time. In the course of time, however, it has become a burdensome and necessarily detrimental monopoly of the more or less arbitrarily privileged whose main concern is to uphold and enhance their position. . . . If the license requirement is abolished by the occupying powers, then those who have benefitted by it will be so firmly entrenched that there will be no room for others. It will then be very difficult to speak of freedom and of the possibility for competition."[216] Dehler was the Attorney General and main prosecuting attorney in the denazification proceedings, and Federal Minister of Justice from 1949 to 1953.

Admittedly, Dehler painted too gloomy a picture of the situation with regard to competition. The old publishers, ousted in 1945, had merged to form well functioning syndicates. They attacked the legal durability of the compulsory leasing contracts which the military government ordered them to conclude with the license holders lodged in their printing press, unless they were the Nazi publishing houses automatically made available through confiscation.

The Western Allies lifted the license requirement in agreement with Article 5 of the constitution, which had been ratified on May 23, 1949. In this same year, the number of newspapers soared from 150 to almost 550. By the end of 1950, it rose another 80. The older newspaper publishers did not become a threat to democracy, nor was anti-Americanism fed to the Germans. The conservatism of the older publishers was even stronger than their antagonism toward the American friends of the licensed press.

The licensed press was not thereby done away with. With few exceptions, it survived the shock to its exclusive position. The old publishers were unable to recover their quality. "All the leading dailies of today, including the *Frankfurter Allgemeine,* which was created on November 1, 1949 from the *Mainzer Allgemeine Zeitung,* have their roots in the licensing laws. The same can be said for the major magazines and book publishers. The names that characterized the newspaper industry of the Federal Republic, names such as Augstein, Bauer, Burda, Bertelsmann (Mohn), Ganske, Gruner & Jahr, Holtzbrinck, and Springer, were not known in the Weimar Republic."[217]

There ensued a rivalry lasting many years, justifiably referred to as the "press war." It came to an end in July 15, 1954, with the merging of the old and licensed organizations that had been in competition up to that point: the *Verein Deutscher Zeitungsverleger* and the *Gesamtverband der Deutschen Zeitungsverleger* combined to form the *Bundesverband Deutscher Zeitungsverleger.*

The *Nürnberger Nachrichten* was among the regional papers licensed shortly after the war's end. The feature supplements of the first issues give an idea of the cultural life of a city that had been almost entirely destroyed.

October 11, 1945: The first issue of the *Nürnberger Nachrichten* appears. It contains six pages, including one on culture. "No burden too heavy for us. Vow of the German Woman." A reflection by Lisolette Krakauer: "We women, especially, will face new duties, meeting them bravely. We are not allowed to rest after these gruesome years. We must remain active, and this we like, for we know that it is again meaningful to work, to care, and to live, for us, and for our loved ones."

An interview with the director of the Nuremburg Opera and Playhouse: "Should we expect an opera to come out shortly, or are the difficulties still too great in this regard?" "No, even in this regard we have done our utmost, and will soon stage Wolfgang Amadeus Mozart's *Magic Flute.*"

A short report on concert life in the United States. A citation of Gottfried Keller's poem, "Die öffentlichen Verleumder" (The Public Slanderers). Under the heading "What We Were Allowed to Read," an essay by Alfred Polgar entitled "Schulaufsatz" (Composition). A couple of verses from "Vaterland" by Friedrich Georg Jünger. Finally, a short story from the *Reader's Digest.*

The cultural rebuilding began matter-of-factly, without programmatic, pathetic declarations. It was such a normal and banal mixture of elements that one might have thought nothing had happened.

Precisely on this point the texts were typical. In the first phase of the early postwar years, the cultural tradition that was carried on was the one that had been received from the nineteenth century, preserved and tended by the middle class before 1933.

There was a constant flow of well-meaning, uplifing prose, intended, for example, for women and young people. "Slowly her young, inexperienced lips parted from his. Her first kiss. She felt the hot current running through her, it was the fulfillment of the unknown and inexplicable longing of her seventeen-year-old soul."

Number 5 of the *Nürnberger Nachrichten* cited a letter written by Friedrich Schiller to Duke Christian of Augustenburg "When aesthetic education finds itself in this double situation of, on the one hand, disarming the raw power of nature and diminishing bestiality, and, on the other, of awakening the independent powers of reason and re-arming the spirit, then and only then will it be fit to serve as a tool of moral education. I vigilantly demand this double influence from an artistic culture, and ask that it find the necessary tools in all that is beautiful and lofty."

This was the hope, that the raw power of nature would disarm and bestiality subside, and that beauty would become the tool of moral education. It was a concept of beauty that believed it could do without judging the individual ego; it lacked the ax "for the frozen ocean within us." Kafka was still not received.[218]

It was typical of these essays to awaken the "contemplative mood." With soothing diligence people sought to "renovate." Good intentions naturally manifested a want of professionalism. The extent to which the German spirit degenerated into a provincial dependency became especially clear. Cosmopolitanism was a distant dream. Moreover, material misery was an impediment to the intake of information and the openness to culture. Though it appears pleasing that the cultural editors in almost all papers abandoned programmatic cultural pronouncements, it was indeed surprising how arbitrarily the work was taken up. For the most part, it contrasted with the pathos that prevailed in the schools and universities with respect to the new beginning.

Touring the Horizon of World Culture

Had the *Neue Zeitung,* "an American newspaper for the German population," not appeared during the rubble years, the cultural development of these years would have taken another turn, and a more negative one at that. It replaced the American army papers and was printed on large paper in the former printing house of the *Volkische Beobachter* in Munich. The editor-in-chief of the *Neue Zeitung* was Hans Habe and, as of January 1946, Hans Wallenberg. Wallenberg was a Berlin-born US citizen who prior to this time had worked in Berlin as the manager of the *Allgemeine Zeitung,* which was founded as the competitor to the Soviet *Tägliche Rundschau.* With the *Neue Zeitung,* these men, along with Erich Kästner, the head of the feature sections, expanded the intellectual and cultural horizons as they had not been expanded by its German publishers for years. Its circulation in May 1946 totalled 1,328,500 copies, which in statistical terms meant one newspaper for every 15 inhabitants of the American occupation zone. On the first anniversary of the newspaper, Hans Wallenberg expressed his thanks to his co-workers, "one thousand within the publishing house, one hundred thousand without," who characterized the overall cultural worth of the paper:

"All of you have exerted yourselves to an extent unparalleled in modern Germany, in order to make the *'Neue Zeitung'* what it is today, a paper that is bought by one and a half million people and read by three times that many; a paper that has placed itself at the center of public criticism and has been rewarded with the confidence of the public. I am convinced that this would not have been possible had we few Americans . . . made the mistake of relying solely on ourselves. I would like to say that our entire publishing house anticipated the coming peace treaty from early on. In small things, if not in the smallest things, we have attempted to uphold that which we have understood to be the daily task of our paper, namely, understanding and communicating. . . . I hope that all of us will be granted the opportunity to reap the fruits of these first constructive years. I hope also that it will be granted us to see that the peace reigning among us here is transformed into a peace among nations, and that this peace among nations becomes also a peace within the human soul."[219]

The mediation and valuation of German exile literature was a significant aspect of the editoral task. In 1946 alone, several articles by F. C. Weiskopf, a communist writer from Prague, appeared on the theme of exile: *Die Schule des Exils, Das Deutsche Buch im Exil, Deutsche Zeitschriften im Exil, Das humanistische Erbe im Exil, Der Sprung in die fremde Sprache,* and *Gertarnte Exilliteratur.* Above all, the works of emigrated authors and journalists were printed. Included among this group were also socialists and communists, like Johannes R. Becher, Stefan Heym, and Anna Seghers. There was hardly any important view of the German situation that was not published in the *Neue Zeitung.* Such commitment, which included the efforts concerning Heinrich Heine, a subject that was generally considered taboo, brought severe attacks upon the *Neue Zeitung.* Both the paper and its editor-in-chief were generally accused of leftist leanings. For this reason, when Wallenberg returned to the US in 1948, some tried to prevent him from becoming broadcasting editor for "Voice of America." In Germany, however, there prevailed the endorsement of an editorial policy committed to informing the public in the best tradition of journalistic liberalism.

Much less successful was *Die Weit,* the British counterpart to the *Neue Zeitung.* This paper appeared for the first time on April 2, 1946, after months of preparation during the first postwar winter. There was no driving principle behind it. The British were somewhat indolent in their approach to re-education. In spite of this, and perhaps precisely because of this and their privileged paper quota, circulation rose rapidly to one million. In the eyes of the public, the paper remained a hybrid, without clear contours. Hans Zehrer, the first editor-in-chief, failed both because of the paper and because of the objections raised by the Hamburg Social Democrats, who considered him intolerable as a man from the *Tat* circle before 1933. He was replaced by Rudolf Küstermeier in the spring of 1946.

The newspaper failed particularly in setting a cultural standard. It was primarily oriented toward politics and economics, but no special push could be expected from these spheres in the years immediately following the war. The population was starving and freezing, and suffering from both intellectual and emotional deprivation. Its focus was on culture as a means of survival, a fact that was missed by the *Welt* and fully recognized by the *Neue Zeitung.*[220]

The occasionally influential historian, Werner Richter, who emigrated to the USA, wrote an attack against the "communist," leftist American journalism in Germany. He claimed "Lasky is also one of these," referring to Melvin J. Lasky, then the publisher of the newly-founded Berlin journal, *Monat.* This "international journal" was connected with Allied journals, many of which had already been planned during the war and were then published immediately after the war by the Allied information Service. Among these, the *Ausblick* provided select political, literary, and generally educational contributions from magazines throughout the world; the *Neue Auslese* reported on contemporary literature; the *Amerikanische Rundschau,* as its name indicates, brought to the fore the historical and contemporary "essence of the American culture and people;" and the *Dokumente* constituted the first German language magazine to appear in the French occupation zone.

Der Monat, appearing for the first time in October 1948, was to be a "forum for an open discussion and debate on the basis of free speech," giving a "hearing to the greatest number of different voices from Germany and every corner of the earth." Melvin J. Lasky, as editor-in-chief, fulfilled this demand with excellence. Lasky, born in 1920, was literary editor of the *New Leader* from 1942 to 1943, from 1944 to 1945 he worked as a war correspondent for this paper, and from 1946 to 1948 as its foreign correspondent. Hellmut Jaesrich worked alongside Lasky on *Der Monat* as the literary conscience of the journal. The table of contents for the first five issues explains the manner in which it attempted to provide a tour of the horizons of world literature. The following themes were given special attention: *"The Fate of the West"* (Bertrand Russell, Franz Borkenau, Arnold J. Toynbee); the *"East-West Antithesis"* (Barbara Ward, Sidney Hook, James Burnham); the *"Hope for a Better World"* (Benedetto Croce, Hans Kohn, Aldous Huxley); the *"Ways to a New Europe"* (Bertrand de Jouvenel, Arthur M. Schlesinger, Jr., Karl von Schumacher, Manuel Gasser, Walter Maria Guggenheimer); and the *"Debate About*

Socialism" (Wilheim Ropke, Paul Tillich, Sidney Hook, Friedrich A. Hayek, Joseph Schumpeter, Willy Brandt); Jean-Paul Sartre treated the theme of *"The Contemporary Crisis of the Intellectual."* Golo Mann debated with Toynbee, Arthur Koestler reported from Tel Aviv, Ritchie Calder from Mexico City, and Hillar Kallas from Helsinki. Cecil Sprigge, Norbert Muhlen, Arnold Toynbee, Manuel Gasser, and Peter Schmid wrote letters from Italy, New York, Istanbul, London and Belgrad, providing highly informative accounts in the best impressionistic, literary style. Contemporary historical themes were treated in *"Lenin's Last Days"* by David Shub, in *"Construction of the Air Bridge"* and *"The New Comintern"* by Franz Borkenau, and in *"China's Tragedy."* Louis Fischer payed tribute to Gandhi, on the first anniversary of his assassination, with *"Saints and Martyrs."* George Orwell and Henry Steele Commager wrote of the "poverty and hope in Great Britain." Authors were greatly honored, and abstracts of their works were often printed. One could read Thomas Wolfe, T. S. Eliot, Thomas Mann's *Doctor Faustus,* George Orwell's *Animal Farm,* W. B. Yeats, and Salvatore Quasimodo. Articles came from H. M. Ledig-Rowohlt, Alfred Kazin, Edouard Roditi, Ernst Robert Curtius, Klaus Pringsheim, W. H. Auden, C. M. Bowra, and others. Among the extensively reviewed books were Carlo Levi's *Christus kam nur bis Eboli,* Thornton Wilder's *The Ides of March,* Winston Churchill's *Memoirs,* Joseph Goebbel's *Tagebüchern 1933 bis 1938,* Aldous Huxley's *Ape and Essence,* Arnold Zweig's *Das Beil von Wandsbek,* Ulrich von Hassel's *Vom Andern Deutschland: Aus den nachgelassenen Tagebüchern 1938 bis 1944,* Theodor Plivier's *Stalingrad,* Paul Serin's *Jenseits des Kapitalismus,* Leo Trotsky's *Stalin,* Jean-Paul Sartre's *Anti-Semite and Jew,* Josef W. Stalin's *Collected Works,* Ernest Hemingway's *For Whom the Bell Tolls,* Klaus Mann's *André Gide,* and Harold Laski's *The American Democracy.* Many of these books were cited in the original, for there were as yet few translations available.

The same concern for timeliness and quality was evidenced in the contributions on topics relating to film, theater, and the plastic arts. Among those people, works or events analyzed were Sergej Eisenstein's last work, Laurence Olivier's portrayal of Hamlet, D. W. Griffith, Jean-Louis Barrault's magic theater, Jean-Paul Sarte's *Dirty Hands,* and Joan Miró, Marc Chagall, and Picasso.

With lofty and hallowed words, the issues of the *Monat* illustrated and criticized the essence of the western tradition. There was hardly a western author of rank who did not write in and for the newspaper. Young authors were discovered and included in the constant discourse.

An editorial comment in the first volume read "Never before did the shadows of war and brutal power hover so dark and threatening above every citizen of almost every country. Therefore, it is not enough simply to understand. One must go beyond this admittedly necessary step and be ready to protest, to rise to the occasion, should this be required. For only when one acts in accordance with insight is one worthy of the motto coined by Immanuel Kant, the greatest of German philosophers, 'The highest task of the human being is to know what one must be in order to be human.'"[221]

The old *Monat* lasted 243 issues, with its final publication appearing in 1968. After Melvin J. Lasky, its editors-in-chief were Fritz René Allemann, Hellmut Jaesrich, Peter Härtling, and Klaus Harpprecht. The attempt was made to modernize the magazine, to "Americanize" it in the negative sense. The spirit of continuous discussion was no longer appropriate now that the Vietnam war had reached its decisive phase. The *Monat* closed in 1971. In 1980, it experienced a short and unsuccessful comeback.

Hans Schwab-Felisch wrote one of the few well-founded evaluations that the magazine received upon its folding. Apparently, in light of the rising anti-Americanism, the gratitude was repressed. The *Monat,* he said, appeared on the German stage as an exponent of American liberalism, a liberalism that still believed in itself and that has stamped an entire postwar generation with its manner of thinking. The great family of those who "had believed in a God that was no longer there" were previously associated with this liberalism. These included former communists turned anti-communists, such as Koestler, Silone, Stephen Spender, and Sidney Hook. What today might pass, without further concrete investigation, as the position of the cold war, a political hostility against communists on the one hand and the statue of liberty on the other, was not so black and white at the time. Then there was an ongoing, high-level discussion.[222]

In October 1965, Helmut Jaesrich wrote of the German-American "cultural springtime," looking back on both the internal and external beginnings of the *Monat.* "It was a time of great dangers and harsh contradictions. It was the time in which a thoroughly defeated and divided Germany spanned both sides of the chasm that transversed the planets. It is possible that the two partnerships into which Germany was called did not help the character of either side. The speed with which the western Germans changed from picking up cigarette butts to driving Mercedes left little time for reflection. The *Monat* sought, along with many German publishers, a *'presse-bien-pensant.'* It did not, of course, always receive the attention of its readers. It sought to control evil, to clarify concepts, to explain the lines of battle, and to eliminate prejudices. It sought to make clear that the opponent was not Russia, but Stalinism, and that neither Marxism nor capitalism needed to tolerate disparagement."[223]

Magazine Euphoria

Hans Schwab-Felisch's "obituary" of the *Monat* appeared in the *Merkur,* a "German magazine for European thought."[224] The *Merkur* is one of the few surviving magazines founded during the early postwar years. A certain "magazine euphoria" pervaded those years. In January 1947, Hartmann Goertz characterized this phenomenon with dramatic pathos, not unfitting for the psychological profile of his era: "It has been about 20 months since the first newspaper appeared in the American zone. There were weeks of total uncertainty, when rumors poured in like avalanches, rolling with the people through the streets, and the little news received through the radios was at best distorted. Then there appeared a newspaper like a light in the darkness. With deep interest and a sigh of relief, the frequently long outdated issues were read, passed on, and often mistrustfully studied and discussed. It was an event to be remembered. And there is something else that needs to be added. Open discussion of political, cultural, and economic questions has already begun to appear natural to us. Sometimes we can estimate the change in the tone of public expression, the gradual development of which we have lived through, only by considering the astonishment of those like the prisoners of war who, upon returning from places far away from Germany, are suddenly confronted with the changed reality. The realization of the uniformity from which we have been freed will then come to us in a flash . . . The time had come for dialogue between equals, the road was finally cleared, and the abundance of issues could hardly be overlooked."[225]

The nation that had wanted a total war, a total victory, and that now had to suffer through a total defeat, had in reality nothing more to say. Spiritually, however, its people identified themselves with those who summoned the courage and skill to voice their own opinions. The autonomy of the overwhelming majority of authors and founders of magazines was legitimized either because they had opposed the Third Reich and been persecuted, or because they felt themselves a part of the inner emigration. They did not depend on re-education at someone else's hands, but encouraged the people to accomplish this with their own powers. With few exceptions, from the *Ruf,* perhaps, they were on the whole positive toward the re-education policies of the Western Allies. In this context as well, however, they sought their own independent stance. In moved and moving words, they declared their will to concentrate on the essentials of surrender, recollection, renewal, change, and construction. The names of the various magazines expressed this commitment: *Aussatt* (Sowing), *Die Sammlung* (Collection), *Begegnung* (Encounter), *Besinnung, Bogen* (Archway), *Einheit* (Unity), *Ende und Anfang* (End and Beginning), *Die Fähre* (The Ferry), *Frischer Wind* (Fresh Air), *Gegenwart* (The Present), *Geist und Tat* (Mind and Deed), *Das Goldene Tor* (The Golden Gate), *Horizont Neubau* (New Construction), *Neues Abendland* (The New West), *Neues Europa* (New Europe), *Neue Ordnung* (New Order), *Prisma* (Prism), *Standpunkt* (Standpoint), *Umschau* (Review), *Weltstimmen* (World Opinions), *Zeitwende* (The Turn of an Era), *Die Pforte* (Door), *Die Kommenden* (The Coming Ones) and others.

In the preface to the first issue of the *Wandlung,* which appeared in November 1945, edited by Dolf Sternberger and Lambert Schneider, Karl Jaspers wrote the following:

"We have lost almost everything, government, economy, secure conditions for our physical well-being. Even worse, we have lost the binding force of universal norms, our moral worth, and the unifying confidence of a people. It is like the end of the Thirty Years' War, when Gryphius wrote:

> I am not speaking of that which is more vexing than death,
> more fierce than plagues, fire, and starvation:
> That your soul's treasure has been wrestled from us.

"Have we really lost everything? No, we survivors are still here. We may well have no property on which to rest, no memories we care to keep, we may well have been sacrificed to the utmost. But that we are alive should have some meaning. Let us rise up quickly in the face of nothingness.

"Only the external events are unequivocal, the silent disappearance of the dictator, the end of an independent German state, the dependence of our every act upon the will of the occupying powers that freed us from the yoke of National Socialism. Our initiative is confined to the scope they allot us.

"One of the opportunities we have to exercise our initiative comes from the permission to start a magazine. We are allowed to speak publicly with one another. Let us see what we have to say to each other!

"We have changed both internally and externally in 12 years. We continue to change in incalculable ways. We wish to participate in this transformation, asking Germans to speak, to share their thoughts, to fashion their images, and to make the fact that we live and the manner in which we live publicly tangible. At the same time, we would like to recognize and make recognizable the world's opinions.

"There must be a beginning. Inasmuch as we begin to support and allow the change to manifest itself, we hope to be on the road to the place where we can lay a new foundation. We are beginning so completely anew that it is now way too early to be certain of this foundation."[226]

In the first issue of the *Frankfurter Hefte,* April 1946, a magazine for culture and politics, Eugen Kogon and Walter Dirks wrote the introductory lines. Dirks, a section editor of the *Frankfurter Zeitung* from 1935 to 1943, was among the inner emigrants of the Catholic left, and after the war became the director of the department of culture for the West German radio. Kogon and Dirks wrote:

"We will seriously concern ourselves with clarity, but the readers will have to exert themselves in any case. The current phrases and obscure words that so easily enter into and evaporate from the brain have rendered thick the atmosphere of thought. We cannot breathe in it. We want good visibility and an accurately functioning reason. The living heart, beating in rhythm with the times for eternal goals, is self-evident.

"Thus we anticipate reflective readers. In this way, we believe we are offering a service for the renewal of Germany. We, means the totality comprised of editors, co-workers, and readers. The darkness surrounding us shall be lifted. All of us wish to cooperate in clearing up the opaqueness and mystery that threatens us, to the extent that this is granted to us who have just come from the abyss, and to the human spirit at all."[227]

Das Goldene Tor (1946) bore the stamp of its publisher, Alfred Döblin, who had turned to Catholicism. This author was commissioned by the French cultural authorities to oversee literary censorship. By the end of 1945, after taking office in Baden-Baden, he had already begun preparations for the foundation of a literary journal:

"Golden rays beam forth from that gate through which poetry, art, and free thought pass. The gate is beautiful, but what is now standing under its wide arch does not look like peace, joy, or contemplation. The shimmering gold of the gate and the cheerful and proud relief don't fit in with the drooping, shabby figures hovering, crouching on the ground, hardly muttering a word to one another . . . To clear the rubble and clean up the spirit we have the instruments of judgment and criticism. We wish to return to their rightful place those good things for which we accept responsibility, which have been distorted and eliminated from our mental horizon. In so doing, we are certain to help close gaps and to grow strong.

"For more than a decade, however, a tremendous amount of our nation's spiritual and intellectual power has lain buried . . . These powers are again at our disposal. We will, however, indulge in no illusions, we will not expect to bring in a harvest that is doubly or triply as rich. It is different in Germany than in France, where in the course of occupation, powers increased with the embittered underground war, and the new and original resistance literature that was to fulfill such a vital function was brought to life. We will think of the obstruction and isolation in Germany. The spirit has not been killed, it lives and moves here again, its recovery is certain.

"Buried and unavailable for the country were those powers that were imprisoned by the thousands and driven into foreign lands. Many in this country await their voices. The 'Golden Gate' allows the exiles in. We will read their words on these pages."[228]

Rudolf Pechel expressed the conservative standpoint in his *Deutsche Rundschau,* which had just been reinstated. "We believe there is no better way to justify the trust given us than by pursuing the battle for the freedom of spirit, for truth, righteousness, and humaneness, for democracy and communication among nations. It is a battle to keep our face clean in the midst of German self-degradation, one which the 'Deutsche Rundschau' fought unremittingly until it was banned in 1942."[229] Very special care and love goes out to the German youth, with the hope of providing a firm foundation for their newly awakened desire for truth and a sense of reality, and of enabling them to engage in honest cooperation with other nations. These prescribed tasks will be tackled with full intellectual freedom and independence, not in the service of any particular party or group, and also not in the service of the occupying powers, but responsible only to the individual conscience and to the great powers of the spirit and humaneness *(Menschlichkeit).*

The *Merkur,* founded by Joachim Moras and Hans Paeschke, abandoned a programmatic declaration in its first issue of January 1947. Yet it was possible to discern its goal, that of a European thinking publication, fairly clearly from Hans Paeschke's essay, "Die Verantwortlichkeit des Geistes," published in this issue. "The task is to find the most comprehensive and exact definition possible of the present times, not one that describes contemporaneity, but that expresses continuity, that is, one that mediates in the current of the times. A creative polarization of tradition and construction is involved. Responsibility for guilt chains us to our past. With this we learn a difficult but good lesson about the meaning of all political freedom, that each person is responsible for the freedom of every other person. From this responsibility, we draw the courage for the formation of the future. This puts us at an obvious distance from avant-garde speech. We have become new so often and in so many frighteningly false ways this century that an *esprit de suite* (consistency) is the first thing we need. This is not only a law of historical experience, but also of self-respect. What could we, at this nadir of our history, carry with us but the respect for the great, universal personalities of our past?"[230]

Some of the magazines received intitutional support. The *Zeichen der Zeit,* for example, was a magazine of the Evangelical Church, and the *Aufbau* belonged to the "Cultural Coalition for a Democratic Renewal of Germany." The latter, even with its communist leanings, manifested a trans-party breadth and a democratic, anti-Fascist program so that already in 1945 it commanded a readership from all over Germany and in this regard was echoed positively in all camps. For the first time in November 1946, the *Hochland* continued the expression of the Catholic tradition under the leadership of its publisher and chief writer, Franz Joseph Schöningh. The first issue honored, among others, the magazine's founder, Carl Muth, as a "European legacy."

In almost every magazine, literary and especially art-related themes played a great role. According to Heinrich Vormweg, literature became a refuge.[231] The association with culture, said Theodor W. Adorno, "had something to do with the dangerous and ambiguous solace and security of provincialism."[232] Of course, this corresponded to the traditional German hierarchy of values, which moved from the peaks of culture to the lowlands of politics. Yet people were also prepared to meet the negative experiences with the consciousness of an educated citizenry, that is, to accept the separation of thought and action, and to work for a political culture and a cultural politics.[233] Thus it is significant that a great number of these magazines alluded to the alliance of culture and politics in their subtitles: "Magazine for Culture and Politics" *(Frankfurter Hefte)*; "Cultural-political Monthly Magazine" *(Aufbau)*; "Bi-monthly Magazine for International Cooperation in Culture, Politics, and Scholarship" *(Neues Europa)*; "Contributions to the Cultural and Political Questions of the Times" *(Ost und West)*; "Magazine for Politics, Culture, and History" *(Neues Abendland)*; "Magazine for Political, Social and Cultural Re-organization" *(Das Neue Wort)*. The editorials confirmed the impression that the combination of these concepts had programmatic value. On the whole, this sphere was often described as the "spiritual" *(das Geistige)*, yet in the understanding of many authors, "culture" encompassed more than this. In connection with culture, the lead articles spoke of "public spirit," of "the ascent of a new culture," and the "reawakening of intellectual life." "In this context, culture signifies the manifest totality of values and orientations that enable people to find direction in their surroundings and to act, and that actually shape them into what is called society. If this seems close to an Anglo-Saxon, Western concept of culture, a distinction can be found in their foundations. In the postwar magazines, culture was frequently disassociated from the chaos and nihilism that destroyed social existence. Thus, this understanding of culture appeared to be of constitutive significance for numerous magazines."

In contrast to the "refuge theory," a new universalism became apparent, one which, with an understanding of a democratic culture, attempted to overcome the division between culture and politics that marked the affirmative culture. In support of this theory is the fact that the *Ruf*, considered the magazine which, more than others, presented current events, also evidenced a predilection for literature. "Literature was for us something other than entertaining fiction. It was capable of influencing, of transforming minds in the long run, not in the short run, of course. We still believed in the written word, in the possibility of changing society through writing."[234]

Many authors understood the political powerlessness of the Germans in a land occupied by the Allies as being, not simply a hindrance, but an opportunity. According to an article in the first issue of the *Gegenwart*, Germany now had time to thoroughly clarify its political notions. In the midst of all the misfortune, it had the fortune of not having to decide immediately, and the duty of not rising up impatiently in the intellectual spheres.

The political culture of postwar Germany was influenced in an extraordinarily positive manner through the many journals. The formation of a democratic and republican identity was promoted, and the intellectual horizons were substantially broadened. In an hour of extreme physical and spiritual misery, of incapacity for critical thought, and of susceptibility to the slightest consolations,[235] the magazines contributed to the sublimation of material misery, the destruction of ideological fantasy, the renewal of critical thought, and the estimation of culture as an aid to living. The spectrum of these magazines was quite broad in every respect, circulation, distribution, duration of existence, thematic direction, and ideological orientation. That need to communicate, which broke through every traditional barrier, was met by them all in stimulating, motivating ways.[236] However, according to Hartmann Goertz, the growing quantity interfered with the quality. The publisher may still be interesting. However, for a long time, the same authors had been appearing. "With respect to the first issue, the principles appear again in sequence in addresses to the readers. I can imagine that by now the readers must be quite tired of principles. And behind these addresses, the floodgates of essay writing open up." The word can often be a flight from reality and its tasks. When one considers the flood of printed material with a critical mind, it seems to be a flight that could be called a flight into the magazine. "Recently, an instructive act was performed in a Munich cabaret. Three well-dressed men fought intensely in front of a rubbish heap made of colored paper, one that could be interpreted as both real and symbolic. The argument seemed to be about great tasks, and in all the moving about only a few catchwords could be understood. In the meantime, nearby on the stage, the rubbish heap of a silent, doggedly working man was changed into a small house made of colored paper, one that could be interpreted as both real and symbolic. The silent man finally entered the stage-house and even put a flowerpot in the window for all to see. Meanwhile, the three men nearby continued to discuss passionately in front of their rubbish heap. Perhaps one of them was the publisher of a magazine."[237]

Soon, however, this displeasure with the magazine died down. The euphoria was serenity in the face of death. Most periodicals died with the currency reform. Then real houses were built. The discussion was no longer about foundations.

Along with newspapers and magazines, weekly papers also experienced a rapid development. Most have remained in business to the present.[238]

In 1946, the *Allgemeine Wochenzeitung der Juden in Deutschland* appeared for the first time. It was an organ of the Jews returning to Germany, founded by Karl Marx, who enjoyed a great international reputation. As of April 1, 1947, the *Rheinische Merkur* was published as a weekly paper under the direction of Franz Albert Kramer. Kramer spent eight years in emigration, returning afterwards to Koblenz. The paper was considered a "messenger of the good news of Catholic Christianity." The old *Rheinische Merkur* from the years 1815 to 1816, published by Joseph Görres, served as its model. In February 1948, the *Deutsche Allgemeine Sonntagsblatt* came into existence, published by Dr. Hanns Lilje, who at that time was bishop of Hannover. It was called an "independent weekly newspaper for politics, economics, and culture." Behind this terminology was the idea of "helping to increase the value of an often misunderstood notion through trans-regional work with lofty political, economic, and cultural aims."[239] *Christ und Welt* was licensed a few days before the currency reform, in June 1948. Eugen Gerstenmeier, director of relief work for the Evangelical Church, took responsibility for this "informative paper." Klaus Mehnert, returning from East Asia, became the editor-in-chief. Additionally, conservative journalists were hired as co-workers, including some whose activities in the Third Reich were not undisputed.

The most significant new publication from among the weekly newspapers proved to be *Die Zeit.* Its license holders were Lowis Lorenz, who had been editor-in-chief of the magazine *Die Woche* until 1944; Richard Tüngel, originally an architect, who after 1933 became an author; Ewald Schmidt de Simoni, business manager for the former *Frankfurter Zeitung;* Gerd Bucerius, attorney, member of the first city parliament of Hamburg called by the military government, and later responsible for the formation of the Hamburg Senate. The first issue appeared on February 21, 1946. "It is important today, not only to remove the rubble from the streets of the bombed cities, but also to remove the spiritual burdens of a declined epoch. This can only happen if we have the courage to speak the plain truth, even when it hurts, which will unfortunately be quite often. Trust can develop only in an atmosphere of incorruptible truthfulness."[240] Gerd Bucerius, later one of the great press tsars of the Federal Republic, tried to achieve continuity in the midst of the changing and conflict-ridden history of the *Zeit.* In 1949, he, who along with Schmidt acted as trustee, bought for the *Zeit* 50 percent of the dividends of the publishing house that published the illustrated *Stern* under Henri Nannen. He thus began his press empire. In 1946 he was 30 years old, belonged to the CDU, was married to a Jewish woman, and had showed himself an active defender and protective assistant of those persecuted by the regime. Ernst Samhaber worked as the first editor, but soon had to resign due to his overly sharp criticism of the occupying powers. On the editorial staff were, among others, Josef Muller-Marein, Marion Gräfin Dönhoff, and Ernst Friedlaender. "All of us, the editors and the license holders, came from the middle class. We found, however, that it was this same class that prepared the way for, or at least submitted to, National Socialism. To be sure, none of us had voted 'middle class' in the last years before Hitler, and thus we all felt ourselves to be vaguely 'leftist.' Ultimately, it was the Social Democrats, apart from the dogmatic communists, who offered the longest and bravest resistance against Hitler's plot. It is apparent, however, that we have learned a different lesson from the catastrophe from that learned by the Social Democrats. An aspect of freedom, we believed, was also freedom from the government. The government, however, oppressed us with an employment bureau, a housing bureau, and on the whole the inevitable administration of want. And the Social Democrats let it be known that our lives and economy will also be under state control in the future. Our decision for the market economy was still not clearly formulated at that time before the currency reform. But it was recognizable, much to the disappointment of the Labor dominated British occupying powers and their Social Democratic friends in Germany."[241]

The first phase of the newspaper's liberal-conservative political course was largely defined by Ernst Friedlaender, the son of a Jewish doctor from Breslau and a volunteer soldier in World War I. He spent the greater part of the Nazi era abroad. In 1946, he moved with his family from Vaduz to Hamburg in order to earn his bread amidst the destruction and hunger. "The 'unindicted,' suspected one surely had things to say that none of us editors of the 'Zeit' could have said."[242] Friedlaender committed himself to the whole of Germany. He wrote on June 17, 1948: "We do not desire a Western government, but a German government, a core of Germany, therefore, for as long as it cannot be the whole of Germany." With respect to the de-nazification debate, he declared March 4, 1948: "Most young Germans know that Nazism has fundamentally deceived them concerning what they had perhaps hoped to find in it. What they had hoped for was a stable and clean society of German people, a true community, which could have suppressed the crippling mutual hostilities of the parties. . . . By thus burrowing into the past, one must end up in the pre-past, in the Weimar generation. With those who had failed in the first Weimar, the second democracy was staged. What more lenient judgment could be passed on the Weimarer than they failed humanly and politically. In 1933 they left nothing behind but discomfort. In the meantime, they have grown much older and not much wiser." Friedlaender questioned the value of political parties because they had learned surprisingly little since 1933. "They have again developed intolerant, isolated, ideological organizations with compulsory beliefs and an automatic party vote. Again they are not primarily ready to fill in for each other in essential tasks. . . . Once more the battle for the government seems more important than work in the government."

In 1947, *Der Spiegel* began its appearance in Hannover as a weekly magazine. Rudolf Augstein started it when he was 24-years-old, and was co-publisher and editor-in-chief from the beginning. After a few years he became sole publisher. He drew from his experience on *Diese Woche,* a short-lived magazine of the British occupying powers, for which he had worked two months as an editor. In his first letter to the "dear *Spiegel* readers", written December 20, 1947, reflecting on his one year of editorial work, he wrote: "It was truly one of our noblest tasks to expose with all frankness the dead seriousness and the political officiousness in the new small states of Germany . . . Un-seriousness conceived of as a political task. If *Der Spiegel* were able to gather all its readers together for a New Year's party, they would be asked to drink a toast with us "to self-irony!" At that time, the *Spiegel*'s official advertising slogan was "Even Mr. Igel (Hedgehog) reads the *Spiegel.*"

"We noticed from the very beginning," recalled Augstein, "the contradictions between the words and deeds of active figures. These contradictions had been unsettling to us from the beginning, and by then we had already suspected that hollowness had in fact become more evident. We went rather far in our mistrust of the active politicians to the point of being unjust. We then had no desire to eat something we knew would offer no nourishment." People became practitioners without a practice. With difficulty, they had to form from the living object a mental concept for the democratic and parliamentary form of government they would plan.[243]

Recounted by Hans Jaene, the genesis of the *Spiegel,*[244] appeared like a journalistic piece of morality from the foundational phase of the Federal Republic. Fantasy and perseverance, the spirit of improvisation and Chutzpah led the way to success.

Major John Chaloner, 23-years-old, representative press control officer of the British military government in Hannover, decided early in 1946 that a news magazine would be good for Germany. He had in mind not so much the American exemplars like *Time,* but the British magazine entitled *News Review.* This publication explained abstract political phenomena, presenting the various personalities as commonplace people. Chaloner planned a German branch of this magazine. A first trial issue, dated March 29, 1946, inspired the collaboration of the British Staff Sergeant-Major Harry Bohrer, originally from Prague, who was sent to Hannover to monitor the newspapers. Also interested in this venture was Staff Sergeant-Major Henry Ormond, a German jurist who emigrated to England, who understood business, and was able to procure money, paper, space, a printing press, means of transportation, and a teletype machine. He also developed the distribution and advertising departments. Since German personnel were sought, Rudolf Augstein was accepted. The first issue of *Diese Woche* appeared on November 16, 1946. On the first page, under the headline "Hunger in Ruhr Valley," was the text inspired by Victor Gollancz's letter to the editor printed in the *New Chronicle.* It read: "The shamelessness of the [British] government continues to grow. Mister Strachey, British Minister of Food Supplies, announces turkeys and other fowl, extra meat, sweets and sugar for Chirstmas. Do these Christian statesmen, then, have no idea of what is happening in Germany at the present time? Apparently not, or they wouldn't make such an idiotic declaration." In no time at all, the 15,000 copies of *Diese Woche* were sold out at one Reichsmark apiece. British authorities expressed their astonishment. Further articles called forth further grievances, even from the Soviets and the French. The British in Berlin's Control Commission ordered the English to retire from the magazine. Major Chaloner, however, received permission to reinstate it under another name as a German magazine with a British license. Three German license holders had to be found. The German editors employed along with Augstein were out of the question. One of them had been in the NSDAP, another had worked as the feature editor of the National Socialist paper, *Niedersächsischen Tageszeitung,* and a third was charged with being a PK man. Only Augstein was left. He alone received, on January 1, 1947, a provisional license as the provisional publisher. He thought up the new title *Der Spiegel.* "If I have brought profit to this paper, this was the greatest profit. The title is simply good." And so Rudolf Augstein, 23, with an education from a Hannoverian *Gymnasium,* and with the experience of three years in the artillery, assumed the responsibility of a weekly magazine, for which a paper contribution for 15,000 copies a week was made, the proverbial quantity that was too much for death and too little for life.

Soon the *Spiegel* went on the black market, going for as much as 15 Reichsmarks an issue. It was popular, even though it offered no great revelations, no sensationalism. And yet, it called truth by its name, especially when it was unpleasant. This was packaged, of course, with skill and cunning, so that the license, while jeopardized, was not withdrawn. The casual and at times contemptuous tone, in conjunction with a love for personal details that was unusual for Germans, brought fresh air to journalism.

Germany Is Again 'In the Air'

The history of postwar radio began in Germany even before the capitulation. On May 4, 1945, this announcement was heard from the Hamburg radio broadcasting station: "This is Radio Hamburg, a station of the Allied military government." As of May 13, 1945, the Soviets broadcasted from a mobile transmission van via Tegel. In Munich, Stuttgart, and Frankfurt, special units of the American occupying forces were able to begin operating broadcasting stations of the military government within a few weeks. In Cologne, broadcasts for the entire British zone began on September 26, 1945, under the name of Northwest German Radio (NWDR). Berlin radio remained under Soviet control after the city's division into four sections. In November 1945, the Americans established a wire broadcast in the American sector (DIAS) that was soon expanded to become a radio station (RIAS). The British followed in June 1946 with a branch office of their NWDR. In the French occupation zone, the former relay station of Koblenz transmitted a regional program. The Southern Broadcasting Station founded in Baden-Baden began operating for the entire French zone on March 31, 1946.

The Radio of Great Germany, one of the most important instruments of propaganda for the National Socialists, was destroyed in the zero hour. The construction of a new form of radio broadcasting was undertaken under the control of the occupation forces. Hans Bredow, a retired Secretary of State and *Reich* Commissioner for the German Radio before 1933, wrote in the *Neue Zeitung* (March 1946) that with the elimination of all the best skills and products, every sphere of the Third Reich had sunk to a catastrophic level. The incessant barrage of propaganda that wore down the soul and stirred unsavory instincts was interrupted by insipid radio shows. The works of what were essentially deceased great masters who were not racially or politically suspect were interspersed in the futile attempt to cover up the spiritual poverty and low level of culture. Instead of serving as an instrument of peace and culture, the hope of the radio pioneers for whom the wireless was to cross all boundaries, the radio of the National Socialists served demagoguery and the undermining of German morality, thus bringing tremendous guilt upon itself. "Now we are again faced with the construction of a new radio station. We have much to make up for. To do this, we must above all learn from the past."[245]

Here, too, was to be found re-education, change, reflection and construction. The people's radio *(Volksempfänger)* had its place on the radio table in the living room or on the cabinet of the parlor kitchen, but now it was directed toward democratization.

In the spring of 1946, officers of the Information Control Division formulated "ten commandments" of radio freedom. The Americans wished to see these guidelines in the preface of every future broadcasting law and perhaps even in the constitution. This was in contrast to the British policy, which traditionally placed little value on written, "paper" decrees. The commandments were as follows:

"1. Representatives of the major religious confessions who express the desire to be heard shall be granted a suitable time for broadcasting.

2. Representatives of different sides of debatable issues of general public interest shall be guaranteed equal radio time.

3. Representatives of organizations of employers and employees permitted by law shall be guaranteed the right to equal radio time.

4. All political parties permitted on regional or broader bases shall receive equal radio time during their participation in local, state or future national elections.

5. The permanent speakers, commentators, or program editors shall not be allowed, on the stations by which they are employed, to lend their names in support of any political party.

6. All news coverage shall be presented with a high level of factual objectivity with respect to content, style and reporting. All commentary, both overt and covert, shall be omitted.

7. News transmission shall use, as much as possible, material coming from free and independent news agencies, or from sources that can be presumed to take an objective standpoint. Information that cannot be positively determined as coming from free, independent, and uninfluenced sources, must be clearly identified.

8. The right of democratically disposed commentators and speakers to criticize injustices, improprieties, or inadequacies of persons or departments of the public administration and of the state or federal government shall be secured and guaranteed by all available means.

9. No program shall be allowed that could give rise to prejudice or discrimination against individuals or groups on the basis of race, religion, or color.

10. Preventative measures shall be taken against the spreading by radio of thoughts or concepts that would greatly offend the moral sensibilities of a large segment of listeners."[246]

With the beginning of 1947, "Germany's voice" in broadcasting again had quality, although it was only heard under the direction and control of the Allies. The expansion of the broadcasting stations had advanced to an astonishing degree.

The program of the Northwest German Radio was under the control of Hugh Carlton Greene, who during the war worked as director and commentator for the German language broadcasts of the BBC.[247] It was partially supported by Hamburg, Cologne, and Berlin. Cologne, whose share in the program was from 30 to 40 percent, already had a German supervisor by this time. The NWDR made intense efforts to fill the cultural and educational gaps that had been left behind by 12 years of the Nazi regime. The cultural and artistic level was considered highly important. *"Runder Tisch"* (round table), a discussion broadcast headed by Axel Eggebrecht, became the model for other radio stations as well. Eggebrecht was an excellent embodiment of the new-old radio journalist type. He was a critical leftist who, during the Weimar Republic, had been a member of the KPD for some years, and was arrested in 1933 and sent to a concentration camp. Along with the liberal civilian Peter von Zahn, he was among the co-founders of the Northwest German Radio. Both were in charge of the publication, *Nordwestdeutschen Hefte,* which appeared in May 1946, promoting material from the programs of the NWDR.

The Southwest Radio provided programs extolled by critics as the best in the sphere of culture. It was almost exclusively in the hands of German editors, supported and supervised by French experts. Heading the network was Friedrich Bischoff, who before 1933 had managed Brelau's radio station. The musical programs were dedicated to those modern composers who had been suppressed during the Third Reich.

The radio stations of the American zone (Munich, Stuttgart, and Frankfurt) were under the directorship of American broadcasting experts. The Munich program was famous for its radio plays, wherein Hellmut M. Backhaus developed his own style for crime thrillers. Elements from folklore and local dialects were readily apparent in the programs. Stuttgart emphasized the loosely structured conversation and so-called "variety shows," literature and radio drama received relatively little space. Radio Frankfurt, which had opened in a family boarding house in Bad Nauheim, moved into the destroyed and makeshift building that was taken over from the

Reich station. Eberhard Beckmann was the manager. The station demanded an openness to the outer world. Critical reflections on modern literature, with special attention given to authors previously banned in Germany, were offered by Stephan Hermlin, a young author who had returned from emigration. The literary scholar and critic Hans Mayer, also returning from emigration, worked for a time with Radio Frankfurt. As chief editor for politics and news, he worked alongside Erich Lissner, chief editor for culture. In the adjoining room, Golo Mann functioned as the American control officer.

Hans Mayer recalls that "Golo Mann oversaw the powerplays and intrigues of a radio station with just as much pleasure as he was later to have with the intrigues of his Wallenstein. What lay in his imagination, I am able to understand quite well today. It had something to do with Montesquieu and his invention of the political principle of the separation of powers. Applied to Radio Frankfurt, it looked something like this, at the top is the military government, that was understood. This became, however, the board of control. Program design and administration was now the responsibility of the German editors, with Beckmann at the top. Beneath him there was an administrative director, and those two chief editors whose position Golo Mann had cleverly figured out . . . I was spontaneous, susceptible to moods, often angry and forward as well. Eberhard Beckmann went through a school of disguise in the Great German *Reich*. He smiled a lot, was consistently obliging, and yet often prone to moving the people around him like figures in a subtle game. A game of power and about power.

"For that very reason we got along well with each other, for what stimulated me was the work, not the power. The present manager of Radio Frankfurt once had a middle class profession, and through no fault of his own did not become successful. The result was that he became almost crazy for external glory and personal favors. For a long time I was a nobody, without a profession, a pass, housing, regular work according to my liking, and naturally without a secure income. Then suddenly I had everything, as good as one could have it in the land of the conquered, as an employee of the conquerors, who could 'fire' from one hour to the next."[248]

As with the press, re-education and the task of rebuilding was, on the whole, successfully accomplished in the radio industry. The western control officers had a keen sense for both proven and new journalistic talents, and gradually entrusted them with more and more responsibility. Thus the broadcasting establishments became centers of democraticization and republican identity. The resume drawn up by the *Neue Zeitung* on March 31, 1947, was justified in its optimism: "And so, 22 months after the capitulation speech of Mr. Dönitz had come to a close on the waves of Flensburg, the voice of Germany is again carried on many waves. Germany is again 'in the air' even if at first still under Allied supervision. Yet the interim balance of achievements is not bad, and for the future promises still more with the free competition of radio stations and programs."[249]

E. Kappes, *Plakatentwurf* (Poster Design), 1947.

Emergency Dwellings in Berlin. PHOTO: L. WINKLER.

Search for Food and Combustible Material in an American Dumpyard in Berlin, 1945.

Black Market in Berlin, 1946.

Tanz
Cabaret
Remdes
St. Pauli

Concentration Camp in Nordhausen after the Liberation, 1945.

Otto Kohtz, *Entwurf sum Wiederaufbau einer Grossstadt* (Design for the Construction of a City), 1945.

Berlin, 1947.

First Approaches despite the Ban on Fraternization, Bavaria in May, 1945. PHOTO: HANS SCHÜRER.

Kurt Schumacher at the SPD Mass Rally in Frankfurt, June 1, 1947.

Konrad Adenauer in West Berlin, Together with Berlin Mayor Ernst Reuter (left) and the Head of the Municipal Councillors, Otto Suhr, 1948.

Stalingrad, Title Page by Theodor Plievier.

THE ART WORLD

Musica Nova

The newly instated radio networks were of decisive significance for the music life of the rubble years. The Southwest Radio in Baden-Baden led the broadcasting networks in the field of modern music. In November 1945, the French military government commissioned Heinrich Strobel to build up the music division of the station. He returned from Paris, where he had emigrated, to a country whose artistic world, including music, was totally desolate. Indeed, ideological resistance to 12 years of march music, battle hymns and "appropriated" classical music cleared the way for something new. Furthermore, there were many modern composers who either had been silenced and forced to retreat during the Third Reich, or who were just beginning their careers.

Due to the efforts of active and courageous pioneers, among whom Strobel was clearly the most significant, a substantial amount of contemporary music developed after 1945 on German soil. "Despite inadequate means, the life of music began to bloom in between the rubble and the hope, carrying within itself the seed of promising developments."[250] In Baden-Baden, Heinrich Strobel found a small archive of shellac records and the remains of a spa orchestra. In a very short time, a serviceable orchestra came into existence, giving its first performance under Otto Klemperer in 1946. Paul Hindemith and Arthur Honegger conducted several works. Then, in 1948, Hans Rosbaud was engaged as head director of the Southwest Radio.

Strobel published the first postwar issue of the magazine *Melos* in November 1946. In it he complained that the greatest proportion of German music lovers had practically no knowledge of the art of the previous 30 years, be it the art of a Chagall or Picasso, an André Gide or a Huxley, a Debussy or a Stravinsky. "And how many German musicians know anything of consequence about the work of their greatest living composer? I am referring to Paul Hindemith."[251]

Yet ignorance was not all that was to be found. Hostility against the "new musicians" was widespread, both among music professionals and among the general public. At the head of the anti-modernists stood Alois Melichar, a composer and songwriter from Munich.[252] Not only could he not expect endorsement from the "classicists," but also not from those who sought to connect with the period immediately before the Third Reich. Indeed, the 1930s represented an epoch of reaction or regression for the new music, in that it pushed populist tendencies into the foreground with the idea of the avant-garde becoming suspect of sectarianism.[253] From the middle of the 1920s, a strong countermovement began, aiming for light, playable piano music for lovers and amateurs, and urging the renewal of chorus literature in the spirit of the youth and workers' movement. Amateur pieces, educational pieces, and school operas turned against the esoteric. For children, pieces were written that could easily be performed in the schools. The lay musician was above all to be inspired to play music actively. Contrary to all this was the complex and complicated modern music. Later, in a review of the Melichar book, *Musik in der Zwangsjacke,* Walter Abendroth, an authoritative, conservative music critic of the *Zeit,* articulated this antimodernism and the way it bridged the gulf between the time before 1933 and the time after 1945. "The extreme revolutionary direction taken by modern music was, like all excessive subversive ideas in the art world, already dying out at the beginning of the 1930s. That which had been fruitfully stimulating about it began, according to the not so radical views of Schönberg, to enter into the course of its logical organic evolutionary development, thereby fulfilling its specific mission. Then came Hitler with his prohibitions, and the extremists emigrated. However, those things that had up to that point hardly played any role, suddenly came to represent the persecuted freedom of the spirit. At the same time, they received a political character given them, in fact, by Hitler himself, through which they became a point of honor for the free world."[254]

Such a statement was certainly more typical of the world of the economic miracle than of the rubble years. Immediately after the war, and for some years following, the new music resonated relatively well with the rebellion against the teachings of harmony. Atonal music provided the counterpoint to sensual-emotional or trivial and sentimental music. In any case, there was greater openness to new music than there was later, when abstraction led to a total absorption with the concrete.

Of course, the understanding of music was also dichotomous during the early postwar years. The restoration of the opera demonstrated that, just as before, perhaps even more than ever, the middle class hoped to transcend itself, by means of opera, to true humanity. Heinrich Strobel, on his first fact-finding tour from Baden-Baden into southwest Germany, was disappointed in what he saw of musical theater. "I saw either the old trash of representational theater, the more embarrassing as the misery lurked from behind every crack of the meagerly painted scenery, or the old *Spielastik,* whose 'proven' effects killed the meaning and spirit of all music. I read opera programs that could hardly be distinguished from those of the 'Thousand Year Reich.'" This included the "rush of operetta."[255]

At the same time, the anti-romantic generation was rediscovered, increasing the number of its richly varied followers, Schönberg, Berg, Webert, Hindemith, Egk, Jarnach, Reutter, Hartmann, Fortner, Blacher, Zimmermann, Klebe, Henze, whose "love for geometry" was fascinating. In many mostly small circles, the new music was passionately discussed. The artists were working not only to comprehend the past as a legacy to be preserved, but as an obstruction to be cleared away. The new music of the future was no longer to be imprisoned in ghettos and secret societies. Especially with the help of the widespread influence of radio and records, it was hoped that a different type of listening generation could be educated.

A number of concert series were performed to promote contemporary music. Already in October 1945, Karl Amadeus Hartmann founded "Musica Viva" in Munich, a model for analogous attempts both in Germany and abroad. In special courses and week long seminars, composers and students of music, as well as interested amateurs, were made familiar with the modern music.

According to a February 1948 newspaper article by Hans Mersmann a prerequisite for training a new generation of music listeners was the invention of individual styles. "They will no longer be defined by limited sectors of a great circle of listeners. We no longer have any need of such circles and secret societies. Rather, those forms which deviate from the representative concerts, such as studios or working groups, will point the way. In this way, the new music will go beyond its own sphere, and will be supplemented and supported by the written word as well. Works of problematic composition will be repeated fully or in part, thereby providing the listener with the opportunity to deepen and correct the first impression. In other types of circles, the record will be given back its old rights. It preserved the new music for us in authentic, often remarkable recordings at a time when we were deprived of it. Today, also, it acquaints us with those works that are unavailable in the circles of our concert life. None of these paths are tied to a specific form. The podium of the concert hall is simply one way of realizing the musical art form."[256]

The international vacation courses for new music, held in the Kranichstein *Jagdschloss* (hunting castle) near Darmstadt, linked with the 'music days' established by the city of Darmstadt, were at first thought of as supplementary extensions of the regular course offerings of German conservatories and colleges. Increasingly, however, they were recognized as an important international forum of modern music. "Since 1946 the Kranichstein Institute of Music in Darmstadt was run under the devoted, purposeful leadership of one man Wolfgang Steineck. The undertaking, rocked in its cradle by opposition and defense, developed as the most impactful meeting point of creative, international music. The response was undoubtedly due to the unintrusive, uncoerced exchange of ideas, and to the interweaving of courses, concerts, lectures, and private evaluations."[257] During August and September, 1946, Wolfgang Fortner rehearsed Brecht-Hindemith's *Lehrstuck* (teaching example). Hermann Heiss lectured on twelve-tone music, and Hindemith's *Ludus tonalis* and his *Fifth String Quartet* were played for the first time in Germany.

Wolfgang Fortner, born in Leipzig in 1907, worked continuously with the Darmstadt vacation courses, and also led the 'Musica Viva' concert series in Heidelberg and Freiburg. His first compositions were influenced by Bach, Reger, Hindemith and Stravinsky. After World War II, he evolved his own original application of the twelve-tone technique. The first performance of his only symphony, which he wrote in 1947, was given in Baden-Baden on May 2, 1948.

In 1947, the program included Bartók, Stravinsky, Hindemith and Schönberg. Rolf Liebermann, Carl Orff, Hermann Heiss, Heinz Schröter and Heinrich Sutermeister gave first performances of some of their works, and Fortner performed his violin concert as well as his *Shakespeare-Songs.* The slow movement of Hans Werner Henze's *First Symphony* was played under the direction of Hermann Scherchen. With the symphonic overtures of *China kampft,* Germany heard the work of Karl Amadeus Hartmann for the first time.

From every occupation zone of Germany, 140 predominantly young people came to the vacation course "to receive explanations of theory and practice from composers, pianists, singers, violinists, conductors, managers, and critics gathered as specialists of contemporary music." Hans Heinz Stuckenschmidt, who participated as a lecturer, claimed that the move toward lifting the understanding of music out of the sphere of hazy emotions and into consciousness with the goal of clarifying undigested concepts such as "linear," "concertante," "atonal," and "polytonal" had been essentially successful. Granted, this did not happen without opposition. The minds and hearts of even these young Germans, a receptive elite, were still haunted by the consequences of the 12 year numbing and political retardation. Foreign works were still considered strange and hostile, and there were cases of serious ignorance and rebellion against everything critical and analytical.[258]

Carl Orff, born in Munich in 1885, experienced an international breakthrough after World War II with his *Carmina burana,* which he had finished already in 1937. Building upon this success, he developed his musical-dramatic and musical-pedagogical work consistently further. In 1949 he concluded his work on *Antigonae.* The opening performance of this opera occurred in the same year as the Salzburg Festival, and was staged by Oskar Fritz Schuh, with scenery by Caspar Neher, and the musical direction of Ferenc Fricsay.

Karl Amadeus Hartmann, born in 1905, had refused to bring out any compositions in the Third Reich, and thus simply put his work in his desk drawers. After the war's end he finished his *Second String Concert* and revised his first four symphonies, which, along with the scenic oratorium *Simplicius Simpliccissimus,* were then performed for the first time. Noris Blacher (b. 1903) also composed many important works during the war that only became known after 1945. In 1948, he received an appointment to the Berlin College of Music. Of those works written during the rubble years, the chamber operas *Die Flut* (1947) and *Die Nachtschwalbe* (1948) were the most prominent.

The avant-garde of the older and younger artists included, along with those mentioned above, the names of Bernd Alois Zimmermann and Gieselher Klebe. The German composers around whom these people oriented themselves to a great extent were Arnold Schönberg, Anton von Webern and Paul Hindemith. Schönberg's twelve-tone technique was fascinating as a principle promising constructive and subjective expression at the same time. Thomas Mann's exposition of this technique in his novel, *Doctor Faustus* (1947), bestowed an additional demonic luster upon it, thus increasing its cultural reputation. Schönberg was the embodiment of the dialectic of enlightenment. He took over from the nineteenth century the messianic belief in unceasing, eternal progress, and, with the assumption that it could open up unimagined possibilities for the future, he extended this belief with amazing thoroughness to every tonal aspect of music. He thus stood in contradiction to the decline of this bourgeois Romantic spirit. "One cannot imagine him absent from the history of music. Decay and decline of the bourgeoisie, certainly. But what a sunset!" These were the words of Hanns Eisler, a Schönberg scholar who returned to East Berlin from America, where, as a German communist, he had been under suspicion for "un-American intrigues."[259]

Schönberg made moving mourning efforts after the war. He composed a cantata entitled *A Survivor From Warsaw* (1947). In his later years, he devoted himself first and foremost to metaphysical and religious questions, to some extent transcending the position of a utopian musical constructivism. He died in Los Angeles, where he had emigrated in 1934.

Anton von Weber died in 1945. Having flown in from Vienna to stay with his daughter in Mittersill, near Salzburg, he walked out the door to breathe some fresh air and was shot by an American guard, because he had stepped over the exit barrier. He became the highest model, going beyond Schönberg, for the musical avant-garde of the second generation. Serial music (an extension of the twelve-tone system, applied to color as well as to pitch), or serialism, crystalized around his name. Already by 1949, at the vacation course in Kranichstein, Oliver Messiaen had composed the first music piece completely structured according to the sequence for the twelve designated pitches, expanding it to other compositional qualities, like rhythm, intensity of volume, and tone color.[260]

Paul Hindemith celebrated a great comeback. According to Ulrich Dibelius, the insecurity that generally prevailed in the stylistic understanding of artists received, in or through Hindemith, triple compensation. "First personally, with the rehabilitation of a musician to his homeland, freed of the humiliation to which he had been subjected by the Nazis. He had been defamed and expelled by the National Socialists even though Furtwängler had called him with more truth than he was aware, a "definite German type." It was then possible, through a new version of the Hindemith school, to advance his once interrupted and obstructed development, gaining endorsement and even securing the practical support of a topnotch group of German composers of the same age or younger, Blacher, Fortner, Jarnach, Orff, Pepping, Reutter. Finally, because everyone felt a general cultural backlog after 12 years of isolation, the lack of truly new, uncompromised and timely music could be compensated by recalling or by imagining the regaining of youthfulness. And with Hindemith's enthronement, demonstrated in concerts, taught during the Darmstadt vacation course for new music, and propagated in the reemerging music magazines, *Melos*, and *Musica* from 1946 and 1947, most had in mind the musical buoyancy of the 1920s, but not the established master who had lectured in America and begun to revise his early works in line with the 'ethical necessities of music.'[261] In addition, Hindemith was widely known in circles of musicians and music lovers because of his earlier appointment in the Berlin College of Music, his cooperation with the representatives of the musical youth movement, and the altercation with the National Socialists that resulted in his departure from Germany in 1938. Hindemith's works were immediately made accessible again through the publishing company of B. Schott's Söhne in Mainz. In contrast to the radical atonality, his creations represented a compromise, he stood for continuity.

On his fiftieth birthday in November 1945, he was celebrated as a master redivivus. By the start of 1946, he had already returned to the German concert hall with great success. According to a report from Hamburg, when Eugen Jochum performed his second postwar philharmonic concert with *Symphonie in E-flat,* Hindemith's work was not discussed, it was simply played, with the conviction and the consciousness of its true artistic significance. Hindemith had not been forgotten. Not only the older people, but also a segment of the musically advanced younger Germans continuously acknowledged him and believed in him. The performance of a work by Hindemith was no longer an experiment.

The opening performance of Hindemith's *Mathis der Maler* took place in the Württemberg Municipal Theater in December 1946. It was above all "Germanness" that was celebrated in this opera of the life of Grunewald, the painter and creator of the Isenheimer Altar.

Paul Hindemith came to Frankfurt in the early summer of 1947, having decided against the idea of making permanent his return from America. The trip was like a "family reunion." He was born in the neighboring city of Hanau, and had passed his entire youth in Frankfurt am Main. In Frankfurt, too, he had conducted the opera, beginning his career on the Main. "The people of Frankfurt knew this, and thus they greeted him. Theirs was not simply a greeting extended to a wonderful musician, but to a member of the family now returning for a visit. There was no lack of Hindemith's old friends in the room, and he himself was amazed to rediscover so many people who had changed so little . . . He reported on his latest works that were then still unknown in Germany. Among them, the most significant was a musical sacrifice to the dead, a type of world requiem, conceived according to a great poem by Walt Whitman *"When Lilacs Last in the Dooryard Bloom'd."* The American poet had commemorated the dead of the American Civil War. He further portrayed how Abraham Lincoln's coffin traveled through the country after his assassination, followed by throngs of people. Hindemith used this English text for his composition in order to give a musical offering to those killed in World War II. He also intended, with this work, to express the living American democracy. He noted that upon Roosevelt's death, when his coffin traveled through the country, it stirred up the same feelings of honor and gratitude in the people as had Abraham Lincoln's casket earlier. He interpreted this as a continuation of the pure democratic sense of life that undulated throughout Walt Whitman's poetry."[262]

The Abraxas Scandal

The musical consciousness of the rubble years felt quite at home with Hindemith, the German American, the American German. If *Mathis der Maler* was in fact "demonic," this was to be understood in a typically German, that is, Faustian, sense of the word.

The cultural consciousness was less comfortable with the character of Mephistopheles. Thus Werner Egk (b. 1901) evoked the greatest musical scandal of the rubble years with his Faust ballet, *Abraxas,* of 1948. Particularly since his work was based on Heinrich Heine's Faust fragments, Egk's ballet focused on the "most devlish" elements of the passions. Egk had already aroused the mistrust of the establishment with the troll scene of his opera, *Peer Gynt,* in 1938. Abraxas symbolized the power that ruled over 365 godheads. Participating in a dance of magical sensuousness were Faust and Margarete; Archiposa, the devil's main consort; Bellastriga, a beautiful, alluring witch, similar to Mephisto in her infernal grace and spirit; and several mythological and historical figures belonging to the court of Charles IV of Spain. The concert version was broadcast by the Southwest Radio, directed by Werner Egk at the invitation of Heinrich Strobel.[263] The world premiere then occurred in June 1948, in the Bavarian State Opera House. It was "one of those unusual, moving phenomena that invited both sympathy and discord."[264]

The "sensuous, stirring attraction," particularly of the "Black Mass" of the third scene, so bothered the Bavarian Minister of Culture, Alois Hundhammer, that he, supported by the Archbishop, closed it down after the fifth performance. In Berlin, advance performances were given for the cathedral chapter, the Senate, the House of Commons, and the League of Women. The objections were few and insignificant, and the ballet ran for 116 performances. In his autobiography, *Die Zeit wartet nicht,* Werner Egk gave an extensive account of this educational piece from the Bavarian Catholic province:

"In autumn, or more specifically, on October 25, 1948, I began to pester the administrative office of the opera with the question, 'When is the performance series of *Abraxas,* under contract with Dr. Hartmann, expected to begin?'

"They leafed in vain through the thick book containing the dates of rehearsals, performances, attendances and absences, and even the foreseeable indispositions of the singing bird. No matter how much they steeped themselves in the book, they found no sign of *Abraxas.* I therefore reported to Dr. Georg Hartmann and continued asking questions until, piece by piece, the unpleasant truth came to light.

"'When, then?' I asked.

'What exactly are you referring to?' A manager has so many things in his head that it often takes a long time to get organized.

'I'm referring to my ballet!'

'Oh, now I understand, it has to do with *Abraxas.*'

'When', I asked, stressing each syllable, 'does my ballet again come up on the program?'

'Oh yes, well in fact . . .' He stopped short, and the thin streamlet of his speech dried up.

'Excuse me?'

'Something has happened.'

I pressed him further. Crumb by crumb, he spit it all out. What came out was by no means pretty. The Minister of Culture had prohibited the re-staging of the ballet.

'Prohibited? That can't be true. Who's in charge of the program, you or the Minister of Culture?'

'You remember, of course, that Dr. D. from the secretariat prevented the sale of your libretto in the Prinzregententheater. That was perhaps 14 days before the performance.'

'The black mass,' I said. 'We have already performed it, without protest, receiving a jubilant response from the press and the population. Isn't that true?'

'Yes, of course.'

'In fact, I seem to remember that a commission, acting under higher orders, had already watched the 'black mass' before the general rehearsal. The authorities had at that time asked for some insignificant changes in order that no souls would be endangered. I still remember what disturbed the commission. When the ballerina was flipped over, she was hanging with her head down. Her little ballet skirt flew open according to the law of gravity. People saw, horror of horrors, her belly covered with thick cotton tricot. Because of this, the commission demanded that this scene be shortened so that people's eyes couldn't linger so long on the cotton tricot. The scene was cut so drastically that no topographical orientation was possible. Then the spotlights were withdrawn and a few steps were altered. That was all.'

'Unfortunately, I can't change the fact that the piece remains prohibited.' No more was said.

"Immediately, I reported to my very beloved Dr. Dieter Sattler, who was at that time Secretary of State in the Ministry of Culture. He was in the best of moods, as usual, and gave me the gossip fresh from the source. 'And so, it went like this, before the premiere the assistant bishop to the Archbishop called on us one day, requesting that the Minister of Culture withdraw *Abraxas* from circulation. They had agreed to run a series that was already being prepared. When the theater reopened after its break, the ballet was to to disappear silently behind the scenes, like the rabbit in the hat.'

'Do you know why?'

'Two female members of the ballet complained to the bishop's assistant.'

'Did they also go to their superiors, the theater manager or the Ministry of Culture?'

'Not that I know of.'

'What did the ladies say to the Bishop's assistant?'

'They complained about the ballet instructor and about your ballet.'

"From the fact that they had written to an ecclesiastical dignitary and not to a secular authority, I concluded that their complaints had to do with offenses against morals and religion.

"Could it be that these were the two ladies who had been unable to press their demands at the time of the casting? One was stiff as a board and yet she wanted to dance some nimble dance to show off her anatomy in its best light. She could have at best been cast in the part of a tree but only with the wind completely still. And the other one? She was not satisfied with the costume designed for her, thinking it veiled her charms too much. She demanded either a costume that would show off what she had, or else another role. If my suspicions are correct, they wrote to the bishop's assistant that they should not be expected to do what they were asked to do in my ballet.

"It didn't occur to me to attempt to go the way of Canossa (site of Henry IV's penitential plea for Pope Gregory VII to lift the ban of excommunication in 1077). Rather, I preferred to write a letter of protest to 250 newspapers, claiming that Article 108 of the Bavarian Constitution had been broken with the ministerial prohibition of my ballet, *Abraxas.*

"There was not much immediate response. A few commentaries and caricatures appeared. Our Minister of Culture, who was already out of favor with the liberals because of his plea on behalf of the penalty of thrashing, and for his Obscene Publications Act, appeared in one newspaper as a blockhead with a nail in his brain. In another he appeared as a fat dog with a full beard, sitting under the boundary post of the free state of Bavaria and making sure that *Abraxas* did not return. Caricatures meant publicity. For a while I regarded myself as the minister's benefactor."[265]

Music as a Means of Survival

"Serious music," a highly significant, typical German generic term for classical music, was ranked high on the value scale of the early postwar years. "After the cultural dismantling of the 'total war,' people simply wanted to hear it again, for consolation and protection against the past, and for compensation and courage in the present. And thanks to these unquestioned restorational tendencies, a concert life, as makeshift as it was active, was already established a few months after the war's end. It was, for the most part, provincial in style. . . . And, with a certain lack of realism given the pervasive want of the necessities of life, ideas and plans for the rebuilding of concert halls and opera houses soon circulated around the newly established government organs. In actuality, however, it was mostly in the emergency shelters, churches, inns, schools, and even private homes that the quickly thrown-together music groups still played. And there, where the new spirit of the postwar times could have stood out the most, the works that were performed were of the casual sort. Perhaps those that under the Nazi regime had been forbidden, tabooed, or in the language of the time, connected to 'undesirable' composers were sometimes given priority over other works. The 'strings-attached' patronage of the small casts and chamber music was an exception to this."[266]

Ulrich Dibelius' analysis is, with respect to the average situation, certainly correct. It it necessary, however, to supplement it with reference to a relatively large number of exceptions. In the large cities in particular, there soon reappeared outstanding orchestras, especially since through the great number of refugees, highly qualified musicians had come into the Western zones seeking work. The newly founded "Bamberger Symphoniker" was comprised largely of such people. There was also no lack of outstanding conductors.

For a fair estimation of the quality of the music life during the rubble years, it is necessary to remember the adverse conditions under which it developed. The musicians, like every one else, were undernourished. In May 1948, the whole cultural establishment of Munich was affected by a pervasive disease traceable to malnutrition. The Minister of Culture, Alois Hundhammer, immediately requested a living allowance for artists from the two-zone administration in Frankfurt. He was praised by the press for this action.[267] Also problematic were the totally inadequate concert halls that stayed ice cold in the winter.

The importance of classical music for these times is evident much more clearly from photographs than from any statistical data. One of the most gripping photographs from this period was taken by Hans Schürer. It shows an audience of women and men listening to Beethoven's *Ninth Symphony*, performed by the Munich Philharmonic Orchestra in a university auditorium in 1945. Their faces reflect rapture, devotion to another world that illuminates the misery like a glimpse of the idea. It was contemplation of art without affectation, submersion without internal coquetry, celebration without pathos. It was music as a means for living, for surviving. Music, Ernst Bloch informs us, because of its immediate power of human expression, possesses, more than any other art form, the ability to absorb the numerous sorrows, desires, and bright moments of the oppressed classes. And at this time practically everyone must have felt oppressed. "And no other art form had so much in excess of the prevailing times and ideology, a surplus which of course does not leave the human realm behind. It is the material for hope, even while feeling the pain caused by time, society and world, and even in death. The 'strike now, desired hour, desired hour, strike now' of the Bach cantata pierces the darkness and offers, by the very fact that its sound exists, incomprehensible consolation." The objectively indefinable aspect expressed and portrayed in the music was but a promising shadow of its virtue. "Whereupon music is that art form of revelatory light which most intensively concerns the unfolding seed of the existence of being, and most extensively, its horizon, *cantus essentiam fontis vocat.*"[268]

Bloch's "principle of hope" was also clearly present in quite another genre of music. It did not, however, come down "from above," from the heaven of geniuses, but instead rose up anonymously from the people, who instead of using the accompaniment of classical instruments, improvised with "dirty tones." For this reason, and also because it was not transcendent-German, but socially immanent-American, the response to it was limited. Jazz, which during the Third Reich was an expression of inner opposition, and an aspect of many young peoples' resistance to Hitler Youth, found a home only in the taverns of the rubble years. Because it stood outside the European tradition, it was not recognized in established or upcoming cultural life. Particularly fatal for its future was its prohibition from the schools. What was missed was the possibility of inspiring young people in music, of making accessible to them an art form that meaningfully carried the feeling of and for freedom, and that evoked an unconventional creativity beyond current art forms.

There developed during the rubble years an "underground" of alternative music culture, lead by jazz fans. It existed in numerous variations, noted Joachim-Ernst Berendt, then an editor for the Southwest Radio, who was among the first in Germany to be competently and courageously engaged with jazz. There were young men and women, who with the rhythm of jazz music literally broke out of themselves in an enthusiasm that for middle class citizens bore all the signs of shocking and repellent behavior. The questions posed by Berendt provide an indirect mirror of the prevailing prejudices of the time. What creates this enthusiasm? What fascinates them about jazz? Are they unstable people who react to every momentary fad with seismographic sensitivity? Are they immature young people who lack the feelings defined by the word "proportion." Are they poorly brought up people lacking those human values that distinguish the Western world?

"It appears impossible to assign a specific social origin to the jazz enthusiasm. Jazz fans come from every circle, workers and students, blue collar and white collar workers, journalists and sales people, technicians and industrialists or the sons and daughters of such folk. At best one can specify a geographic point of origin, for jazz fans tend to be city people, marked by that vague modernity that stigmatizes them as international. They are people caught in the net of responsibilities and relationships, of attentions and precautions, of desires and responses, of hustle and bustle, a net that does not let go of modern people, even in their most free moments, perhaps on the way from or to their jobs. These are almost always, as long as they are young, people for whom the 'life in all its seriousness' began earlier than it did one or two generations previously, and who, however, will never admit that there is something unfamiliar or noteworthy in this."[269]

It is instructive to note that Theodor W. Adorno, the middle class revolutionary, the ingenious philosopher of a new musical aesthetics and the incisive observer and critic of the music scene, failed to recognize the youthful elements of jazz. Music, for him, was precisely "that other," and jazz, in contrast, like so many of his contemporaries, "the ground floor." "It was once the case that the aesthetic sphere, as a realm with its own rules, issued forth from the magical taboo that distinguished between the sacred and the profane, keeping itself pure. Now the profane takes its revenge on the descendants of magic, of art. The latter will be allowed to stay alive only if the right of being different is renounced and if it submits to the predominance of the profane, to which the taboo passes over in the end. Nothing must be allowed to exist that is not like that which already is. Jazz is the false liquidation of art. Instead of bringing about Utopia, it wipes it off the map."[270]

Fine Arts Abandon the Catacombs

In a talk on art and artists given in 1946, Ernst Wiechert claimed that the German essence has found its immortal expression, through long centuries, in music, poetry, fine arts, philosophy, and the sciences. These things have shaped the eyes of those who throughout generations have looked upon them, and through their eyes, their hearts have also been shaped. "It has been formed on goodness, wisdom, patience, humaneness, and above all and with all on love. It has allowed us to live together in the great house of humanity, constructed by the nations of the earth, among which we were not the least." Now, however, it has become clear. Deep down in the original soil of our people, deep under Christianity, beauty, wisdom, and humaneness, lay a jungle, undisturbed and unchanged since the stone age, and in this jungle lurked the beast, half awake, half dreaming, untamed, uncontrolled, undisturbed by ten thousand years of effort, devotion, and love. In the Third Reich, this earth spirit was let loose, and the terrified human face stared wordlessly into its red hot eyes. "At no time in human history have the promises from the other side of the stars become so questionable as they have today. At no other time has such a luminous thread of true happiness been spun around the hands of those already able to promise things on the earth, if only in pictures and sounds. Prophets and demons have fallen into the abyss from which they came. Yet the face of that one whom the demons futilely tried to undermine with all their power, that face has remained unchanged, shining over us. It is the face of the good earth, of art and of love." Wiechert, with his characteristic metaphorical pathos conjured up in art a glimpse of the idea that lost souls would find the way, that those in the darkness of doubt and despair would find light, the suffering, an ointment, and the outlaw, a glimmer of great justice. Wiechert, while clearly leaving the ground of reality, also offered concrete criticism of the daily activities of the art world. "No reasonable person will deny that the Americans do their best to clean our house, but neither will they deny that it is not right that the mega-artificial artists of the Third Reich such as Thorak or Breker, who inscribed the ethos of the Third Reich eternally in concrete and marble, were discharged after a few weeks in prison so they could make busts of American generals."[271]

Many artists who had hoped for the end of the Third Reich while in inner or outer emigration asked themselves whether the great catharsis would take place, or whether the danger existed that the followers, opportunists, conformists, and accommodators would again succeed.

A few days after the war's end, the painter Ernst Wilhelm Nay (b. 1902) wrote the art dealer Günther Franke, who had found refuge on the Starnberg Sea. A fellow soldier, who had been discharged into this area, delivered the letter. "What more will happen? Certainly one can assume that there will be interest in art . . . Hopefully art will now regain its freedom after these 13 evil years."[272]

There were soon passionate debates on questions of style. Which style was suitable for the times. Expressionism, surrealism, realism, abstractionism, or absolute art? In a lecture given in the spring of 1946, the authoritative art historian, Franz Roh, argued for a strong union whose task it would be to solve the material problems of those engaged in the fine arts, and to secure their political and economic influence. With respect to the question of style, he said, "My beloved colleagues, whether you paint barricades or meadows dotted with timid violets, is all the same to us, assuming both represent works of art."[273] However, such peaceful coexistence of styles was not in conformity with the spiritual consciousness of this agitated era. The creative thoughts and designs of the past were passionately questioned as to the value they could have for the present and future.

With the total defeat, the opportunity had come to rehabilitate the art that Nazi ideology had defamed as "degenerate." The good spiritual cultural climate of the rubble years was apparent in the fact that this restoration took place with greater participation of the population than could have been expected in light of developments before 1945. Granted, conservative sectors also expressed significant opposing views, earning the reproach of representing pre- or post-Fascist tendencies.

Expressionism, of course, was also relativized in other ways as well. With all due respect for its historical accomplishments, there has been much development. In one of the first exhibitions in Munich, the painter Fritz Burkhardt presented classical expressionistic and "degenerate" graphics alongside the works of the newest Munich art. An accompanying pamphlet stated that "the art of the present, as it has developed outside the German sphere in the open and inside Germany's 'underground,' is no longer congruent with that which we show in the more retrospective segment of our exhibition, namely, with expressionism, whose golden age already passed by 30 years ago. Yet this bygone era was the presupposition for the following one, and the understanding of its essence is also the precondition for the understanding of the art of our day."[274]

More incisively still, art critic Friedrich Adama von Scheltema stated in the second issue of *Prima,* a journal published by Hans Eberhard Friedrich since November 1946, that expressionism, including even the extremes of Picasso and Kandinsky, had already run its course before World War I, and that today, after all the epoch-making events, it could hardly be classified as modern. He further warned against a return to expressionism, saying that in his opinion it came from the same spiritual soil that brought forth the worst blossoms of Nazism. Karl Scheffler, too, in his book *Die fetten und die mageren Jahre* (The Fat and Lean Years) (1946), also saw this connection, and therefore rejected expressionism. Finally, in 1949, H. Ludecke reproached expressionism for being an "art of disharmony, of being-out-of-accord, of uneasiness and negation." This "pseudo-revolutionary art with emotionally real and rebellious impulses" failed as the style of the petty bourgeoisie, and should therefore be avoided.[275]

Along with expressionism, surrealism received special attention in the rubble years. It represented a spiritual movement, "nothing materialistic, which does not exclude the possibility that most surrealists are extreme Marxists. There was an emphasis on the need for internationalism and an equally clear anti-nationalistic disposition. And, more political still, the surrealists of Paris were no collaborators . . . When today in Germany or in Berlin some artists are characterized as surrealists, . . . it can be assumed that these artists were also not collaborators or opportunists." None of them exhibited in the great art exhibition in Munich in 1937. These were Heinz Trökes' words, appearing in 1947 in *Kunstwerk,* a magazine founded by Woldemar-Klein-Verlag, a publishing company in Baden-Baden and probably the most important journalistic forum for modern art during this time.[276]

Trökes, born in 1913, was part of a generation that consciously lived with National Socialism from the beginning. In 1933, after completing his graduation exam *(Abitur),* he transferred to a school of arts and crafts in Krefeld, where he studied under Johannes Itten, former master of the Bauhaus school. Even in the Third Reich, one could still find, in the art schools and academies, small circles and pockets of resistance that remained connected with modern art, thus having withstood complete regimentation. With Itten and later with Georg Muche, Trökes came in direct contact with the outlawed Bauhaus ideas. In 1937, during his first trip to Paris, he visited Vasily Kandinsky. When, in 1938, the Berlin Gallery of Nierendorf, which, incidently, had managed a certain opposition against the official doctrines of art, arranged an exposition for Trökes, it was immediately closed down by the National Socialists. This marked the end of a career that had not yet begun, and the beginning of intense activity, which for Trökes' surrealistic creations meant 'underground art.' "Trökes had not resigned, and he had not served the brown-shirted wielders of power. For a halfway talented painter it would have been laughably simple, even without pictures of Hitler, to enter the *Haus der Kunst* with approved, conventional landscapes. Trökes preferred to design textiles which he had learned in Krefeld, and also to pursue his fantastic surrealist path in the art realm. From literary circles, he found Jean Paul and James Joyce congenial. They accompanied him through the Third Reich and through the war, when he served as an anti-aircraft gunner in Berlin. On the book lining of one of his first sketchbooks, begun early in 1945 and finished in May, 1945, are inscribed the following words of Jean Paul: 'Beneath the earth is sleeping, above the earth is dreaming, but between sleeping and dreaming I see the lights wandering like stars.'"[277]

The landscape left behind by the war, both real and mental-spiritual, with big cities turned into rubble heaps, the juxtaposition of hope and despair, readiness to build and demoralization, and the all pervasive idyll of Pan, was itself, said Barbara Klie, a giant "masterpiece of surrealistic painting." And the pictures reproduced this model. This art did not aspire to compensate for the overall lack of prosperity. Neither the security of the fifties nor the boredom of the sixties hovered over the quarters, which were not lived in, but simply occupied. If anything from this final period can be positively ascertained, it is the memory that the contrasting relationships between art and life and between a calm life and a completely unsettled art was not valid then. The massive warning signals forged in iron by the sculptor Hans Uhlmann, and Karl Hartung's collossus carved from boulders, Alexander Camaros' thin lines of wire rope, and the glimmering landscapes of craters by Trökes, Max Zimmermann and other surrealists, "reproduced the evil unreality, the illusory loss, that anyone could find, every day, just one block away, one day away. At that time, Werner Heldt traveled back and forth between his eastern Pankow and the western sectors. In the rubble dunes reflected in black canals, he discovered 'Berlin on the Sea,' once a dim vision, now a reality."[278]

"Berlin was . . . in fact a sphere between the Reichs, surrealistic," noted Werner Gilles in August 1947. And Hans Sedlmayr asked, "Is there any decomposition more surrealistic than the pictures of the devastated cities?"[279] Surrealism wished to see the unexpected, unlikely, and unfamiliar expressed in art. In fact, however, this was present in real life, and did not need to be first conjured up in the imagination, in dreams, or by chance. Hans Egon Holthusen, in 1947, referred to those who had come through the war and the disjointed reality which followed, as "contemporaries of an amorphous and anarchic world, shipwrecked people whose lives consist of continuous and stressful provisional arrangements; driftwood of a crumbled civilization; inhabitants of a fantastic dreamland stretching out between the garbage dumps and the rubble heaps . . . Eye- and body-witnesses of a catastrophe that drowned the world . . ., of fire and of public insanity; miserable survivors and returnees who barely escaped with their lives—all strangely entangled in the contradiction between the impossibility of their living conditions and the possibility of living."[280]

Such "shipwreck mood" pervades the pictures of Karl Hofer. He was born in 1878, and in 1920 began teaching in the College of Fine Arts in Berlin. As one of the artists dismissed by the National Socialists in 1933, he found forceful metaphors for the approaching disaster: specters, masks, starving, blind, and crazy people, dances of death, rubble fields, and demolition nights were the variations of the theme of "damaged persons." *Der Gefangene* (1933) anticipated the concentration camp; *Der Turmbläser* (1935) gives an idea of an air raid siren; *Die Wächter* (1936) predicts a long night. In 1937 Hofer painted a *Mann in Ruinen,* an anticipation of a destroyed city. Between 1938 and 1943, more than 600 of his works were lost, half in a Fascist raid, and the other half in a bomb attack that destroyed his studio. In his memoirs, Hofer reported that he had never sold so well as after the ban on his work and exhibitions. He took this as proof that realistic symbolic, or surrealistic art could not be fully suppressed by the National Socialists.

As did Gottfried Benn's stoic aesthetics, "Nothing but with icing on the top," Fascism and the war made Hofer deeply distrustful of the future. His postwar pictures oppose the euphoria of new beginning and change with a profound pessimism and a great skepticism. Pictures such as *Totentanz, Im Neubau, Atomserenade,* and *Die Blinden* make it clear that human activity is vain and foolish, irredeemably lost and cut off from salvation. *Die Blinden* shows four people, clinging to each other, stumbling disoriented through a forest of dead, rotten trees.

In a letter to Hermann Hesse at the end of 1948, Hofer concluded, "We are coming to recognize that the most detestable, criminal human activity is politics." "Politics, whether dressed in conservative, democratic, or socialistic garb, whether of the right, left, or center was all the same to Hofer. It always had to do with power and was always run with crime and force. The misery of the world was due to there always being a claim, a right, an idea, or a worldview to fight for or enforce. These keep ominous events alive. For many artists, therefore, only *one* attitude was morally defensible, refusal. Against every claim and demand of 'mediocre and blindly raging worldviews' they obstinately insisted on their individual freedom and independence. 'In light of the present political social order,' said Albert Camus in a much noted article, 'it is futile and laughable when one demands vindication or involvement from us.'"[281]

Abstract art, like the other modern art forms outlawed during the Third Reich, found a new, significant resonance with many in the rubble years, for it transcended the present dismal reality toward the actual and essential. In 1946, Wilhelm Uhde declared that "surrealism, in a manner as original as it was astonishing, made it its business to combine human emotion with things. One thus need not be surprised when one encounters abstract art that makes a clean sweep of all feelings and objects."[282]

Just as the first great wave of abstract art before World War I represented a response to the plush world of the Wilhelmian culture, it became, after 1945, a way out of the gloomy concreteness of the rubble-scape. The abstract was not only more spiritual than the concrete, it was also more "true," assuming one interpreted art as an extension of consciousness, a venture into unknown territory, as did Willi Baumeister, the central figure of abstract paining. *Das Unbekannte in der Kunst* (The Unknown in Art), which first appeared in 1947, was written by Baumeister during the war, throughout which he had found shelter as a worker in the Technical Institute in Wuppertal. Reality proved to be merely a jumping off point for the picture. The object was simply a window leading into the unknown world of forms. The totality showed unusual boldness, breaking every convention. At the same time, it was self-evident, simple, "natural," and exemplary. In his understanding, geniuses were not only discoverers and inventors, the greater their importance, the more universal will be their handling of every question and situation. Genius is manifested in the greatest simplicity, in that it builds itself step by step, employing logic, hypothesis, encirclement, practical research, and intuition always at the right moment. With respect to method of discovery, the genius of art and of science is similar. Granted, in contrast to science, art makes no use of proofs. Art demands faith in art. Seen as a whole from without, however, science can also not be "proven," but presupposes a faith in science. There is thus a close inner relationship between art and science.

When Baumeister was called to the Academy of Art in Stuttgart in 1946, he began a phase of his work that was highly significant for postwar art. "Baumeister stands with Beckmann, Max Ernst, and perhaps also Feininger as one of the few great artists whose postwar work is not inferior to the work before that time. As with Beckmann, themes from the mythical realm predominate in his work. Their methods, however, differed, for Baumeister translated the mythical into the abstract. Of course, the mythical elements were not the reason for the attraction his work held for students, no matter how numerous his formal discoveries, inspired by memories of Mexican temple pictures and African rock pictures, by mental and written images of China and the ancient orient. What fascinated young people was his ever-seeking, investigating, analyzing method of painting. To them, soberness was more important than mythical content, even though it did not lend itself to direct symbolical interpretation. Baumeister remained, like Josef Albers, a student as well as a teacher. To the very end, he was open towards many impulses and stimulations which never appeared as foreign particles in his work. His goal was never the isolated 'beautiful picture,' instead, he always sought the chance for new working groups to form. The individual discovery was not important to him, but rather the discovery of rich soil. Even more, he was concerned with the method of creativity."[283]

At the first great exhibition of Willi Baumeister's work in September 1947, Franz Roh delivered a kind of monologue on abstract art between "him and myself." On the basis of the significant exhibits of the Franke Gallery, the critic expressed his uncertainty with respect to the classification of Baumeister:

"Nature was poured over the canvas in Nolde's art, with green marshland breathing moisture and heavy clouds steaming over the sea. Beckmann jammed streaks of land and figures like barricades over his canvas. Marc embedded his creatures in presence, encircled the animals in color, and only seldom did the forms assume independence. With Baumeister, however, we have difficulty. Unreadable, strange ciphers flutter before whitewashed walls. Runic forms float about, incomprehensible as the early cave drawings. Sharp lines intersect mysterious agglomerations. Something moves me, yet I often lose the ground from under my feet . . . Painting without objects seems to me like an interesting schema for a composition, more like a preparation for the actual work of painting. Is the enjoyment of the painting thereby not cut in half? Old masters like Giotto, Mantegna, and Brueghel can also be interpreted as abstract, meaning that their paintings can be looked at like colored architecture. Nevertheless, they carry within themselves the miracle of objectification. Abstract art thus appears puritanical to me, somewhat renunciatory. . . . On the other hand, there is something more to be said. If I compare the opera with absolute music, then in the opera all sound is centered on the object, the story, which is missing. In its place, however, something new comes forth, as in abstract art. Rhythm, color and shapes are experienced as ends in themselves, pure and distinct from everything else. We now experience the laws that lie behind all things. Elsewhere, colors and forms become more and more specialized, associated with specific figures or landscapes. Here, however, emotions are aroused that are partially specific and partially general." Franz Roh eventually came to the conclusion that "absolute painting" would not replace the painting that emphasized objects, both forms would accompany one another in the future. Each had its own magic, as long as able artists were there to attend to it.[284]

Those people with a strong will to rebuild, influenced by "the magic of the future," were especially inspired by abstract art. The dreariness of the early postwar years faded in light of the richness of new forms and colors that could be "utilized." Melancholy defined by the past, such as Karl Hofer, who severely challenged abstract art, and especially Willi Baumeister, was blotted out by futuristic art. It was this futurism that later, in the design of the world of the economic miracle, changed in the direction of a playful and cheery freshness. If the abstract art of the rubble years signified a transfer into a progressivism aimed at a new essence, in the fifties the dialectics of abstract art brought about a regression of the spiritual-abstract to the formal-abstract, thereby becoming concrete as "form design" without binding itself to it. Thus art aspired to be free from the prison of reality. The reception of Joan Miró in particular, as well as of other abstract artists who detached themselves from cubism and entered the sphere of applied and practical art, reversed a development that began under quite different auspices after the zero hour.

The most significant center for new abstractionism developed in Munich, eventually joining the Zen group founded in 1949, of which Willi Baumeister, Rupprecht Geiger, and Fritz Winter were members. Ernst Wilhelm Nay began his postwar career in Frankfurt.

Geiger circulated a letter marking the field of tension in which abstract artistic creations developed. "Endless attacks from those looking backward were directed against the de-concretized portrayal . . . Recognizing this renewed threat, the group felt responsible to become even more active in their written and spoken efforts to disseminate their new ideas." Among the honorary members of the group was the German-American Hilla von Rebay, who met Kadinsky, Chagall, Léger, and Delaunay in the 1920s after her studies in Dusseldorf, Munich, and Paris. She then established a private museum in Berlin in 1929 for nonrepresentational art, and published a magazine entitled *Das Geistreich.* She inspired Solomon R. Guggenheim's interest in abstract art, thereby initiating the Guggenheim collection, of which she was the first director. While visiting Munich after the war, she was shocked by the prevailing misery, yet also inspired by the resurgence of abstract painting. She not only furnished the Munich painters with care-packages, but she put together a selection of 50 works of abstract art from the Guggenheim collection for an exhibition that traveled to Paris, Zurich, Stuttgart, Munich, Hamburg, Düsseldorf, Braunschweig, Amsterdam, and London.[285]

Fritz Winter became the head of the young avant-garde in Munich after his return from a war prison. Prior to the war, he had been working on the theme of nature, creating pictures and sketches in the 1930s with names like "Waldgrund," "In den Zweigen" or "Pflanzliches." "In the 1940s, however, Winter moved far away from this. His sketches became gloomy, taking on a wild flow like crystal formations that lost their rigidity through fractures and diffractions, appearing as if in motion. Dramatic use of light rendered the sketches explosive. Their titles spoke of anxiety and pain. The abstract form is for Winter an expression of psychic states. Now in 1949, these forms have calmed down. They are more compact, and differ from one another without the strong intertwining of forms that marked his earlier drawings."[286]

In the art of Ernst Wilhelm Nay, Ernst Jünger discovered the "stamp of both primitivism and awareness" already in 1943. With his abstract use of color, he was a vital representative of the euphoric phase of reconstruction. His stirring creations, Nay, himself, occasionally spoke of "enraged painting," stood in contrast to the "works of mourning" undertaken, for example, by Max Beckmann with his backward directed visions. With Nay, one can clearly follow the decline of the reputation of abstract art beginning with the latter phases of the economic miracle. In 1964, his art colleague Hans Platschek thought he could polemically and critically uncover the uncommitted nature of Nay's work by separating out the individual elements of his *Freiburger Bild.* There were 211 color discs, of which 141 were intact, and "the remaining 70 were only recognizible as half or quarter discs or less than that. This does not account for the 49 dots that, perhaps for a change, are spread over the canvas. The painting is 6.34 meters wide and 2.51 meters high. Twice the number of color discs could easily have fit into it, three times as many, indeed, the master could have included ten times as many if necessary. We'll say nothing of the dots!" In the rubble years in any case, people experienced the "magic" of this art, the sensual picture of a spiritual world. The world of ruins was thereby transcended, and the catharsis was accomplished *more geometrico.*

Nay's painting *Kythera* was presented as a typical work from 1947 in the exhibition, "German Art from 1898 to 1973," held in the Hamburg Hall of Art. The programme's reference to this painting included the following comments. "Characteristics of the reconstruction are clearly and insightfully expressed. Who acts accordingly? The motivation of private initiative serves other goals. The urbane system of life would almost imperceptibly be sacrificed to the fetish of production capacity. The first signs of East-West tension occurred when a critic of the Soviet Union reproached the organizers of an exhibition in Baden-Baden for a lack of objectivity with respect to 'social trends.'"[287]

Other trends appearing immediately after the war were also branded "aesthetic escape movements." The flight from the "gray world" into "color zones" was, however, often a means of survival, apart from the fact that the flight from the overcast North into the clarity of the South is a basic component of German culture and cultural history. ("I, too, in Arcadia.") Who could find fault with art for seeking to exchange the gloomy reality of the Third Reich, the war and the rubble years for the cheerfulness of a southern landscape, for which the ambivalence of ancient myths remained present?

Werner Gilles wrestled significantly with the Orpheus myth in 1947. The history of the singer and poet Orpheus dealt with love and death, with a journey through the underworld and resurrection, with joy and sorrow, despair and hope. For Gilles, it symbolized the destiny of a humanity loved and destroyed by the gods, a humanity exposed to the limit situations of life. With the *Orpheus-Zyklus* he hoped to render visible that which lurked behind the obvious. For this it was not necessary either to illustrate or to accuse the past in its entirety.

Gilles was born in 1894, studied with Lyonel Feininger, among others, and lived mostly in southern Italy, until he was drafted by the military in 1941. Commenting on the beginning of his postwar creations, in which figures from myths and sagas occupied a large space, he said. "Only a few days had passed since the war's end, and a new world appeared before me in a new light. Over night, the chains were broken, and a carefully concealed unconscious blossomed forth full of hope . . . There ensued an entire cycle of pastels, apparitions, dreams and visions . . ."[288] Characters from fairy tales (St. Georg, St. Martin, and Charon) helped reduce the suffering and mystery of death through the "wonderous" representation of miracle, deliverance, and salvation, thereby lifting present reality into eternity.

A certain fluid structure characterizes "escapist" art, so that one finds an overlap of realism, surrealism, expressionism, and abstractionism. The rule of "free nature" became a metaphor for redemption and grass grew over everything. Eberhard Hempel discussed "the beauty of ruins" in a 1948 issue of *Zeitschrift fur Kunst.* "Not only we Germans, but many other European nations will have to get used to living among ruins. The oppressive feelings of irreplaceable loss must first take over the soul. But an eye that is open to artistic impressions soon discovers that the greater unity, present in the emergence of the basic structure, often confers a beauty that the previous, variously decorated plaster structures did not possess. This effect will continue to grow with time, as soon as the disintegrating walls surrender to free nature."[289]

Werner Heldt, a friend of Werner Gilles, experienced harsh times during the Third Reich, living in constant anxiety of arrest. He named some of the works he painted after 1946 *Berlin am Meer.* The pessimistic fatalism of the artist who, like Max Beckmann, feared the threat of collectivism, and the "revolt of the masses," was calmed by "nature." "In my paintings, I have always presented the victory of nature over human achievements. Beneath Berlin's asphalt pavement is everywhere the sand of our mark. And earlier, it was once the ocean's floor. Yet human works also belong to nature. Homes spring up on the shores, then wither and rot. Humans populate the cities like termites." An organic cycle prevails. The cities created by humans exist under the inexorable law of nature and of life, they grow and decay. *Berlin am Meer.* "These are paintings of an incomprehensible, elementary event, paintings of a tragic and fatal destiny. The city sinks back into nature and its decline is the beginning of another era on earth."[290]

"Art in the Catacombs." With this *topos,* Bruno E. Werner described the situation of all those in the Third Reich who strove for a new statement, a new power of expression, and for forms corresponding with their experience of that time. None of these artists, who were mostly between 55 and 70 years old, were allowed to exhibit in Germany after 1937. Some, including Karl Hofer, Ernst Barlach, Emil Nolde, Karl Schmidt-Rottluff, Max Pechstein, Erich Heckel, and Otto Dix, remained in the country and worked in hiding. Others, such as Max Beckmann, Max Ernst, Oskar Kokoschka, and Josef Scharl, left Germany in order to begin a new life, often with great difficulty. The young artists, who stood on the shoulders of their teachers, encountered similar fates. They, too, worked in the catacombs, more solitary still, with only a few friends who visited them. Or else they went abroad. Many were forgotten.[291]

The emergence from the catacombs began with zero hour. The artists who were part of either the inner or the outer emigration had full trunks of paintings. Those who were famous before 1933 had it easier, but even some of these were no longer able to become successful. The younger and unknown artists had to establish connections all over again. There were also those artists who had made compromises during the Third Reich. The figure sculptors, in particular, such as Georg Kolbe (d. 1947), had been welcomed by the National Socialists. It was difficult to free themselves from incrimination. In the first important postwar publication about painters and sculptors in Munich, Hans Eckstein wrote, "No. There is no new style, no new 'direction,' that hasn't already been around for ten years . . . People enjoy what has already been achieved and vary the results of yesterday."[292]

Departure and escape from the catacombs was not simple. People traveled through the country with water colors, paintings and even small sculptures in their knapsacks. They visited museums, hoping for new interest, even when buying was out of the question. They hoped for private showings, often housed in perilous surroundings. The "Frankfurt Kunstkabinett' of Hanna Bekkar vom Rath, located on the second floor of a house in Frankfurt, was at first only reachable by means of a makeshift wood staircase on the exterior of a house.[293] The first postwar private gallery in Germany was opened in Berlin by Gerd Rosen in August 1945 in the devastated rooms of what was formerly a shop for textiles and military. The opening speech, "On the Freedom of Art" was given by Edwin Redslob, an historian of art and culture who from 1949 to 1954 was rector and prorector, respectively, of the Free University of Berlin. The Günther Franke Gallery was re-established in Munich in 1946, occupying a large studio in a stucco villa. Its first exhibit was a presentation of Xaver Fuhr, followed by five Beckmann shows from each period of his work, a large memorial exhibit of Franz Marc's work, and an overview of the works of Oskar Schlemmer.

The exhibitions performed an important mediating function right after the war. The first exhibition of German art after the war took place in Berlin-Lichterfelde, in a house on Kamillenstrasse 4, during early spring 1945. It was put together by Hans Uhlmann, a Berlin sculptor who, during the rule of the National Socialists had been condemned to total isolation from the art world. He traveled around Berlin by bicycle, seeking out his old colleagues who had also been prohibited from working and exhibiting during the Third Reich.[294]

There were several other exhibitions during these years, including a presentation of Nolde's works in 1948 by the Kestner Society of Hannover. There were two, however, that decisively shaped the artistic understanding of the postwar years, one in the middle, the other toward the end of the rubble years. In February 1947, the Augsburg Schaetzler Palace held a showing of "extreme art." It featured an exclusive presentation of works by artists unable to show their works in public during the Third Reich, meaning either that they lived in exile, or that they went secretly into inner emigration. Among those represented were painters Josef Scharl, Gunther Strupp, Georg Rohde, Richard Ott, Ernst Geitlinger, Werner Gilles, Max Ackermann, Willi Baumeister, Conrad Westphahl, Fritz Winter, Karl Kunz, and Rupprecht Geiger. Of the visitors to this event, the *Neuen Zeitung* of February 3, 1947, had this to say:

"Some wore tall fur caps and short, full beards like truck drivers or Russian prisoners of war. Others had on Basque caps, and wore glasses over their red noses, while still others covered their heads with wool caps and earmuffs. Some wore hats. Thick scarves were wound around their necks, and underneath their gray coats one would occasionally see the bulge of soldier- or ski-boots. The women who were there could hardly be distinguished from the men. The smoke of warm air billowed from their mouths, and they shifted from foot to foot to warm their toes. It was 25° C. outside, and unheated inside, but they seemed to be in a good mood and quite animated. I suspect they remained in front of one picture to draw its shape in the air with their gloved fingers, or in front of another in order to establish how splendidly vermilion stood out against a cobalt blue. Obviously, these people must have been crazy, for they came with no other purpose than to see this exhibition, traveling in icy trains from Munich, Tübingen, Stuttgart, Staffelsee, and who knows where else, all the way to Augsburg. They did not come to do business, but simply to see an exhibition! Normal people would just shrug their shoulders over such things."[295]

In Augsburg, only 14 painters, most of them abstract artists, were introduced. What was provocative was the direction of style. In 1949, however, four years after the war's end and one year after the currency reform, the Cologne Artists' League *(Kunstverein)* and the city of Cologne sponsored an exhibition of the whole of contemporary German art. This program was initiated by Toni Feldkirchen, at that time the director of the Cologne Artists' League. Presented were 496 works by 131 artists, including Nolde, Heckel, Hofer, Dix, Beckmann, Nay, Pankok, Pechstein, Schmidt-Rottluff, Baumeister, Meistermann, Trier, and Winter.

Modern art represented, especially for the younger generation, an unknown terrain even at this time, despite the fact that right after the war, with the special support of the Allied officers of culture, an intensive "education in modern art" was instituted. "Education can help. Since it has to do with art, it is artistic education. The neglect of art must be overcome and made up for. . . . So, art education! Education in taste through appointed specialists, in universities, adult evening classes, at public events, through the teachers, artists, educated people, and the trade unions. It is about time. This will affect Germany's youth. It will affect the value and relevance of German art." Erich Kästner wrote these words in January 1946, on the occasion of an exhibition of contemporary German painters in Augsburg, which solicited public reaction through a type of "suggestion box." What was demonstrated was that "the most intolerant, stupid, and base observations came from school children, male and female students and other young people."[296]

In the universities, in particular, there developed a conservative opposition to modern art. The seismograph was deemed responsible for the earthquake. People feared that the autonomy of the arts would unleash total chaos. In 1948, Hans Sedlmayr, art historian at the University of Vienna from 1936 to 1945, and from 1951 at the University of Munich, published his book *Verlust der Mitte: Kunst des 19. und 20. Jahrhunderts* as a symptom and symbol of the times. Its motto came from Pascal. "To abandon the center is to abandon humanity." Anti-modernism had found a very important foundation, one which was constantly overflowing into polemic.

"Painting is in modern times the most unrestricted of all art forms. Free of ties to those public tasks for which it creates, free of obligatory themes, creating only 'for itself' or for the anonymity of the exhibit, it is threatened by the 'accident of arbitrariness.' What Jaspers said of the mentally productive people of this time holds true especially for the painters. 'The secure boundaries provided by a whole are lacking. No binding command comes from the world. One must take the risk of establishing one's own order. Without response, or with a false response and without true opponents, one becomes ambiguous toward oneself.' 'The possibilities seem to open up unheard of prospects. Yet the possibilities threaten to follow in rapid succession. To find one's way back from the dispersion requires almost superhuman strength.' In the colors that have been set free, where they are no longer hemmed in by plastic and architectonic counterweights, there resides an element of formlessness and chaos."

Loss of center refers to a departure from the human, from humanity, the loss of an image of humanity, and a descent into the inorganic, into chaos:

"The relationship of the individuals to themselves is disturbed. They observe themselves, as is immediately apparent in portraits, with mistrust, anxiety, and despair. They feel as if delivered unto death. Their world of reason and passion is torn asunder. This split is reflected in the conflict between the cult of reason in modern architecture and the cult of the irrational in modern painting."

Sedlmayr's intentions, which were directed toward an aesthetic theocracy, culminated in his "sole prescription." In the midst of new situations, hold fast to the eternal image of humanity, restore it! This eternal image could not be discovered by humanity alone, or we would again be standing with the God of the philosophers. Humans cannot be understood without the faith that they are, potentially, in the image God, and have a specific place in the admittedly disturbed world order. "This is the solid point. We will not find the handle outside, in generalities, but inside of ourselves. The entire diagnosis of this epoch will only be effective if it is applied to oneself for self-knowledge and self-change. . . . One should not lose confidence that the individual, in healing himself or herself, can contribute to the healing of the whole. For there is a solidarity in suffering. The sickness of the whole also originated in the 'disease of one element.' And it will only be overcome by those who in themselves have radically overcome the general derangement, and have renewed themselves . . . However, renewal can only be achieved when the situation is experienced as sickness, when one suffers from it, and when one is ashamed of the decline of humanity, almost to the point of despair. One must at the same time take suffering upon oneself and try to give it meaning. 'Therein lies the secret, suffering generates greater healing power.' Hope is where people suffer most deeply under these circumstances."[297]

Sedlmayr's book became a bestseller, bringing strong criticism upon itself. At the second German Art Historical Conference in 1949, Werner Haftmann declared, in a blazing polemic, that all losses in the newer art were above all positive witnesses to freedom. Willi Baumeister attacked Sedlmayr in a speech given in Darmstadt entitled *"Das Menschenbild unserer Zeit"* (1950). He accused his NS past on the one hand, and uncovered his methodological tricks on the other, that is, the replacement of the historical and aesthetic criteria of "good" and "bad" with the moral criteria of "good" and "evil." "Sedlmayr is hardly a democrat, and still renders the church a veritable service. His theory is as single-minded as are the racial theories of Rosenberg . . . Sedlmayr sees no difference between humanity and degeneration. He only sees degeneration in humanity. I protest the allegation that modern art is without ethical value and has no ties to the past or religion."[298]

At this time, the concern with radicality as it had been defined by the rubble era, as a concern with discovering the roots of existence and the world, was already intertwined with conservative political and economic tendencies. In the country of the great center, the upsetting questions posed by modern art were experienced as disturbing factors. Nevertheless, they still caused scandals.

Resurgence of the Theater

In 1942, at 31 years of age, the singer Martha Mödl received her first engagement at the Municipal Theater of Remscheid. Shortly thereafter, both the city and the theater were hit by air attacks. The artist received an industrial conscription, and began putting fuses into grenades. She was unable at that time to accept a contract to perform in Düsseldorf. With the arrival of zero hour, she hoped the offer was still good. She set off by foot, shortly after the capitulation, from Remscheid to Düsseldorf. There she was taken in, and began a career that was to win her a worldwide reputation. This episode illustrates the enthusiasm with which people tried to resuscitate the theater immediatly after the war's end. The road was rocky, but many marched on it, literally and figuratively.

Theater companies sprung up everywhere. They were varied as chance played a large role in their constitution. The ensembles were comprised of local residents, refugees, war returnees, and people returning from emigration. Amateurs played alongside professionals, and opponents of National Socialism alongside those who had accommodated themselves to it. In many cities, centers of postwar theater were established where famous people from days past, gave performances. A large number of theaters had been destroyed or severely damaged, and the occupying forces had confiscated many of the houses that remained intact, using them as clubs or moviehouses for soldiers. Performances were held in substitute quarters.

What did the theater have to offer during this transition into a new society and way of life? It was effective in recovering human experiential possibilities. In these wretched times, people desired cultural enjoyments, and believed the stage could provide moral and political education. Goebbels, as plenipotentiary of the Reich, closed all the theaters by September 1, 1944, for the purpose of total war. This fearsome time was now at an end, and the need to recover was tremendous. Hitler had robbed the German theater of its best trait, internationalism. "Since there was no tradition to go back to, there was nothing left for those who continued to perform under the dictator to do but to defend some aspects and, over the years, to salvage what was alive in the 1920s. However, cut off from the movements of world theater, there was no other choice for such people as Fehling, Grundgens, Hilpert, Erich Engel, Caspar Neher, Felsenstein, and Schweikart but to remain in the position they had already attained."[299]

Still, however, they received enthusiastic support from a public thirsty for the amusement and uplift of theatrical art. When Käthe Dorsch returned to Berlin, she was overwhelmed by a standing ovation. "Her sweet, sincere womanliness and her restrained charm infatuated not only her partners, but especially the public, who gladly overlooked the weaknesses in the performance and celebrated Käthe Dorsch. They celebrated the great artist, who is perhaps an even greater human being, with total and unending devotion."[300]

Special expectations were attached to the return of emigrated actresses, actors, and directors, which included a number of Jews and communists. Ernst Deutsch, who went forth as a "fiery young man," returned as a character actor through Vienna (1947) and the Salzburg Festival (1951), ending up in Berlin at the request of Karl Heinz Stroux. After a sixteen-year absence, Therese Giehse performed again at the Munich Kammerspiele in September 1949. Elisabeth Bergner made a guest appearance in Germany in 1949, and in September 1951, Adolf Wohlbrück was brought to Düsseldorf by Grundgens. Curt Goetz, together with his wife, the actress Valerie von Martens, wished to show his indebtedness to Germany by making it laugh again.[301] Albert Bassermann and Else Schiff-Bassermann incorporated an aspect of the history of Weimar theater. "It is all the same, whether you wear the clothes of a king, a beggar, or a criminal. The friendly, beautiful sound of your ailing voice, your eyes, and your soothing hands are, thanks to perfect technique, not only confined to the limited hours of an evening at the theater. They go beyond you into all times and all places. Unrestricted, you are the master of your genius." With these words, Alexander Moissi congratulated Albert Bassermann on his sixtieth birthday. When, in 1934, the Leipzig Theater rejected his wife as a non-Aryan, he went into exile in the United States. "However, when the German request for his return reached the almost eighty-year-old actor, who in the meantime had become an extraordinary English-speaking actor in New York and Hollywood, he wired, 'I'm coming.' Before returning either to Vienna or to his home in Berlin, he went to Zurich, where he performed his star role as the architect Solness, his first reappearance on a German-speaking stage. He was overwhelmed with applause. Almina was played by the partner of his life, Else Bassermann."[302]

Gustav Hartung was among the first stage directors, returning in November 1945. He had hoped to revive his former Heidelberg Festival, but he died in February 1946, while staging *Maria Stuart*. Ludwig Berger, who survived in Amsterdam, began working in Berlin in December 1947.

Fritz Kortner came to Berlin at the end of 1947 in an American military train. He was a significant actor who was to develop, in the next few years, into perhaps the most important German theater director. Kortner describes his "uncomfortable return" in his autobiography, *Aller Tage Abend*, "I trudged, with lead in my feet, through the demolished city, and was often recognized and looked at with astonishment. That someone would voluntarily enter this starving hell caused many heads to shake. When I went for the first time into the theater, it was the Kurfurstendamm Theater, the public greeted me with applause, perhaps out of gratitude for the consolation they derived from the fact that someone had returned to live with them. My eyes became moist. The performance that I perforce endured to the end was inconceivably atrocious. I remained sitting out of politeness. In fact, shortly after the curtain went up, I wanted to run away, back to America. A cheeky cast, uncivilized humor, a theatrical gaiety foreign to humanity, it was an offense to the eyes, ears, heart, and mind. Days later, I felt bad about this run down, dissolute, anxiety-producing comedy. There was not much else to laugh about, either. Meetings with old acquaintances were forced. Even seeing Erich Engel again, a visit which I had ultimately sought out, was an uneasy experience, and topics of conversation were slow to surface.

"When I left America, I lost weight systematically and probably also due to the excitement. I, who tend to be on the stout side, was the thinnest I had ever been. Here in Berlin I felt fat like Falstaff. I suspected and noted that my weight, which seemed extravagant only in relation to the Berliners, whose wasted frames were a discredit to the victors, must have had a provocative effect. I had also dressed too well, again a purely relative matter. All this troubled me. I saw myself through the eyes of an observer: an overstuffed American who can have no idea of those torments of hell that people had endured. I noticed, and it seemed inexplicable at first, that that which I suffered did not surface in the consciousness of most of those I met. I mentioned, in an effort to defend myself, for the role of a Jew pampered by fate was not to my liking, that in my family alone eleven relatives had been gassed. For this I received polite condolences. I fought for the recognition of my equal rights to misfortune, to misery. I wanted to express my thoughts. We, who together wander around, confused, competing with each other over the suffering we occasionally bore, we were indeed, whether Aryan or Jew, now again Christian *and* Jew, survivors of one and the same catastrophe. And we had similar experiences of survival, as of suffering. I seemed to have little luck with this argument. Most people persisted in the feeling that no suffering was equal to theirs. Perhaps they needed the consciousness of having borne the greatest injustice to calm their subconscious minds."[303]

Theatrical performances first resumed in Berlin.[304] The first premiere took place in the Renaissance Theater on May 27, only three and a half weeks after the German capitulation. Franz Schönthan's farce, entitled *Der Raub der Sabinerinnen (The Rape of the Sabines)*, was a stage play warmed up for municipal theater from before the "pause." June 26th saw the reopening of the beloved Deutsches Theater, which survived in the midst of the rubble of the city center. Its first performance was Friedrich Schiller's *Der Parasit*, which had also been featured in the municipal theater's program for 1943. Shortly thereafter, of course, the piece was banned, for the Soviets disliked its ending. "The web of the lie ensnares the best, the honest ones cannot get through, and obsequious mediocrity goes further than winged talent. Appearances rule the world, and righteousness comes only on the stage." Each of the concerned parties were paid off with 500 Reichsmark and a box of food. The next attempt was Thornton Wilder's *Our Town*, directed by Bruno Hübner. The text was available, for Gustaf Grundgen had been able to get it in a round about way after its premiere in Zurich in 1939.

After the entrance of American, English and French troops, the English commissioned Karl-Heinz Martin for the Renaissance Theater. However, after the opening premieres on July of 7 of Schnitzler's *Gruner Kakadu* (The Green Cockatoo) and Wedekind's Kammersänger *(The Tenor)*, the theater was confiscated for the purpose of maintaining the troops. One of the theater directors, Kurt Raeck, together with Victor de Kowa, was called back to organize entertainment for the troops. In compensation, Martin was given a license for the Hebbel Theater, which opened on August 15 with the *Three Penny Opera*.

The municipal stages of Friendenau presented the first postwar opera on August 31, with a performance of Fossini's *Barber of Seville* that even featured piano accompaniment and a small string orchestra. A pensioned singer had rehearsed the work, keeping expenditures to a minimum.

On October 6, Jürgen Fehlin staged the original *Faust* in the hall of a garden restaurant in Lichterfeld. Joana Maria Gorvin played Gretchen, and Otto Eduard Hasse, Mephisto. "The man who stood up there, bowing his thanks for the overwhelming applause given him and his co-star by an enthusiastic audience, is over sixty years old. Yet he is so young, that 25 years after his first Berlin performance, he once again manages to chase out the boredom, convention, and mediocrity of the scenes, and to fill them with a supernatural element."

"Max Reinhardt's Deutsche Theater," newly renamed by the senate, reopened on September 7 with Lessing's *Nathan*. Paul Wegener played the title role.

Boleslaw Barlog, who had previously worked as a theater assistant and a film director, created the Schlosspark Theater out of a Steglitz moviehouse. Licensed by the Americans, it opened on November 3, 1945, with *Holuspokus* by Curt Goetz.

In total, at least 121 premieres took place in Berlin in the seven months from June to December, 1945. The performances were held not only in the theaters, but also in inns, public halls, school auditoriums, and movie theaters. One of the shortest lived undertakings was the "Volkstheater," opened in the Pankower Tivoli Movie House, which played Tolstoy's *The Living Corpse*. The cast consisted of 80 persons. In ten days, 6000 people came to see the play. Soon the troupe disappeared without a trace. Nineteen operettas were performed, as well as 11 operas, over 50 farces, musical comedies, revues, and boulevard pieces. Shakespeare's *Midsummernight's Dream* was presented three times, and only six classical performances and six dozen works from twentieth century dramatic literature.[305]

Friedrich Luft (b. 1911), who reported regularly on Berlin theater for the *Neue Zeitung*, began a "Sunday Theater Column" in the radio broadcast of the American zone (AIAS) in February 1946. This program was eventually to claim legendary fame. In his first report, he said, "Yesterday I had the opportunity to travel throughout the city by car. It was ghastly. People have become used to the rubble of their surroundings, of their way to work, and of their districts. But I suddenly became conscious of how little of Berlin remains. I wondered if we weren't fooling ourselves. I passed a billboard covered with innumerable announcements of theaters, operas, and concerts. Afterwards, I noticed in the advertising section of the newspaper that theatrical performances were being held in nearly 200 locations. Really! Everywhere. In every district. At least a half-dozen concerts take place daily. In every district. Two opera houses perform continuously, what city in the world still has this? Isn't it possible that an unhealthy art boom has taken place, and that it would be better to engage in more robust activities? Might it be that the theater and cinema impulse has something thoughtless and frivolous about it?" It was expected that the answer would be yes, given what remained to be sorted out and accomplished, and given the imperiled and dangerous situation of the city both in the past and at that time. Yet Luft answered in the negative, in what was then a typically despairing expression, "No, art is no Sunday recreation or ornament of daily life. It is no knick-knack on the display cabinet. Art is necessary, especially now in the midst of misery."[306]

Friedrich Luft embodied a new generation of critics who, despite their isolation during the Third Reich, provided competent and brilliant commentaries on artistic events. They were influenced by the theater critics of the Weimar Republic, the most important of whom no longer worked in Germany after the war, except perhaps while traveling through. Alfred Polgar and Julius Bab, both of whom died in 1955, had emigrated to the United States; Alfred Kerr, who died in 1948, had moved to England. The new theater critics quickly gained respect. They distinguished themselves from earlier commentary, and emphasized their pedagogical, social-political responsibilities. "The pleasureful savoring of impressionistic criticism since, for example, the beginning of this century, tastes today like a stale meal. Yet the old gourmets, who were already dying out by 1928, at least trusted their own noses. They were in no way isolated, and were able to give, through hints and associations, some understandable idea of their impressions. Today's critics can no longer count on all their readers having the educational background of the last 150 years. That should pose no problem for the stage, for nothing is more frightening than a public that attends the theater exclusively for 'education.' For the critics, however, it means they must first clarify the factual situation that was once presupposed. . . . The task of today's critic? Society has had an interest in the theater for around 200 years. If this society disintegrates, the proportion of theater-goers will also slip. Then we will lean against the crooked walls, and the doors will no longer open. The critic is in the peculiar position of having to clarify the means by which any piece or performance is evaluated."[307]

In the three western occupation zones, the theatrical enterprise began later than in Berlin, where the cultural competition of the four Allies accelerated activity. Most performances took place in makeshift sites. Of the 262 theaters in existence in 1937, 28 were destroyed in 1945, and almost all were more or less damaged. Statistics from August 1947, indicate that 86 percent of all stages were either destroyed or seriously damaged. Of the provisional theaters, 46 percent were in halls without stages; 31 percent were in club houses and cinemas with more or less usable stages; 15 percent had managed to arrange some sort of stage in a theater, in rehearsal rooms or foyers; and 7.5 percent occupied emergency quarters in gymnasiums. Over 300 theaters required new technical installations.[308] New constructions were not even under consideration until the 1950s; rather, the concern was for the consolidation and improvement of the alternative quarters.

The dates of the first performances in the west zones were as follows: In Essen, on July 20, 1945 *(Im Weissen Rössi)*; in Hamburg, on August 29, 1945 (Hofmannsthal's *Jedermann*); in Hannover, on September 3, 1945 and in Frankfurt on September 5, 1945 (*Ingeborg* by Curt Goetz); in Munich on September 8, 1945, in Dusseldorf on September 23, 1945, in Mannheim on November 11, 1945, in Darmstadt on December 15, 1945, and in Bochum on December 17, 1945 (Grillparzer's *Weh dem, der lügt, Woe to Him Who Lies)*.[309]

During the rubble years, people became quite intoxicated with the theater. Head producer of the municipal theater in Erfurt, Lutz Besch's observations in the Soviet zone's magazine *Diogenes* applied as well to the western zones. "Most performances took place in the afternoons and evenings. Almost every stage had a traveling performance . . . in the majority of cities, two theater houses were running . . . The number of monthly performances was between 40 and 50, yes, even as many as 55 or more!"[310] In autumn of 1945, the division of adult education of Berlin's town council received 400 applications to open theaters. In addition, there were 100 applications for cabarets. In the second postwar performance season, the United States military government issued 400 theater licenses to its zone and its sector of Berlin. In 1947, there were 74 stable theaters in North Rhine-Westphalia, as well as an undetermined number of wandering troupes. The growth rate was great in the other zones as well.

The multiformity of theater life in those days can be illustrated by an overview of events in 1947. This will bring out the predominantly conservative characteristics of German postwar theater.

Due to his ten-year employment as director of the Berlin State Theater, Gustaf Grundgens was at first rejected by the denazification commission. While director, he was reproached on the one hand for ambitious opportunism, and on the other for his artistic, uncompromising attitude. In March 1947, however, he was entrusted with the management of the Dusseldorfer Schauspielhaus.

Grundgens, who preferred conservative authors such as T. S. Eliot and Christopher Fry, was not unjustly criticized, for he largely blocked the way for experimentation. "However, the reason for this did not lie in idealistically overstated demands made on 'art.' With him, it was the concept of solidity that prevailed. Perserverance in solidity was for Grundgens, whom Suhrkamp called a tightrope dancer 'without a safety net,' more than a question of art, it was an existential question. This was not a contradiction; on the contrary, art requires above all precision, solidity of the actual object, security for the sake of that which cannot be secured. The strong accent on form and the formal, the hostility against 'our search for originality,' the agreement with Ihering's promotion of 'practical stage direction,' or 'stage direction that built up style,' all seemed more important to Grundgens than the 'search for unique and unmistakable genius.' Consider also his statement, 'I do not think it is so important today whether good or bad theater is performed in Germany. Of far greater significance is whether theater is performed rightly or wrongly.' Another variation on his theme of 'solidity.''"[311]

The Hamburg Theater, which in February 1947 closed down due to lack of electricity, had until then staged mostly French and American works. According to a report of the times, the theater lacked an audience that appreciated problematic pieces.[312] In this city of big business, shipping, and trade, people's relation to the theater was through season tickets. "But one should not portray the Hamburg public in so poor a light. It does enjoy theater. This much must be said for it. It has made the best of the many small theaters which have been started in the most unlikely places, and has filled them night after night. No theater has yet had to close due to disinterest. However, no forward impulse has emerged from this love of the theater. Inasmuch as it does not spring from a naive need for entertainment, a sound but still unfruitful source of cultural life, this love for the theater is more a return to what remains of the bourgeois *Bildungstheater* (educational theater) which was still in existence in Germany until 1933." But the world is now much more out of joint than it was in 1918. Though it was easier then to hold onto the past, people searched for new paths; now, however, people try to discover the old paths in the midst of the rubble. "Here, for example, *Don Carlos* was seen as a bourgeois marriage tragedy; *As You Like It* as a merry Fasching masquerade; and *The Three Penny Opera* suddenly became a cheerful fairytale. These performances are basically less a result of the director's stylistic derangement than they are a reflection of some gruesome 'as-if-dance' presented by a German consciousness still stunned by catastrophe." No new stimulation can be expected from a theater that simply follows the predominant impulses of the average audience.

Darmstadt was almost completely destroyed by a night bomb attack of the Royal Air Force in September 1944. Twelve thousand people died. The theater reopened on December 15, 1945, with a performance of *Iphigenia* directed by Karl Heinz Stroux in the Orangery with 370 seats. After Stroux's departure, a report by Heinz Rode in November 1947[313] lamented the lack of leadership in the theatrical world. There were, however, some extraordinary accomplishments in opera. The "Darmstadt Syle," which abandoned the representational stage, took a chance on doing *Freischutz*, drawing out its romanticism with only music and movement, without the help of magical scenery. "We still hear and see something in this unspeakably afflicted city, above whose ruins the shadow of 'tall Ludwig now looms large like a ghostly lighthouse.' Rallying points of the will to create and foster culture have long been active. Belying the gloomy idea that 'nothing is going on here, Darmstadt has become a provincial nest.' Indeed Darmstadt had a college, a theater, an 'art school in the artists' colony,' which also had studios in the Kranichstein Castle and in the Hochzeitsturm, and an art publishing company which, under the name 'Vincent,' became the 'Gunther-Franke of Darmstadt' due to Robert D'Hooghe's enterprising spirit."

Frankfurt. It was here that Heinz Hilpert was appointed head manager of the Frankfurt municipal theaters. Hilpert had once been the manager of Berlin's Deutscher Theater, and after the war he first went to Constance. The buildings in Frankfurt had been demolished. The opera found acoustically defective accommodations in the "*Borsensaal.*" Plays were performed in a former gymnasium in Sachsenhausen, although for 'great' pieces, the "*Borsensaal*" was used. "Whoever knows Hilpert's working pace," wrote Rode,[314] "understands the impatience and the not overly rose mood of this man possessed by the theater. He was also quite preoccupied with building up a theater company. Is it the particularly miserable housing conditions of what is becoming a central administrative city that causes so many newly appointed talents to leave? Was the extensive period of provisional theatrical leadership responsible for the failure to bring high-ranking artists to Frankfurt immediately after the war? In spite of this, there is no need for a pessimistic view of the theatrical future of a city that is preparing for the Year of Goethe and the Centennial of the first German parliament . . . In any case, the public is as much in love with the theater today as it ever was. Seats for Lessing's *Nathan,* for example, were sold out 50 times this summer at the courtyard of a Carmelite cloister. The next great theatrical event to take place here will be Zuckmayer's *The Devil's General,* which will be Hilbert's first production since taking over his new office. It will be the first German performance, opening on November 25."

Theater in Stuttgart. The state theater performed in two houses under the direction of Karl Heinz Ruppel. Bruno E. Werner praised it as being of a quality not seen in Stuttgart for a long time. In the Kammertheater, in a tastefully arranged, snow white, former rehearsal room, Federico Garcia Lorca's *Blood Wedding* and Ibsen's *Ghosts* were performed. Hermine Körner, one of the last classical tragedy actresses, co-starred with Erich Ponto in both pieces. Now, along with the state theater and the young people's theater, there existed the new theater with two houses. At the time of Rode's report, Brecht's *Three Penny Opera* was playing there, "Before, it set the world afire as accusation, today, as a lively performance and not simply because of the fascination with Kurt Weill's music." It was a high-spirited performance, for which the young theater-goers clapped enthusiastically.[315]

Erich Engel, who had directed the Munich Kammerspiele since 1945, left this post in the summer of 1947. His reasons for leaving were grounded in certain difficulties he had accomodating to the atmosphere of the city and to the fact that his position left him too little time for actual directing. His successor was Hans Schweikart, who had already worked at the Kammerspiele under Otto Falckenberg who died that same year. The state of Bavaria seemed to take hold of the theater business, beginning in the fall of 1945 with operas and operettas, and shortly thereafter staging plays. The appointment of a state secretary for arts, Dieter Sattler, further strengthened Bavaria's image of supporting the arts. In an address delivered to a convention of theater directors in October 1947, Sattler claimed that the state theaters, besides representing Bavaria to the world, should also contribute to the reeducation of the German people, reopening the windows to the world by showing the recent works of English, French, American and German authors who had been banned during the Third Reich. Finally, they were also expected to provide a diversion from the cares of daily life, and to spread optimism. Thus, the call to eternal values, to a humane image, resounded again and again.[316]

The manager of the state theater, Paul Verhoeven, knew how to keep extraordinary actors in his company. Among those he worked with were Heidemarie Hatheyer, Maria Wimmer, Elisabeth Flickenschildt, Erich Ponto, Wolfgang Buttner, Peter Pasetti, and Inge Langen. All the performances at the Theater am Brunnenhof der Residenz were produced on a stage of the size used for chamber theater. During the cold, winter vacation of 1947, several of these were expanded by using the debris from the Residenz. "It was not enough that the state theaters had to put up with considerable shortages of coal and food supplies, but they also had a managerial crisis. Verhoeven had suffered a heart attack and wanted to devote himself to more artistic, private work. Furthermore, his relationship with the Minister of Culture, Hundhammer, was not the best. All the while Verhoeven was manager, Hundhammer never visited the theater once. Verhoeven did not extend his contract, and a successor had to be found. Negotiations with Heinz Hilpert fell through largely because of the incompatability of Hilpert's opinions with the demands by the Minister of Culture for unreserved consideration of the Catholic Bavarian mentality. Finally, after puzzling for a long time over acceptable candidates, they appointed Alois Johann Lippl as manager. He announced that he would provide a theater that was open to the world, representative of western Christianity and of native culture."[317]

Recklinghausen was an exceptional theater locale of this time, with its Ruhr Valley Festivals. The first president of the Federal Republic of Germany, Theodor Heuss, provided the motto for the inauguration of this festival, "I gave coal for art, I gave art for coal." An actual history of the Ruhr Valley Festival was much more matter-of-fact.[318] In the postwar winter of 1946, Otto Burrmeister, who was then managing director of Hamburg's German Theater, went by truck to the Ruhr Valley with some of his co-workers and committee members. They went to get coal, for it was so cold in the theaters that the freezing artists were striking.

Burrmeister came from a simple background, and had only attended primary school *(Volkschule)*. He was a Social Democrat and a union man, and sat through the Third Reich in prison. He was a self-educated man whose ideals were those of the German classicists Goethe, Schiller and Herder. He dreamed of a new, democratic Germany, one in which the "bourgeois" art and culture would also be shared with the working class. During their trip through the Ruhr Valley, the group came to a side entrance of the "King Ludwig 4/5" mine in Recklinghausen-Suderwich. The guard standing there had previously been a seaman, and raved about Hamburg, especially St. Pauli. He convinced the staff council to help "the poor people from Hamburg." "You got the coal for which we previously cheated the English." The mines had to deliver coal to England.

In thanks for this "sacrificial," in fact illegal, supply of coal, the Hamburg Theater went to Recklinghausen for a guest tour. The city and the miners organized the performances. Half of the tickets were sold to the general population, and the other half to employees of the mine. The artists were given lodging in private homes throughout the city and fed stew at the mines. On June 28, 1947, the tour was opened with a performance of *The Marriage of Figaro*. Further performances included *Don Pasquale*, a *Russian Comedy Evening* with one act plays by Chekhov and Tolstoy at the Playhouse, and Michael Horward's *Das Verschlossene Haus* at the Thalis-Theater. The entire tour cost 25,000 Reichsmarks, payed for by the Hamburg Senate. The response was tremendous. Hamburg's mayor, Max

Brauer, was so inspired that at a farewell party he suggested they continue with the guest tours. Why should only Salzburg and Beirut have Festivals, why not the Ruhr Valley as well? In 1947, the Salzburg Festival achieved a new and greater significance with the performance of Gottfried von Einem's opera *Dantons Tod.* In 1948, Herbert von Karajan made his debut as the Festival's conductor, and Wilhelm Furtwängler also returned. From 1951 on, Richard Wagner was again raised up on the "Green Hill" of Beirut. In 1946, new Festivals originated in Bregenz.

Otto Burrmeister originated a second plan as well, He went to visit Hans Böckler, who was then the chairman of the DGB, reaching him during a break in a conference with union leaders in northern Germany. He proposed that the union organize the "Ruhr Valley Festival" together with the city of Recklinghausen. Böckler returned to the conference room, coming back after half an hour. "I bring you, Colleague Burrmeister," he said, the affirmative vote of the German union." Burrmeister became the cultural advisor of the DGB and then the director of the Ruhr Valley Festival.

While the large theaters were striving to overcome their difficulties, and the first preparations for the reconstruction or new construction of theaters were underway, freelance groups made a virtue out of necessity. With the *Zimmertheater* (room theater), theaters without curtains or platforms, were created. It was a new form of drama, one of which found one of its most exceptional representatives in Helmuth Gmelin. Already before the war, he had developed the concept of a miniature stage. After he was freed from pretrial confinement in Hamburg-Fühlsbuttel, he began to work again as a theatrical director. He also became president of a theater company that was founded in 1948 with the merging of regional groups. Having successfully directed Ottofritz Gaillard's *Deutsches Stanislawski-Buch* in Berlin in 1946, he began, in July 1947, his theatrical work on the uppermost floor of a house on Hamburg's Alsterschaussee. In March of the next year, his "*Zimmertheater*" opened in a Biedermeier villa with Hebbel's *Maria Magdalene.*[319] Wera Liessen, the first female dramatist, gave the following report of the play, "On a genuine farm table there smoked a genuine kerosene lamp, and the remaining state lights came from . . . reflections made of some old tin cans. Above the door of the room, which also led into the room where the audience was seated, there hung a sign 'This Way to the Cabinet Maker.' Gmelin, who himself played Master Anthony, portrayed the cabinet maker so skillfully that the people sitting in the first rows could feel the sawdust on their feet. The audience sat so near that they felt as if they could take the soupspoon from Master

Anthony's hand. 'Not an accidental hit, but a well-planned, conscientious piece of work.' Such was the judgment of the press, and night after night the audience stumbled down the stairway, unlit due to the times, with the feeling of having something very precious."

Other little theaters were created in Bremen, Mainz, and Sommerhausen am Main. The painter Luigi Malipiero opened his little theater in a room of the Sommerhausen town hall in 1948. For the Goethe Year of 1949, with five actors, he presented both parts of *Faust* in one evening. Then in autumn 1950 he moved into a gate house.

The stricken times left their mark on stage management style, which drew its inspiration from the prevailing scarcity. Actors and actresses wore street clothes on stage, only wearing costumes if they were available. Even the dearth of scenery affected style. In November 1946, for example, the state theater of Kassel performed *Aida*, Verdi's 'most splendid opera,' on the temporary stage of the city hall's blue room. The scenery consisted simply of three columns, a platform and curtains, all in dark blue. Through the skillful arrangement of columns, every scene, whether at the temple, in the king's court, or on the banks of the Nile, evoked a different sense of space. The experiment won singular acclaim.[320] In the place of the representational stage, the stage itself was brought back to consciousness. "Movement" and props were more important than spectacular scenery. "A theater that intends to serve truth, including the painful, fearsome truth, must also give up those sublimer tricks it has mastered with the help of a refined stage technology. Modern drama demands that actors and actresses act from their inner being, not from their ability, which is taken for granted. Thus it demands reality, and not deception, from the set as well. Reality should not be confused with realism. Rather, it means that the fictive being of the theater is fundamently affirmed, and not conjured away by some coarse or more sophisticated trickery. Basically, this is nothing other than a harkening back to the fundamentals of theater. The stage, the naked, 'demystified' stage, has again become a working platform, not only in the technical, but also in the artistic sense. Was it any different with Shakespeare's theater?"[321]

When, in August 1947, the set designers and technical directers gathered for an international conference in Hamburg, they declared that the lack of production space and materials that had forced them to simplify their scenery had been throughly beneficial. The voluntary renunciation of the magic of shifting scenery required a stage design that brought theater to consider the basic realities of life. To leave behind everything but the essential is the art of providing the necessary for the representation of the essential. A work of art demands inventiveness and skill. In conjunction with the conference, there was an exhibition whose motto was "Our Necessity, Our Virtue." Here one was shown how to achieve the best effects with scant means, there were also several examples demonstrating ingenious use of substitutions. There were elegant dress suits made from lining, rococo outfits made from jute, costumes from paper, pewter pots from tin cans, armor made from powdered egg canisters, and curtains from Nazi flags. Theater, said Hamburg's Senator Landahl in his opening address, cannot count on support from state or city subsidies after the currency reform. Consequently, the reduction of scenery is not only a question of new style, but also of self-preservation. Throughout the discussions, it was agreed that the complicated and time-consuming theatrical equipment, with sliding, revolving, and trap-door platforms, was gone for good. Special consideration was to be given to the seating so that the audience could be more closely connected to the stage.[322]

There were several reasons for the enthusiasm for the theater during the rubble years. For one thing, there were few opportunities for recreation and enjoyment. Thus, along with radio and cinema, the theater provided an important escape from the dismal, everyday life to higher cultural values. Furthermore, it offered consolation for the material loss that had been suffered, compensating as well for the decline in social prestige associated with this loss. Practically everyone felt declassified, whether as a refugee, a bombing victim, a denazified person, a war returnee, or an unemployed worker . . . A visit to the theater served as a sign of recovered social respectability. It was a reflection of better times for the bourgeoisie. The newly formed theater-goers associations, the *Freie Volksbühne* going back to 1947,[323] and Dr. Kasten's *Besucherring* to 1949, helped resolve the problems, quite difficult at the time, of getting tickets and transportation. In these early years especially, they also took an interest in the intellectual questions posed by the theater.

The rapid flowering of theater life, particularly the play, after the total defeat, was largely due to the fact that during and after the persecution, high level German-speaking theater existed outside of Germany, free of National Socialist influence. The Zurich Playhouse showed itself as a bastion of the free spirit and refuge for many who had to leave Germany and then Greater Germany. Up to 1933, its work had been provincial and mainly concerned with lucrative entertainment. Soon, however, the new task was comprehended, namely that of taking a stand against the barbarous attack on humanity and of providing spiritual opposition. During the 1934 season, Ferdinand Bruckner's *Die Rassen* and Friedrich Wolf's *Professor Mamlock* were performed in Zurich. Radical forces from the right created disturbances among the audience with stinkbombs and the clamor of chairs, beer glasses, and steel rods.

"There were a couple of wild weeks. Many people became nervous, and the well-behaved *Neue Zürcher Zeitung* printed an article calling for 'more tact,' addressing the playhouse, not the rioting opposition. It was . . . the greatest and most significant victory of the playhouse, that it did not lose its nerve at this uncomfortable time, and that it not only remained true to its convictions, but also dared to express them loudly and clearly. The direct attacks were thereby ended, the 'revivalists' retreated peevishly, and free German thought was brought to the playhouse stage, without the dynamic interruptions."[324]

In 1938, Oskar Wälterlin took over the directorship of the playhouse. The new repertoire was perhaps even more decisive and uncompromising than ever. Brecht, Giraudoux, Zuckmayer, Wilder, and Bruckner were either performed for the first time, or were performed in the German language for the first time. Dramaturgist Kurt Hirschfeld had a special ability to sense burning issues and modern actors. An ensemble of high level talent was formed, including, among others, Maria Becker, Therese Giehse, Ernst Ginsberg, Emil Stöhr, Wolfgang Heinz, Hurt Horwitz, Wolfgang Langhoff, and Karl Paryla. The special style of the playhouse was molded by Oskar Wälterlin's characteristic staging, as well as by Leonard Steckel and Leopold Lindtberg, supported by set designer Theo Otto. At the center of attention stood the person of the times, involved in countless transformations, needs, temptations, in false glory and deserved misery. Kurt Hirschfeld wrote an essay in which he sketched the task of the playhouse as follows:

> "The task was to reinstate the theater as an effective cultural institution, to define its intellectual role and to restore its functions at a time when German theater was simply a tool for propaganda.
> "To bring about discussion of artistic, ethical, political, and religious problems at a time when discussion seems to have lost to blind following.
> "To represent and preserve the image of the human in all its multiformity, and thereby to provide a counter-position to the destructive forces of Fascism.
> "To build a sober, humane style in the face of the blustering, bru-

tal style of the official German theater. With the new style, it is possible to express the contents of works and to stimulate and promote discussion of them."[325]

With the end of the war, the Zurich Playhouse again demonstrated its central significance. Its material assistance should not be underestimated. On the day the capitulation of the German army took effect, on May 9, 1945, Wolfgang Langhoff organized an "assistance action for Germany." Zurich actors produced plays by Giraudoux, Jean-Paul Sartre, Friedrich Wolf, Thornton Wilder, and Ferdinand Bruckner for their German colleagues. The playhouse became an information bureau. Food and clothing, as well as props, material for curtains, and text books were collected. Above all, the Zurich Playhouse was an intellectual crossroads of great significance. Already by May 6, Leonard Steckel, theater chairman and stage manager, had made "notes for the ideational rebuilding of the theater in free Germany." . . . "In all probability, Germany will have no permanent theaters in the beginning of the postwar period. Guest troupes, partly organized and sent out by the occupying forces, will perform in the villages on improvised stages." Steckel hoped that the administrators and censors of the occupying forces would recognize that theater could be an "important voice for democratic ideas of government. Then it would not be long before the curtains would rise somewhere in the midst of the rubble of the German cities, and a festival performance would inaugurate a new, liberal theatrical season."[326]

It was of enormous significance for such a "liberal theatrical season" that Zurich offered a comprehensive selection of contemporary dramatic literature. Among the plays performed were: Camus' *The Just* (1950); Claudel's *The Satin Slipper* (1944); Eliot's *Family Reunion* (1945) and *Murder in the Cathedral* (1947); Giraudoux's *Undine* (1940), *Sodom and Gomorrah* (1944), and *The Madwoman of Chaillot* (1946); Garcia Lorca's *Blood Wedding* (1944); Arthur Miller's *Death of a Salesman* (1950); O'Neill's *Mourning Becomes Electra* (1943) and *The Iceman Cometh* (1948); Sartre's *The Flies* and *Dirty Hands* (1948); Wilder's *Our Town* (1939); and Tennessee William's *The Glass Menagerie* (1947) and *A Streetcar Named Desire* (1949).[327] Also performed in Zurich were the works of a number of authors banned in Germany, such as Kaiser, Bruckner, Wolf, Brecht, Werfel, Hasenclever, Bruno Frank, and Horvath. Highly important for Swiss drama were the contacts made between Max Frisch, Friedrich Dürrenmatt, and the epic theater of Brecht, as well as the parable style of Thornton Wilder and John Steinbeck. Another line of development was drawn from Zurich to Brecht's Berliner Ensemble, and to the German Theater in East Berlin. In 1947, Brecht came from Paris, visited his schoolmate Caspar Heher, and became aquainted with Oskar Wälterlin. He began to demonstrate the experimental theater's "aesthetic position, or at least outline an aesthetics for this theater." The result was the *Kleine Organon fur das Theater,* a summary of his theory. On June 5, 1948, his *Mr. Puntila and His Servant Matti* was staged for the first time, with Leonard Steckel as Puntila and Gustav Knuth as the servant, with Therese Giehse as smuggler Emma, and with Helen Vita, Regine Lutz and Blandine Ebinger. Although Brecht directed the play, his name couldn't appear on the program because of the immigration office, and thus Kurt Hirschfeld was listed as director.[328]

Brecht ultimately returned to Berlin, arriving on October 22, 1948 after a fifteen-year absence. He formed the "Berliner Ensemble," the condition of his settling in East Berlin. It played first in the German Theater and in 1954 moved into its own quarters in the Theater am Schiffbauerdamm.

Hirschfeld encouraged Max Frisch to write for theater. The "attempt at a requiem," *Nun singen sie wieder (Now They Are Singing Again),* was performed on Easter 1945, and the romance, *Santa Cruz,* in 1946. In the same year, after a trip through a devastated Germany, *Die chinesische Mauer (The Chinese Wall)* appeared as a warning in the face of collectivist suicide ("the Flood is not irreparable"). This was followed three years later by *Als der Krieg zu Ende war (When the War Was Over).* Durrenmatt's Anabaptist play, *Es steht geschrieben (It is Written),* was presented under the direction of Kurt Horwotz in 1947. In 1919, his "historical comedy" *Romulus der Grosse (Romulus the Great)* came out. In general, however, Durrenmatt had to carry on his work outside his country.

The authors and works which the Zurich Playhouse made accessible, mostly in German-language premieres, before and after 1945, found their way into Germany relatively quickly. Leonard Steckel's prognosis that there would be no permanent theater in Germany immediately following the war did not prove true. Instead, the curtains went up rather quickly amidst the rubble of the German cities. Thus it was so important that the self-inflicted ghetto into which the world of theater had entered during the Third Reich be broken on the stage. The German theater directors, managers, and dramaturgists made use of the opportunity offered them by Zurich in its function as "governor."

Theatrical Competition Among the Allies, German Moderns, and Classicists

After having been condemned to 12 years of stuffy provincialism, large segments of the population enjoyed the international diversification which the Allies, through theatrical competition, were able to offer. At first the Allies cleansed the repertoires of National Socialist plays, and rapidly reinstated the works that had a clean record, including of course the classics. Frequently, old stage directions were revitalized. Above all, the concern was to quickly import German translations of plays written in their own languages.

The situation of the United States was particularly convenient, for included in the US zone were important theatrical cities such as Munich, Frankfurt, Stuttgart, Wiesbaden, Mannheim, Bremen, and Kassel, as well as the US sector of Berlin with its Hebbel and Schlosspark Theater. Britain had a similar head start, with Hamburg and the Rhine-Ruhr area. The only theater city in the French occupation zone was Baden-Baden.

The official dramatic canon of the United States was comprised of 60 translated works, of which about 45 were actually brought to the stage. The list of translated French plays contained 98 pieces, and that of the British, 15, all of them contemporary works. The Reichsmark was not exchangeable, and was thus practically worthless outside of Germany. Therefore, the military governments acquired the translation and performance rights for a specific time period, and served as agents for the distribution of theatrical works. They valued the theater "especially as an instrument of cultural propaganda and reeducation. Moreover, they did not want the reputation of being hostile to culture. Third, they soon broke into competition with each other. They wanted to impress each other, especially the Western Allies with respect to the Soviets, and vice-versa. Before long, the conquerors wanted to impress the conquered as well, for they needed an infantry in the war between the systems. They were therefore quick to offer bread and entertainment, especially in Berlin and Vienna, the two major cities with sectors governed by the four occupying forces."[329]

In contrast to the reality of American theater of this time, for which the pleasures of Broadway played a great role, the cultural program of the US military government was aimed at ideological reeducation, on the other side of the communication and recreation industries. Those pieces chosen for translation either presented the United States in a positive light or "contributed to Western discourse." Despite such a fastidious program of democratization, more than half of all the performances were comedies, some from Broadway, boulevard pieces, farces, slapstick, and detective stories.

While on the one hand the American military government was anxious to avoid works containing negative depictions of American life, the cultural officials, on the other hand, tended to act against censorship. Thus the official in Berlin criticized the fact that works which critiqued life in America were equally as taboo as those by communists or communist sympathizers. Works by Arthur Miller or Clifford Odets, for example, were not performed, but uncritically positive plays by William Saroyan or Paul Osborn were. The anti-communist policies of Harry S. Truman resulted in the removal of the first hour liberals from the theater department of the American military government. "Thus the department head, Benno Frank, had to retire from his office after speaking on behalf of hiring Brecht for Munich's Kammerspiele. The Foreign Secretary in Washington made it known that the Marxist Brecht was not to be supported, for he had recently been suspected by the United States of being involved in communist activities." [330] American theater officials and Western theater critics defended the modern dramatists against this narrow mindedness by pointing to the alleged "optimism" of their works. Thornton Wilder was hardly to be considered a pessimist, for he had demonstrated that in fact humans had survived previous catastrophes, the ice age, the flood, World War II, and would therefore be likely to survive future ones as well. Moreover, these works constantly contrasted the principle of evil, Creon, Aegisthus, Medea, with that of pure goodness, Antigone, Orestes, Elektra, Jason.

In a thorough analysis based on the 24 plays which the theater and music division of the American military government's Bureau of Information Control published for use on German stage, Walter Kiaulehn attempted, in January 1947, to draw some conclusions about the audience. The allure of these plays was that of a journey of discovery. Whoever has read these plays, thought Kiaulehn, must really know what moves the heart, mind and soul of the human beings that have once seen and experienced these as living theater, as their theater. From among the many insignificant things one might encounter, Kiaulehn found the success of Wilder's *Skin of Our Teeth* and Elmer L. Rice's *Adding Machine* especially revealing.[331]

From the official British canon of plays, Boynton Priestley's socially critical family pieces, *An Inspector is Coming* and *Time and the Conways* were particularly successful. T. S. Eliot soon came to German theater via Zurich, where *Murder in the Cathedral* was performed in June 1947. Bruno E. Werner gave a talk on the occasion of the three West German performances of this play during the fall of that same year, in Cologne, Göttingen and Munich. He spoke of the fact that the American-born Eliot, who became a citizen of England and a Catholic convert, belonged to that class of European personalities who not only considered Christianity the living heir of antiquity, but who saw the preservation of European culture only in terms of a renaissance of Christian faith. His Christian drama expressed an openness to the world that left narrow provincialism and petty bourgeois morality far behind. It remains a question whether content and form achieve the aims of theater, i.e., to thrill, capture and shock. At least, however, Eliot's play could make one thing.[332]

The most frequently performed of the plays translated from the French were Anouilh's *Antigone*, Sartre's *The Flies*, and Camus' *The Plague*. With *Antigone*, people were deeply struck by the "justice" which the author bestowed on both positions, that of the state's reason embodied by Creon, and of the protesting youth represented by Antigone. They were able to rediscover the discord of their own situations through the dialogue between the two characters. Indeed, those who had taken the route of inner resistance to National Socialism continuously looked for and found "reasonable" arguments for accommodation and cooperation for the sake of the government, the nation, the law . . .

With Jean Giraudoux, audiences were treated with "enchanting and clever dialogue." He was an author who could preach reason to the "stupidity of people and events" without being patronizing. In a review of *The Trojan War Will Not Take Place*, which was performed in the Munich Kammerspiele in spring 1946, it was stated that "this teacher from Frankfurt wore no shabby dress coat, but rather an elegant, silk-lined tuxedo. The actors toss their positions and insights across the stage as if they were in no way heavy with thought, but rather feather light balls. One is reminded of a first class variety show, where the artists sling lead balls in the air, smilingly catch them on their necks as if it was nothing, and then, defying the law of gravity, let them roll up their arms."[333]

Western theater, the intensity of which determined the German stages of the rubble years, was, despite the ideology of reeducation, multi-dimensional and multi-faceted. It is possible, however, to distinguish three fundamental currents running throughout:[334]

The first is the existential one, which treats the liberation of the individual on a predominnatly abstract and philosophical level. With Sartre, for example, freedom is not a social concept, but an inner, psychic state. One should keep this in mind when reading his ambiguous statements, "We were never more free than when under

German occupation." In *The Flies*, Orestes acts "for the mass, but without the mass," he accomplishes the liberating act for its own sake, and after accomplishing it, leaves the people, whose future remains uncertain. One thus notes a certain depoliticization of the theater. The Marxists argued against this individualistic-psychological conception of freedom.

Second, there is the current of irrational historical fatalism. The course of the world and of life seems emptied of meaning, and everything is the same. History is seen as the result of natural catastrophes. Human beings, as in Wilder's *The Skin of Our Teeth*, do well to bow their heads so that they won't be noticed. Or else they can rebel and offer themselves as a sacrifice like Anouilh's *Antigone*. There is indeed no realistic chance for a pure ethos, although the idea of one shines through the failures. Such a position of resistance does not offer practical suggestions for action. Those proven right in the end, however, are not those without conscience but those sacrificing themselves for the ideal. When Antigone and Haemon, Creon's son, allow themselves to be entombed together and to die in the grave, Creon remains behind a broken person.

The tendency of "magical realism" contributing to both to these currents is, according to Gunter Groll, an expression of the helplessness, nostalgia, escapism, and fundamental anxiety of the epoch.[335] "The affirmation of the immaterial" is especially apparent in the strong comeback made by religious drama since 1945 with works by Eliot, Claudel, François Mauriac, and Christopher Fry. "Magical realism could play a prominent role in the aesthetic discussion of the postwar years, for it dealt with obvious and universal phenomena like death and other metaphysical issues. But only because magical was understood in the widest possible sense could the magical theater be described as a dominating and characteristic current of the times. Every fantasy and parable, everything surrealistic and visionary, in short, everything that went beyond the obvious surface reflection of reality, was considered magical realism. Thus every other aesthetic method was seen as insignificant and dispensible. In the end, Gunter Groll never offered an historical explanation of his theories. He spoke of 'feeling,' an 'unconscious reaction to the times' and of the 'general situation of our times' without giving further definitions. He ignored the fact that neither escapism nor anxiety can exist independently, but are actually dependent on and capable of being influenced by historical-societal situations and forces. The connection between the cultural policies of the Western powers and the 'cold war' should have been seen in this light. Magical realism was indeed promoted as the aesthetic tool which would suppress and obstruct a rational and realistic handling and surmounting of the material and spiritual problems of the postwar years."[336]

With respect to German drama, significant works came only from those authors who either opposed Fascism or who were part of the inner or outer emigration. A journal entry by Alfred Kantorowicz in Berlin, February 26, 1947, describes the situation: "What stands out are the reunions with old friends who had survived, either inside or outside of Germany. The experiences and fates of every one were enough to fill books. The times had driven everyone to extremes, of heroism and moral cowardice, inhumanity and sacrificial courage, perseverance and despair, boldness and cunning, faith and cynicism, roguishness and selflessness, magnanimity and meanness, yet everything was so confused and entangled that ten Grimmelhausens would not be able to condense the chaotic and contradictory material into one allegorical fate." That hardly any German author, with the exception of Wolfgang Borchert, had written a significant period piece, may have had its ground in this chaos. "We were so happy, so optimistic in our cultural activities. We still had no idea that oft mentioned drawers would be proven empty. We still thought that with one shove all would proceed from where it perforce had stopped in 1933. The weeks of beautiful delusions and illusions!"[338] In spite of everything, Friedrich Wolf (b. 1888) experienced a comeback. Wolf had been a military doctor in World War I, and then spent time in a mental hospital for refusing to fight. He was a member of the USPD, and in 1933 emigrated via Switzerland and France to the Soviet Union, where since 1941 he had published anti-fascist material. In the meantime he had returned, working in the Soviet zone for the reconstruction of radio and theater. In April 1947, he wrote a letter to Erwin Piscator in New York. In it he remarked that he felt as if he were being unearthed like an Egyptian mummy at the hands of archaeologists. *Cyankali* (1929) was running at the Hebbel Theater, and *Die Matrosen von Cattaro (The Sailors of Cantaro)* (1930) was playing at the Theater am Schiffbauerdamm. "'*Mamlock*' has been here more than 90 times with Walter Franck, and is the box office hit of Munich. For my better pieces, however, such as *Was der Mensch säet, Patriots, Dr. Wanner*, and *The Last Experiment (Die letzte Probe)*, the stage wardens lack the necesary courage. Why? Because these works throw open the question of our compatriots' guilt, and this is not wanted today. Moreover, the old forces are again quite in the foreground. Democracy seems compatible with this, for the Nazi Pg's still constitute the uncontested majority today."[339]

Professor Mamlock was a tragedy of a mixed marriage that ended with the suicide of the title figure, a Jewish surgeon. Its performance in Berlin in 1935 was accompanied by an evening of discussion in the Deutscher Theater. A "theater letter" of April 1946, described the two events, "When Fredrich Wolf, the playwright returning from emigration in Russia, spoke of the flight of German men on the side of the partisans, the following cry came from the audience, 'The swines have stabbed our brothers in the back.' There were riots in the hall and agitated demands for the removal of the 'pro-fascist.' Then Fred Denger, the twenty-five year-old dramatist, called out at the rioting crowd. 'Not so! Help them! They are young people!' Such is the situation of the playwright. The youth, with whom he is concerned, are disconcerted, headstrong, and profoundly skeptical even in the theater. They mistrust everything. Help them? But how? Friedrich Wolf had sought to cleanse the spiritual terrain with *Professor Mamlock.* For weeks, the evil misjudgments of 1933 had been dramatized in a Jewish destiny. The writer had touched the youth. He could show us letters containing talk of the gratitude and changed thinking of young people. The work cleared away the rubble and made room for the foundations of something new."[340]

The postwar years were not easy ones for young dramatists. Along with Friedrich Wolf, Georg Kaiser and Gunther Weisenborn experienced some measure of fame. Kaiser wrote *Der Soldat Tanaka,* aimed directly at the Berlin-Tokyo Axis powers, and *Das Floss der Medusa* (1945) *(The Raft of Medusa),* a more general description of the human condition. Gunther Weisenborn's success came with his play, *Die Illegalen* (1945). Of the pieces written on the theme of returning home from the war, including Fred Denger's *Wir heissen Euch hoffen,* only Borchert's *Drausen vor der Tur (The Outsider)* experienced a breakthrough, and that posthumously. It stood apart from the prevailing trends, making use of expressionistic dramatic forms. The play premiered in the Hamburger Kammerspiele under the direction of Wolfgang Liebeneiner who later shot the film version, entitled *Liebe 47*. The most moving aspect of the drama became clear in an interview given by the author on the occasion of its Hamburg premiere. Bochert, it appeared, had gone a decisive step further than most of the writers of his time. He approached the edge of the abyss. Others had turned their backs on the abyss, holding onto their memories and deriving hope from them. *The Outsider* was without hope. The despairing question "Is there then no answer?" faded away in the sea of apathy. "The audience, expecting the ordinary, found no designation of the genre of this piece on the play bill. Was it a drama? A tragedy? Since the essence of the drama was concerned with the confrontation between two worlds, the dialogue, first heard as a radio play on the Hamburg station before making its way to 16 theaters, was truly dramatic. If the world of those who had survived the war, not the other world in which one lived backwardly, that is, the bourgeois, antiquated world, the world in which the image of the past is thought real, would in fact become nonexistent, then drama would connect with tragedy."[341]

The greatest stage hit for many years after the war was *The Devil's General*, written by a theater expert from the Weimar Republic, Carl Zuckmayer. The play was performed 3238 times between 1947 and 1950. With a sure sense for vivid characters, and at the same time a great empathy for the specific situation, this piece brought a "blossoming vitality" to modern German drama, offering a "direct perception of human existence in all its fullness."[342] The storm of applause, bestowed especially upon General Harras, was meant for the idol with whom the small time nominal NS party member gladly identified. The tragic, unpolitical person who because of loving "something" passionately, in this case, flying, is seduced by demonic powers and atones bravely.

The currency reform of 1948 marked a decisive turning point for theater.[343] In Bavaria alone, 300 theaters, orchestras and related industries were closed down. On September 11, 1948, the *Hessischen Nachrichten* announced,"The Kassel State Theater is fighting for its existence. It advertises, organizes lotteries, and solicits public cooperation. Its most prominent talents play soccer, and the manager even admits to begging in order to save the institution." On September 27, the *Stuttgarter Zeitung* reported "In the next few days, the state assembly's theater committee will discuss state subsidy for the theater. One can only hope that Bavaria will not serve as an example for other states." The Bavarian minister of finance had declared the state theater unnecessary. The Munich press spoke of the impending "dismantling of culture." The Frankfurt stages announced 150 cancellations by August 1949, in February 1950, the closing of both houses was decreed. However, by popular vote, 50,000 Frankfurt citizens decided in favor of the theater, whereupon all parties of the city parliament ratified new means. Harry Buckwitz was elected General Manager.

Subsidies for theaters were drastically reduced everywhere. In the fiscal year of 1949, the municipal stages of Essen received only 827,000 marks instead of one million; those of Dortmund were alloted 625,000 instead of 1,255,000 marks; and those of Wuppertal only 629,000 instead of 833,000 marks. In a survey of pay rates taken by the *Neue Zeitung* in the Autumn 1949, Harry Buckwitz estimated that the average wage for the Munich Kammerspiele was around 750 marks gross, 550 net. At the end of the 1948 season, Grundgens had the most successful acts continue to perform so that he could pay full wages. There were cuts in the Soviet Union.

In this emergency period, Bertolt Brecht's *Mutter Courage (Mother Courage)* provided a model for the theater of the fifties. Returning to Berlin in October 1948, he first directed with Erich Engel this play on January 11, 1949. It was an example of "bright, cheerful, instructive and entertaining theater." Before that time, Brecht refused to allow any performances of *Courage* to take place. He had wanted to procure for Helene Wiegel an enduring entreé as an actress, and he aimed for a demonstrative performance of "his" theater. At the same time, this performance coincided with the climax of the East-West confrontation. As Brecht introduced a new phase in the history of postwar German theater, many people, and not only the "cold warriors," posed the question, "May, can, or should Brecht continue to be performed?"

"The two great West Berlin newspapers, *Der Tagesspiegel and Der Telegraf* remained silent about the performance. They had boycotted the East Berlin Theater since the blow up by the SED of the House of Commons of united Berlin. The Soviet blockade of access roads to West Berlin was already in effect during the rehearsals of *Courage*. The greater part of the city was served by Allied airlifts. Despite this, Brecht held fast to his plan of permanently setting up his theater in Berlin. Five days before the premiere, however, on January 6, 1949, he was hit with the 'stinking breath of the province.' The SED Mayor *(Oberburgomeister)* Ebert made it clear to him that for the time being he would not receive the Schiffbauerdamm Theater. It was not available until 1953, when after the rebuilding of the *Volksbühne*, Fritz Wisten transfered his ensemble there. The Berliner Ensemble, however, was indeed founded with Helene Weigel as the lead, opening at the Deutsche Theater in November 1949, with Brecht's *Puntila*. Brecht had spent the previous summer in Switzerland. There he obtained what, before his definitive move to East Berlin, he considered 'enormously important,' an Austrian visa. He explained in a letter in April 1949, 'Now, if I settle in any one part of Germany, I cannot thereby be considered dead to the other parts.'"[344]

The National Socialists "incorporated" classical German literature into their ideology with much propagandist pomp. They had the support of a Germanistic literature that since the nineteenth century had grown increasingly national and nationalistic. Thus, German literature was refashioned into an altar for the nationalist *(volkischen)* spirit. When this was not possible, they resorted to deleting lines, for example, from Schiller's *Don Carlos*, "Sire, give us freedom of speech!" Certain pieces, such as Lessing's *Nathan*, were banned as "unGerman." In 1941, Hitler even outlawed *Wilhelm Tell*.

In general, however, the German classicists were propagated as "*Fuhrer*," as models of heroism. Stefan Georg and his circle had paved the way for such stylizing. In addition, the "agents of society," especially the schools and universities, had for decades been zealously engaged in polishing the German spirit. For them, this meant substituting myth for enlightenment, pathos for ethos, and bondage for emancipation. Instead of grace and dignity, "aristocracy and decline" prevailed. The possible misinterpretation of Schiller already criticized by Friedrich Nietzsche, who claimed he had been made into the "Moral trumpeter of Säckingen" (title of a play by Schiller) exemplifies how, with the help of a false cult of the classicists, abysmal barbarity was covered by a brilliant facade. Gerhard Schuhmann, as a young author had a sky rocketing career in the NSDAP, and extolled Hitler and the German classicists, especially Hölderlin and Schiller, as messianic cult figures. Schuhmann was, among other things, Presiding member of the Reich's Academy of Writers, a member of the Reich Cultural Senate, and first president of the Hölderlin Society, founded in 1943.[345]

Such perversion of the German spirit confirmed Franz Grillparzer's ominous claim that German culture would evolve from humanity, through nationality, to bestiality. Paul Rilla, in 1945, critiqued the National Socialists' attempts to legitimate their theater by referring to the German classicists. Never, he claimed, has a more blood-stained insult been thrown at the ideas of the German classicists than by the National Socialists. "The century of Lessing, Herder, and Kant, the century of Schiller and Goethe, never has the historical truth been so falsified into its opposite as with the insolent use of this national tradition by the National Socialists."[346]

Already during the Third Reich, the classical productions of Gustaf Gründgens, Heinz Hilpert, Jürgen Fehling and Otto Falckenberg represented a subtle protest against such usurpation. The stronger presence of classical drama in the postwar repertoires, and earlier in exile performances, for example, in Zurich, are conscious opposition to the misuse of the humanist idealist values by the Third Reich. Many theaters opened after the war with *Nathan the Wise*. In frequency of performances during the 1945 season, Lessing's play placed third, followed by Goethe's *Iphigenie* and Schiller's *Intrigue and Love (Kabale und Liebe).*

Berthold Viertel, author, director, translator and friend of Bertolt Brecht, was amazed to discover, upon his 1948 trip to West Germany from the United States, that the shallow pathos of earlier classical performances continued to have its effect. He called this old-new style "Reichs Chancellery Style" *(Reichskanzleistil),* having observed it on the stages of Berlin, Düsseldorf, and Vienna. "A rare mixture has crystalized and obviously become established here, a rootless ecstasy or a cold, boastful rhetoric, which emphasized and overemphasized the official and representative parts of the production, and then changed abruptly with an all too delicate discretion that escaped into the quiet, the private and subprivate. Mania and depression followed each other without clear transitions or breaks." The frenzied tone of violent rhetoric, the strained voice that was meant to persuade, this paroxysm that brought foam to the actor's lips, was in any case quite effective in exciting the admiration of the public, who "regularly acknowledged the explosive tirades with enthusiastic applause." The delicate points reminded him of the enforced discretion of that time when freedom yielded to the views of timid secretiveness, when not only political contradictions, but also the private human sphere which could not be forced into conformity, had to seek refuge in the whispering hideouts of locked rooms. "The unique circumstances of official and private speech struck me as being extremely significant for this style of expression. There was absolutely no natural balance between the two. The result, therefore, was the impoverishment of spiritual possibilities and technical means of expression."[347]

Such observations were intended to characterize the overall relation to classical literature during the rubble years. On the one hand, the total collapse had sensitized people to the "beauty, truth and goodness" beyond affirmative culture and the representive pathos of "our classicists." On the other hand, there were no radical attempts to wrestle with, or to "get to the roots" of the inheritance of the times. Viertel questioned the great devotion to the classicists. Did this theater, which performed before ruins, serve today as an escape from misery, an evasion of decision, and a pretense of that unity and freedom which it still does not and cannot provide? Is it not the case that most of these classical performances were pretenses of a culture that cannot be had without being truly earned? The road to Peter Stein's production of *Tasso* in March 1969 was still a long one.

More Cabarets than Undemolished Houses

From the scoffers' bench, neither the sublime nor the shallow, the secretive nor the puffed up rhetoric had any more right to exist. The time was over for big words and fatal deeds. The result was a clearing, a rubble. Because absurdity was considered fatal, the National Socialists waged a bitter war against the floor shows of the big cities. The free spirited urbanity of the Weimar cabarets jeopardized their bombastic provincialism. Thus the "Tucholskys and Consorts" were banned, persecuted, and exterminated. Cabarets continued to be an important weapon against Fascism in major exile centers. Even in Germany, when political humor was subject to the death penalty, it could never be totally silenced.

The Third Reich had hardly disappeared before it became evident that the value of disrespect had not been completely forgotten. With the liberation from the totalitarian yoke, the mouths of protesters and scoffers were no longer gagged. An amazing cabaret boom began. In August 1945, Erich Kästner pointed out that "if all the plans of the past weeks materialize, there will soon be more cabarets than undemolished houses."[348]

"The lid finally came off the container of public opinion. Here it was finally possible to divulge long forbidden thoughts with freedom and audacity. One could twitch the beards of yesterdays's idols, and one was allowed to scoff openly at the fundamental errors of an entire epoch."[349]

Many of the cabaret projects of the postwar years were able to materialize because of the readiness of the Western occupying powers to support them. As long as they, themselves, were not the focus of attack, they saw the cabarets as a very practical instrument for enlightenment. The cabaret was to become an important forum for the expression of political opinion. "The political element was unmistakable, regardless of whether the cabaret was traveling or stationary, in a theater or in a tavern, concerned with literary quality or more in the style of a light revue or musical. In contrast to the average audience of the Weimar Republic, the cabaret fans were not limited to an elite group. Rather, largely because of radio broadcasts, the shows began to catch the attention of an increasingly broad spectrum of the population."[350]

The *Schaubude* of Munich had already opened in the Kammerspiele by August 1945. Ursula Herking, the dominant figure of the ensemble, had matured in Werner Finck's *Catacombs* that had actually been able to "hibernate" until 1935. Erich Kästner was soon to become the most important author, and the program was marked by his "leftist meloncholy." He began with "Elegie mit Ei," a poem that appeared in the author's first publication, *Herz auf Taille*. This poem was an especially appropriate lyrical commentary on the situation of the summer of 1945. Kästner captured the mood of the younger generation, their desire to free themselves from the guilt of their fathers and to demand the right to make their own mistakes, their inability to believe in anything, and yet their resolve to work:

It is in life disgustingly the case,
that after questions, question marks appear.
Things feel no duty to the human race.
but only smile when we have finished here.

Who knows what dreams the flower sees?
Who knows if many blacks have yellow hair?
And why does fruit hang high on trees?
And why the whistling of the air?

We will not view our future through a window.
It's with our past, together in one bed.
When humans came, the primates did not vanish.
And "block" is usually firmly joined with "head."

We'll soon become as youthful as our fathers,
we shoulder all the burdens of the past
those major criminals ask their little heirs
to share with them a hearty guilt repast.

They wished to fight, and gave to us the cudgel.
They gladly fought with rifle, knife, and pride.
We sow the grass above their leaders' graves.
We're slowing down, and much improved besides!

We wish again to bury the tradition.
It sat in the window, growing big in size.
We wish to finally make use of our vision
and have a place on which to set our eyes.

We want to finally make our own mistakes.
We don't believe in anything, not we.
And yet to work and laugh we have resolved.
Is it possible for you to see?

Are we at the start or at the end?
We laugh in the face of countless mysteries.
We spit—pfui, Herr Kästner—in our hands
And shoulder our responsibilities.[351]

After "a sorrowful, wintry experience of reconstruction" the *Schaubude* was able to obtain its own hall in the spring of 1946. The *Neue Zeitung* printed a review of the opening program in the new location. According to the article, the program, entitled *Bilderbogen für Erwachsene* (Pictures for Adults), provided literary entertainment with its well balanced mixture of biting satire, uncomplicated fun, and genuine feeling:

"Among those rebuked were the Austrians, the country peasants, the informer in the city, the young girl seeking business prospects, and even the sacred institutions of the military government. Kästner's song, 'State and Individual,' played by Bum Krüger, and his skit 'Youth and Politics,' as well as the sketch 'Reeducation of Education' by Axel von Ambesser, and supported in part by Gustav Tolle's play bills, aimed the most searching spotlights on the government and governors under whose rule we had lived until one year ago. Their psychological effect was so remarkable that the public was much less united in its applause than it was, for example, with Kästner's charmingly biting couplet 'Oh, my beloved Austria' or Krüger's playful *'Amis'* (Yankees). Going straight to the heart were pieces such as Kästner's *'Plädoyer einer Frau'* (A Woman's Plea), interpreted by Inge Bartsch, and his *'Briefkasten'* (Letterbox), a song referring to all mothers, and sung by Margaret Hagen in such a way that one would like to think there would never be another 'heroic mother' or 'noble mourning.' Then there was the Bavarian element, gently mocked by Ambesser and personified most originally by Sepp Nigg and Margaret Hagen. Herbert Witt's *'Zunftiges Zukunftiges'* (Fair Things of the Future), was one in which the Yankees became Bavarian and Munich blossomed in new life. It is a small declaration of love by the immigrants to the country of their choice, bashfully concealed in thorny roses. Ursula Herking had her second major success with this act. Her first and most enduring success had been with Kastner's *'Marschlied 1945'* the fight song of a tough and illusionless optimism which made one hope not only that this depiction of times would some day become real, but that it would be real in the present. At the end of his first program, Kastner brought the audience directly out into the impending rubble clearing."[352]

Those texts of Kästner which directly captured the misery of the postwar years were more elegiac than satirical, more concerned with mood than with sharp analysis. His view of the times was most clearly manifested in *Deutsche Ringelspiel* (1947).

"Some characteristic figures of our day enter one by one into footlights, looking like marionettes going round in a circle:"

The "snow covered refugee woman," "do you have hearts of iron;" the jovial profiteer, conspicuously fat, with a derby on his head and a cunning smile on his face; the old prisoner of war returnign home, "your home is in Nowhere;" the women, swaying with the rhythmn of tango; the poet in street clothes, with a lyre in his hand, "you are the people that never listen to your poets;" the young girl, embodying the "poor youth;" the party politician, wearing an election poster with fictitious wording, "my party is the only one;" the wild teenager carrying a bag; the adversary, straddle-legged, hands idly stashed in his pockets, wearing old breeches and black riding boots.

Every figure sang his or her song. After everybody's act, there appeared on a pedestal, "in the dimness of the center stage, that allegorical figure which until that point had existed only in presentiment, Time, her face"—like justice, she wore a blindfold; her concluding song:

> My realm is small and infinitely wide.
> My name is time.
> I am the time that crawls and speeds.
> I cause and heal the wounds that bleed.
> I have no heart, I cannot see.
> And good and bad are nought to me.
> To me, they're one in unity.
> I bear no hate, and pity none.
> I am Time.

In the following she grows increasingly icy, scornful, and unapproachable:

> Of one thing there can be no doubt:
> you're far too loud!
> I cannot hear the seconds now.
> The hourly step is muffled now.
> I hear you pray and curse and scream,

and shoot your bullets in between,
it's only you, just you I hear . . .
so to my words you must give ear:
you must at last be still!

Now somewhat less cool, somewhat more humane.

You're but a speck of dust upon Time's dress,
stop your warring foolishness!
A tiny spot is your great earth,
spinning with you in the universe.
Microbes are not wont to shout
but if wisdom's not what you're about
you could at least not be so loud!
Hush! Hear the tick of eternity.
I am Time, listen to me!

While the musical clock starts up again and the figures renew their rotating movements, the curtain goes down."[353]

The merging of "magical realism" with historical interpretation is unmistakable. In fact, it would be useless to try to stop this from happening. The world in any case continues to turn, urged on by time. Human beings, as "a speck of dust upon Time's dress," would therefore do well to duck their heads and keep quiet.

Werner Finck defined his solo cabaret as "humorous futuristic art of big city folk," directed against bureaucracy, mismanagement, workers' stress, and political inertia. In November 1945, he showed up "for work!" After the closing of the "*Catacombs*," he had been sent to a concentration camp. Some of his colleagues managed to get him out. He then played with the UFA and was forbidden to hold a job. He was barred from the Reich's Academy of Writers and drafted into the army, where he received the Iron Cross Second Class and the Eastern Medal. In 1942, he was again detained for investigation, and was thereafter made a soldier again. He ended up in an Italian prison, from which he was eventually released.

In his *Silvesterrede 1945* (New Year's Eve Speech, 1945), he stated that there was no need to shed tears over the past year. "At the beginning of this year we were still rich *(reich).* I will spell that Reich: R as in *Ruhmsucht* (passion for glory). E as in *Eitelkeit* (vanity). I as in *Irrtum (error).* C as in *Casarenwahn* (Caesarean madness). H as in *Heroeninflation* (hero-inflation). Finally, we are the opposite of rich.

What a few years ago was circling as a subversive joke, has long since become the reality. An optimist said, 'After the war we will all go begging,' and a pessimist answered, 'Who will we beg from?' Oh, you sad, miserable, damaged postwar years . . . The old have fallen, and new life, we hope for it. But when our luck turns bad, we will see new ruins. Listen, dear friends, they are proclaiming the new year. The fools are bellowing and howling! The wise ones smile and tremble. Welcome, 1946! You have a pleasant license number. The digits add up to an even number. Your front two legs add up to ten, as do your two hind ones. Leave us in peace! Change our misery, give us new illusions! You shall live, nineteenhundredfortysix!"[354]

Like Kästner and other cabaret people, Finck regarded the contemporary situation without illusions. The program with which he opened in 1946 was entitled *Kritik der reinen Unvernunft* (Critique of Pure Unreason). Later, he wanted to found an alternative party called the "Society of Happy Hopeless Humans." Its goal was not to have a goal. "By this time it has become clear that Finck's concept of humor, so effective in subverting Fascist slogans and rendering them laughable, was ultimately a form of political nihilism. It went from being disdainful of National Socialist politics to scorning all-politics whatsoever. Even the perspective of a Schweyk (Character in a famous novel by Hasek. Brecht revives this figure, in his play *Schweyk im Zweiten Weltkrieg*.) served that attitude on which it was primarily dependent, that of keeping itself as much as possible out of politics."[355]

Günter Neumann's cabaret *Ulenspiegel* was oriented around the revue style, which had ties both to the 1920s and to the American musical. *Alles Theater* (1947) was directed by Gustaf Grundgens, who had once directed the cabaret revue *Alles Schwindel* in the Theater am Kurfurstendamm under Max Reinhardt. No sensational novelties, no ground-breaking cultural achievements, no revolutionizing of the cabaret was to be expected here. The author criticized in a friendly, engaging manner not only the events of the time, but also the difficult life of Berlin, especially as it pertained to the theater. "Everything is so charmingly carried out, the irony is so conciliatory, that we hope to meet with the public's approval."[356]

This comment anticipated the tenor of the subsequent and even more successful revue, *Schwarzer Jahrmarkt*. Politics appeared as a circus, with the average German citizen as the "stupid clown," and all of life as an amusement park, a colorful, fuzzy, and occasionally grotesque mixture of attractions and abnormalilites. Everything revolved in a circle, as in Kastner's *Ringelspiel*.[357] Satirical points were wrapped in mild, prosaic philosophy. To be sure, the "coal" comes first, but the heart is most important. Given the harmful times, people gratefully accepted a certain belittlement. This tendency also defined the *Insulaner* (The Islander), a satirical journal founded in 1948 by Gunter Neumann. Since it declined after the currency reform, its contributions were made into illegal advertisements for the RIAS station. It was intended to be a single broadcast, but it met with so much response that it was followed by almost 150 more.

The cabarets ran into difficulties with the censorship of the occupying forces. Along with the cabarets, other well-known shows included the *"Hinterbliebenen"* (The Survivors) from 1945, the *"Amnestierten"* (The Pardoned), and the *"Kom(m)odchen"* (Little Bureau, Little Comedy), both opening in 1947. The regionally employed American theater officials complained of increasing anti-Americanism. In September 1947, the Bavarian Theater Control Board threatened their license holders with extremely severe measures. "The next spot check we make at one of your shows will, if it turns out negative, cost you dearly. The license holder is responsible for every word spoken in his or her show, even if the artist in question just happens to improvise on that particular evening."[358] The ruling authorities handled the situation in various ways. The Frankfurt *Palette* was simply advised to eliminate an aggressive and tasteless political joke from the program. In Munich, the program of the *Bunte Wurfel* (Colored Dice), which had painted an unhappy picture of events following the occupation, had to be changed. It had summarized the intrusion of American culture into Germany with words such as "cigarettes, chocolate, and penicillin." The director of a cabaret in Giessen had his performance permit taken away after he had depicted the numerous black soldiers in the area as gypsies . . . Granted, often what proved offensive had nothing to do with politics, but with obscenities, sheer nonsense, and high prices. Not only the American theater officials, but also the German ones, required a certain "level."

In February and March 1948, the Information Control Board of Hesse sent observers to visit all the cabaret shows of Frankfurt, Wiesbaden, Kassel and the surrounding areas. They were to prepare written reports of their observations. Among other things, these reports showed that the number of programs dealing directly with the politics of the occupying powers was relatively small. In Kassel and Frankfurt, it was only around 5 percent of the shows, and in Wiesbaden about 20 percent. The alleged reason for this was that authors and actors held themselves back out of fear that the military government would either ban their programs or withdraw their licenses. It could also have been part of the aftermath of the authoritarian Nazi regime. Typical occupation themes were: denazification, fräuleins of American soldiers "*(Ami-Fräuleins),*" gum-chewing US soldiers, their preference for swing, and their dietery situation. Authors and actors were clearly freer to criticize the German government. "Approximately 25 percent of all the jokes are directed against German politicians, their programs and their activities. Jokes against the German government are made much more spontaneously, without fear or hesitancy. The authors know that the American, and not the German, authorities control the licenses for the cabarets. Therefore, they are not reluctant to attack German politicans, from the Minister President on down."[359] The following themes were especially popular: the ineffectiveness and corruption of food and housing officials; the general food situation; the bi-zonal elections; the "Burgomasters;" the black market, "Hurrah, we're still alive, everyone knows how, but no one speaks of it;" the absurdity of the paper rations, a flood of placards and questionnaires alongside a dearth of good school books; the corruption of officials and merchants; the frivolity of the "Fräulein;" Bavarian particularism; railroad employees; police; the danger of playing with thoughts of war when militarism is not yet extinquished; the attempt of many Germans to improve their standard of living by claiming to have been persecuted; and the tendency to deny personal guilt.

The *Schaubude* was praised in 1946 as "by far the best cabaret," it was "superbly literary." The program *Vorwiegend heiter—leichte Niederschläge* (Mostly fair, slightly overcast) of 1947, came under sharp attack. It was reproached for its poor taste and lack of wisdom, for stupidity, immodesty, tactlessness, and arrogance of the Germans with respect to Americans. Its political contents, however, were the main focus of criticism.[360] When Americans were represented on public stages as black market dealers and political failures, when it was implied that American men raped German women with the slightest provocation, this was interpreted as a malicious and dangerous attack on the United States occupation forces. When the *Hinterbliebenen* appeared at the *Schaubude* four months later, one sketch became a stumbling block. It criticized the plan of the Bavarian Minister of Culture, Alois Hundhammer, which suggested that refugees from the various zones be divided up and settled according to religious denomination. According to Hans Ludwig Held, director of the municipal library, honorary professor of the University of Munich, first chairman of the Munich *Volkshochschule,* and highly influential in German postwar cultural politics, the incriminated text contained various sentences "which even for a liberally minded person, or at least for the Bavarian context, must seem imprudent and superfluous." CSU city council member Max Gerstl claimed that the *Hinterbliebenen* could provide a ready foundation for a new form of Nazism, or even Bolshevism. The right wing of the CSU, however, was not able to succeed in this. The program proceeded unchanged, although the scandal continued to grow.

The problem of the rebellious cabaret eventually "resolved" itself. After the currency reform, most of the cabarets closed their doors. Interest in satirical and cabaret style criticism, which was frequently only lightweight, rapidly declined. People preferred to spend their money on urgently needed material goods.

An Internal and External Look at the Movies

The National Socialist film industry, which was consolidated into a state-owned industry, UFA-Film GmbH, in 1942, continued to produce until the last days of World War II. "The last reserves of the nation's spiritual powers should be awakened. If there is no faith in victory or trust in the leadership, then at least blind obedience should be practiced with respect to the authority of the state and the party. Harmony between plot and propagandist, opportunist intention was preserved, whether in movies such as *Kohlberg,* which seemed to portray endurance at any cost, or *Die Frau meiner Träume,* disguised as an unpolitical show inviting an escape from reality. In studios at the time of the unconditional surrender, there were more than 30 movies about to be released. These had already been conceived in 1944 with the collaboration of the Ministry of Propaganda and the film industry. At the end of 1945, the last edition of the German weekly newsreel *Deutsche Wochenschau* reached the few cinemas that were still open."[361]

Until the end of 1945, 1,150 cinemas were reopened in the Western occupation zones, compared to the 6,484 cinemas of 1944. The number almost doubled in 1946 to 2,125, and increased to 2,850 in the end of 1947, to 2,950 in the end of 1948, and to 3,360 in the end of 1949.[362]

Along with the radio, the cinema offered one of the few opportunities for entertainment and information. It comprised the center of social and cultural life both in the city and in the country. One sat again "in a darkened room, facing one of those magic white walls, upon which the old enchantment of a photographic pseudo-reality was developed." Hermann Kadow provided an "internal and external look at the movies" for the *Frankfurter Hefte* in August

1946. He stated that, especially in the rural areas, where most of the small movie houses remained, the audience, a new mix due to war evacuations, again let itself be fed the old pleasures, not, however, with that unconditional enthusiasm that prevailed so naturally before the destruction of the old world. "The judgments and opinions have become markedly more critical. One feels that the dreams whose photographic reality is depicted on the screen are no longer quite correct, at least not in Germany any more, and perhaps no longer in Europe. Tragedy is smiled at, for people possess a personal treasury of tragic experiences unreached by the fantasies of the film writers. Even comedy is pitied, because one suspects that tragedy and comedy are related on a deeper level. In their present form, comedies seemed dumb, empty, and somewhat boring. Nevertheless, people go to the cinema because here life's hollowness at least has a friendly, hairy wart which lends levity to the devastated German face and even beautifies the gray monotony of daily German life." Underlying this metaphorical talk was the fact that, for the most part, films from the USA, England, France and the USSR were made available in the respective occupation zones, with very little exchanging. Furthermore, the cinema listings increasingly consisted of "those surviving German films which were free of Nazis and militia and served sheer entertainment or educational functions." Only occasionally were films such as *Die Todesmühlen* offered, which asked more of the audience than a noncommittal response. The documentary film, *Die Todesmühlen,* by Hans H. Burger, was removed from distribution in 1946. It was composed of shots of concentration camps taken by the Allies after the liberation, portraying the shared guilt of the majority of the German population. This was followed in 1947 by a film with a similar goal, *Nürnberg und seine Lehren.*

The newsreel was an important instrument of Allied film production in the first postwar years. *The World in Film,* produced by the English and the Americans, was brought into German theaters as early as May 18, 1945. The central focus was the presentation of the occupying powers as guarantors of justice and facilitators of democratic political reconstruction. At first, there were extensive reports on the prosecution of Nazi criminals. However, beginning in the summer of 1946, the tendency was to refrain from blaming the German population as a whole. At the same time, the entertainment function grew to constitute one third of the newsreel content, which, by the way, omitted reports from Soviet and French zones in the first years.[364]

With respect to German film production, the film industry said Hermann Kadow was "sliced and heavily amputated in its most powerful financial area and in its most important extremities." Indeed, the Berlin-Babelsberg film studios that centralized their work during the Third Reich suffered relatively little. In East Berlin, the DEFA was founded on this basis. It worked closely with the Soviet military administration to release, on October 15, 1946, Wolfgang Staudte's *Die Mörder sind unter uns (The Murderers Are Among us),* the first postwar German film. The DEFA also produced *Der Augenseuge,* the newsreel distributed in the Soviet occupation zone.

In the Western occupied zones, the first British licensed film, *Sag die Wahrheit* (Tell the Truth) followed. It was a trivial comedy under the direction of Helmut Weiss. In July 1947, the Hamburg Camera-Film GmbH produced, under the artistic direction of Helmut Käutner, the movie *In jenen Tagen* (In Those Days). An old car that, after the war, had been stripped by two mechanics of all serviceable parts, narrated its fluctuating history in seven episodes. It reported of people who suffered political and racial persecution during the Third Reich, who participated in resistance movements and were murdered, and who died in the war or escaped from the eastern parts of greater Germany.

At this time, in the British zone, there were six licensed production companies and one association of film directors. The theater owners organized themselves, and film distribution was transferred into German hands. The most pressing problems were the acquisition of raw materials and the shortage of studios.

Good filmscripts and suitable directors were also hard to find. Despite this, the financial situation continued to improve. Films costing 600,000 Marks, which was considered quite high, began to earn a profit. Since the number of theaters had declined, it naturally took longer than previously. For example, only five copies of Käutner's film, *In jenen Tagen,* could be produced due to the shortage of materials.[365]

The first American licensed film, produced in West Berlin and first shown in December 1947, was called *Und über uns der Himmel!*. It was directed by Josef von Baky and featured Hans Albers in the title role. In it, a man returns home from the war. He breaks into the new Berlin life, moving between hunger, misery, swindling and the claws of the black market. His son also comes home from the war, and is blind. He, however, regains his sight, and sees his father wandering down the path of the prevailing vices. "He rebels, separates from his father's house, goes to work and in the end leads his beloved father out of poverty and back to decency. They want to try the honest way." The joy of seeing the art of film, which had taken a long reprieve, start up again under technically sound and affectionate guidance, was not unambiguous. There was the question of whether such an optimistic actor, a star who joyously rolled up his sleeves, conjuring up many memories of early films, could appear in a contemporary rubble film without interrupting the consciousness of the viewers. It was doubtless a success, and yet one might have wished that things didn't start out with routine, but with something new and revolutionary. One might have hoped for a documentary of the times, a daring venture, an experiment on new ground. Obviously, the filmmaking pause was only an interruption. The industry continued, admittedly without ideology and propaganda, along familiar paths.[366]

Various hopes were attached to the filmmaking pause caused by the collapse. In 1945, film director Harold Braun thought that because of technical and personal difficulties, the break could have a deeper, necessary meaning. He claimed it was a dietary experience, that after times of especially concentrated and stressful life, there is no better means of regeneration than a prescribed time of fasting, no matter how difficult this might seem to an individual. Perhaps the German filmmaking pause would help bring about some insights that would make our misery appear virtuous. The German film of the last 13 years, he thought, did have the questionable privilege of attracting the special attention and care of the dictatorial regime. The propagandist possibilities of the film were made the dominating feature. The future production of films should be ideationally oriented. The order of free artistic play needs attention, and humor needs to be experienced anew. If there is to be a common denominator for all these tasks that have become so foreign, and that must now be accomplished, it can only be the demand "that the films on which we wish to work should assist people in dealing more easily with their difficult lives." So long as enthusiastic rehearsals are already taking place upon the remaining German stages, and the curtain is rising here and there; so long as the creators of cabaret put their heads together and figure out new acts; so long as new casts of actors and actresses emerge daily, rehearsing today in empty rooms what they tomorrow will present to the public while traveling through the country; so long as the great circle of producing actors are feverishly working and planning, the film people have nothing to do but keep their hands in their pockets and reflect with a heavy heart. One day the hour will again strike for German film to be prepared to assist with life. "Whether we like it or not, nobody today should pretend, not in life, not in theater, not in film, as if the guilt, craziness, death and anxiety of the past years has not existed at all. We do not wish only to produce period pieces, but films, whether they be cheerful, timeless, or requiring costumes, fed from the dark well of our fate, that help us to stand our ground with this fate."[367]

The result of this "film fast" in the following years was varied, yet with few exceptions, not striking quality. The films of the rubble years lacked the courage for radicality, in both content and form. Therefore, people looked with awe and envy at Italian films which introduced a new phase in film history with neo-realism. Roberto Rossellini's masterpiece, *Open City* (1944) and then *Paisan* (1947) and *Germany, Zero Hour* (1947), depicted the collapse of Fascism in the documentary style of a chronicle. Vittoria De Sica, on the other hand, mostly in collaboration with the author, Cesare Zavattini, placed dramatic stress on plot from the beginning, with works such as *Shoe Shiner* (1946) and *Bicycle Thief* (1948).[368]

While in Zurich in November 1947, Erich Kästner saw the movie, *Shoe Shiner.* He was deeply impressed. "The Italian film, *Sciuscia,* by De Sica, is one of the most shocking social films produced since *Panzerkreuzer Potemkin.* It depicts the fate of children coming from the black market into a youth prison, where they degenerated psychologically and physically. All attempts should be made to attain several copies of this masterpiece for Germany, not just because of the content which moves us, but to inform the public of the staggering progress of the artistic Italian film since the war's end. When one recalls the former Italian films and compares them with *Sciuscia* or with Rossellini's films, bearing in mind the abject conditions under which they were produced, one is confronted with a mystery. This unbelievable progress, bordering on miracle, permits the hope that also in other areas of destroyed Europe and on various broken branches of culture, blossoms could bloom overnight."[369]

In light of the Italian film progress, the question of German period films was seriously discussed. In the beginning of 1948, the *Neue Zeitung* encouraged discussion. Bruno E. Werner sketched the terrain of the discussion:

The German film must not avoid the theme of the present. "Present" connotes that living expanse of consciousness which spans about 20 years. In this context, the most important films are *The Murderers Are Among Us, Ehe im Schatten* (Marriage in the Shadows), *In jenen Tagen* (In Those Days), *Über uns der Himmel,* and *Zwischen Gestern und Morgen.*

Some demanded that in period films, things should be true, even if angels crossed the screen or miracles occurred. Others were ready to let themselves be entertained by popular actors, gags, and other elements of suspense. The film in Berlin, in which Hans Albers played the lead, was applauded enthusiastically by many, while others left the theater, fuming with rage. The former enjoyed seeing their Hans again, how he managed his return to a world of ruins, how he sang with a rough voice, wistfully observing mother and child, inciting a tremendous brawl, finally gripping a black market dealer with the grasp of an excavator and throwing him into the water. The others thought that cruel sport was being made of the German ruins, that the divsion into a dreadful misery and a dreadful black market from which the hero breaks free, was bourgeois cinema. They thought that someone forgot to include the shooting of the last scene of the film premiere at Nollendorffplatz, where men in tails and women in evening gowns crowded around the richly arranged, free buffet that was delivered "from the heavens above" for guests of honor after the performance.

The filmmakers, however, explained that the film was not meant for art specialists, but for the multitudes, to whom the harsh present or politics can only be presented in homeopathic doses, for they expected other things from a movie. Against this opinion, critics said that these practitioners merely mastered their "old tricks," and that the cold professional routine with which they mixed the ingredients of the film kitchen according to proven recipes were the very obstacle standing in the way of the resurgence of film. As an example, they pointed to the Italian films *Leben in Frieden* and *Shoe Shiner.* These films stirred the whole world by featuring new faces and new directors who produced shocking and exhilarating works emerging from a new spirit. There was no danger that falsified contemporary history would confuse native minds and the perceptions of foreigners. In Italy, it was clear that people had reaped great human and artistic benefit from misery.[370]

In his contribution to the discussion, Eugen Kogon said that whenever he returned to his small town Taunus in the evening, the people were standing in long lines in front of the only movie theater there. "No film producer in Germany should dare tell us that he must abide by public taste today! In five or ten years perhaps. Now it is in his sovereign hand to let our lives pass by like a dream, and our dreams like our lives." There are two types of realities, he continued, that of our fantasy, and the concrete one. The sound person is at home in each. He or she does not want to remain with only one of them. If the mundane, everyday things played with like building blocks for at most 90 years get on their nerves, they step on the magic carpet made by either their own or others' imaginative powers, thus rising above the cares of daily life. "What follows is that the person whom we, the audience, have left behind, steps out of the entire, the full, the disgusting and grandiose reality before us. This person is ourselves, the way we are and the way we would like to see ourselves depicted. Of what use is the question whether the German film should portray our world, the world of this Germany with its rubble and raggedness? Would it not be possible to shoot comedies in living quarters with heating pipes hanging from the doors of balconies, so that we get cramps from laughter rather than from starvation? Or could we not shoot the last scenes in barracks where the misery would stop our hearts from beating, where the tragedy of a family escaping from Bucovina with child, horse and wagon or where a resettlement from southern Tyrol would allow the "consolidation of the German people?" When the past, rather than the present and nonreality, spanning earth, the future and the beyond, steps into imaginary tracks like the English film *A Matter of Life and Death*, which, naturally, has not yet been shown here, then in its own way it is real and therefore effective. It is a question of art, and thus of the artist, an old question, not new in the least."[371]

According to Inge Scholl, if film was to have a future, it would be only as artistic film. Figuratively speaking, the film should get out of the studio and into reality, the present, and life. Where the present molds the film, the hollow faces in the film fade away, having less to say to us than at any other time. The camera, she felt, was much too stiff and unmoving. It did not capture the psychological movements of events through the play of closeness and distance, of digression and ingression. "Thus, it is my opinion that today, the what is much less important than the why. A film may portray a contemporary or historical theme, it may be shot inside or in the open air, if only it enters into the great contemporary movements of which today's arts are a part. It must carry within itself the spirit of experiment and daring. Thus, the courage of progress should be expressed not only in the contemporary theme of the film, but especially in its mediums and forms as well."[372]

With the currency reform, even small risks were no longer of interest. Directors and producers interpreted and anticipated the taste of the masses as a longing for the perfumed idyll. Still there was rubble, yet no one wanted to see rubble films anymore. The wave of sentimental folk films entered the cinema, and the box office thrived.

> " . . . Stars of my homeland,
> on foreign soil they also light my way.
> As secret words of tender love,

I gladly hear the words they have to say.
Beautiful eventide,
the sky is like a diamond.
A thousand stars set in a circle wide,
a friendly gift from my beloved's hand.
From far away I dream of my homeland."

Though this song, representing the new mood of the newly constituted Federal Republic, had already been composed in 1942, *Capri-Fischer* carried the copyright imprint of 1943, the regression into sentimentality became a flood. The UFA style was indestructible. The first German postwar folk film, which again reveled fully in operatic enthusiasm, was called *Schwarzwaldmädel* (Black Forest Maiden) (1950).

Book Shortage

During the rubble years, to be an author meant to struggle with daily need. Of course, above the insufficient economic substructure was an overarching heaven of ideas where utopias abounded.

On the one hand, there were authors and poets who, impressed by the catastrophic war, captured the images of devastation either realistically or surrealistically. On the other hand, there were authors and writers, frequently continuing their mode of inwardness, who sketched out silver point pictures of details from natural idylls. There thus existed one kind of literature that turned again to the world with a love of life and all its possibilities, and another kind that, with doubt or despair, agnosticism or faith, searched for the answer to the question of purpose. There were the old, the older, and the formerly successful, the exiled and the injured. They looked back on a significant work, or at least thought they possessed something of the kind. Full of pride and melancholy, they recalled the past, perhaps the Weimar Republic. They emphasized their opposition to the Nazis if they had been involved at all, and minimized or remained silent about their accommodation to the Third Reich, and now praised the new horizons either self-critically or didactically, morosely or enthusiastically. There were younger people, who because of military service or experience in war prisons were in fact older than the youth of other times, who now saw opportunities coming their way and reached out for them. These had hardly yet begun to write during the Third Reich, or had only worked for the drawers of their desks. If, perhaps, they had written something, they left it unmentioned, considering it an unimportant preliminary exercise. They now joined together in active literary groups and circles, working intensely in radio, newspapers, and magazines.

The feeling of a new start intermingled with apocalyptic visions. Spirit wandered here and there among different worlds, and the "light," though just beginning to break, was shining predominantly in the West. The Occident was questionable, and yet its traditions were still thought to promote life. The classics were not empty illusions. As before and now more than ever, they begged for a Goethe from within. Granted, the *topos* of cultural stability was often simply an imaginary castle of escape. Some suppressed the approach of modernity, which others, mindful of the earlier hollow provincialism, vehemently greeted. Would the dreams of a brave, new world bring out a paradise on earth or end with a "1984?"

The rubble years, as they were reflected in literature, were years of affliction, difficult years of beautiful hope. They brought a recognition of necessity, of resourceful assistants at work in a time of need. Zero hour had struck, would hour one be missed? Did zero hour, or hour one, really exist? Clearings were reforested, and deserted fields remained among the growing forests.

We return to the material substructure of the literary life. It was of little use to write manuscripts, for no books could be produced. Only after the total surrender, when the shock of the collapse had passed, were people thinking about the possibilities of publishing and dealing with books. The first licenses were conferred. There followed a "slow enrichment of the book market with reprints and new editions from all spheres of literature. The number of works of notable worth and essential significance was not small. However, the shortage of paper, book binding materials and machines, and printing presses, as well as numerous difficulties with production and delivery, made it in most cases impossible to go beyond the limit of 5,000 copies per title or work."[373] By the end of 1946, there were already more than 2,000 book dealers again in the three Western zones. On the average, each dealer received two to three copies of each new work.

In the course of the years 1945 to 1947, 5,000 new books or newly reprinted books appeared in Germany. The catalogue provided for Berlin's German Book Exhibition in June 1947, stated that there were 4,913 titles, noting, however, that it did not pretend to be complete. Thus, when figuring the standard edition at 5,000 copies, this made for a total number of 25 million volumes. These, however, often referred to the titles of pamphlets and tracts containing 40 or

50, sometimes only 12 or even eight, pages. This number also included textbooks and parallel editions.

The "questionableness of the German book production" was analyzed by Manuel Gasser in August 1947.[374] Most publishers were content simply to recognize the phenomenon of shortage. An exception to this was Ernst Rowohlt, who in spite of everything was able to fight for the paper for his new rotary press novels, which reached a circulation of 100,000 copies. They had long since stopped trying to solve the problem of bringing meaning and order into marketing. They worked, like most respectable people in Germany today, for the sake of working, hoping that some day it would be possible to reestablish contact between the book and the appropriate reader. It was the opinion of Eugen Claassen, co-partner of the Claassen and Goverts publishing house in Hamburg, that it would be best to distribute the few existing books on the basis of reports by traveling personnel. He thought that close contact with the dealer, who would promise a jealous supervision of the distribution, would offer the best possible guarantee of intelligent management of the low, all-too-low circulation. Peter Suhrkramp, at that time still trustee for the German inheritance of S. Fischer, explained, "If I put together some letters in haphazard type, print this nonsense, have it bound and sell it, I can be sure to sell the entire editon in a few days without receiving one word of protest in return." His distribution system proved to be the most complicated, time-consuming, and yet also the most exacting. He asked his friends and trusted people all over Germany to send him lists of intellectually interested people. He compiled whole card files of exact details concerning their level and type of education, their preference of either fine arts or sciences, their interest for either educational literature or fiction.

"The situation might have been called tragic, had this miserable shortage of paper and technological assistance not been accompanied by a pronounced stagnation of intellectual output. There was not a publisher in all of Germany who did not complain of the non-appearance of literature stashed away in drawers, or of the obvious unavailability of those works which should have been produced at home during the Nazi terror. There was not one who did not notice that the young authors lacked the resilience for great projects, and the prerequisites for settling accounts with the times. Not one, who could find something halfway decent in this onslaught of lyrical effusiveness, confessional and experiential literature. And what can one say, when one learns that young publishers even have licenses and paper, but do not know how to begin to make use of these treasures, and have the gall to ask the older publishers for copyrights to bestsellers that have been sold out-of-print."

This sharp critique by Manuel Gasser was responded to in an open letter written by Ernst Heimeran, "Every printed work has a spiritual and a material presupposition. When, for example, there are no authors, the best paper is of no help. If there is no paper, the most capable authors and publishers become incapable of developing themselves. Is there a lack of authors? When one reads the list of members of the Association for the Protection of Rights of German Authors, one finds 500 names for Bavaria alone. Thus, one could assume that there is enough creative talent for the diminished book production, which, moreover, only allows new publications in exceptional cases, and at six-month intervals. Yet when one asks for outstanding new talents who can be thought of as international figures, one is embarrassed. Internal and external misery explain the shortage of great, creative achievements. Yet there remains the fact that, qualitatively understood, the lack of books begins with the lack of authors."[375]

Regarding the external difficulties, the Publication Branch of the Information Control Division (ICD) distributed the paper that was available for books and magazines, about six percent of the entire paper output. The Allied authorities first worked without German cooperation, but later engaged German committees. In Bavaria during the first quarter of 1947, 198 metric tons of paper were available for books, and 185 tons for magazines. In the second quarter, there were 11 metric tons for books, and 171 for magazines, and in the third quarter, 70 metric tons for books and 220 for magazines. Six metric tons were required for the publication of 5,000 copies of Ernst Weichert's two-volume work, *Jerominkinder.*

Licenses, at least from the ICS, were only given to select publishers. In Bavaria in September 1947, there were 90 licensed book and magazine publishers, in contrast to the 200 prior to 1933. In light of the production difficulties, the ICD was extremely hesitant to give out further licenses. The German committee argued for the licensing of at least "all those publishers by profession or calling whose reputations are unblemished." "The trade association of Bavarian publishers subjected the cumulative publications of its members to a type of efficiency test. The result: two publishing houses seemed basically dispensible. Around two dozen publications were deemed bad and superfluous, and alongside these were just as many outstanding ones. The overall picture of 600 titles was of average quality. This balance will doubtless encourage greater self-criticism, but it also puts the generalized 'questionableness' of productivity in its proper place. Contemporary authors represented, such as Barth, Benz, Bergengruen, Buschor, Claudius, Diesel, Dorfler, Edschmid, Flake, Graf, Groth, Jaspers, Kaphan, Kogon, Le Fort, Meissinger, Niemöller, Ortner, Penzoldt, Pfandl, Radecki, Roth, Scheffler, Schnack, Schneider, Sellmair, Stepun, Taube, Vossler, Wiechert, Windisch; foreigners such as Barzun, Buck, Churchill, Curie, Gide, Mead, Munthe, Steinbeck; publishing companies like Biederstein (Beck), Desch, Ehrenwirth, Happel, Hanser, Kaiser, Kosel, Leibniz (Oldenbourg), List, Munchner Verlag (Bruckmann), Piper, Rinn, Schnell & Steiner, Schöningh, and Urban & Schwarzenberg, seem to prove that noteworthy works are coming out of Bavaria from various fields."

The miserable book predicament apparent in Ernst Heimeran's balance sheet was especially serious in the area of scholarly, university text material. At the end of 1947, students of the School of Journalism at the University of Munich conducted their first opinion poll modeled on the Gallup poll. Seventy-eight percent of the students owned fewer than ten textbooks. Class notes were taken on packaging paper and on the backs of old notebooks. In order to borrow a book from the university libraries, whose holdings had been reduced by the bomb attacks, one had to get on a waiting list weeks in advance. When, in 1948, the rotary printing machines turned out college books in unbound sheets, this was considered a significant step forward. Paper was "apportioned" according to the number of students and "in consideration of the scope of the individual work." Preference was given to the medical field, which received 30 percent of the available paper supplies, the largest single allotment. Fifty-six titles were to be printed, although only 11 came out. Paper expenditures were especially high for medical works, it was said. A manual for gynecological operations alone required seven tons of paper for 5,000 copies.[376]

In accord with the overall educational euphoria, the intense discussions of German book production during the rubble years constantly referred to the need for pedagogically-linked complulsory measures. Only in this way, it was thought, could the best use be made of the paper quotas imposed by economic necessity.

It was Eugen Kogon's opinion, expressed in the *Frankfurter Hefte* in September 1947, that while there must be free initiative, planning was also important. At that time, the *Frankfurter Hefte* had a circulation of 50,000. The publisher, he maintained, had a great task to fulfill, but Clemens Munster's assertion, likewise appearing in the *Frankfurter Hefte,* June 1946, applies as much now as it did before, "That most books have been destroyed and are no longer available, that the situation urgently calls for clarifying, interpreting, and orienting ideas, that the educational state of an entire generation constitutes a vacuum. It is hard to overlook the fact that this very generation is touched by experiences that will make their burden difficult to bear throughout their lives. These unique opportunities and tasks may inspire the publishers." Despite this, while there were certainly some good books, the majority of material appearing on the German book market was useless. "All of this has developed in the midst of our rather extensive confusion. How is one supposed to put out publications that are reasonable and responsive to the times with these extremely low quantities of paper? A difficult piece of work."[377]

A model, high caliber library was envisioned, one that served the intellectually interested population in compliance with the decisions of the publisher. Of course, such a conception contradicted the desired freedom of spirit, which was also to be reflected in a free book market and a free publishing enterprise.

Thus it was the case that, in the years directly following the war, there were hardly any "clear lines" discernible with respect to German book publication. Randomness dominated, or, to state it more positively, the windows that were opened to brighten up a darkened cultural presence were still very small, and were oriented in every possible direction, without a clear "geometry." Within the framework of a description of Germany's spiritual situation, the London *Evening Standard* of February 1947 spoke of a "cultural black-out," from deficient book production due to paper scarcity. This was considered an "insurmountable obstacle to the successful reeducation of German youth and the revival of democratic thinking." Calling the book Germany's "No. 1 scarce commodity," the paper warned against intellectual starvation in Germany. At the same time, the first German book exhibition, *"Deutsches Buchschaffen"* (German Book Production) of all four zones took place in the Oetker Hall in Bielefeld. This indicated that the situation was serious, but not as bad as it was made out to be. What the 320 German publishing houses managed to accomplish and continue to accomplish daily, shortages, technical difficulties, and other handicaps notwithstanding, bordered on miracle.

By gathering together the four zones, this first presentation of German publishers underscored Germany's unity at least in the area of cultural rebuilding. Around 4,000 books from 260 book publishers were brought together, as were nearly 120 magazines from a total of 80 magazine publishers. In addition, there were abundant special displays dealing with foreign book production, especially from the United States, England, France, Switzerland, Italy and Belgium, and with books produced in emigration, mainly in conjunction with the publishing program of Bermann Fischer in Stockholm. Other displays featured the art of book making, book printing, binding, production, treasures for the bibliophile, prewar book production, and advertising graphics.

The condition of libraries was also bleak. With the destruction of many buildings during the war, valuable book supplies were lost. There was often no space to store those books that were removed before the bomb attacks. A wide spectrum of modern literature was eliminated during the Third Reich. Of course, a number of shrewd library directors were careful to see that the works were not destroyed, but packed away in cellars, thus surviving the "Thousand Year Reich."

At first there were few possibilities of restoring supplies. The Allies did in fact improve the situation through book contributions and with the establishment of their own libraries. By August 1946, there existed a "reading room" called *"Die Brücke"* (the bridge) in the English zone. Hamburg, too, set up an English reading room of the same name, and already in the first week it had 6,000 visitors. The Americans established four libraries in Bavaria. The first "American Library" in Munich contained 3,000 American books and 300 volumes of emigration literature, including works by Franz Werfel, Thomas Mann, and Lion Feuchtwanger. From 100 to 150 avid readers came daily to the library. A thousand library cards were passed out to steady readers at five Reichsmarks apiece. The libraries of Augsburg, Erlangen, and Regensburg were smaller. Libraries in Würzburg, Nuremberg, Passau and Garmisch were in the planning stages. In other areas of the American occupation zone, i.e. in Berlin, Frankfurt, Stuttgart, Heidelberg, Wiesbaden, Mannheim, Karlsruhe, Ulm, and Kassel, libraries were likewise organized, and were enthusiastically received by the German public.[378]

Peter Hartling, who was 14 years old in 1947, described the library situation from the point of view of a small city book user, in the Swabian town of Nurtingen. The town had two libraries, that of the American occupying powers and of the *Arbeiterwohlfahrt* (social security organization).

"As a fourteen-year-old avid reader, I used both libraries with enthusiasm and curiosity. Even today, I can still remember almost word for word the three books that I first borrowed. They were: Max Herrmann-Neisse's *Heimatfern,* a book of poetry published by Aufbau in 1945; *Geheimnis und Gewalt,* a great and now almost forgotten two-volume work of recollections, written by Georg K. Glaser and published in Switzerland in 1945; and a thin, rust colored cardboard bound book which I read over and over again, carrying it with me constantly, and which the librarian finally presented to me as a gift. This was Joseph Roth's *Leviathan*, published in 1947 by Querido in Amsterdam.

"Through reading, I came upon a world that was new to me. I experienced riots and resistance, persecution and murder, the loneliness of a stranger and only evasive answers to my questions. Such authors were not to be found in the schools. The teachers did not even know their names. And yet neither did they speak any more of Hitler, the deadly enemy of these writers. We read Raabe's *Else of the Fir-Tree* and meditated for hours on Carossa's *Brunnen-Gedicht* (Poem of the Well). Even years later, one teacher refused to lecture on a story by Thomas Mann. He did not think he should acquaint us with someone who had fled, like a coward, abusing and soiling his country. When we refuted him, he ridiculed us as ignorant fools.

"I was not alone in this. The young librarian of the *Arbeiterwohlfahrt* took my questions and doubts seriously, and she introduced me to her husband when she couldn't answer my questions. He was the painter Fritz Ruoff, a friend of Grieshaber. He was able to report on his own views. At the beginning of the Nazi era, he was carried off to a camp in Heuberg, after which he had to sweep the streets of Nurtingen. Taciturn and discreet, he made little of this, and unlike many others, was able to survive fairly well.

"And so in his stead, he let others speak, added names to a litany of rage and lamentation, piled up in front of me the books, newspapers and magazines that he had kept hidden and with which he had consoled and strengthened himself. No, Kolbenheyer, Blunck, Vesper, Melusisch, Grimm and Dwinger had never been the true representatives of German literature, despite the attempts to make us believe they were. We had been swindled out of a great fortune. He spread them out before me in fragments, and pressed me to read, piece by piece, from the collected quotations of *Verboten und Verbrannt* (Banned and Burned) by Drews and Kantorowicz. He gave me René Schachhofer's anthology, *Vom Schweigen Befreit* (Freed from Silence) to take home."[379]

Everywhere there were people who, often at great sacrifice, had saved the German book culture from the Third Reich. From private libraries, many works that had been kept "in the second row" were now available for personal use, thus reacquainting people with the outlawed authors.

Newspapers and magazines, led by the *Neue Zeitung* and *Der Monat* which also carried Georg K. Glaser's book of recollections in several long segments, concerned themselves with the mediation of exile and foreign language literature.

F. C. Weiskopf's series of articles, which he began writing for the *Neue Zeitung* in February 1947, provided pathbreaking, highly informative and analytical accounts of themes related to German exile literature.[380] This literature, profoundly dissassociated from the writings of authors who remained in Germany, developed in extraordinary ways. "Both branches of German literature found themselves limited from further development by unnatural living conditions and unusual difficulties. And yet, while literature became increasingly moribund or silent under the whip of the Reich's chamber of culture, exile literature gave up neither its life nor its voice. Despite the variety of forms, temperaments, and views of life and art, the core of exile literature was unified by the consciousness of the inheritance of a great humanistic tradition which had been scandalously betrayed and dishonored by the Nazis. Upon his return from exile, Alfred Döblin wrote an article on the *Two German Literatures,* asking about the 'situation of the emigration literature of 1933 to 1945.' . . . 'What did one do out there? . . . In general, one got on as well as one could. Many heavy books of attack were written. The German situation was endlessly reflected upon. The struggle did not let up. It was taken up with incisiveness in novels, poetry, drama, and also in biography. Sometimes it was directly portrayed and criticized, and at other times it was dealt with in transparent historical parallels. Only a few slipped away or escaped into mythical clouds. Many went under and died. But I don't have the impression that the emigration made the authors weak and defeatist. In comparing the two literatures, I would like to assert that the foreign literature did, for the most part, preserve the fresh and fighting vigor of these authors.'"

Weiskopf divided his overview of German exile literature into several categories:

FIRST SETTLING OF ACCOUNTS. Expelled from their homeland, the writers attempted to reach clarity regarding the expanding government of injustice, and to spread this insight. Much space was given to the theme of concentration camps: They have stirred the conscience of the world and, as perhaps no other means of enlightenment, helped to render the brown barbarity visible. In this group, one finds Willi

Bredel's novel, *Die Prüfung* (The Test), Ferdinand Bruckner's play, *Die Rassen* (Races), Lion Feuchtwanger's novel, *Die Geschwister Oppenheim* (The Oppenheim Siblings), Walter Hornung's chronicle, *Dachau,* Wolfgang Langhoff's true story, *Die Moorsoldaten,* Ernst Toller's play, *Pastor Hall,* and Friedrich Wolf's tragedy, *Professor Mamlock.*

BOOKS DEALING WITH THE ROOTS OF HITLERISM. The desire to clarify the National Socialist rise to power was, from the beginning, predominantly accompanied by the efforts to unveil the secret of its being and development. Among those who dealt with this theme in novels and political historical writings were Johannes R. Becher *(Abschied)* (Departure), Alfred Döblin *(Arbeiter und Soldaten 1918)* (Workers and Soldiers 1918), Oskar Maria Graf *(Der Abgrund)* (The Abyss), Konrad Heiden *(Geburt der Dritten Reiches)* (Birth of the Third Reich), Hermann Kesten, who took special care of the emigrants, *(Die Zwillinge von Nuremberg* (The Twins from Nuremberg), Erich Maria Remarque *(Drei Kameradan)* (Three Comrades), Anna Seghers *(Der Kopflohn)* (A Price on the Head), and Theodor Wolff *(Der Krieg des Pontius Pilatus 1914–1934)* (The War of Pontius Pilate 1914–1934).

STEEPED IN HISTORY. One of the most interesting of the literary discussions, carried on with enthusiasm among exiles in Paris, Prague, Moscow, and Copenhagen, and then in New York, London, and Los Angeles on the podiums of the local gathering places and in their newspaper columns, dealt with the historical novel. The criticism was advanced that the use of historical material could become a flight into the ivory tower. However, many agreed with Ludwig Marcuse that the historical novel occasionally enlightened the present more than portrayals of actual events. Again it was Alfred Döblin who hit the crux of the problem in his essay *"Der historische Roman und wir"* (The Historical Novel and We) when he wrote, "We are not surrounded by a society in which we have grown up, and whose language is our own. We've been dismissed from the field of force of the society in which we used to live, and we are not attached to a new one. There are few things that the actively engaged person needs and that would serve to inspire life. A good part of daily life that surrounds us remains, at least for a long time, silent. This is so for all emigrants. This situation creates in the storyteller a certain compulsion to write historical fiction. It is a necessity. Of itself, the historical novel is obviously not a necessary phenomenon. But when the writer is an emigrant, it is likely that he or she will produce historical novels. It is understandable that, given the empty present, one might desire to look for historical parallels, locate oneself historically, and find vindication. There is the need for meaning, the tendency to console oneself and to take revenge, at least in the imagination."

The historical had a similar significance in the areas of drama and biography as well. Weiskopf mentioned Brecht's *Mother Courage* and *Galileo*, Ferdinand Bruckner's *Simon Bolivar* and *Die Geburt der Neuen Welt* (Birth of the New World), Lion Feuchtwanger's *Der falsche Nero* (The Wrong Nero), Bruno Frank's *Cervantes*, Heinrich Eduard Jacob's *Johann Strauss und das 19.Jahrhundert*, Hermann Kesten's *Ferdinand und Isabella*, Siegfried Kracauer's *Jacques Offenbach und das Paris seiner Zeit* (Jacques Offenbach and the Paris of his day), Emil Ludwig's *Cleopatra*, Heinrich Mann's *Die Jugend des Königs Henri Quatre (Young Henry of Navarre)* and *Die Vollendung des Königs Henri Quatre* (The Perfection of Henry of Navarre), Ludwig Marcuse's *Ignatius von Loyola, Diktator der Seelen* (Ignatius of Loyola, Dictator of Souls), Gustav Mayer's *Friedrich Engels*, Robert Neumann's *Struensee*, Werner Richter's *Kaiser Friedrich III*, Joseph Roth's *Die Hundert Tage* (The Hundred Days), Friedrich Wolf's *Beaumarchais*, Arnold Zweig's *Bonaparte in Jaffa*, and Stefan Zweig's *Castellio gegen Calvin (The Right to Heresy: Castellio against Calvin.)*

THE BUILDING OF GREAT BRIDGES. Robert Musil, who was severely affected by sickness and the misery of emigration, was urged by his friends in Switzerland to interrupt his work on the third volume of his novel *Der Mann ohne Eigenshaften*. They argued that exile was in any case not the most appropriate situation in which to work on and finish a broadly conceived book. Musil responded, "When one has begun to build a great bridge, one cannot, of course, stop work midway. One must make effort to finish it, even in the midst of floods and storms." The rough manuscript of *Der Mann ohne Eigenshaften* was finished, but the third volume did not come out in book form until after the author's death. "Others also had ideas similar to Robert Musil, and continued unflinchingly to build the 'great bridge,' whose foundation they had already laid many years before emigrating. Lion Feuchtwanger finished his 'Flavius-Josephus trilogy,' Arnold Zweig completed his 'Grischa Cycle' with the volumes *Erziehung vor Verdun* (Education at Verdun) and *Einsetzung eines Königs* (Appointment of a King), Jacob Wassermann continued the theme of *Etzel Andergast* in Joseph Kerkhovens dritte Existenz (Joseph Kerkhoven's Third Existence.) Thomas Mann finished the epic novel of Joseph and his brothers."

THE EXILE AS THEME. What theme could be more appropriate for an exiled writer to take up than the theme of the exile? Günther Anders, Johannes R. Becher, Albert Ehrenstein, Oskar Maria Graf, Walter Hasenclever, Stephan Hermlin, Stefan Heyme, Mascha Kaleko, Else Lasker-Schüler, Fritz von Unruh, Berthold Viertel, Franz Werfel, Alfred Wolfenstein, Karl Wolfskehl, Paul Zech, and Carl Zuckmayer have written verses about the exile. Some have written volumes of poetry completely or largely devoted to this theme. Among these were Berthold Brecht's *Gedichte im Exil* (Poetry in Exile), Franz Theodor Csokor's *Das Schwarze Schiff* (The Black Ship), Max Hermann-Neisse *Um uns die Fremde* (Strangeness Around Us), and Alfred Kerr's *Melodien.* Weiskopf also mentioned the following documentary books and works of narrative prose: *Unholdes Frankreich* (Unkind France) and *Exil* by Lion Feuchtwanger; *Der Reisepass* (The Passport) by Bruno Frank; *Kind aller Lander* (Child from all Countries) by Irmgard Keun; *Der Vulkan* by Klaus Mann; *Ein Man fallt aus Deutschland* (A Man Falls out of Germany) by Konrad Merz; *Arc de Triomphe* by Erich Maria Remarque; and *Zwei an der Grenze* (Two on the Border) by Friedrich Wolf. Moreover, there were the anthologies such as *Die Vertriebenen: Dichtung der Emigration,* (The Exiles: Poetry of the Emigration), *Das Wort der Verfolgten: Gedichte und Prosa* (Words of the Persecuted: Poetry and Prose); and *Briefe und Aufrufe deutscher Flüchtlinge* (Letters and Proclamations of German Refugees). Finally, there were many treatises, essays and pamphlets written in the style of Wolf Franck's *Führer durch die Emigration* (Leader through the Emigration); Alfred Kantorowicz's *In unserem Lager is Deutschland* (On Our Side is Germany); and Heinrich Mann's *Der Sinn dieser Emigration* (The Meaning of this Emigration.)

THE FATE OF THE JEWS. This theme already played a significant role in the treatments of the concentration camps. With the increasing persecution of the German and then of the European Jews, this theme became more and more central. Berthold Brecht wrote *Die Jüdische Frau* (The Jewish Woman), which was later taken up into a series of scenes entitled *Furcht und Elend des Dritten Reiches (The Private Life of the Master Race).* Paul Zech wrote *Nur ein Judenweib* (Only a Jewish Woman); Else Dormitzer wrote *Theresienstädter Bilder* (Pictures of Theresienstadt); and George Mannheimer, *Leider eines Juden* (Songs of a Jew). Karl Wolfskehl wrote *Die Stimme ruft* (The Voice Calls); and Egon Erwin Kisch, *Geschichten aus sieben Ghettos* (Stories from Seven Ghettos). Also significant was the area of sociological and historical literature: Max Brod's *Rassentheorie und Judentum*

(Racial Theories and Judaism); Alfred Döblin's *Flucht und Wandlung des Judenvolkes* (Flight and Transformation of the Jewish People); *Die Aufgabe des Judentums* (The Task of the Jews) by Lion Feuchtwanger and Arnold Zweig; *Israel unter den Volkern* (Israel Among the Nations) by Erich Kahler; *Das Schicksal der deutschen Juden* (The Fate of the German Jews) by Josef Kastein; *Kriegstagebuch eines Juden* (War Diary of a Jew) by Julius Marx; and *Bilanz der deutschen Judenheit* by Arnold Zweig.

AUSTRIAN MATERIAL. The events of February 1934 in Austria, the fight against Austrian Fascism put up by workers from Vienna, Linz, Wiener Neustadt and Bruck and ending in heroic defeat, provided a number of exiled authors with material for dramatic works, novellas and novels. Among them were Anna Segher, with *Der Weg durch den Februar* (The Road Through February) and Friedrich Wolf with his *Floridsdorf.* The echo of the February struggles was also especially strong in the poetry of Stefan Heym, Berthold Viertel, and Erich Weinert. In another sense, the fantasy of the exiled writers was inspired by Austria in the forms of memory and dream, or trauma, whether the writers were from Austria, Czechoslovakia, or Germany. For example, Joseph Roth's *Kapuzinergruft* (Capuchin Tomb), F. C. Weiskopf's *Abschied vom Frieden* (Farewell from Peace), and Otto Zoff's *Der ewige Aufbruch* (The Eternal Beginning).

SPAIN. In the November 1938 issue of *Der Deutsche Schriftsteller,* a magazine of the Association for the Protection of German authors in Paris, it was claimed that "twenty three German authors fought on the front of the Spanish war of Liberation." They fought as soldiers, officers, war commissioners and doctors of the "international brigades," but they did not forget that they were writers. Many lyrics were written, as well as short stories, narrative pieces, novels, plays, documentaries, and reports. Among these: Willi Bredel's *Begegnung am Ebro* (Encounter at Ebro); Bertolt Brecht's *Die Gewehre der Frau Carrar (Señora Carrar's Rifles);* Eduard Claudius's *Grüne Oliven und nackte Berge* (Green Olives and Bare Muntains); *Tschapajew, das Bataillon der 21 Nationalitäten* (Tschapajew, The Batallion of 21 Nationalities), edited by Alfred Kantorowicz; *Die Kinder von Guernica* (The Children from Guernica) by Hermann Kesten; *Drei Kühe* (Three Cows) by Egon Erwin Kisch; *El Hell* by Rudolf Leonhard; *Als Katholik im republikanischen Spanien* (A Catholic in Republican Spain) by Hubertus Prince of Lowenstein; and *Der kugelfeste Hidalgo* (The Bullet Proof Noble) by Franz Werfel.

THE INTERNAL VIEW. In a speech given to Yugoslavian members of PEN, Ernst Toller stressed the idea that "the gift of a writer could be a blessing and a curse, a prerogative and an obligation, and that with his or her inner eye, the writer could pierce through walls of steel of the kind that Hitler had built around Germany." With this, he linked the demand to "expose to the world what the inner eye had seen." More than a few exiled authors fulfilled these demands. They attempted to expose to the world what they perceived inwardly, what they discovered from the study of underground reports, Nazi documents, newspapers and radio speeches, and what became clear to them through discussions with refugees and later with prisoners of war. They did this through poetry, Albert Ehrenstein, Stefan Heym, Alfred Wolfenstein; through theater pieces such as *Das trojanische Pferd* (The Trojan Horse) by Friedrich Wolf; and in novels and novellas such as *Dein Unbekannter Bruder* (Your Unknown Brother) by Willi Bredel, *Die Brüder Lautensack* (The Lautensack Brothers) by Lion Feuchtwanger, *Nach Mitternacht* (After Midnight) by Irmgard Keun, *Mephisto* by Klaus Mann, *Es waren ihrer Sechs* (They Were Six) by Alfred Neumann, *Das siebte Kreuz* (The Seventh Cross) by Anna Seghers, and *Das Beil von Wandsbek* (Wandsbek's Hatchet) by Arnold Zweig. The revelation of what occurred behind Nazi steel walls included an exposition of Hitler's war both inland and on the front line. In this way, the "barbarizing" of hundreds of thousands of German soldiers was brought to light. Relevant authors and their works are: *Schlacht um Moskau,* the dramatic poetry of Johannes R. Bechner; *Stalingrad,* a novel by Theodor Plivier; *Himmelfahrtskommando,* (Dangerous Mission) a novel by F. C. Weiskopf; *Dr. Wanner,* a play by Friedrich Wolf; and Carl Zuckmayer's *The Devil's General.*

THE SUFFERING OF AN ENTIRE CONTINENT. The exiled authors, having found refuge in other lands, were easily able to empathize with the suffering of those countries and races that had been crushed and dominated by Hitler. In his novel, *Die Totenjäger* (Death Hunters), Leo Katz recounted the devastation of Rumania by Nazi murderers. Bruno Frank, through his novel *Die Tochter* (The Daughter), was able to search deeply into the suffering Polish people. Ferdinand Bruckner chose the Norwegian war of independence as a theme for his drama *Denn seine Zeit is Kurz* (For His Time is Short). Franz Theodor Csokor wrote a Yugoslavian partisan piece, *Der verlorene Sohn* (The Lost Son); Lion Feuchtwanger's novel, *Simone,* portrayed the France of Nazi occupation and the resistance. Bruno Frei wrote a sequence of scenes entitled *Partisanen in Kärnten* (Partisans in Kärnten). Stefan Heym's novel, *Die Geiseln* (The Hostages), deals with the Czech underground resistance. In his novel, *Lidice,* Heinrich Mann commenorated a Bohemian village that was razed to the ground by the Nazis.

RELATIONS TO THE HOMELAND DURING EXILE. Although the poets and novelists were banned and hunted from one country of asylum to another, pursued by threats and slanders from their fatherland, they still did not give up their homeland. They described it in melancholy and cheerful, despairing and hopeful verses. In the stone sea of New York, Ernst Waldinger celebrated the Austrian village countryside. In Palestine, Louis Fürnberg dreamed of Bohemia, and Artur Zanker heard Slovakian shepherd's pipes in the London fog. Johannes R. Becher saw the Neckar in the Moscow river, and Paul Zech wrote poetry about the German countryside while under the southern cross. Also included in this category are Leonhard Frank's *Deutsche Novelle,* Oskar Maria Graf's *Des Leben einer Mutter* (The Life of a Mother), Ernst Lothar's *Der Engel mit der Posaune* (The Angel with the Trumpet), Joachim Maass' *Das magische Jahr* (The Magic Year), Anna Segher's *Der Ausflug der toten Madchen* (Excurstion of Dead Girls), Carl Zuckmayer's *Der Seelenbräu,* and Arnold Zweig's *Versunkene Tage* (Lost Days).

FOREIGN COUNTRIES. In the course of their flight and involuntary world tour, the exiled writers entered many foreign lands, hidden corners of the earth, abandoned surroundings, and exotic places. This wide, colorful world was reflected, if perhaps less than one might expect, in their works: in the lyrics of Albert Ehrenstein, Max Herrmann-Neisse, Else Lasker-Schuler, Berthold Viertel, and Paul Zech; in narratives, such as Theodor Plivier's *Im letzten Winkel der Erde* (In the Last Corner of the Earth), Rene Schickele's *Die Flaschenpost* (The Bottle Post), Bodo Uhse's *Der Weg zum Rio Grande* (The Road to Rio Grande), and Carl Zuckmayer's *Salvare, oder Die Magdalena von Bozen* (Salvare, or the Magdalene from Bozen); in travel literature and reports, like Lion Feuchtwanger's *Moskau 1937,* Otto Heller's *Auf dem Baikal* (On the Baikal), Egon Erwin Kisch's *Abenteuer in fünf Kontinenten* (Adventure in Five Continents), *Landung in Australien* (Landing in Australia), and *Entdeckungen in Mexico* (Discoveries in Mexico), Else Lasker-Schuler's Hebraerland (Land of the Hebrews), and Stefan Zweig's *Brasilien* (Brazil). Naturally, homesickness prevailed.

POLEMICAL WRITINGS. The exile brought forth countless works of a polemical nature, both short and long, in pamphlet and book form. Among them were Johannes R. Becher's *Deutsche Lehre* (German Lesson), Wilhelm Herzog's *Hymnen und Pamphlete* (Hymns and Pamphlets), Alfred Kerr's *Die Diktatur des Hausknecht's* (The Dictatorship of a Servant), Heinrich Mann's *Hass,* (Hate), *Mut* (Courage), and *Es kommt der Tag* (The Day is Coming), Thomas Mann's *Ein Briefwechsel* (An Exchange of Letters), *Achtung, Europa* (Europe, Beware) and *Deutsche Horer!* (German Listeners!), Konrad Heiden's and Rodolf Olden's Hitler-Portraits, and Norbert Muehlen's *Der Zauberer: Leben und Anleihen des Doktor Hjalmar Horace Greely Schacht* (The Magician: Life and Borrowings of Doctor Hjalmar Horace Greely Schacht.) The manner in which Thomas Mann concluded one of his radio broadcasts was characteristic of this entire genre. "Hitler has sometimes been compared with Napoleon. I find this a tasteless comparison, for the Corsican was a demigod in comparison with the bloody dissembler whom you Germans have for a while taken for a great man. And the universal dominion with which the son of the revolution then threatened the world, was mild, perhaps benevolently tyrannical, compared to the filthy horrors that Hitler would bring about. But listen to the lines of 'Des Epimenides Erwachen' with which Goethe, upon Napoleon's downfall, condemned in advance the Hitler peril:

> Like he who, poorly misadvised
> with spirit over brazen
> follows that French Corsican
> in deed, but as a German.
> He always feels, both late and soon
> for him, a law forever:
> Despite all power and effort spent
> misfortune leaves him never.'"

JEST, SATIRE, IRONY. According to F. C. Weiskopf, Erich Kästner, as one of the genuine inner emigrants, rightly belonged in a presentation of exile literature. Kästner thought, when he was again allowed to write in Germany, that German literature had only one eye. It lacked the "smiling eye." Whoever knew firsthand this skyrocketing climb of National Socialism and the invasion of this excessive humorlessness into world history, was tempted to believe, especially on rainy days, that the lack of humor was a national German trait. Though laughter also frequently left the exiles, satire, wit, humor and profounder meaning blossomed. Relevant authors and their works are: Bertold Brecht's *Satire für den deutschen Freiheitssender* (Satires for German Freedom Broadcasts) and his play *Der aufhaltsame Aufsteig des Arturo Ui* (The Avoidable Rise of Arturo Ui); Mascha Kalekos' *Verse für Zeitgenossen* (Lines for Contemporaries); Walter Mehring's *Und Euch zum Trotz* (And in Defiance of You); Georg Kaiser's play *Klawitter;* and that of Franz Werfel, entitled *Jacobowsky und der Oberst (Jacobowsky and the Colonel).* Further narrative prose pieces include Brecht's *Dreigroschen-Roman* (Three Penny Novel), Oskar Maria Graf's *Anton Sittinger,* Hermann Kesten's *Oberst Kock* (Colonel Kock), Walter Mehring's *Müller* (Miller), and Roda Roda's *Roda Roda und die 40 Schurken* (Roda Roda and the 40 rogues).

HISTORICAL AND PHILOSOPHICAL WORKS, AS WELL AS WORKS OF CULTURAL AND LITERARY HISTORY. Apart from works that were written for a specialized audience, many of the works originating in exile were great scholarly pieces that could easily claim a place in the ranks of literature. Among these were *Der Irrweg einer Nation: Ein Beitrag zum Verständnis deutscher Geschichte* (A Nation Gone Astray: A Contribution to the Understanding of German History) by Alexander Abusch, *Philosophie der Gegenwart* (Contemporary Philosophy) by Ernst von Aster, *Erbschaft dieser Zeit* (Today's Inheritance) and *Freiheit und Ordnung* (Freedom and Order) by Ernst Bloch, *Die Philosophie im 17. und 18. Jahrhundert* (Philosophy: 17th and 19th Centuries) by Ernst Cassirer, *Mein Weltbild* (My Picture of the World) by Albert Einstein, *Der österreichische Volkscharakter* (The Austrian National Character) by Ernst Fischer, *Der Mann Moses und die monotheistische Religion (Moses and Monotheism)* by Sigumd Freud, *Sechstausend Jahr Brot* (Bread for Six Thousand Years) by Heinrich Eduard Jacob, *Der deutsche Charakter in der Geschichte Europas* (The German Character in the History of Europe) by Ernst Kahler, *Demokratie und Sozialismus* (Democracy and Socialism) by Arthur Rosenberg, and *Die Hugenotten* (The Hugenots) by Otto Zoff.

COUNTLESS WORKS ON LITERARY HISTORY ALSO APPEARED. *Der lebendige Heine im germanischen Norden* (The Living Heine in the German North) by Walter Berendson, *James Joyce und die Gegenwart* (James Joyce and the Present Times) by Hermann Broch, *Franz Kafka* and *Heinrich Heine* by Max Brod, *Die deutsche Literatur im Auslande* (German Literature Abroad) by Alfred Döblin, *Thomas Mann's Roman 'Joseph und seine Brüder'* (Thomas Mann's 'Joseph and His Brothers') by Käthe Hamburger, *Süsskind von Trimberg* (Susskind of Trimberg) by Josef Kastein, *Thomas Mann in seiner Zeit* (Thomas

Mann and his Times) by Ferdinand Lion, *Gottfried Keller* and *Zur Geschichte des Realismus* (On the History of Realism) by Georg Lukács, *Handbuch des Kritikers* (Handbook for the Critic) by Alfred Polgar, *Liebe und Ärgernis des D. H. Lawrence* (The Loves and Scandals of D. H. Lawrence) by René Schickele and *Franz Kafka, Deutung seiner Werke* (Franz Kafka: An Interpretation) by Herbert Tauber.

RECOLLECTIONS AND AUTOBIOGRAPHIES. "What choice do we exiles have but to live off memories and to write memoirs," said Joseph Roth at a gathering of the PEN club in Paris early in the gloomy year of 1939. Rudolf Olden, however, countered with "we will write memoirs after we have returned from exile. We should now be looking at the present and toward the future." Several memoirs and autobiographical novels were written in exile: Otto Braun's *Von Weimar zu Hitler* (From Weimar to Hitler); Egon Erwin Kisch's *Jahrmarkt der Sensationen* (Festival of Sensations); Theodor Lessing's *Einmal un nicht wieder* (One Time and Never Again); Heinrich Mann's *Ein Zeitalter wird besichtigt* (Review of an Epoch); Ludwig Renn's *Adel im Untergang* (The Decline of Aristocracy); Roda Roda's *Ein Mann von mittlerer Intelligenz* (A Man of Average Intelligence); Carl Sternheim's *Vorkriegseuropa im Gleichnis meines Lebens* (Pre-War Europe in the Parable of my Life); Ernst Toller's *Eine Jugend in Deutschland* (Youth in Germany); Wilhelm Unde's *Von Bismark bis Picasso* (From Bismark to Picasso); and Stafan Zweig's *Die Welt von Gestern (The World of Yesterday).*

LEGENDS, FAIRY TALES, MYTHS AND MYSTERIES. Dark times, and the times of exile were indeed dark, increase the attention given to themes of the "world beyond." This, however, does not mean that these writings were escapist, for they did concern themselves with the contemporary world, its problems, needs and desires. Works fitting this category are: Hermann Broch's *Der Tod des Vergil (The Death of Virgil);* Thomas Mann's *Die vertauschten Köpfe* (Reversed Heads); Joseph Roth's *Antichrist* and *Die Legende vom heiligen Trinker* (The Legend of the Holy Drinker); Anna Seghers' *Die schönsten Sagen vom Räuber Wojnok* (The Most Beautiful Sayings of the Robber Wojnok); Franz Werfel's *Das Lied von Bernadette (The Song of Bernadette)* and *Stern der Ungeborenen* (Star of the Unborn); and Stefan Zweig's *Legenden* (Legend).

In his last category, F. C. Weiskopf mentioned various kinds of short works, e.g. aphorisms, anecdotes, miniatures, literary conversations, and books for children and teenagers, as well as a series of entertainment literature in the best sense of the word.

On the whole, German exile literature achieved an extraordinary amount, both quantitatively, with a bibliography comprised of around 2,500 titles, and qualitatively. It was therefore possible for liberated Germany to use this inheritance. However, it was not only paper that was lacking for the printing of important books, there was also a shortage of the necessary knowledge and literary consciousness. The reemerging publishing houses were hesitant to include the full extent of exile literature in their programs. In view of the interest of the general public, the work of mourning was not given priority. One suspects, and rightly, as can be seen particularly after the currency reform, that the readers were most interested in appropriating the Western literature of the times.

Publishing Conditions

Many publishing companies had originated either during the rule of the Kaisers or with the Weimar Republic. They were therefore attached to old traditions. Some emigrated, and established branch offices abroad. The editors of those publishers that remained abroad were well informed, and the cultural osmosis between those within and those outside of Germany had not ceased. Furthermore, with the emigrants and the Allied cultural officers, there were a large number of people available to give advice. Still, however, it was difficult, in light of the tremendous backlog, to make the right decisions, especially since the material prerequisites for a comprehensive expansion were not available.

In the spring of 1960, the following publishing houses were reestablished and opened again for business. In Wiesbaden: Insel Verlag; Dieterich'sche Verlagbuchhandlung; and Verlag Brockhaus. In the British zone of Berlin: the publishing houses of Springer; Walter de Gruyter; S. Fischer; and Herbig. In Hamburg: Goverts; Christina Wegner; Marion von Schröder, and Wolfgang Krüger. In Tübingen: J.C.B. Mohr and Rainer Wunderlich. Herder in Freiburg, and in Munich, the Zinnen-Verlag Kurt Desch and the publishing houses of Piper and Carl Hanser. Rowohlt opened in Stuttgart, and shortly was established in Hamburg.[381]

In these days, it was still difficult for publishers to receive copyrights from foreign authors, and they were largely dependent on the fiduciary support of the Allied authorities. The reading public anxiously awaited the appearance of the books published by the significant Bermann Fischer publishers and which has been published previously in the United States and Sweden. The Bermann Fischer company stood at the center of the literary emigration, and possessed the publishing rights of the most important foreign books.

In 1925, Gottfried Bermann, a Jewish doctor from Gleiwitz and an assistant in a surgical clinic in Berlin, married the daughter of the publisher, Samuel Fischer, and joined the S. Fischer Verlag. He became its director in 1932. After the Nazis took power, he emigrated to Vienna with the outlawed part of the company, narrowly escaping the SS in 1938. Two years after the reopening of the company in Stockholm, he moved with his family to the United States, and continued to direct the Stockholm firm from there.

In his autobiography, Bermann Fischer reported how, in the middle of September 1945, he received the first news of Peter Suhrkamp, who had continued to direct the branch of the company that had remained in Germany. At first, he received a letter that Suhrkamp had addressed to the American journalist Louis P. Lochner, who was staying in Berlin. " . . . All this time, I have regarded my publishing activity as a governorship or a trusteeship. I would be very grateful to you, Mr. Lochner, if you could help to connect Dr. Bermann Fischer and myself soon with respect to these last questions . . ." Then there came a handwritten, personal letter, which, as he described in his autobiography, deeply affected Bermann Fischer:

"Berlin, August 3, 1945

Dear Gottfried and Tutti Bermann,

The last news of you came to me via Hesse, in 1943. Since then, our destiny has hit us like an avalanche. On November 22–23, 1943, our apartment on the old Dernburgstrasse was destroyed by the bombings; early in the morning of December 4, with the attack on Leipzig, the distribution at Fleischer was also destroyed, as were the books in stock and those in process by Spamer, Poeschel, Haag Drugulin, and the Bibliogr. Institute. On February 15, 1944, our alternative quarters on Brahmsstrasse in Grunewald were destroyed, and on April 13 I was arrested by the Gestapo on charges of high treason. Since then, I stayed in various prisons and, in the beginning of January 1945, I entered the concentration camp of Sachsenhausen on the Oranienburg. I was released from there on February 8 with a serious case of pneumomia and pleurisy. I lay in the hospital in Potsdam waiting to die, until Potsdam was destroyed on April 14–15. Still very sick, I experienced the Russian entry of April 27. To top it all off, in the last days of April, the publishing house on Lützowstrasse was destroyed. My wife and I survived through this chain of experiences but we live and are about to begin working again. That will be difficult, in light of the fact that we will work among those who still have not understood and for whom it will be difficult to understand, who gather together their goods, antlike, among the rubble and the ruins, too tired to take heaven seriously, much less notice the glimmer of spirit and in the heart. I am trying to bring friends together into some kind of community, in order to undertake the mission laid upon us in the midst of ruin.

Incidently, I await you daily so that I can again place in your hands that which we took over from Mr. Fischer, what I for nine years have administered alone and personally. Outwardly, only rubble remains, but the reputation has remained pure and clean. You could, without shame, and perhaps without giving up what you have built up meanwhile there and in Stockholm, begin again here on a good foundation."[382]

According to Bermann Fischer, it was as though the dead had risen. "We had thought that the end of this time of horrors would come some day. But how strong are our imaginative powers! Now, it was no longer an empty thought. Incomprehensible, this letter was real, tangible, carrying the trusted handwriting of one who had disappeared into the unknown, of one who called to us in deepest need, and who wanted now to place in our hands the inheritance of that segment of the S. Fischer publishing company that had been wrested from us, that we had long since considered lost. There was only one thing to do in the face of this fate: to give assistance and support until the paths would meet again."[383] It was still illegal for Americans to conduct businesses in Germany. The books had to be made available to the book trade through a transfer of the publishing license to a German company. Thus Bermann Fischer asked Suhrkamp whether he had a license from the Control Commission for the opening or further business of the company, and whether he thought he would want to carry on with his company and reconnect with the Fischer organization, and in what manner. Suhrkamp responded that he held a license for the continuance of his company as the first publishing house in the British sector of Berlin. Furthermore, he said, "As you surely know, the change of the firm's name in 1942 occurred on the orders of the secretariate only after a long dispute. Now one of my first considerations was whether or not I should right away sign with S. Fischer Verlag once more. I decided, however, by avoiding any presumptions about your disposition, that for the time being I would call it Suhrkamp Verlag, formally S. Fischer Verlag." He again emphasized that he had never considered his task as anything but a trusteeship for the Fischer family, and that he expected them to again take possession of the company.[384]

In May, 1947, Bermann Fischer came to Germany. He met Suhrkamp in Berlin. After many days of dealings with the American authorities, Bermann Fischer transfered the publishing license of some of his important books to the American army, which on its part agreed to hand the rights over to the Suhrkamp Verlag. He also saw to it that the necessary paper would be available for the printing of these books. With this final hurdle crossed, the first book series of the Suhrkamp Verlag was begun, consisting mainly of books published in exile by the S. Fischer Verlag. As of 1948, there appeared in this series, for each publication, 50,000 copies that sold like hotcakes. Included were such works as Ernest Hemingway's *For Whom the Bell Tolls,* Herman Hesse's *Narziss und Goldmund,* Thomas Mann's *Ausgewahlte Erzählungen* (Selected Stories), followed by Ernst Penzoldt's *Die Powenzbande,* Willaim Saroyan's *Menschliche Komödie* (Human Comedy), Stefan Zqeig's *Sternstunden der Menschheit (The Ride of Fortune)* and *Amok,* Carl Zuckmayer's *Salware,* Hugo von Hofmannsthal's *Deutsches Lesebuch* (German Reader), and Stefan Zweig's *Die Welt von Gestern (The World of Yesterday).*

Bermann Fischer transferred to the Suhrkamp Verlag, which in 1946 had begun its own production of mostly smaller brochures, further licenses for, among other works: Thomas Mann's *Doctor Faustus* and *Joseph der Ernährer (Joseph the Provider,* the fourth volume of his Joseph-tetrology); Franz Werfel's *Song of Bernadette;* Thornton Wilder's *The Ides of March* and the stage rights for Wilder's plays; Franz Werfel's successful piece, *Jacobowsky and the Colonel;* and Carl Zuckmayer's equally popular *The Devil's General.*

In light of the growing East-West tension, Berlin seemed too dangerous a place for a publishing house. Therefore, Bermann Fischer recommended that Suhrkamp establish the Suhrkamp Verlag, formerly S. Fischer, in Frankfurt in 1947. Already by 1948, it had relieved itself of practically all its business in Berlin. Differences with Suhrkamp, who directed the Frankfurter and Berlin companies, became apparent in the beginning of 1949. Disagreements over diverging conceptions of the task and future perspective of the company finally resulted in their separation into two publishing houses.

However, before the separation became legal, Eugen Kogon was able to formulate an amicable agreement which was finally accepted by both parties. It was finalized at the reparations office in the district courts of Frankfurt am Main and Berlin on April 26, 1950:

"On the occasion of attempts by National Socialist forces to take possession of the S. Fischer Verlag, Dr. Gottfried Bermann Fischer and Peter Suhkramp attempted to defend their company against these endeavors, finding, in 1936, a way to maintain the name, substance and tradition of the publishing house and to keep it legal and effective. As this was achieved partly abroad and partly at home, both partners sought to rebuild the German firm, which had been destroyed by the war in the meantime. Both partners regarded their cooperation to be based on a trusteeship rooted in a mutually agreed upon goal. The following terms of agreement shall serve now to enforce joint efforts toward, on the one side, reestablishing the S. Fischer Verlag in its original form, and on the other, preserving those publishing activities developed under the name of Peter Suhrkamp as Peter Suhrkamp Verlag."[385]

The Fine Art of Words

Upon arriving in Frankfurt in October 1945, Hans Mayer was visited by Stephan Hermlin, who asked him to come "along." "Where to? To friends and to hear a poet read his works. I must have looked dumb. I had expected about everything, but a poetry reading in the destroyed city of Frankfurt on my first morning in Germany?

"But it did happen, and it was no deception to have called it a poetry reading. It took place in a middle-class residence in the west end of Frankfurt. The house was not destroyed, but in bad shape. The bombs had not fallen there. About 10 people came together in a nice, light living room filled with books. The sister of our host served 'real' tea, and there were some cookies. I remained cool and polite, everything seemed anachronistic to me. Wasn't I in Germany? What could these Germans have committed? Whose hands did I shake? . . . Or was everything OK? Was I in fact sitting together with good people, people who also went through difficulties during the Third Reich?

"The poet of this reading was a thin blond man in his mid-thirties, wearing a wornout uniform. He was thus a retired soldier. He had experienced and survived the war in Italy, which was mentioned during the talk. I felt very uneasy and would have liked to go, but Hermlin seemed to feel comfortable. Since I knew his severe, often too severe, political moralism, I thought everything there must be all right. Then the soldier read.

"Sonnets. A comprehensive cycle. Nothing was left out. Every sonnet, as was soon recognized, belonged to the composition. It had to do with war and with Italy and with the abstruse contrast between the two, war and Italy. There was no question that a talented lyricist was reading. The sonnets did not lie, neither by being rash nor by pretending false suffering. What we heard was the 'Venezianische Credo,' and the soldier in the threadbare uniform was Rudolf Hagelstange."[386]

Born in 1912, Hagelstange studied German philology in Berlin and became an editor of a serial section. Having served as a soldier in France and Italy, he was sent to a PW camp in 1945. After his discharge, he lived in Unteruhldingen on Lake Constance. He was one of the young writers just appearing on the scene. This generation still articulated the moral shock in the "fine art of words." It was hoped that strict form would be the best means of countering chaos. The prevalence of a literary tradition that had not developed during the Nazi rule but rather had become deprived, was enormous. Even when authors sought open-mindedly and resolutely to deal with the recent past and their own situation, they remained bound to it. Thus there prevailed a drive to escape intellectually from the present, to imagine a saved world, and to find shelter in romanticism and metaphysics."[387] For most of them, writing did not mean radical stock-taking, as was attempted lyrically by Gunter Eich shortly after the end of the war. Rather, it meant the conservation of the "linguistic inheritance," even though the shattered times should have caused them to doubt this inheritance.

Such formalism was even more widespread among the very popular nature poets. Obviously, "their" Hölderlin, Rilke, George and Hofmannsthal must have resounded continuously in their ears. For the most part, they responded uncreatively, though at times imaginatively, to the respective tendencies of the inner emigration.

In April 1947, Hans Mayer characterized the "wandering paths of German lyricists and publishers" as "the rustling in the shave grass."

> 'It sounds, like the word evening,
> and it conveys much more than many words,
> said thoughtlessly . . .'

A moment, please! Isn't this . . . How does it go in Hofmannsthal?

'. . . and yet, much is said with evening.
A word dripping with profundity and grief,
like rich honey from a honeycomb.'

With Victor Scheiterbauer's volume, *Glans zwischen Disteln and Dornen* (1946),[388] Mayer took an unimportant product to task. But even with writers who became successful, no reductionism could prevent their works from having an air of imitation about them. In an analysis of the lyrical view of life held by postwar Germans, Peter Rühmkorf argued that from a poetic point of view these gray years were by no means as golden as our recollection sometimes makes them seem.[389] The beautiful hand-in-hand of art and poverty, expression and privation, hunger and momentum and initiative is a fiction of the later overdose of prosperity. "It cannot be denied that the period between 1945 and 1947 had its own aura, consisting of enthusiasm for change and desire to survive. And yet, all good intentions did not lead to poems that could compare with what was called lyric after World War I. Above all, it is becoming clear that this period did not have its hunger-stricken face and that it did not produce an epoch-making style. The opposite seems true. It is astonishing that the first postwar publications had nothing to do with the turning and shaking of the foundations, with change or with a new beginning, and that the supercatastrophe produced little more than perfect mediocracy." People freed themselves from a time that had grown too big by affirming small and humble things. Heroic flatulence was answered with "cabaret." Green enclaves were wrestled from horror. The emerging public wanted again to become the little woman at home, after the infernal dance. Starvation was our daily ration and horror a daily occurrence. There was now a widespread desire for calm in the times. "What was of interest now were not stimulants but tranquilizers, not flight of fancy and storming of hell but comfort, support and the stability of tradition. And these were offered and promised already by the titles of most publications of that time: F. G. Jüngers *Das Weinberghaus* (The House in the Vineyard) and *Die Silberdistelklause* (The Carline Thistle Hermitage); R. A. Schröder's *Alten Mannes Sommer* (Old Man's Summer); Hans Carossa's *Abendländische Elegie* (Elegy of the West); Rudolf Hagelstange's *Venezianisches Credo* (Venetian Credo); Oda Schäfer's *Irdisches Geleit* (Earthly Escort); Albrecht Goes' *Die Herberge* (The Hostel); Anton Schnack's *Mittagswein* (Wine at Noon); Joseph Weinheber's *Hier ist das Wort* (Here is the Word); Georg von der Vring's *Verse für Minette* (Verses for Minette); Georg Britting's *Die Begeg-*

nung (The Encounter); Ernst Waldinger's *Die kühlen Bauernstuben* (The Cool Rooms of the Farming House); and Elisabeth Langässer's *Der Laubmann und die Rose* (The Leaf Man and the Rose).

The objection that there were still other publications beside the poetic hermitage of carline thistles, such as Haushofer's *Moabiter Sonette* (Moabit Sonnets), Nelly Sach's *Die Wohnungen des Todes* (In the Habitations of Death) and Marie Luise Kaschnitz's *Totentanz und Gedichte zur Zeit* (Dance of Death and Contemporary Poetry), overlooks the strikingly disproportionate ratios. "And where, after all, were the youth and the war returnees, the deeply troubled young people who are now 25 to 30 years old? Where did they make their appearances, define themselves as a generation, and paint the town red, no, pour red paint over the town? And where, the question is long overdue, were the traces, or even a scent, of a literature of awakening and change, a stylistic venture, a linguistic new beginning and a change in the sentence structure? That the traces weren't here, in this recurrence of Rilke, goes without saying. Hans Egon Holthusen wrote in 1947:

> 'Your death rises like a towering rock
> full of superiority and strength.
> I am fading, and my trifling grievance
> is like a man lost in the rocks.'

Was it perhaps that too much experience, an excess of external peril and inner unrest, caused them to lose their voice, their ability to articulate? Was it perhaps that the reality experienced did not fit into any form, space or style? The problem was best expressed by Wolfgang Borchert, the most talented prose writer of the young generation of returnees: '. . .who then, ach!, who knows a rhyme to the death-rattle of a battered lung, a rhyme to the shouts of execution, who knows the meter for the bark of automatic rifles . . .?'"

Apart from Borchert, who although he was himself quite agitated in his expressions, was a master of metaphoric language, many of the authors of that time knew how to a rhyme to horror. Advance and victory, the wild ecstasy of success, withdrawal, the bitter wine of defeat. The truth was figuratively and lyrically packaged. "This is the return home. This is valid. Oh tender, oh heavenly poverty of the last soldiers?" This was how Holthusen wrote about the "years in the labyrinth" in his *Trilogie des Krieges* (War Trilogy, 1946). He touched the nerve of the times, because he reflected "beautifully" on time and death.[390] In 1942 he let his "man before Stalingrad" describe the landscape of the war, on which "even the red thistles burned up." "God marked them off with a diamond/ out of sheer bitterness."

In one of the first cultural magazines of the postwar years, in 1945, Holthusen's poem *Tabula rasa* appeared. Following are its first lines: "To put an end to. To set a beginning,/ The unheard of, which frightens and weakens us."[391] Exactly this did not happen. What had already been heard "continued to be heard." The beginning was not preceded by an end.

The lyrical world view of the rubble years is characterized by a unique paradox. The dark reality was to be supplanted by beautiful art. The distancing from reality made the convergence with essence possible. While a conversation about trees signaled resistance in the totalitarian state, for everything was to be put into service, now poetic sublimation meant relief from daily labor. Those who had been without "intellectual goods" for 12 years, who were now "without means," equipped themselves with the word. "The sonnet, created against the unspirit, became a mere fashion of the resistance."[392] One was really to stand "Here in the Present," the title of a volume of poems by Holthusen in 1949 when one actually withdrew from it through pure composition. Wolfdietrich Schnurre formulated it as follows, "The more questionable my outer life became, the more bitterly my hostility to reality grew, and the more recklessly I destroyed the relations to all that was actively alive. I shut myself off. I withdrew into the ivory tower." Later he interpreted his statement, "Try to understand what it was, what it meant, for a twenty-five-year old in 1945, to have been on the wrong side for six and a half meaningless years of war. Please, try to understand the scruples and the pangs of conscience that preceded and accompanied my two acts of desertion. Furthermore, please, try to understand the most profound consequences of the significance of this, I would almost like to say, controlled schizophrenia that led to continuous crossing of boundaries and changes of fronts touching my very being. And then, I would like to ask you whether a seemingly exalted position, such as the one in the super temporal realm, in the ivory tower, has not continued to be defended because somebody wanted finally to hold onto his terrain, instead of 'betraying' it again. The obstinate defense of this cloudy position was due to a misunderstood will to survive. We knew what was going on. The great absurdity had given us its mark of Cain. For a long time, we wrote in the scanty shorthand of the person who had just barely made it. But since so many illustrious intellectuals had leaned over this banister, we did not want to leave the long-since-demolished ruins of the tower. We overlooked, however, the fact that even the bats had already left it."[393]

Inside the Ruins of the Ivory Tower

The illustrious intellectuals who leaned gracefully over the banister of the ruins of the ivory tower were the successful artists, the expert survivors of the declines and shipwrecks. They stylized their ability to survive into great solitude, sought to stay away from the simple folk, and observed leaves and stones as well as turbulences and explosions. They felt they belonged to the "few" who knew where the truth lay. In Ernst Jünger's novel *Auf den Marmorklippen* (1939), two worlds are contrasted. On the marble cliffs of Marina, there lives a humane and noble clan of longstanding culture, farming grapes and grain. It possesses erudition and churches, high magic and the arts. The ideal coastline of the settlement is saturated with Burgundian ritual. The other world is the land of the "shady characters." It is marked by the slyness of a hunter, a vital superiority, and is led by a demonically strong lord, the "chief forester." Though the longstanding culture is defeated, it does not perish. The knights board their ships and disappear into the ocean.[394]

Surviving in the ark. The rule of Hitler was evil, but the democratic leveling was also a horror. The marble cliffs are now endangered by Americanization. One can avoid the masses with a certain carriage. "Jünger," a thinker of magic aristocracy, "knows of the old human models, the knight, the cavalier, the king and the saint. But their possibility seems to have been lost in the modern world of the masses. Does he doubt their substance altogether? Even in the human realm, the substitutes prevail. The gnawing pain can be numbed by drugs, but there is no means of total alleviation. Remorsefully and with a type of bad conscience, the human slowly returns from the abyss of nothingness. Reverence and memory are not sufficient for the rebirth of the eternal. But Jünger knows that understanding, memory and reverence are already human participations in reality."[395]

Tired of metropolitan hypersensibility at the beginning of the Third Reich, Gottfreid Benn was fascinated by populist irrationalism and the semiconscious, antienlightenment historico-morphological state which Fascism represented. Later he analyzed this state as a philistine rebellion that became abysmal in its numbness:

"They are a people of the masses without a defined taste, on the whole untouched by the moral and aesthetic refinement of the bordering civilizations, of philosophically confused idealistic concepts, prosaically somber and dull. They are a practical people who, as their development has shown, found only a biological escape from the spiritualization brought about by romanticism or universalism. They have permitted the rise of an antisemitic movement whose phraseology conjured up the people's lowest ideals, that is, settlements of small houses in which sexual relations are subsidized by tax laws. In their kitchens one can find homemade rape-seed oil, omelets made from home incubated eggs, and home grown barley. They wear native *Kurkeln* and regional flannel. And their art and inner life consists of soldier's songs blaring over the radio. In these things, a people recognizes itself. A horizontal bar for gymnastics in the garden and a bonfire on a hill on Midsummer's Eve. This is the full blooded German. With a shooting range and a stein full of beer, the Germans are in their element. And now they look with expectation at the educated nations, anticipating, with the naiveté of a child, something awesome and amazing."[396]

In view of the "realm of the lower demons,"[397] style turns into attitude and morality. For Benn, the poem was the product of the great lyrical self that could only receive warmth from the pathos of loneliness. It was the most important result of art's attempt, in the face of the general disintegration of content, to experience the self as content and to form a new style from these experiences. In the face of general nihilism, there remained only the transcendence of creative desire. Lyric should either be exorbitant, or should not exist at all. In this sense, the "absolute poem" is the "poem without faith, the poem without hope, the poem that addresses nobody, the poem made of words that you construct fascinatingly."[398] Form is the highest content and being is the existential mission of the artist, his aim. The new gods are order and form, the new principles are expression, character and style. Everything else signifies decline.

The small and the smaller lyrical selves of the postwar years were hanging on the lips of the great lyrical super self. Benn's parlando pronounced the message that the world was out of joint and could not be glued together anymore. However, if one could but capture it poetically, one would be able to survive it. This was nothing but the pride of the defeated who understood their inner victory.

The illustrious intellectuals of the literary aristocracy waved an aesthetic "stay solitary" to the young writers. And indeed, the generation of the rubble years, having been thrown into the loss of orientation of the total collapse, joyfully seized the knowledge that, as Jünger said in his *Marmorklippen*, "the destruction does not find its home in the elements and its delusion swirls on the surface like images in the fog that cannot withstand the sun." And the lost generation suspected that "if we were to live in such indestructable cells, we would come out of each phase of destruction as though we were passing through open doors from one festive chamber into ever more splendid ones." And the returnees who then learned that they had been misused by the "shady characters" and who did not trust the present change, were gripped by a "shudder in the innermost self." In view of the abiding values provided by the authors, they recognized that "there were still some noble ones among us in whose hearts the knowledge of the great order is alive and confirmed." And as they were led to follow these high examples, they pledged, "in the future we shall rather die lonely with the free, than march triumphantly with the slaves."[399]

Beyond the River of Life

The message of those who had leaned over the banister, calling for the abandonment of all world-affirming activity, found its response. Hermann Kasack's novel *Die Stadt hinter dem Strom* (*The City Beyond the River,* 1947) was influenced both by the use of allegorical metaphors and parable-like abstract constructions found in Jünger's work and in Franz Kafka's great posthumous novels. This novel was so well received not the least because it went beyond surrealistically and symbolically the depiction of the brutal facticity of horrible events. The events were transposed into a no-man's-land that somewhat resembled the no-man's-land in which people lived daily, though more in the sense of "remnants of the day" appearing within a dreamlike landscape that extended into metaphorical dimensions. In a letter from the town administration, Dr. Robert Lindhoff is asked "to come." He takes a train, crosses a large stream and arrives at the main station of the city. He meets Anna, his sweetheart, who had departed a few months previously and he meets his father. Suddenly he realizes that he has crossed the river of life, and is now in the city of death. The city beyond the stream, however, is only an intermediate realm, a region between the realm of the living and the realm of the ultimately forgotten ones, the zone of last remembrance. One day, Lindhoff returns to life. But what message could he bring? All his loved ones and acquaintances will eventually have to leave even the intermediate realm of the city beyond the stream. They will be called to enter the realm of the unreachable. The living are not permitted to pursue them. "When I finished the book in the summer of 1946," reports the author, "I was 50 years old."

"It is the right point in time not to let oneself be confused either by fame or by banishment. As a chronicler, moreover, I went through hell, which we call euphemistically our time on earth. I had suffered vividly the glasslike, figurative situation of our reality, finding myself invulnerable and changed. The reader, too, who through the method of narrative becomes the chronicler's companion and neighbor, could, I think, look differently at reality after these experiences, less fearfully, more at ease, and, though not comforted, certainly freed from the exaggerated seriousness of his or her personal importance. . . . Like a seismograph registers the variations of the earth's crust, I wrote down the tremors of our present existence without considering dogmas and ideologies. The poetic diagnosis shows that the European of the twentieth Christian century looks quite helpless. That is not my fault. But it would be a fault to idealize reality. The task of an author consists of being the conscience of the time. Otherwise writing would be a vain game.[400]

Most critics bothered less with Kasack's metaphysics. What they found problematic was rather the "city" which they recognized as an image of the contemporary time and world. The *Tagesspiegel* wrote, "Our century of mass man, mass murder, mass love, and mass craze, of total systems, dark powers and the emancipation of the spirit, approaching the perversion of automatic, specialized and materialized thinking, is mirrored on the level of a higher dimension where the reality near death seems to become transparent. We are horrified, for it is as if we were foreseeing our own future."[401]

In Elisabeth Langgässer's novel *Das unauslöschliche Siegel,* which was valued as a great literary event in 1946, individual events are dissolved into transpersonal ones. These events happen within a world theater that is determined by the "excessive" powers of baptism and grace. In a review, Erich Pfeiffer-Belli is deeply moved by the fact that a work like this could be written during the frightful spiritual silence of Hitler's Third Reich, a work possessing such a unique power of expression, with an icy spirituality and an almost chaotic richness of internal pictures. "It is a book that speaks of a peculiar love-hate relationship beween blood and spirit. With its transcendent longing, its passionate faith, questioning and doubt, it is truly unique in the world of the new German literature. This original work is the more admirable as it is the work of a woman whom fate has especially tested and made suffer, precisely because of this Third Reich, but also endowed with special grace, as proven on every page of this book." He sees vision alternating with "supernaturalism," and stridency with the greatest tenderness. Through the author's bold grip, the chaos of the world and of humanity seems ordered at least for a moment. "Perhaps only those readers, who, full of presentiment and faith, know themselves close to the faithfulness of Langgässer at least during the reading, will recognize from which depths and from which sources she draws the power of expression, the purposeful interpretation and her faith, all of which are involved in the attempt to describe the downfall and the new creation of a world."[402]

The reception of the book as well as the rhapsodic critics indicate an important trend in the literary consciousness of the rubble years, that an allegorical, mystic-mythical relationship with reality was preferred to direct realistic description. People had been exposed to a senseless reality for too long, and now craved an interpretation *sub specie aeternitatis.*

Old and New Language

"Time rushes on like it had on seven-league boots. It has been two years since we left the barbed wire for good. A singing black soldier drove us to the station of the small town in Upper Bavaria. Taking our seabags we climbed off the truck, and there we stood in our black uniforms with the letters PW painted on our backs, in freedom. We were home again. Germany waited for us, we were told everywhere. Wandering through its ruins felt like walking through a foreign land. First we had to get used to the nightmarish feeling that seemed to overpower the inhabitants. That was two years ago."

The above quotation was written by Walter Kolbenhoff in 1948, when he was 40 years old. His contribution was announced as a "voice from the young generation of writers."[403] Again and again, this generation was asked why there was no young literature in Germany and what caused this silence. Where was the literature that faced the present without avoiding it, that did not care about art products but about providing the truth of its statements? "I felt compelled to think of my friend G. when reading these questions. He was released at about the same time from war prison. This young man had been an apprentice typesetter. He had struggled with an iron-willed industriousness to gain education, and he wrote many small pieces. In 1936 he was imprisoned on charges of high treason, spending several years behind bars. There then followed years of uncertainty and the impossibility of publishing any writings. The war came, and he was put into the famous division 999 and sent to Africa. He then lived for a couple of years in prison behind barbed wire. Now he sits and writes in a small, dark and cold room in northern Berlin. The numerous experiences of his adventurous life threaten to make him explode. He says, 'Give me time! Every minute is precious. Please, wait, I have a lot to say.'"

As mentioned, Kolbenhoff has been at home for two years visiting a good number of young writers. He knows their feelings. Nobody could understand them better than one who, together with them, dragged his rifle across the roads of Europe, who got to know the hells of Sevastopol, El Alamein and Montecassino, and who on quiet evenings stared, weary and exhausted, through the barbed wire of PW camps. "Give us time? What are two years? Everything is destroyed, why should our souls not be destroyed?" One should read the polished articles and stories of the "old." These are sparkling pearls, the skillful first class writings of expert literary figures. "I take my hat off to their fascinating skill that was trained and cultivated in long olympic years. But I venture to affirm that the former typesetter from Berlin will in a short time be writing things that will move our hearts more passionately and grip our conscience more strongly than the glittering sentences of the others. Don't forget, they crawled with bleeding hearts through the cities of their own fatherland, they crawled through debris and mud, they felt the iron boot in their necks and did not break." In Kolbenhoff, too, one notices the paradox of the "style of the rubble years." They wanted to break open the old patterns of speech, of thinking and feeling, and yet articulate according to popular "metaphoric dramaturgy." Indeed, this generation did not have the time for exercises in style. The new freedom, however, which after years of dread now claimed to liberate their hearts enthusiastically, was tied to the pathos of the "old" language. "Perhaps their sentences will not sparkle as much," yet, they did. "They speak the language of the present. They will express that which as of now has remained unspoken by the tortured, lost and crazed people to whom they belong." They spoke the language of the past, and what they expressed had been expressed in this way before . . .

How does this sound, asked Hellmuth von Cube in a reply to Kolbenhoff's essay? This sound is quite familiar to us. It not only sounds, it is. It is the same tragic pathos, the same mixture of sentimentality and arrogance, the same front-soldier mentality, the same appeal to heart and conscience. There is the same hardly concealed animosity against spirit and all that belongs to it, freedom, grace, irony, smiling insight, love of form, and aristocratic bearing. It is the same spirit that the demagogues and their following of the petite bourgeoisie brought against the intellectuals 15 years earlier. The tone and the melodies of that music soon turned into the shout of the masses, the scream from the concentration camps, and the thunder of guns. And the wise people beyond the Elbe River, tuned to the balalaika of cultural dictatorship, do not sound much different. Herr Kolbenhoff, I am sure, was no National Socialist. But there is only a tiny step from his words to the decision to put the spirit under guard and to talk sense into the playful, light-minded muses. In any case, he is more concerned with the spirit of the time than with the time of the spirit."[404]

In this dispute, the richly metaphoric Kolbenhoff turned the tables and rejected Cube's criticism as "metaphoric polemic." Ultimately, such disputes circled around the problem of the "old" and "new" language. In the Third Reich, the language of dialectics was persecuted and banished. It had never become very influential. It was pushed aside and forgotten. The National Socialist nomenclature had left shell-like concepts of unimaginable barbarity behind, such as Nordicization, master race, extermination of Jews, human experiments, gassing, and the final solution. . . . To this now was added the vocabulary of the bureaucracy of reeducation: denazification tribunal, nominal participants, *Persilschein,* meaning discharged from any involvement with National Socialism . . . and a jargon that rigorously democratized human relations, boss, babysitter, teenager, fan. . . .[405]

Like "formal language," political language on the whole was determined by "affirmative patterns of speech," which now were "employed for the military victories of democracy." During his newspaper work, Hans Habe noticed that apparently only a few German journalists remained untouched by the bacillus of Hitler language. "One of the best German journalists brought me an excellent article in which he denounced the language of the inhuman creature, asking for the return to German language. It was the excellent article of a man with the best of intentions, and yet, we were not able to print it because it was written in Hitler German."[406] What, however, comprised "Hitler German" could not easily be determined. If one disregarded contents, one found a pathos of oppression, as well as of freedom. Metaphors could serve both freedom and repression.

In November 1945, Dolf Sternberger began his column "Aus dem Wörterbuch des Unmenschen" (From the Dictionary of the Inhuman) in the first issue of the journal *Die Wandlung.* This series, in which also Gerhard Storz and W. E. Süskind were instrumental, continued for three years. Its intention was to point out and to deal with, through language analysis, the degeneration of words and concepts in the Third Reich. A democratic language as the articulation of humane attitude and morality was to replace the forced sentence structure, stunted grammar, and the monstruous and crippled vocabulary expressive of despotism. Among others, the following words were denounced: (In this list, the German words are retained. Most of the translations do not carry the same problematic usage that the German word carried within the ideological context of the Third Reich.) *Anliegen* (request); *Ausrichtung* (alignment); *Betreuung* (control); *charakterlich* (of character); *Durchführen* (carry through); *Einsatz* (involvement); *Frauenarbeit* (women's work); *Gestaltung* (shaping); *Kulturschaffende* (those creating culture); *Lager* (camp); *leistungsmassig* (concerning efficiency); *mädel;* (girl); *Menschenbehandlung* (treatment of people); *organisieren* (to organize); *Propaganda* (propaganda); *Schulung* (training); *Vertreter* (representative); and *Zeitgeschehen* (current affairs).

"Language is the gift of human beings only, the confusing and liberating, the treasonous and illuminating, the expanding and shackling, the loosening and the binding, the saving and the dangerous medium and seal of human nature. The extent and the kind of language that one speaks determines the extent and the kind of knowledge that one can gain about things, the world and nature. And every word spoken changes the world in which one moves, changes the person speaking and his or her place in the world. Therefore, there is nothing about language that is meaningless, and nothing is so essential as the *façon de parler.* The ruin of language is the ruin of the person. Let us be on our guard! Words and sentences may be both gardens and dungeons, into which we lock ourselves by speaking. And the definition, that language is the gift of human beings only, or that it is a human gift, does not offer security, because the notion of the human includes the possibility and reality of the inhuman. Otherwise this notion is inadequate. Therefore, we must examine this very point, for we know inhumanity. Human beings as inhuman also have their vocabulary, their specific grammar, and their specific sentence structure. We would like to trace their vocabulary and recognize in language the objects to which it gives meaning. Regretably, it is no foreign language, but this dictionary has a task contrary to the other and familiar dictionaries, that is, it is to make this language foreign to us. . . ."[407]

Contrary to a pseudo-idealistic intoxication of words, "noise of words," and an ideology-oriented jargon, "language of inhumans," enlightened desire aimed at a new language that was "realistic." "Today's writing youth has not recovered from the tremendous shock of the last years and is withdrawing into an imaginary, romantic world. An example of this is the colossal increase of lyricists who, for the most part, write good things. These romantics, however, stil live in another time and their models are mainly Rilke, George, Heyse, Alverdes and others. They do not speak in a contemporary language. We will let all those young writers who have talent and something to say speak up in the *Skorpion.* Our language will be modern and yet there will be enough room for real talents." With these words, Hans Werner Richter stated, in November 1947, his intention to found a new journal. The *Skorpion* was to be a mouthpiece for the growing young German literature and to be sponsored by the "Gruppe 47" (Group 47).[408]

Among the young authors meeting in the house of the writer Ilse Schneider-Lengyel in the Allgäu were Walter Kolbenhoff, Alfred Andersch, Wolfdietrich Schnurre, Heinz Friedrich, Ernst Kreuder, Walter A. Guggenheimer, Wolfgang Bächler, Friedrich Minssen, Nicolaus Sombart, Günter Eich, Walter Hilsbecher and Walter Heist. Most of them were former collaborators on the prohibited *Ruf.*

"In the same sense that we thought the political concepts of the past were no longer applicable, we held the literary schools of the past to be outmoded. I even considered the period of the literary revolution, from naturalism to expressionism, to be over for good. There was to come about a new literature after this collapse and not a new school that would only continue the experiments of form undertaken by the old one. This literature was to stand in close relation with reality, similar to the neo-realism that was just beginning in Italy. This literature was to serve political commitment and truth. We believed that in the long run it would, though indirectly, influence the social and political development. What we did not want, however, was literature of agitation. This would have been unliterature *(Un-Literatur),* propaganda, and we had been saturated with that by the Third Reich and by the parties before that. What about language? We had . . . turned against the slave language of the Third Reich, which we had called *Kalligraphie,* and against the party and propaganda language of the Third Reich. The slave language was the language of the inner emigration whose critique of the dictatorship was esoterically coded, known only to the initiate and the like minded. What about the official language of the Third Reich? We in the *Ruf* had also been accused of having used this language, which was, so to speak, the language of our enemies. That may be true. The young people returning from World War II had grown up and lived in the housing of this language. At first, they were unable to avoid it. But the following radical period of clearing caused the change."[409]

Richter gave an extensive report on the first meeting of the "Group 47." It vividly portrays the new style of language and speech which was aspired to by this group.

"We sit in a circle on the floor of Ilse Schneider-Lengyel's living room, some more lying than sitting. We are listening, strenuously, concentratedly, rarely expressing our affirmation or displeasure through nods, laughter or other gestures. No one interrupts with shouts or remarks. The reader always takes his or her seat beside me. It is self-evident, it just happened. After the first reading by Wolfdietrich Schnurre, I asked, 'Well, please, some criticism. What do you have to say to it?' And suddenly something begins to happen in a form that nobody expected. The tone of the critical utterances is coarse, the sentences short, tight and unequivocal. Nobody minces matters. Every word read is weighed as to whether it is useable or outdated and used up through the years of dictatorship, the time of the great wear and tear of language. Every sentence is examined, every unnecessary frill reproved. Big words that have lost their meaning and content are discarded, such as heart, pain, desire and sorrow *(Herz, Schmerz, Lust, Leid).* What endures before the ears of the participants are the tight declarative sentences. Gertrude Stein and Ernest Hemingway are in a way present in the room without anybody noticing. Dialogue and the spoken style predominate. 'Yes,' says he, or also 'no,' and the 'no' and the 'yes' endure. Yet, already the next word composition 'Yes, my dear' is scornfully discarded. Who, after all, still uses 'my dear,' and if he does so, he uses it in speech, but is unable to put it in writing. If he in fact does write it, it would be in an ironic sense. But irony is missing in the first years of the new beginning.

"What also finds expression without being noticed is the declarative language of the 'common soldier,' the reduction of language to the necessary, a turning away from the idleness of beautiful words and a turning towards their unmediated relation to reality. They have all learned it among the nation's masses where they have lived day by day for years, in the companies, in the barracks, in the camps and the PW camps. During that time they lived always on the border of human existence, thereby becoming distrustful and keen."[410]

A few months later, in *Tausend Gramm,* a volume of short stories by new story tellers, Wolfgang Weyrauch named the literature which had become visible through this private and intimate meeting at the Bannwald Lake "clearing literature" *(Kahlschlagliteratur).* The artistic language cultivated by the bourgeoisie, the stylized "penmanship" in all its variations, was now taboo. The bourgeois artistic language was taboo. It appeared outmoded, rusty and untruthful.

"There was nothing that endured in light of the reality in which we lived. There was a need for a new language that would make this reality transparent, a language of direct expression, clear, unequivocal and precise."[411]

At a meeting in Inzighofen in 1950, Günter Eich received the award of the "Group 47," its first award. This recognition was given to him in part for the following poem, *Frankischtibetanischer Kirschgarten.*

The scarecrow with fluttering sleeves,
whom does he seize?
The rabbit skin in branches
scares the starlings but not me.

The swinging scythe,
tin foil lifted high
little tin windmills turn
wind-rattled in the sky.

The sparrows' chatter is far away
and street noise too is fading,
upon the sloping cherry orchard
invisible shapes are praying.

Read upon the empty banners:
om mani padme hum,
the signs that come from lands surrounding
Lhasa and Kumbum.

And hear from regions such as these
the prayers that multiply
when mills so strangely whirl around
on cherry trees up high.[412]

The presentation of the award was characteristic of the quick change that had occurred in the consciousness of language. The "clearing literature" had come to an end after hardly having begun. While reduction first served the concretization of and the fixation on a real, historical world, now it aimed at supertemporal universality. The "pure poem" characterizes the beginning of change, and the time of "magic poetic" in which the material things "fade," returns with this spiritual transfigurative style. "In this connection, in spite of the political motivation, the effects of the 'hermetical' poetic language of Paul Celan is recognizable. Contrary to the intention of the author, the numerous political and autobiographical references remain so highly coded for the reader, who also brings along his or her formally acquired reading and interpretative habits, that the poems also allow for purely formal aesthetical and uplifting interpretations, thus cancelling the enlightening impulses of the poems. The award to Eich in 1950 may be seen as symptomatic of the development of literary language in the fifties."[413]

Literature Awards

The development of the "new literature" was dichotomous. Some stayed consciously or unconsciously on the path to inwardness and conservative preservation. These were introspective, fostering their isolated "authenticity." Others sought to gain a multitude of experiences, to open up, and to connect with world literature and its movements. The province, though, was not always provincial, and the metropolis not always urban. The inward path discovered values that especially nationalist and National Socialist petite bourgeoisie despised and destroyed. The rehabilitated "yellow literature," preoccupied with fashions and trends, most often did not find the time and the strength for in-depth reflection.

Apart from all the differentiation necessary for the evaluation of individual authors and works, it is possible to make the general observation that the literature which failed to open toward the outside, continuing to believe that essence could only be found in a "vertical direction," got stuck in skillful superficiality with a pretence of depth. Such tendencies of isolation were very widespread, supported by the public taste. This fact is proven by the literature awards after 1945 that Friedrich Kroll rightly referred to as sign posts into restoration.[414]

The tradition of these awards goes back to the Weimar Republic: the Lessing Prize of the Free and Hanseatic City of Hamburg was established in 1930; the Georg Büchner Prize in 1923, reestablished in 1945, and since 1949 awarded by the German Academy of Language and Writing; the Immermann Prize of the City of Düsseldorf in 1935, reestablished in 1947; the Literature Prize of the City of Munich in 1927, reestablished in 1947; and the Wilhelm Raage Prize of the City of Braunschweig, reestablished in 1946. These and other literature prizes were discontinued during the war years and for the most part not taken up for some time after the collapse. The Georg

Büchner Prize was a significant exception to this. Beginning in 1933, it was no longer awarded until the end of World War II. In 1945, the prize went to the hardly known Hans Schiebelhuth and in 1946 Fritz Usinger, two authors whose beginnings were connected to the active "Darmstadter Dichterkreis" (Darmstadt Circle of Poets). Usinger had published a number of volumes of poetry between 1933 and 1945 in Germany. After expressionistic attempts under Stefan George's influence, he came to write in strict lyrical forms such as the sonnet, ode, hymn and elegy.

In 1945, the city of Munich conferred its Literature Prize on Peter Dörfler, an often sentimental narrative writer, deeply rooted in his land, who had actively published during the Third Reich. According to Friedhelm Kroll, what Joseph Bernhard said about Dörfler in the *Nahdbuch der deutschen Gegenwartsliteratur* (edited by Hermann Kunisch) could have been said on the occasion of quite a number of award ceremonies. "Trusting in the principle of immanent Christianity, he remained in control and true to his disposition and existence in the midst of the confusion of polarities. His basically priest-like nature, aiming at the salvation of all things, determined also his poetic life work, open to spaces and times and full of life's warmth and faithful wisdom."[415] This quotation sums up all themes that warrant receiving a prize, elevating them metaphysically and salvifically.

In 1947 the Literature Prize of the City of Munich went to Gertrud von Le Fort, in 1948 to Ernst Penzoldt, and in 1949 to Georg Schwarz.

In 1923, Ernst Wiechert received the last Raabe Prize before the National Socialist takeover. In 1944 it went to Ricarda Huch, in 1947 to Fritz von Unruh, in 1948 to Werner Bergengruben, and in 1949 to Ina Seidel. The Lessing Prize, awarded to the historian of literature Freidrich Gundolf in 1930, went to Rudolf Alexander Schröder in 1947.

The Immermann Prize of the City of Düsseldorf was the main prize for Fascist authors during the Third Reich. It was not reinstituted until 1947, when it was given to Emil Barth. According to Heinrich Vormweg, this occasion was more than just an expression of regional specificity. Barth wrote his *Aufzeichnungen und Meditationen* (Notations and Meditations) between 1943 and 1945 in Haan/Rheinland. It was then published in 1946 under the title *Lemuria.* This diary can be seen as a textbook case of a "voice of the inner emigration," as a testimony of one who was permanently fleeing from current affairs, and as an attempt to rescue historically concrete confrontations on a higher and more detached level. In

Vormweg's view, there was no question that the reception of Barth's diary after 1945 had representative significance. "The 'spiritual German' public heard this message faithfully. The tradition of inwardness, held publicly in this way and conceded to by the Nazis, became the ideological basis and foundation of legitimization for the inner emigration. In every way, Emil Barth's diary signals a fundamental tendency of the immediate postwar time, its determining fundamental tendency."[416]

The Fontane Prize was newly founded in 1948. It was first received by Hermann Kasack for his work *Die Stadt hinter dem Strom (The City Beyond the River).* He was followed by Friedrich Georg Jünger, a master of "heroic songs and strict form."

The fact that Günter Eich received the prize of the "Group 47" only appeared to stand in contrast to the trend in prize presentation. Indeed, as one of the initiators of the clearing literature, he irritated the "jingling word style" of the inner emigration with his terse, realistic style. At the time of the presentation of the prize, he was already on the way back to coded esotericism. Moreover, Eich may be viewed as a representative of the continuity that spans from the antimodernism of the "Kolonne" Circle of 1929 to 1930, to which he belonged, through the years of the Third Reich, during which he continued to publish, to the postwar years. The "Group 47" furnished him, though, with the aura of a literary novitiate. The "Group 47" claimed to be an organ for the new beginning of literature, an authority of legitimization that prided itself on its interpretation of both the literature of the Weimar Republic and the anti-Fascist literature of the exile as sunken worlds of literature with which one could no longer connect. At the same time, the "Group 47" held the authors of the exile in high regard. "In this light, the 'Group 47' appears, so to speak, as the executioner of the will of the 'Kolonne' Circle, insofar as it was essential for the 'attenuation of modern style' and its fusion with 'a metaphysical meditative literature.' In this sense, the 'young generation' also helped to pave the road for a moderate, or more precisely, for a restorative modernity."[417]

The authors of the exile were suspected of ideology. Anti-fascist authors figured among hardly any of the prize lists. Instead, the writers of modernity, tuned into the mood of restoration, rose to become the prized authors of the total new beginning, of the "stocktaking." Their real image was distorted through the myth that all authors of the young generation stood at the beginning of their literary socialization.

"Do You Think, For Example, That Zurich . . ."

Gottfried Benn was a key figure of the poetic worldview of the rubble years, insofar as his writing brought together irrationalism and rationalism, escape from and longing for the world. On the one hand, he saw a mistake in the brain. "A bluff for the middle class. Whether one walks upright or swims vertically, all is a matter of habit. It has mis-thought all of my associations. The cosmos rushes by. I am standing at the shore, gray, steep, and dead. My branches are still hanging into the water that flows by, but they are only looking inward, into the growing nightfall of their blood, into the growing coldness of their parts. I am separated and myself. I am not moving anymore.

"Where to? Where to? Why such a long path? What is it that we should gather around? That for one moment I stopped thinking and I didn't lose my extremities?

"I am associating with something. Something is happening within me. Now I only feel the brain. It lies like a braid on my head. It gives me nausea from the top on down. Everywhere, it is at work go, yellow, yellow, brain, brain. It is hanging down between my legs . . . I clearly feel it knocking on my ankles.

"Oh how much I would like to live this way again, grass, sand, flowers, a wide field. In mild and cool waves, the earth carries everything toward me. No more head. I am being lived."[418]

On the other hand, it was especially Benn who pointed the way into the "promised land" of metropolitan urban freedom for all those, especially younger ones, who, having carried the classicists in their heads, got stuck at Carossa or Hautmann. The motto was "stay close." "The lyricist cannot know enough, cannot work enough. He or she must be close to everything, must be oriented around where the world is today, on what hour the sun stands directly over the earth today. The great matadors say that one has to fight close up to the bull, and then perhaps there will be victory. A poem should not leave anything to chance. What Valéry wrote about Moltke, that 'to this cool hero the real enemy is chance' may also be applied to the lyricists. They must linguistically secure their poems against incursions and possible disturbances. They, themselves, must clean up their front. They must have nostrils, Neitzsche remarked that his genius lay in his nostrils, nostrils at all starting places and paddocks, at those intellectual points where material and ideational dialectics separate from one another like two sea monsters spewing at each other with spirit and poison, with books and strikes; and there, where the newest creation of Schiaparelli, made of ash gray linen and pineapple yellow organdy, indicates a change in fashion. Out of everything come colors, the imponderable nuances, the *valeurs,* out of everything comes the poem."[419]

The young generation identified with Benn's ambivalence. It did not quite know whether to make a virtue out of necessity and remain "internal," or whether it should leave behind the fortress of the soul, raze the walls of metaphorical haughtiness, and throw itself into the whirlpool of metropolitan modernity.

> Do you think, for example, that Zurich
> is a city more profound,
> a place where wonders and blessings
> can ever and always be found?
>
> Do you think that from Havana,
> hibiscus red and white,
> there falls an eternal manna
> to save you from your plight?
>
> On station roads and *rue,*
> on the boulevard, lido and lane,
> even on fifth avenue,
> emptiness hits you again.
>
> Alas! to travel is futile.
> Only late do you come to yourself.
> Stay and preserve it calmly
> that I that defines itself.[420]

When Erich Kästner came to Zurich for the first time after the war in 1947, he marveled at the "metropolitan melody" that, it was believed, would never resound again in German cities.[421] What a feeling to roll over asphalt, pulled by smooth, well-fed horses, and to see open carriages with rosy-cheeked brides and grooms. The coachmen wear shiny silk top hats, and fluttering strings on their coats. There are plates of almonds and coffee beans on the counters of bars, and guests serve themselves with indifference. There are well-stocked shoe shops with nylon stockings in the windows. English, American, Turkish, and Greek cigarettes are available everywhere. There are matches. Their boxes have two striking surfaces which to Kästner seems almost a sin. The shop assistants are smooth like silk. The barber is concerned, asking whether the razor is indeed sharp enough. Baskets of strawberries stand in front of the shops stacked almost to the curb. Mounds of vegetables are piled behind the windows. Before dinner, a cart richly covered with hors d'oeuvres is pulled up. There are glittering jewlery shops, plentiful confectioner's shops, sound banks, book shops in which one may buy an unlimited number of books, travel agencies, department and clothing stores with Persian carpets, clocks, cameras; perfume shops, and full newsstands. "This was once also our world, and now we stare at it as if over a book of fairy tales like children who cannot read and look at the pictures with wonder."

Upon returning home to Schwabing, while standing at the window and reflecting on his days in Zurich, Kästner notices an old gentleman with his dachshund coming up the street. With measured steps they pass by the rubble heaps now overgrown with weeds. But the measuredness is not quite real. Suddenly, with a half-filled linen bag, the man climbs carefully and bashfully up on one of the overgrown heaps of debris, searching around in the green weeds. "What's he pulling out? What is he bringing into the barn? Dandelion and sorrel leaves! His wife had sent him out to harvest some vegetables and lettuce. Hastily he pushes the nourishing weeds into his gray bag, climbs carefully down again, shakes the dust out of his trousers, and walks as elastically as a rheumatic attaché around the corner."

Kästner participated in the congress of the PEN Club. He met with "unforgotten friends and acquaintances, especially with publishers, writers and actors that escaped the threats and death of the Third Reich and thus had to face other miseries, anxieties and pains." Of the German and Austrian writers, he met with Werner Bergengruen, Ossip Kalenter, and N. O. Skarpi who now lived in Switzerland; Thomas Mann from California; Alfred Kerr, Robert Neumann, Friedrich Burschell, Richard Friedenthal, Hilde Spiel and Peter de Mendelssohn from London: Franz Csokor from Rome; and Max Tau from Oslo. Erich Kästner delivered to the congress of the PEN Club the newly passed declaration of the "Association for the Protection of German Writers" founded in May 1946:

"Those among the German writers who withstood the seductions and barbarity of the authoritarian political systems bring to the PEN Club at its 19th congress friendly greetings and best wishes. They deeply regret that two years after the end of all war activities, the difficulties still seem insurmountable, thus preventing real peace . . . While they are of the opinion, which they thus make known to their own people, that the virtue of the defeated is humility, they believe that they have the right to say that the virtue of the victors is magnanimity. They appeal to that humility and to this magnanimity with the greatest concern that the system of life in Europe is in impending danger of being totally destroyed. They expect from the discerning German writers an understanding of the great task that arises today in the struggle against any surviving attitude of injustice and inhumanity. They hope that the discerning writers in other countries will make known among the victorious peoples the insight of how alone the endangered are to be saved, namely, through a general act of humanity, consisting not of words but of deeds. This act would be the first step toward the intended goal of the establishment of a better world."[422] In 1948, the "German PEN Center" was reestablished in Göttingen. In 1952, it was divided into the "German PEN Center of the Federal Republic" and the "German PEN Center of East and West," the latter of which renamed itself the "PEN Center of the German Democratic Republic."

Goethe the Helper in Need

To save that which is endangered, daring deeds of humanity, Goethe proved of special assistance during the rubble years. At the same time, the controversies surrounding the Goethe Prize and the Goethe anniversery reflected the difficulties which the depressed, divided nation experienced in the process of gaining a new identity.

In February of 1947, Hans Mayer expressed the opinion that each generation enters upon the inheritance of the past always anew with new discoveries and also new injustices.[423] Such an extreme "dialectical" relationship to the classics, however, was in no way typical for the rubble years. The grand old master Goethe, as well as Schiller, was, without change, honored widely. "He was ours, he is ours, and he will be ours." Such a suggestion, with the help of which they continued to understand themselves as a people of poets and thinkers *(ein Volk der Dichter und Denker),* assisted in the transcendence of the gloomy reality. Those among the rhapsodic who had more integrity acknowledged the fact that these people in their recent history were especially a people of judges and executioners *(ein Volk der Richter und Henker).* Hence, they sought to prove with even greater pathos that such an error could be overcome if one would only absorb Goethe with the full power of one's feelings.

In an aphoristic formulation, Werner Bergengruen asserted that the development of the last 150 years could be summarized in the following: from I. G. Cotta to I. G. Farben. (I. G. Farben was a giant German chemical trust infamous for its dealings with the Hitler government and which even took advantage of the extermination camp of Auschwitz.) Thus, turning, change, and reflection must begin. "The road of evil paved from Weimar to Buchenwald must not become the road of our death." Albrecht Goes, born in 1908 and a minister since 1930, was a folk lyricist of Christian humanist persuasion. Later in *Unruhige Nacht* (Disquieting Night) (1950) and *Das Brandopfer* (Victim of Fire) (1954), he composed two stories which sensitively described the barbarity of the Third Reich through the examples of a soldier sentenced to death and the National Socialist persecution of the Jews. In 1947, Albrecht Goes wrote about "Goethe's poems in our time" calling for the Goethe from within. "The voices of wisdom and of grace, the voices of love and of patience have never, not even in the darkest years, stopped beckoning. Goethe, as we are often told, is one of the main voices in this area. . . . Whom is the voice addressing? Humanity. Its people. The people of its language. Yes. At first, though, it calls the individual. It does not wait for the acclamation of the multitude. It waits for the joy of the wanderer. . . . Finally, we would like to ask whether we already know the means of recovery when we know the sickness? Is the sickness the atomization of life, the destruction of the whole into parts? Similar things have already been indicated in Bergengruen's warning. If so, recovery would have to search and find its point of departure and final goal in wholeness. In the West, there is no place of stronger resistance to division than in the work of Goethe . . ."[424]

The Goethe Prize of Frankfurt, established in 1927 with Stefan George as its first recipient, was given to, among others, Gerhart Hauptmann, Hermann Stehr, Ricarda Huch, Albert Schweitzer, Sigmund Freud and Georg Kolbe. After a pause during the last two war years, it went to the physicist Max Planck in 1945. Then, in 1946, Hermann Hesse received it. The governing body to whom also belonged representatives of the Goethe Society, the Free German Hochstift and the University of Frankfurt, wanted to honor a writer "whose ideas serve the foundation of our spiritual reconstruction." "The essential German, the Swabian writer Hermann Hesse withdrew already early from the conflicts of Germany and moved to the Latin clarity and the Italian beauty of southern Switzerland in Montagnola near Lugano. He still lives there today, forever a harbinger of freedom and of conscience. It was from there that, after the collapse, he repeatedly affirmed his inseparable connectedness with the fate of his homeland, and confessed his faith in Germany."[425] At that very time, the publishing house of Suhrkamp prepared an edition of Hesse's *The Glass Bead Game.*

As the bicentenial of Goethe's birthday, the year 1949 offered a unique opportunity to present to the world the "authentic," the other, the actually very different internal Germany. For the first time after the war, cultural-political opportunities were used in cultural-touristic ways on a large scale, amalgamating classics and commerce. "Goethe's Germany invites you!" Goethe, furnished with all affirmative blessings, was to help Germany to turn again into the peaceful community of the cultural nations.

After 16 years, Thomas Mann again stepped onto German soil. He delivered his speech for the occasion of the Goethe year in Frankfurt, where he was also honored with the Goethe Prize of Frankfurt, and in Weimar, thus emphasizing the connection of the two states. "What was Goethe's advice to us needy humans? The contemporaries were often intimidated by an objectivism that was unwilling to separate and evaluate, the objectivism of art and nature. It was their nature, an element of comprehensive doubt, which, if we are to trust their context, let them utter sentences that already contained the opposite. 'He based his matters on nothing' *(Er hat sein Sach' auf nichts gestellt')* was the morally uneasy phrase with which Schiller's wife, Charlotte, expressed this experience. But this 'nothing' is another name for 'everything,' for that which includes all human, the thousandfold vitality of Proteus who slips into all forms to know all, to understand all, to be all, who demands to live in everybody's shoes. Here, nothing and everything are one, like Mephistopheles and Faust are one in the person of their creator, who lets them make their contract on the foundation of a total abandonment to life that reinterprets the infernal into an all-comprehensive humanness. The 'good Germany' is the strength that is blessed by the muse, moral greatness. Thus a German could become exemplary, not only the model and completion of a people, but of humanity, into whose self he expands his self."[426]

Thomas Mann's willingness to commemorate Goethe in East and West gave occasion to criticism. Fiedrich Sieburg thought that the way from Frankfurt to Weimar (the city of Weimar lay in the Soviet occupied zone), though short, became the cross roads for the writer of *Doctor Faustus.* "Thomas Mann does not have any luck with Germany, but who does anyway!"[427] Thomas Mann responded to these protests, "What is decisive is that my visit was to acknowledge the fatherland as a whole, and that it seemed unfair to stay away from the population of the Soviet zone, to ignore them."[428] In response to that and in light of the political oppression in the Soviet occupied zone, Eugen Kogon asked the writer to stand up for real humanity and not only to hold fast to a merely abstract humanity. "If you are not of the same opinion, the only, though questionable, but at least understandable way out for you, I think, is to remain publicly silent in Weimar for Goethe's and for your own reputation."[429]

In the *Taglichen Rundschau* of the Eastern zone (a frequently used name for the soviet occupied zone) Wolfgang Harich wrote, "Impudent disapproval and 'well-meant advice' from the side of those dividing Germany did not dissuade Thomas Mann from visiting Weimar. He broke through the 'Iron Curtain' that was fabricated, by the reaction, out of lies and defamations, in order to document through his presence here that he cannot and will not recognize the zones and demarcation lines. Now, what does Thomas Mann find here in the new anti-Fascist democratic system of the Eastern zone? He is finding a new Germany that is in the process of changing completely, in which even the roots of Fascism have been eradicated. He is finding a social order whose structure is the real guarantee that the powers of reaction and war, at least in this part of his homeland, will never rise again. He is finding working people, workers, farmers, engineers, scientists and artists whose whole work is dedicated to the service of peaceful construction. Every day and hour they prove that it is possible in Germany, for their own sake and the sake of humanity, to care, without war mongers, saber-rattling militarists, 'nationalist' demagogues and profiteering monopolists and bankers, much better and with much more hope for the present and future than ever before in our tragic history . . ."[430]

Inspite of all official efforts not to dim the glitter of the cult of Goethe, there were many fierce disputes, at least among the academics, about the right understanding of Goethe. The point of departure in the dispute concerning Karl Jaspers harkened back relatively far. When receiving the Goethe Prize of Frankfurt in 1947, Jaspers pleaded for a critical appropriation. Goethe, he maintained, should not be a model for imitation. There were some dangers with him that he himself did not succumb to. "There is only one step from the seriousness of the man who develops into a complete human being to the egocentric isolation from the world, from the liberating translation of experience into writing to aesthetic aloofness, from devotion to the great moment to an irresponsible vivacity of merely the next moment, from the depth of Goethean thoughts to the obscurity of blurred thinking, from the real soaring of Goethe's wisdom to the indescisiveness of insubstantiality, from complete openness to begin without character. It is the doom of German education after Goethe that the latter paths were traveled. So many wanted each to be a small Goethe. Goethe served as the reason and excuse for everything. But Goethe should not be cited to provide justification for anything." In order to continue living spiritually we must bring about a revolution in the appropriation of Goethe. With all due respect, Goethean images of the past cannot be taken over and the cult of Goethe should not be continued.[431]

This deeply affected a cultural consciousness that before and after 1945 adorned itself with Goethe and the classics, in the first place in support of political withdrawal and then as the equipment of democratic involvement. Ernst Robert Curtius polemicized against Karl Jaspers in the Swiss paper *Die Tat.* The article of the romance scholar from Bonn was then reprinted by the *Zeit* on April 28, 1949. "This is the year of Goethe's anniversary. In the name of all those who appreciate Goethe most deeply, we deplore that a philosopher of international renown has compromised the reputation of the German mind and German philosophy through both a base and arrogant correction of Goethe."[432]

The Austrian romance scholar, Leo Spitzer, who had emigrated to the USA, wrote the following in the *Wandlungen* about the Jaspers-Curtius dispute, "Why should a thoughtful philosopher, who is morally concerned about his fatherland and who is in a tragic mood, quite justifiably so in light of the tragic circumstances of the world, not be permitted to think in the Goethe year about the possible evil consequences of the cult of Goethe and to express this publicly? Is the uncritical fatherland and the commemoration of the highly self-critical Goethe served with the militarily-oriented, rigidly humorless, year long choruses of praise, such as 'from the Adige River to the Straits of Belt? (A phrase from the German national hymn.) Is such a mass hypocrisy superior to the bold reflective formulation of the question? With what right, before God, the nation and himself, does this philologist charge his philosophical colleague with three 'acts,' thus passing from self-righteous agitation to the assault of a coarsely denunciatory pamplet?"[433] Borrowing a word from Fichte, Curtius spoke of the three "acts" of Jaspers that had an unsettling effect on his respect for Jaspers, that is, that he admitted Germany's collective guilt, confessed his belief in the Jewish-Christian mixed religion, and censored Goethe.

New Hope: The Fateful Year of 1948

The will and enthusiasm for construction, proceeding gradually, tirelessly and relentlessly, drew its strength from the longing for the Americanization of life, from the motive to take part in American prosperity. That the dreams of a blossoming became ripe so quickly, that the Federal Republic constituted itself out of the Western zones and that the economic miracle issued forth from the rubble landscape, was, however, in no small part due to the political development of the West. At the Potsdam Conference in July and August 1945, the Americans, dismayed in light of the unbridgeable contrasts between democratic and totalitarian systems of government, recognized that its system of market economy and the Soviets' systems of central economy were mutually exclusive. This applied also to the German condominium. Only two possibilities distinguished themselves: either the separation of the Soviet occupied zone from the Western zones or the inclusion of Germany into the Western or Soviet economic systems.

"Neither the Soviets nor the English and Americans were receptive to the former possibility. The second solution was rejected both by the Russians and the Western powers. There were no official plans for the establishment of a Western state in London and Washington. Such a development had not appeared as an acute danger, but did not seem to be precluded as a future possibility, were the miserable situation in Germany to continue. No matter for what reasons and through what means the Western zones came under Soviet influence, this would mean the loss of the four zones of Germany for the West and thus for America. The Western Allies feared that a Germany oriented to communism could bring about effects in the bordering states, especially in France, that would lend further stimulus to communism.

"The USA was also concerned with the French occupying power, and not only in regard to the question of economic unity, reparations and foreign trade. Later, during the conference of the secretaries of state in March and April 1947, Clay once mentioned that the Russians 'are as stubborn as the horse dealers,' but also that 'we are dealing day by day on the basis of a reasonable give and take, thereby not doing too badly. The French, with their claim on the Saarland and demand for the internationalization of the Ruhr District, are much more uncompromising.' France asked unceasingly for the removal of the Ruhr District and the Rhineland, for the purpose of the dismemberment of Germany and for economic interests, and also because of fear that the line of demarcation could be moved from the Elbe River to the Rhine. These regions, separated in this way, were to offer much more security against Soviet expansion under the constant influence of France than if they were to remain with Germany. America and England, however, opposed this French plan in order to prevent Germany's loss of economic independence due to the removal of the Rhine and Ruhr Districts after the loss of the regions East of the Oder-Neisse line. Otherwise Germany would become economically dependent on America, a boarder of America.

"In this situation, the American secretary of state took the initiative. When it became clear that General Clay's call for an end to all dismantling did not bring the expected effect, Burnes asked the three other zones to unite economically with the American zone. Neither France nor the Soviet Union were inspired by this offer, Great Britain, however, accepted. America and England hoped that the unification of their zones would lead to an economic upswing and that this in turn would affect the other zones and their occupying powers like a magnet.

"On September 6, 1946, James Byrnes, as the first secretary of state after the capitulation, gave a sensational speech to an invited circle of Germans and members of the military government in the Stuttgart Opera. Its contents were immediately released in press and radio. This speech marked an official turn in America's foreign policy towards Germany, already prefigured inconspicuously in practice. But now, the first time in front of Germans, Burnes pronounced the old American demands: the removal of the economic barriers between the zones in the condominium, the revision of the industrial plan, the prohibition of withdrawal and rejection of the separation of the Rhine-Ruhr District."[434]

Burnes also suggested the adoption of the model of the state *(Länder)* councils of the US zone for the double zone and its possible extention to the entire occupied area. He maintained that the government should not be established by the Allies but that it should consist of a German national council comprised of the incumbent minister presidents of the states. The national council would also be charged with the preparation of a draft of a federal constitution for Germany. Among other things, Byrnes said that Germany's liberation from militarism would allow its people to put its great abilities into the service of peace so that it might again become a respected member of the United Nations one day.[435]

Byrnes' speech promised great hope. Not only was it a political but also an important cultural-historical event. The Military Governor of the American occupied zone, General Lucius D. Clay, played a significant role in the relatively speedy changeover. Already in May of 1946, he had ordered a temporary stop to all dismantling in the American zone, and signed responsibility for the merger of the American and British zones into the bi-zone, the united economic district on January 1, 1947. His consistent politics, focused on the improvement of the situation in Western Germany, found its decisive field of operation in the realization of the European Recovery Plan (ERP) also called Mashall Plan, after the US Secretary of State.[436]

In July 1947, the American government instructed General Clay with new guidelines for an "orderly and blossoming Europe," in which the economic contributions of a stable and productive Germany would be as necessary as the limitations of the German power. These guidelines were to insure the impossibility of a renewed rise of German military power. Regulations decreed for all areas of public life, politics, economy, administration, law, and culture, were to guarantee that Germany would progress on the path of peaceful and democratic reconstruction.

In December of 1947 before the beginning of the meeting of the secretaries of state, George C. Marshall demanded the final stop of reparations on January 1 of the following year. This announcement was especially directed against the USSR. "I wish it to be clearly understood that the United States is not prepared to agree to any program of reparations from current production as a price for the unification of Germany. . . . In western Germany the United States and Great Britain are pouring in food to keep Germans alive. As I have said, this is costing some 700 million dollars a year. At the same time, in eastern Germany, assets are being taken out at a rate and value which we estimate to be over 500 million dollars a year. Also in that area German businesses, through one device or another, are being brought under Soviet ownership and placed in a gigantic Soviet trust."[437] After the ratification of the US emergency program, Marshall's announced bill was to be presented to the Congress for ratification. It was estimated that until 1948 $1.5 billion dollars were needed to start the long term program of assistance.

The year 1948 was the actual fateful year of German postwar history. The extremely dynamic development of the Western occupied zones began after the miscarried conference of the secretaries of state in London in December of 1947. The Marshall Plan was ratified in April. The attempt of the USSR to completely incorporate the city of Berlin by shutting it up failed because of the resolution of the Western Allies, especially of General Clay who established an air lift that secured the maintenance of the city, though with great sacrifices. On May 12, 1949, after 322 days, the Soviet Union ended the blockade. The administration of the four powers for Germany and Berlin broke apart, leading ultimately to the establishment of two partial states of Germany. After a convention of constitutional experts at Herrenchiemsee that had been called by the minister presidents in July, the Parliamentary Council was installed on September 1 and charged with the draft of a constitution for Germany. In the session of May 8, 1949 which ended on May 9 at 12:40 AM, 53 representatives voted for the ratification of the constitution by the unanimous vote of the SPD, CDU and FDP. The votes against the ratification came from two representatives of the Catholic Center party, the two representatives of the German Party of Lower Saxony, the two communists, and the Bavarian CSU with the exception of two representatives from Franconia.

The most important domestic decision which also led to essential changes in cultural life was made in June 1948. On June 20, the currency reform took place in the zones occupied by the Western powers. One day after this, price control and the government control of many goods was eliminated. The aim of this currency reform was to clean up German finance, completely ruined during the war. Due to the financing of armaments then, surplus money stood in grotesque disproportion to the supply of goods. While the controlled economy and the controlled prices did prevent an inflationary development, there was, however, almost nothing available at the fixed prices. The real values were reflected in the black market. The currency reform drastically decreased the circulation of money and radically reduced the indebtedness of the state. On the fixed day, everybody received forty German Marks and two months later again twenty German Marks. All of the remaining cash was cut to a tenth of its original value: for 100 ReichMarks in an account, 6.50 Marks were returned. Obligations were dealt with in a similar manner, with the exception of mortgages which were converted 1:1, because the government did not want to favor too much the owners of tangible assets.

The miracle occured. People trusted the new money. Goods that had been held back for a long time suddenly appeared on the market. From one day to the next, the windows exhibited a range of goods that nobody had thought possible. Professor Ludwig Erhard, Director of Administration for the Economy of the United Economic Districts and thus essential to the economic reform, was proven right in his opinion that currency reform and economic reform were inseparably connected. The one would not have been possible without the other.

Liberalism's Cultural Ideal and Day X

"Free market" was the magic word of progress, and planned economy was renounced. Private ownership and competition, the basic principles of capitalism, were recognized as the propelling forces of the economic engine. It was expected, of course, that they would also be in line with social responsibility. Liberalism was to be determined by rethinking, which included as well a recollection of the "permanent essence of liberalism."

What is liberalism? Wilhelm Ropke, a national economist who emigrated in 1933, became a professor in Genf in 1937, and went on to become one of the most important "prethinkers" of the new socio-economic concept, posed this question in his book, *Das Kulturideal des Liberalismus*, which came out in 1947.

"It is *humanistic*. This means that it presupposes that humans are capable of good and find ultimate fulfillment through society, that their destiny points beyond material existence, and that they deserve respect for their unique qualities and thus may not be used as a mere means. It is in this sense individualistic, or, if one prefers, *personalistic*. Thus, according to Christian teaching which states that every human soul is directly related to God, and will return to God as an exclusive whole, the individual person is ultimately real and not society, despite the fact that humans can only find fulfillment in the service of and possibly even through sacrificing for the community. Liberalism is therefore *anti-authoritarian*. While it is prepared to render unto Caesar that which belongs to Caesar, it is on guard against any communitarian romanticism that makes the government organization into an object of a mystical cult, into a type of superorganism, or even into a God. It likewise resists Caesar if he demands more than his due. Hence, liberalism is *universal* inasmuch as it is humanistic, personalistic, and anti-authoritarian, respecting the human as such, and inasmuch as it guards against the idolatry of the state, it resists the turning of patriotism into nationalism, and therby also Machiavellianism and imperialism. Thus it is ultimately *rationalistic* not only in the critical, philosophical sense, but also in that as humanists, liberals attribute reason to all people; as personalists, they see this reason as the highest human power; as anti-authoritarian and universal social philosophers, however, they make reason the judge before which all human folly, lies, and evil must answer."[438]

The concrete effects of the cultural ideal of liberalism, namely the Day X, the day of the currency reform, can be seen in a recollection by Ursula Kardorff, then a reporter at the Nuremberg Trials. "The currency reform came overnight. I made only a short entry in my diary. 'Meanwhile, the currency reform came upon us with the result that I sat there without a penny, for because of bureaucratic errors I am unable to receive my allotted 40 Marks here in Nuremberg. I find it quite funny, but I can't get upset about it.' At some time or other I then also received the brand new, crackling bills in Nuremberg, my "head money," per capita quota, of what now became the newest world in our vocabulary, the 'German Mark,' so baptized by the American, Eduard Tenenbaum. The bills depicted confidence inspiring, well rounded women. With my quota I bought four red rimmed wine glasses, a bottle of wine, a corkscrew, and a ticket for the film *Kinder des Olymp* (Children of Olympia), for which I had to hand out five D Marks in Nuremberg. In the evenings, the glasses were emptied by visitors to my place. On the weekend, again in the village, I met a farming woman who offered me twenty fresh eggs for two D Marks. For the first time I knew that it was true. A new age was dawning."[439]

The *Neue Zeitung,* which otherwise appeared only twice weekly, published a special issue on the legal documents and the first legislative acts regarding the currency reform. On June 27, it published a comprehensive report of public opinion entitled "One week of new money. From Day X to Day X + 6."[440] Wherever one looked in the American, French, or British zones, the effect of the currency reform was the same. Passionate love for the "Neumark." Every buyer and seller wanted to possess them. The greater and speedier the supply, the better they felt. There developed a situation that hadn't been experienced for years. While there was an astonishing supply of reasonably priced items, the customers hesitated, for they still had too few Marks at their disposal.

In Frankfurt, there were mouth watering cakes, but because they were still too expensive, they were only marvelled at through the glass by "window shoppers." There was an over abundance of fresh fruit and vegetables.

In Darmstadt, the freshest butter ever was sold at five Marks a pound.

In Heidelberg, a pound of peaches went for one Mark. Farmers were already offering new pears. Green salad, which hadn't been seen for years, was available for thirty new Pfennings. Whoever thought fifteen Pfennings was too much for a lemon, received a half-rotten one as a sales pitch.

In Kassel, the farmers offered eggs at DM 1.10 and a pound of butter for 30 Marks. These were boycotted, and thus the prices sank to 20 Pfennings and DM 1.50, respectively.

In Stuttgart, there were more vegetables than could have been imagined, but few sold.

The citizens of Munich used their quota for shoe repairs and unforeseen emergencies. Butchers sold out their inventories in order to have cash on hand. Farmers happily sold the cattle on faith and trust.

In the French zone, a representative of the central committee for nutrition announced that the main staples would continue to be strictly regulated.

In the British zone, fish could be sold freely, at the discretion of the stores. There was not yet, however, sufficient meat on the market.

"'Welcome' appeared invisibly on the doorways to the shops and visibly in the expressions of the salespeople. After the first shock was overcome, shops were again in business on Monday, and some did unexpectedly well. This could well be, however, because their expectations were minimal. The most frequent requests came for scarce items such as socks, fabric, nails, baby outfits, sewing thread, enamel ware, razor blades, dishes, shoelaces and rubber bands. There was also a great, though at first definitely mainly a platonic interest in radios, refrigerators, irons, which fell from 25 Marks on Monday to 14 Marks on Thursday, and bicycles. Completely "dead" at the moment are craft items, the tiles that went for 30 Reichs Marks remained untouched at DM 1.80, perfumes, furs and jewelry. Watches, in contrast, going for between 30 and 90 Marks, sell like hotcakes. The warehouses are swarming with people, but 80 percent are just trying to get a sense of what is going on. People are seizing opportunities.

"One could also see wonderful things at average prices. Three part stoves at DM 70, gas cookers for DM 50, four tube radios for DM 475, popular receivers for DM 129, tablelamp batteries at DM 0.40, sewing machines for DM 250, bicycles for DM 80, women's hose for DM 4, bicycle tubes for DM 2, leather bags starting at DM 8, men's suits for DM 90, tennis rackets for DM 60, shoelaces for DM 0.30, gloves for DM 6, ties for DM 2.50, preserve jars for DM 1, Junghans wristwatches with 15 stones for DM 80, alarm clocks and desk clocks for DM 18, elastic suspenders for DM 4, Meissner porcelain service for DM 500, and a Olympia from Opel for DM 5900. The first automobiles paid for in cash were sold in Wiesbaden to a department store, a municipal institution, and the finance administration."

One of the most well known figures of the postwar years, the person who jumped trains, was practically nonexistent already in the course of the first week after the currency reform. Private automobile traffic had been sharply reduced, yet as long as they had money, people could ride the taxi to their hearts' content. "On Tuesday, after seven hours of waiting, a taxi driver took in a sum of three marks." Tourist areas asked for visitors. On the door of a hotel stood the following sign, "I grant credit to visitors of the spa who are momentarily short on cash."

Panic broke out on the black market. The motto was, "We must still underbid the officially established minimum price!" Thus, green bean coffee sank to DM 20 per pund, and American cigarettes, offered at DM 45 a carton, stayed on the shelves.

The producers of ready built wood homes were already involved in a price war. Many registered for work in the labor market. Most cash sales were obtained by the dealers of farming equipment and machines; even objects valued at around DM 400 were sold in great quantities. Banks had to work overtime. People worked at least 12 hours daily, and the need for credit was considerable. Indeed, up to DM 20 from the quotas was already being put into savings accounts. On June 22, the record savings of DM 1600 was held by a cigarette dealer in Munich.

By this time, and for some time thereafter, culture was again an unsalable commodity. The concrete aesthetics of the new consumer goods was considered much more fascinating than art products. Because there was a longing to enjoy a better, happier, and more beautiful life at the basic level of existence, it was possible to dispense with the sublimation and projection of the superstructure.

Creations of the spirit stood at the end of the line. This was the "bitter experience echoed in all reports and commentaries on the period. Culture is suddenly no longer in demand, and it is here that the threat of economic collapse is most apparent."

Theaters saw their admission tickets, which shortly before were still an exchange commodity, grow moldy. They drew the consequences of a more or less radical accomodation. Many, of course, like the Hamburg state theaters, and the municipal theaters of Munich, Hannover, Kassel and Nuremberg, had sold advance tickets for up to the end of the month in the old currency. Many had even sold subscriptions for the following season in the old currency. They therefore performed before full houses during the first days after the currency reform. Stuttgart, Düsseldorf, Baden-Baden and Koblenz reduced the price of admission 50 percent, with little success. Bremen attempted to sell tickets in Marks, and sold from 18 to 30 tickets per theater during the first day. Heidelberg asked 4 and 5 Marks and had to cancel the performances for June 21 through 23. Several theaters grasped at panic measures. The Frankfurt opera, for example, had in fact sold out at 30, 40 and 50 Pfennings; the Frankfurt cinemas asked their old prices in the new currency and were therefore half-full in the afternoons and quite full in the evenings.

In spite of everything, *The Devil's General* also achieved good advance sales with the old prices in the new currency. Theater recesses were postponed or cancelled completely. The situation of the traveling troupes, cabarets, and circuses was even more desperate. Hundreds of artists were stranded without travel money to return home. Tours were canceled, guest performances could no longer take place due to the shortage of travel fees and honoraria. A pair of dancers, for example, was ready to go on with their Augsburg engagement for DM 5 to 10 a day, but the hotel alone cost DM 7. Concert halls were empty, and most of the planned evenings were cancelled.

Subscription tickets were advertized in newspapers and magazines. The great death of newspapers began shortly. The publisher Lamberg Schneider recalls how deeply depressed he was in the face of the sudden lack of interest shown by his readers once they had to show their mental participation by paying with hard Deutsche Marks. "It was not very easy to steer the publishing house through all these paths." The high circulation rates suddenly became extremely low, and editing and production costs were as high as they were in years of prosperity.[441] The new *Ruf* was also among the new magazines to fold in the following months. In the sixth issue of 1949, the editors declared tersely, "With this issue, 'Der Ruf' takes leave of its faithful readers and friends. During these last months, the editors and publishers have used all their powers to ensure that during the span of time between publications, which in earlier times of peace was comfortably sufficient, they could guarantee the appearance of the magazine and cover the unforeseen expenses and cost increases. Despite the interest that the 'Ruf' could get from among its circle of readers, all efforts have been in vain. Thus the firm sees itself forced to discontinue the magazine for the present."[442]

When Lambert Schneider's publishing firm announced that the fall 1949 issue of *Die Wandlung* would be the final one, co-publisher Dolf Sternberger concluded:

"*Die Wandlung* did not have the support of any organization, any church or party. Now in Europe, we live between parties and churches, and often enough the 'flight from freedom' takes the form of an explicit or inexplicit conversion, almost as often as does party affiliation or association. . . . And so this magazine had no dogmatic backing, not even that of a 'liberal' ideology, to say nothing of such organizations. Every one of its publishers and authors worked as an individual, as a person . . . Peace is far away. The readiness for peace is being tested more each day, while the idea of a future war becomes more gruesome. Meanwhile, in Germany, resentment and the lingering desire for fear is still widespread. We live near the world's line of demarcation. Europe is a fragment whose real prospect for life lies only in its being an element within a comprehensive Atlantic system. German nationalism can only, by misunderstanding itself, serve as a tool and accomplice of a new party dictatorship. Given the continuing discord in the world, the desire to preserve an inner neutrality could cost human value. The most noble concepts are, when applied, most ambiguous, peace, freedom, and justice. These tensions can hardly be borne. True peace can not lie in slavery and oppression, and true freedom must not be bought and contaminated with the crime of an atomic war. We now live with these contradictions, this danger. Whoever does not decide will be lost. And yet, we wanted happiness and security finally, after so much spiteful and dangerous living.

"This is the situation in which the magazine is being discontinued. When we began, we believed we would face many difficulties, but that we would also have a brighter future. Even that has changed. Of course, we are not giving up. The publisher and the intimate co-workers of the *Wandlung* will remain closely tied to each other and will unite with fellow spirits in the attempt to begin publishing again. Under a sign long trusted in Germany, namely under the name of the *Neuen Rundschau,* they will seek anew the sympathy and attention of their readers. Thus this is not a farewell, but only a form of transition. We will see each other again."[443]

All in all, the currency reform brought to light the fact that the "flight into the magazine" really was a flight, and that the magazine euphoria was in fact a euphoria, a "merriment in the face of the end." The crisis of culture that took place with the currency reform was of great significance in the sense understood by depth psychology. It showed that much of what had, during the rubble years, been perceived as great spiritual transformation and reflection, as moral renewal, in fact served only to compensate the materialism of which one had been deprived. However, as Dolf Sternberger's typical pessimistic-optimistic summary shows, it also initiated a new phase of cultural development, with different phenomena, currents, achievements, and successes.

The Most Important Cultural Events of the Postwar Years

Obviously in anticipation of the approaching end of the culture of the rubble years and in expectation of further not-yet-foreseeable events, the *Neue Zeitung* in February of 1948 asked other German newspapers what the colleagues from their essay and cultural departments would judge to be the most important cultural events of the postwar years. The summarized responses to this question are to conclude the culture-historical survey of the time of origin of the Federal Republic, the "years of beautiful affliction" and the years after the "Zero Hour" (which was no such thing). Thirty newspapers were asked, including some from the Soviet occupied zone. Among them were: *Münchner Merkur, Rheinischer Merkur, Rheinische Post, Die Zeit, Die Welt, Tagliche Rundschau, Telegraph, Der Kurier, Der Tagesspiegel, Leipziger Zeitung, Stuttgarter Zeitung, Kolnische Rundschau, Neue Deutschland, Frankfurter Neue Presse, Frankfurter Rundschau, Westdeutsches Tageblatt* (the *Frankfurter Allgemeine Zeitung* did not exist then). Following are the most important responses:[444]

THE TWO VISITS OF VICTOR GOLLANCZ IN GERMANY AND HIS PUBLICATIONS CONCERNING THEM IN THE ENGLISH PRESS AND IN HIS BOOKS. The fact that an Englishman, a Jew, applied himself most fervently for a defeated, outcast and despised people, using every means at his disposal, "may appear astonishing, but it may not seem to be a 'culture-political event.' We, however, are of the opinion that culture enters exactly at that point where Victor Gollancz begins, and that all spiritual efforts for a people remain ineffective if it hungers, is cold and is denied the most primitive necessities of life" wrote Vilma Sturm in the *Rheinischer Merkur.*

THE EXHIBITION IN 1947 WHICH ATTRACTED 55,000 VISITORS WITHIN A TWO-WEEK PERIOD. "It was as much educational as pleasing to observe the earnest, even piously 'disinterested delight' of the majority of the visitors that denied themselves hasty and forward judgments even of most modern paintings that were, for the most part, problematical. This was the answer to 12 sterile years of dictatorship in which a classic, say van Gogh, was considered one of the degenerates and the color postcard was made the canon. Here, France opened up in all its greatness, breadth and spontaneous generosity, that was so often veiled by the dense mists of politics," said Franz Josef Schöningh, in the *Süddeutsche Zeitung,* Munich.

ONE WILL NOT FIND TOO MANY EVENTS, OMISSIONS PREDOMINATED. There was too much talking and too little production. Instead of artificially prolonging the time of constriction, because of the problems of copyrights and monopolies of translation for Swiss publishers, we should have opened the gates wide to the powerful stream of the world's creativity from which Germany had been shut off for so long. "Apparently, only the French have recognized this necessity and used this opportunity, at least Sartre is being played on all stages, while Heidegger's works are only available in France. For instance, even the new books of Thomas Mann, Hermann Hesse and the posthumous works of Stefan Zweig are not available at all or only published in minute editions." We would need something like an intellectual Marshall Plan. It is not good that men like Hamsun and Carossa are defamed for reasons of their political mistakes, not to speak of Ernst Jünger. Only muddle-headed fellows could think of accusing Thomas Mann of a lack of political sensitivity, while every reasonable person takes him as what he is: a great and worthy writer. People in the plastic arts have not learned that a reversal of a pattern is in itself not an indication of development. All the "cultural weeks" could not obscure the fact that people of this country do not have much interest in the unprofitable arts. Therefore, the mental jobs at the newspapers rank last. "I almost answered your poll thus, the most important cultural-political event is the fact that last week I was able to obtain a stovepipe. Now in the evenings I am able to read Thomas Mann's *Doctor Faustus* which I think is the most important book of the postwar years," said Henri Nannen, in *Abendpost,* Hannover.

"I REGARD THE LECTURES ON THE WORK OF KARL BARTH AT THE UNIVERSITY OF BONN AND THE LECTURES HE HELD ALL AROUND GERMANY IN 1947 AND 1948 AS THE MOST IMPORTANT CULTURAL EVENT." Those who want to save the Western person, especially the young Western person, should not oppose existentialism, for it would mean the opposition of truth and reality. They should rather affirm existentialism and take it into that which the "victor" has to say, so as to save it from itself. "As far as I can see, this is only being done by the proclamation of the New Testament. I do not mean this in the form that the church preaches, which dares nothing and thinks of itself as not being capable, but rather in the radical, uncompromising, paradoxical and enormous form, in the original form in which the dialectics of Karl Barth attempt it." wrote Manfred Hausmann in the *Weserkurier,* Bremen.

THE PERFORMANCE OF THORNTON WILDER'S *THE SKIN OF OUR TEETH,* "because it showed us that the continuity of history is not only destroyed for the present but that it had already been destroyed on deeper levels. This is an insight the danger of which we have been trying to repress habitually for decades." Then the performance of Claudel's *The Satin Slipper* and *Joan of Arc on the Stake.* Both pieces show clearly that the times are dramatically addressed better with examples than with calm and uninterruptedly flowing stories. Finally, the congress of writers in October 1947 in Berlin because "It showed that rational dispute and communication about controversial questions, still believed possible in various regions in Germany, especially in southern and western Germany, is increasingly facing insurmountable obstacles. The reason is that the rational foundation of socialism as well as that of any opposite way of thinking is in danger of languishing. As Raymond Aron expressed, what remain are 'this-wordly religions' that refuse to be addressed, let alone speak by themselves or, least of all, make the work of writers possible or meaningful," said Carl Linfert in the *Kurier,* Berlin.

"THE MOST IMPORTANT EVENT WAS THE FOUNDATION OF THE 'CULTURAL FEDERATION FOR THE DEMOCRATIC RENEWAL OF GERMANY.' That we owe to the initiative of Johannes R. Becher, Bernhard Kellermann, Dr. Ferdinand Friedensburg, Paul Wegener, Professor Eduard Spranger, Pfarrer Dilschneider and others." Due to the Cultural Federation, numerous discussions could take place in recent years. Spiritual people of all professions, scientists, ministers, writers, actors, journalists and physicians, painters and musicians, educators and publishers, representatives of all types of ideologies, Christians of both confessions (meaning Catholics and Protestants), and quarreling liberals and Marxists, discussed together the historical conditions of Fascism, its precursors in the German history of thought, the root of the heretical racial doctrine, anti-Semitism, the leader principle, the theory of living space, militarism and "heroic" nihilism. "The enlightening work of the Cultural Federation about the origin and nature of Fascism is without parallel in postwar Germany. There is no occupying power, not a single party, no other political or cultural organization, no university, no publisher and no theater that has dedicated itself with such sacred, burning enthusiasm to the task of the reeducation of our guilt-stricken and deeply confused, helpless and demoralized people, and that tried with such devotion to lead especially the German youth that had been poisoned by Fascism to embrace the great liberal and humanitarian ideals of humanity, than the Cultural Federation." Sadly, the Cultural Federation was prohibited in the American and English Sector of Berlin in October and November of 1947. This took place after it had earnestly tried to make contact with the representatives of American and English cultural life, and after numerous Americans and English had talked at the events of the Cultural Federation about the cultural movements and cultural political institutions of their homelands. "There is, however, also a positive side to the prohibition. It shows the German intellectuals who the enemies of the democratic renewal of Germany are, and it proves to the former that their solidarity is more necessary today than ever before," wrote Wolfgang Harich in the *Tagliche Rundschau,* Berlin.

IN THE THEATER. The encounter with Zuckmayer's *The Devils General,* because this work teaches that it is possible today to compose a period piece according to effective dramaturgical principles without the necessity of transforming the stage into a pulpit. Furthermore, the excellent German premiere in Hamburg gave occasion to apologize to a public that had often been considered dumb. "[The audience] laughed and got angry in the way the author intended, and no shadow of Nazistic resentment (with very few exceptions) dimmed its reception by the audience. This is perhaps the first valid sign that Hitlerism is internally overcome, and that there is no reason to be afraid of a 'mythos' in the days to come. On the book table, the encounter with Kasack's *The City beyond the River,* because this clearly written novel shows in visions, as grandiose as they are shocking, that an authoritarian system, though capable of existing, is not life but a state of the dead. In the area of music, the encounter with Hindemith's 'Mathis' in Düsseldorf, because this unique work revealed new inspiration, new belief and new forms in the midst of a chaos that is pregnant with both future and danger, and in which art is involved. . . . In the area of the plastic arts, the encounter with masters of the Old Rhenish School in Cologne. Brought to light again from air raid shelters, Lochner's 'Madonna' showed beyond the total wars, halfway peaceful times, and beyond hunger and existential worries there exists the eternal," wrote Josef Marien in *Die Zeit,* Hamburg.

TO THE PEOPLE AT LAKE CONSTANCE THE FOLLOWING EVENTS WERE UNFORGETABLE. The first postwar performance of Goethe's *Iphigenie* with the young Lola Müthel in December of 1945; the internationally acclaimed Cultural Weeks of Constance with French visiting actors and American plays in June 1946; the German premiere of Bertolt Brech't *Mother Courage* with Lina Carstens, recorded Carl Weichardt in *Der Südkurier,* Constance.

"AMONG THE EVENTS THAT LEFT THE MOST ENDURING IMPRESSION UPON US. The plays *The Flies* by Jean-Paul Sartre and *The Devil's General* by Carl Zuckmayer are comparable in radiance and spiritual plastic effect." *The Flies,* because of the indivisible claim for freedom that the author depicted so enthusiastically and formulated so fascinatingly. *The Devil's General* was a projection of the German catastrophe that did not get stuck in a conventional black and white depiction but spoke of an effort that balanced guilt and tragic entanglement. It is the confession of a writer who does not repay hate with hate, a confession "of a Germany of our best dreams, of a life that amidst all despair is nevertheless worth living, something we accept gratefully in the hopelessness of our days," said Werner Tamms in the *Westdeutsches Tageblatt,* Dorthmund.

CARL ZUCKMAYER'S *THE DEVIL'S* GENERAL. As a period piece it hits the mark, towering over all other appearances in this area, because it formulates the question in order to demand an internal decision, hence speaking to us all. Furthermore, it shows such a subtle knowledge of the situation of the Germany of Hitler, unsuspected of an emigrant. At the same time, he stays away from that black and white portrayal that mars the dramatic harmony between style and antagonism and thus fails to leave a deep artistic impression. Lastly, in its depiction of wrestling and struggling, searching and erring, and of the guilt and atonement of real people, it awakens honest reflection and true understanding in the German people, as well as for the German people, wrote Heinz Stephan in the *Kölnische Rundschau,* Cologne.

"I FIND THE STRUGGLE ABOUT THE 'SCHOOL REFORM' TO BE THE MOST SIGNIFICANT CULTURAL-POLITICAL EVENT OF THE POSTWAR YEARS. This event does not merely concern Bavaria or southern Germany, as is frequently assumed in Bavaria. Rather, I see in the mutually opposing tendencies, that are expressed in the various comments of German experts among and against each other, and in their relationship to the attitudes of the military government, a decisive symptom of the contemporary sickness of Germany. I think that the very possibility of a change in our consciousness lies in the attitude toward the problem of school reform. The question is whether to go forward or to stay back, to be open-minded or to withdraw into isolation. The concept of humanism must be understood differently today. We are facing the decision of whether the historical movement of the spiritual liberation of the human being, that is, his or her development into an independent personal being, will continue to expand into the area of education, or whether we should be content with the reception of old forms," wrote Herbert Hohenemser in the *Münchner Merkur.*

The above assertions about education made by the journalist Hohenemser, later department head for culture in Munich, may be applied generally. The question for the next decades was whether the historical movement that at last had brought enlightenment, emancipation, and a radically questioning discourse to this "belated nation" in 1945 would continue; whether German culture would actively open itself to the democratic republican idea, setting the latter, as a prefigurement of a humane existence, rightside up; whether the basic values that were soon to be written into the basic law of the Federal Republic of Germany would become internalized and actually practiced day by day in constitutional reality. In short, would the liberation that was identifiable during the rubble years become reality in the "civil right of culture" and thus lead into collective progress? Such days are still at a distance.

Used Book Store on Kurfürstendamm in Berlin, 1947. PHOTO: FRIEDRICH SEIDENSTÜCKER.

First Day of Classes at the Amalienschule in Munich, Fall of 1945. PHOTO: W. B. FRANCÉ.

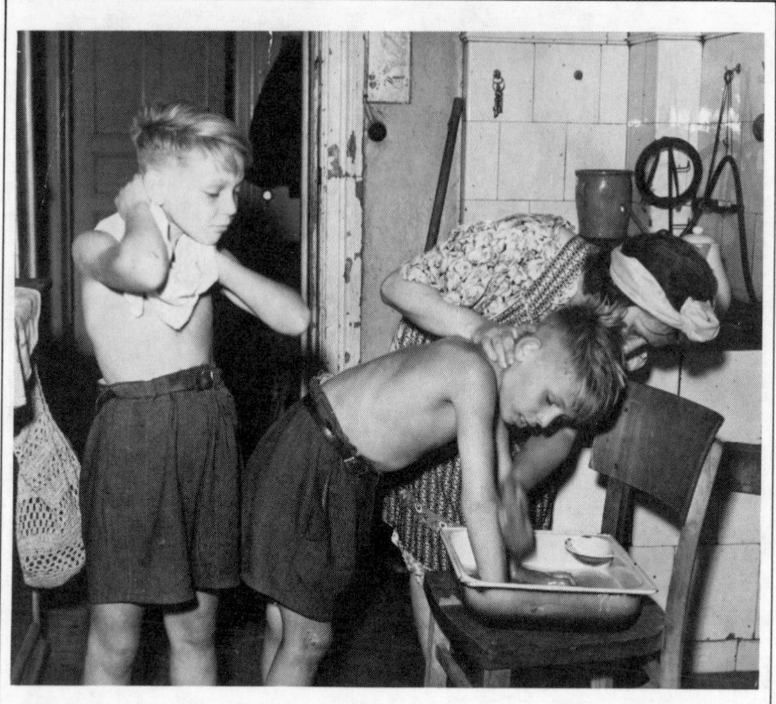

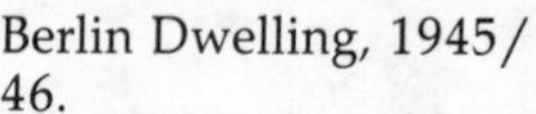

Berlin Dwelling, 1945/46.

At the Havel River in Berlin, ca. 1946.

At the Main Train Depot in Munich, 1949. PHOTO: HANS SCHÜRER.

Selling the *Süddeutschen Zeitung* in Munich, 1946. PHOTO: HANS SCHÜRER.

The First Wireless Newscast by Radio Munich, 1946. PHOTO: HANS SCHÜRER.

Concert of Chamber of Music Performed in the Destroyed Grottenhof of the Munich Royal Court, 1945. PHOTO: HANS SCHÜRER.

The First Postwar Concert of the Munich Philharmonic, Beethoven's Ninth Symphony, Performed in the Main Auditorium of the University, 1945. PHOTO: HANS SCHÜRER.

Artist Unknown, Exhibition Poster, 1947.

Poster, 1945/46. DESIGN: C. HANSMANN.

Wolfgang Borchert's *Draussen vor der Tur* at the Hamburg Playhouse, 1947, with Hermann Lenschau and Hans Quest.

Opening of the Munich Playhouse, 1947.

The Film, *Todesmühlen,* in Munich's Luitpold Theater, 1945.

Scene from Wolfgang Staudte's Film, *Die Morder sind unter uns*, 1946, with Hildegard Knef and W. Borchert.

Book Store in Munich, 1946. PHOTO: W. B. FRANCÉ.

Distribution of the New DM on June 21, 1948 in Munich.

Closing Session of the Parliament after the Ratification of the Constitution on May 23, 1949.

APPENDIX

NOTES

* The word "emigration" was commonly used in Germany during this time, and carried a much broader meaning than that normally given it.

** Though often translated as "folk" because the English word derives from the same root, the English word doesn't carry the rich connotations of the German *"Volk."* Several shades of meaning can be rendered with the German adjective *"volkisch"*, a people sharing a common historical, national, cultural, ethnic, and (often contrived) racial heritage. At times the word simply means "people," in which case it will be translated as such. When, however, it carries the fuller German meeting, a translation will be attempted, but the German word will also be indicated parenthetically.

1 Walter Höllerer, *Der andere Gast* (Munich 1952), 21.

2 cf. Dieter Franck, *Jahre unseres Lebens. 1945–1949* (Munich, Zurich 1980), 32f.

3 Erich Kästner, *Notabene 45, Ein Tagebuch,* in *Gersammelte Schriften für Erwachsene,* vol. 6 (Munich, Zurich, n.p.), 83.

4 Wolfgang Borchert, *Draussen for der Tür und ausgewählte Erzählungen* (Hamburg: 1956), 8, 23.

5 Hartmut von Hentig, *Aufgeräumte Erfahrung. Texte zur eigenen Person* (Munich, Vienna 1983), 39.

6 Thomas Mann, "Deutsche Hörer! Fünfundfünfzig Radiosendungen nach Deutschland," in *Werke. Das essayistische werk,* paperpack version in 8 vols., ed., Hans Bürgin., 3rd vol.: *Politische Schriften und Reden* (Frankfurt am Main and Hamburg 1968), 35.

7 Günter Eich, "Inventur," in *Gesammelte Werke,* vol. 1 (Frankfurt am Main: 1973), 35.

8 Günter Eich, "Latrine," 36. Joachim Kaiser, "Wieviel gelogen wird. Auch eine Erinnerung an die Stunde Null," *Süddeutsche Zeitung,* 4, 28–29, 1979.

9 Joachim Kaiser: "How Much They Lied", also "Rememberance of the Zero Hour"; *Süddeutsche Zeitung,* April 28/29, 1979.

10 cf. Herbert Marcuse, "Über den affirmativen Charakter der Kultur," in *Kultur und Gesellschaft I* (Frankfurt am Main 1965), 63ff.

11 Wolfgang Langhoff, "Ein Deutschland-Brief," *Neue Zeitung,* 2, 18 1946. Henceforth abbreviated as NZ.

12 Wolfgang Borchert, "Das ist unser Manifest," cited in Klaus Wagenbach, *Lesebuch. Deutsche Literatur zwischen 1945 und 1959* (Berlin 1980), 13.

13 Thornton Wilder, "The Skin of Our Teeth," in *Three Plays by Thornton Wilder,* Bantam Library of World Drama (New York 1966), 128.

14 Walter Kolbenhoff: "Ein kleines oberbayerisches Dorf," NZ, 12, 20, 1946.

15 Kyra Stromberg, "Heidelberger Feuerwerk," *Der Kurier* (Berlin), 8, 5, 1947.

16 Letter from 9, 25, 1946, cited in Peter Kritzer, *Wilhelm Hoegner. Politische Biographie eines bayerischen Sozialdemokraten* (Munich 1979), 306.

17 Georg Britting, *Lebenslauf eines dicken Mannes der Hamlet hiess* (Dusseldorf 1949), 252, 260.

18 Edmund Nick, "Carl Orffs 'Bernauerin,'" NZ, 7, 11, 1947.

19 Erich Kästner, *Notabene 45,* 203, 200ff, 204.

20 Hans Mayer, *Ein Deutscher auf Widerruf. Erinnerungen (I)* (Frankfurt am Main 1982), 313.

21 cf. Henric L. Wuermeling, *Die weisse Liste. Umbruch der politischen Kultur in Deutschland 1945* (Berlin 1981).

22 To this and the following, cf. Theodor Eschenburg, *Jahre der Besatzung 1945–1949. Geschichte der Bundesrepublick Deutschland in fünf Bänden,* edited by Karl Dietrich Bracher, Theodor Eschenburg, Joachim C. Fest, and Eberhard Jäckel, vol 1 (Stuttgart, Wiesbaden 1983), 22ff.

23 Gustav Roeder, "Der Demokrat. Zum Hundertsten von Theodor Heuss," *N'ürnberger Zeitung,* 1, 29, 1984.

24 Michael Kienzle and Dirk Mende, *Theodor Heuss. Politik durch Kultur. 1949–1959. Katalog und Austellung* (Bonn 1984), 51.

25 cf. Max Goegler and Gregor Richter, eds., *Das Land Württemberg-Hohenzollern 1945–1952, Darstellungen und Erinnerungen* (Sigmaringen 1983).

26 Hartmut von Hentig: "Beweger, Anreger und Beförderer. Helmut Becker zum 70. Geburtstag," *Die Zeit,* 5, 13, 1983.

27 cited in Helmut Becker and Carl Nedelmann, *Psychoanalyse und Politik* (Frankfurt am Main 1983), 13f.

28 Alexander Mitscherlich, *Medizin ohne Menschlichkeit. Dokumente des Nürnberger Ärzteprozesses,* eds., Alexander Mitscherlich and Fred

Mielke (Heidelberg 1949), Introduction to the edition in Frankfurt am Main and Hamburg in 1960), 14f.

29 Vgl. Wolfgang Frühwald, "Märzenbier und Seidenhimmel. Zur Darstellung der Stadt-Persönlichkeit Münchens in der deutschen Nachkriegsliteratur," in Friedrich Prinz, *Trümmerzeit in München. Kultur und Gesellschaft einer deutschen Grotzstadt im Aufbruch 1945–1949* (München 1984) 231.

30 Marion Gräffin Dönhoff, *Namen die keiner mehr nennt. Ostpreutzen—Menschen und Geschichte* (München 1964), 33f.

31 Max Frisch, *Tagebuch 1946–1949* (München, Zürich 1965), 30f., 35, 37.

32 Alexander Mitscherlich, "Ödipus und Kaspar Hauser," *Der Monat,* 25 (1950), 16f., reprinted in *Gesammelte Schriften VII. Politisch-publizistische Aufsätze 3* (Frankfurt am Main 1983), 151 ff.

33 Herman Nohl, "Die geistige Lage im gegenwärtigen Deutschland," *Die Sammlung* (November 1947), 604.

34 Marie Luise Kaschnitz, "Von der Verwandlung," in *Menschen und Dinge 1945* (Heidelberg 1946), 97.

35 Erich Kästner, " . . . und dann fuhr ich nach Dresden," NZ, 9., 30 1946.

36 Alfred Kerr,, "Fünf Tage Deutschland," NZ, 7., 18. 8.11., 1947.

37 Peter de Mendelssohn, "Gegenstrahlungen," *Der Monat,* 14 (1949), 173f.

38 Siegfried Unseld, *Begegnungen mit Hermann Hesse* (Frankfurt am Main 1975), 37.

39 To the following, see Siegfried Unseld, *Begegnungen mit Hermann Hesse,* 28, 35 f.

40 Program to the new staging of "Schwarzen Jahrmarket" (Nurnberg 1975).

41 To the following, see Peter Roos, *Genius loci. Gespräche über Literatur und Tübingen* (Pfullingen 1978). 33f., 55, 81 f.

42 Peter Roos, *Genius loci.* 81 f.

43 Isaac Deutscher, "Bayerische Landstratzen," in Bernd Schmidt and Hannes Schwenger, *Die Stunde Eins, Erzählungen, Reportagen, Essays aus der Nachkriegszeit* (München 1982), 21 ff.

44 Hans Werner Richter, "Unterhaltungen am Schienenstrang," *Der Ruf,* 10.1. 1946, 6 ff.

45 Dolf Sternberger, "Reise in Deutschland," *Die Wandlung,* 1 (1945–46), 7 ff.

46 Klaus R. Scherpe, "Erzwungener Alltag. Wahrgenommene und gedachte Wirklichkeit in der Reportageliteratur der Nachkriegszeit," in Jost Hermand, Helmut Peitsch and Klaus R. Scherpe, eds., *Nachkriegsliteratur in Westdeutschland 1945–49. Schreibweisen, Gattungen, Institutionen. Literatur im historischen Prozetz,* New Series 3, Argument-Sonderband (Berlin 1982), 35 ff.

47 Wolfgang Borchert, "Generation ohne Abschied," in *Drautzen vor der Tür und ausgewählte Erzählungen* (Hamburg 1956), 125.

48 Karl-Heinz Jantzen, "Eine Welt brach zusammen," *Die Zeit,* 5. 9. 1975.

49 Alexander and Margarete Mitscherlich, *Die Unfahigkeit zu trauern. Grundlagen kollektiven Verhaltens* (München 1967) 78 f.

50 Josef Müller-Marein, "Es war eine Kleiderfrage. Vor dreitzig Jahren: Plötzlich war der tausend-jährige Spuk vorbei," *Die Zeit,* 5. 9. 1975.

51 Marion Vriesländer, "Das neue Modeschaffen," NZ, 5. 31. 1946.

52 Joachim Fest, "Erziehung zur Skepsis. Gedken aus Anlatz einer Selbstvorstellung," *Neue Sammlung,* 4 (1983), 335.

53 Walther von Hollander, "Das Schicksal der Dreitzigjährigen," NZ 4. 22. 1948.

54 Winfried Maatz, *Die Fünfzigjährigen. Porträt einer verratenen Generation.* (Hamburg 1980), 12 ff.

55 A note by Martin Bormann about a talk with Hitler from 1. 29. 1944. cited in *Ausgewählte Dokumente zur Geschichte des Nationalsozialismus 1933–1945 (1),* ed. H. A. Jacobsen and W. Jochmann (Bielefeld 1961).

56 For this and the following, see Angela Vogel, "Familie," in Wolfgang Benz, ed., *Die Bundesrepublik Deutschland. Geschichte in drei Bänden.* Vol. 2: *Gesellschaft.* Frankfurt am Main 1983, 98 ff.

57 Helmut Schelsky, *Wandlungen der deutschen Familie der Gegenwart* (Stuttgart 1953), 48.

58 Martha Maria Gehrke, "Das Erlebnis von Suppe und Bett," *Frankfurter Rundschau,* 5. 10. 1975.

59 Inge Stolten, ed., *Der Hunger nach Erfahrung. Frauen nach '45.* (Berlin, Bonn 1981).

60 Hierzu Angela Vogel, *"Familie,"* 103 ff.

61 Karl Schnog, "Wann wird das sein?", *Ulenspiegel,* 5 (1948), 2.

62 Walter Kolbenhoff. "'Wenn ich unsichtbar wäre' Kinder schreiben uber einen alten Wunschtraum," NZ, 4. 4. 1948.

63 "Wer bekommt die Care-Pakete?" NZ, 10. 11. 1946.

64 F. H. Rein, "Hunger physiologisches und politisches Problem," NZ, 11. 18. 1946.

65 Spectator, "Victor Gollancz. Rettet Europa jetzt. Der Kampf eines grotzen Menschen gegen die Not," NZ, 11. 18. 1946.

66 Margaret Boveri, "Ich stehle Holt," in Fritz Heinrich Ryssel, ed., *Unser täglich Legen* (Freiburg im Breisgau 1948), 259.

67 *Telegraf,* 6. 24. 1947. cf. also Paul W. Meyer, *Die Zigarette als Generaltauschware im deutschen Schwarzen Markt," 1945 bis 1948—ein Beitrag zur Geldgeschichte und Geldtheorie* (Augsburg 1984).

68 Thaddäus Troll, "Vom Schwarzen Markt," in Hans A. Rümelin, ed., *So lebten wir . . . Ein Querschnitt durch 1947* (Willsbach 1984), 62 f.

69 Heinrich Jaenecke, "Die Jahre auf der Strafbank. Aus der Schwarzmarktzeit—Blick zurück in Scham," review of Frank Gruber, Gerhard Richter, *Die Schwarzmarktzeit—Deutschland zwischen 1945 und 1948* (Hamburg 1979), *Die Zeit.*

70 Adolf Guggenbühl, "Die deutsche Tragödie," NZ, 1. 25. 1948. 71. Walter Dirks, "Die Bauern," *Frankfurter Hefte* 10 (1947), 979 f.

71 Walter Dirks: "The Peasants"; *Frankfurter Hefte*, issue 10/1947, page 979 f.

72 Clemens Münster, "Das Dorf und die Not," *Frankfurter Hefte*, 9 (1946), 790.

73 Ernest L. Wynder, "Penicillin, Streptomyzin, Paludrin. Wundermittel, die keine Wundermittel sind. Die Vereinigten Staaten führend," NZ 2. 1. 1946.

74 "Eine erfolgreiche Konferenz," NZ, 3. 8. 1946.

75 Rudolf Krämer-Badoni, "Zustand einer Grotzstadtbevölkerung am Beispiel Frankfurts," *Die Wandlung*, 9 (1947), 831 ff.

76 Otto Bartning, "Ketzerische Gedanken am Rande der Trümmerhaufen," *Frankfurter Hefte*, 1 (1946), 64.

77 "Grotzstadt der Zukunft. Pläne zum Wiederaufbau Berlins," NZ, 8. 23. 1946.

78 cf. Vittorio M. Lampugnani, "Wiederaufbau? Unmöglich. Deutsche Stadtplanung nach 1945. Keine 'Stunde Null'," *Frankfuter Allgemeine Zeitung*, 8. 24. 1983. cf. the booklets on these themes: *Wieder-Aufbau oder Neubeginn?, Die Legende von der "Stunde Nulle." Bauwelt* (1981) and 48 (1984). Die Legende von der "Stunde Nulle." Bauwelt (1981) and 48 (1984).

79 Alfons Leitl, "Erwägungen und Tatsachen zum deutschen Städte-Aufbau," *Frankfurter Hefte*, 4 (1946), 64.

80 cf. Vittorio M. Lampugnani, "Wiederaufbau? Unmöglich."

81 Bruno E. Werner, "Romantik und Wirklichkeit. Gedanken über den Wiederaufbau," NZ, 7. 25. 1947.

82 Erich Kästner, *"Gesammelte Schriften für Erwachsene,"* vol. 7: *Vermischte Beiträge II* (Munich, Zurich 1969), 15.

83 cf. Werner Burkhardt, "Musik der Stunde Null," *Zeit-Magazin*, Nr. 46 and 47 (1983), 37 f.

84 Oliver Hassencamp, *Der Sieg nach dem Krieg. Die gute schlechte Zeit* (Munich, Berlin, n. p.), 109 ff.

85 Oliver Hassencamp, *Der Sieg nach dem Krieg*, 31 f.

86 Werner Burckhardt, "Musik der Stunde Null," 47 (1983), 44 f.

87 Thomas Mann, "Deutsche Hörer! Fünfundfünfzig Radiosendungen nach Deutschland," 289.

88 cited in Peter Hamm, "While zur Ohnmacht. Ein Porträt des katholischen Schriftstellers Reinhold Schneider," *Die Zeit*, 4. 10. 1984.

89 Reinhold Schneider, *Das Unzerstörbare* (Freiburg i. B. 1945), 3 ff.

90 Sigrid Undset, "Die Umerziehlung der Deutschen," NZ 10. 25. 1945.

91 Karl Jaspers, "Antwort an Sigrid Undset," NZ, 11. 4. 1945.

92 "Jaspers' Weggang von Heidelberg," NZ, 3. 25. 1948.

93 cited in J. F. G. Grossert, *Die grotze Kontroverse Ein Briefwechsel um Deutschland* (Hamburg, Genf, Paris 1963), 19.

94 cited in J. F. G. Grosser. *Die grotze Kontroverse,* 24 f.

95 Thomas Mann, "Warum ich nicht nach Deutschland zurückgehe," 180.

96 Herman Hesse, "Brief nach Deutschland," NZ, 8. 2. 1946.

97 Walter Muschg, "Der Ptolemäer. Abschied von Gottfried Benn," in *Die Zerstörung der deutschen Literatur* (Munich, n. p.), 140.

98 Alfred Weber, *Abschied von der bisherigen Geschichte. Überwindung des Nihilismus?* (Hamburg 1946), 8.

99 Alfred Weber, *Abschied von der bisherigen Geschichte,* 221, 231, 252 f.

100 Friedrich Meinecke, *Die deutsche Katastrophe. Betrachtungen und Erinnerungen* (Wiesbaden 1946), 7 f., 174 ff.

101 c.f. Hermann Glaser, *Weltliteratur der Gegenwart. Dargestellt in Problemkreisen* (Frankfurt am Main, Berlin, Wein 1970), 165 f.

102 c.f. Hans Mayer. *Von Lessing bis Thomas Mann. Wandlungen der bürgerlichen Literatur in Deutschland* (Pfullingen 1949).

103 Thomas Mann, *Doktor Faustus. Das Legen des deutschen Tonsetzers Adrian Leverkühn erzählt von einem Freunde* (Frankfurt am Main 1981), 510.

104 Nelly Sachs, "In den Wohnungen des Todes," in *Das Leiden Israels.* (Frankfurt am Main 1964), 79.

105 Ernst Niekisch, *Das Reich der niederen Dämonen* (Hamburg 1953), 111.

106 Erich Kästner, "Streiflichter aus Nürnberg, NZ 11. 23. 1945.

107 Hans Mayer, *Ein Deutscher auf Widerruf. Erinnerungen (1)* (Frankfurt am Main 1982), 351 f.

108 Adolf Guggenbühl, "Die deutsche Tragödie (II)" NZ 1. 29. 1948.

109 cited in Klaus Hohfield, ed., *Dokumente der Deutschen Politik und Geschichte,* 20 f.

110 To this and the following, see Martin Greschat, "Die Evangelische Kirche," in Wolfgang Benz, ed., *Die Bunders-republik Deutschland. Geschichte in drei Bänden.* Vol. 2: *Gesellschaft.* (Frankfurt am Main 1983), 265 ff.

111 cited in Franklin Hamlin Littell, *The German Phoenix* (Garden City, N.Y. 1960), 189.

112 Karl Barth, *Offene Briefe* 1945–1968 (Zürich 1984).

113 c.f. Heinrich Albertz, "Martin Niemöller. Ein Christ und deutscher Patriot," *Die Zeit,* 3. 16. 1984.—Anton Andreas Guha, "Eiferer und Versöhnender. Martin Niemöller—Ein Mensch des Widerspruchs," *Vorwärts,* 3. 15. 1984.—Karl Grobe, "Ein Mensch mit seinem Widerspruch. Zum Tode von Martin Niemöller," *Frankfurter Rundschau,* 3. 8. 1984.—Christian Schütze, "Guter Pastor und Bekenner. Zum Tode Martin Niemöllers," *Suddeutsche Zietung,* 3. 9. 1984.—Heinrich Stubbe, "Ein reiner Tor im Fegefeure. Der Weg des früheren hessischen Kirchenpräsidenten," *Rheinischer Merkur/Christ und Welt,* 3. 9. 1984.

114 Speech of Pastor Niemöllers in the Neustädter Kirche in Erlangen, NZ 2. 1. 1946, 2. 15. 1946.

115 To this and the following, see Günter Hollenstein, "Die Katholische Kirche," in Wolfgang Benz, ed., *Die Bundesrepublik Deutschland,* 238 ff.

116 Walter Jens, "Unsere Vernichtung. Eine Rede über Juden und Deutsche," Frankfurter Allgemeine Zeitung, 3. 22. 1980.

117 "An unsere Leser," *Frankfurter Hefte,* (1946), 2.

118 Eugen Kogon, "Gericht und Gewissen," *Frankfurter Hefte,* 1. (1946), 25 ff., 37.

119 Walter Dirks, "Das gesellschaftspolitische Engagement der deutschen Katholiken seit 1945," *Frankfurter Hefte,* 11 (1964) 761 f.

120 Konrad Adenauer, *Erinnerungen. 1945–1953* (Stuttgart 1965), 51.

121 c.f. Konrad Adenauer, *Briefe 1947–1949. Rhöndorfer Ausgabe,* ed. Rudolf Morsey and Hans-Peter Schwarz, commissioned by Stiftung Bundeskranzler-Adenauer-Haus, ed. Hans Peter Mensing. (Berlin 1984).

122 Christoph Meekel, *Suchbild. Über meinen Vater* (Düsseldorf 1980), 28 ff.

123 Hans Dieter Schäfer, *Das gespaltene Bewutzstein. Über deutsche Kultur und Lebenswirklichkeit 1933–1945* (Munich 1981), 7, 10, 54.

124 cited in Hans Dieter Schäfer, ed., *Am Rande der Nacht. Moderne Klassik im Dritten Reich. Ein Lesebuch* (Frankfurt am Main, Berlin, Wein 1984), 289.

125 Peter Buchta, "Der Porträtist des deutschen Charakters. Zum Tode des Filmregisseurs Wolfgang Staudte," *Süddeutsche Zeitung,* 22. 21. 1. 1984.

126 *Das Kunstwerk,* 1.2 (1948), 36.

127 Klaus Mann, *Der Wendepunkt. Ein Lebensbericht* (Frankfurt am Main and Hamburg 1963), 427, 439 ff.

128 cited in Bayerische Landeszentrale für Heimatdienst, *Nach dem Zusammenbruch. Zur Zeitgeschichte seit 1945 (I). Wandzeitung Heimat und Staat.* Number 7 (1961).

129 for the following, see Melvin J. Lasky, "Die kurze Geschichte des Morgenthau-Plans. Ein dokumentarischer Rückblick," *Der Monat,* 10 (1949), 7 ff.

130 "Die 'weitze Liste' deutscher Kultur. Ausschaltung nationalsozialistischer Elemente aus dem Kunstleben, NZ, 10. 25. 1945.

131 Alexander Mitscherlich, "Analyse des Stars. Ein Beitrag zum Fall Furtwängler," NZ, 7. 8. 1946.

132 "Steht Kunst über Politik? Furtwangler vor der Entnazifizierungskommission," NZ 12. 16. 1946.

133 cited in Hans Daiber: *Deutsches Theater seit 1945. Bundesrepublik Deutschland, Deutsche Demokratische Republik, Österreich, Schweiz* (Stuttgart 1976), 42.

134 c.f. Hans Daiber: *Deutsches Theater seit 1945,* 45.

135 For this and the following, see Hans Daiber. *Deutsches Theater seit 1945,* 42 ff.

136 For the following, "Georg Meistermann. Die Legende von der Stunde Null. Über die Umwege bei der Vergangenheitsbe-wältigung," *Sud-deutsche Zeitung,* 14. 2. 15. 1981.

137 Georg Meistermann, "Die Legend von der Stunde Null."

138 "Ein Brief Erich Ebermayers. Ein politisches und sittliches Dokument," NZ, 11. 8. 1945.

139 cited in Hans Daiber, *Deutsches Theater seit 1945,* 46.

140 Hans Werner Richter. Wie entstand und was war die Gruppe 47? in Hans Z. Neunzig *Werner Richter und die Gruppe 47.* Frankfurt am Main, Berlin, Wein, 1981, 34.

141 Alfred Andersch, "Das junge Europa formt sein Gesicht," *Der Ruf,* 1 (1946); Hans A. Neunzig, ed., *Der Ruf. Unabhängige Blätter für die junge Generation. Eine Auswahl. (Munich 1976), 19 ff.*

142 Hans Werner Richter, "Wie entstand und was war die Gruppe 47?" 38; c.f. Erich Kuby, "Der legendäre 'Ruf'. Über die Installation amerikanischer Gedanken," *Transatlantik,* 9 (1984), 16 ff.

143 c.f. Alfons Söllner, ed., *Zur Ärchäologie der Demokratie in Deutschland. Analysen politischer Emigranten im amerikanischen Geheimdienst* (Frankfurt am Main 1982) Ferner Michael Thomas. *Deutschland, England über alles. Rückkehr als Besatzungsoffizier* (Berlin 1984).

144 "Gespräch mit einem Verleger. Ernst Rowohlt über seinen Ro-Ro-Ro-Plan," NZ 12. 9. 1946.

145 cited in Peter Mendelssohn, "Abbruch des geistigen Gettos, in *Bayerischer Rundfunk: Radio Revue. Die Jahre nach 45.* Manuscript of program. 1. 2. 1981, 7 f.

146 "General Eisenhower an die 'Neue Zeitung' Zum Geleit," NZ 10. 18. 1945.

147 Otto Zoff, *Tagebücher aus der Emigration (1939–1944)* (Heidelberg 1968), 192 f.

148 c.f. Peter Kritzer, *Wilhelm Hoegner. Politische Biographie eines bayerischen Sozialdemokraten.* (München 1979).

149 cited in Hans-Albert Walter, *Tradition und Erbe. Das 'andere' Deutschland in West und Ost.* Bayerischer Rundfunk. Funkmanuskript (Munich, n.p.), 11. c.f. Gerhard Hirschfeld, *Exil in Grotzbrittannien. Zur Emigration aus dem nationalsozialistischen Deutschland* (Stuttgart 1983). Also John Russel Taylor: *Fremde im Paradies. Emigranten in Hollywood 1933–1950.* (Berlin 1984).

150 Richard Drews and Alfred Kantorowicz, *Verboten und verbrannt. Deutsche Literatur 12 Jahre unterdrückt* (Berlin and Munich 1947), 9 f.

151 Paul E. Lüth, *Literatur als Geschichte. Deutsche Dichtung von 1885–1947,* 2 vols. (Wiesbaden 1947), 580.

152 "Gestrichene Namen," NZ 10. 21. 1945; c.f. also NZ, 10. 21. 1945.

153 For this and the following, see Theodor Eschenburg, *Jahre der Besatzung. 1945–1949. Geschichte der Bundesrepublik Deutschland in fünf Bänden,* eds. Karl Dietrich Bracher, Theodor Eschenburg, Joachim C. Fest, Eberhart Jäckel. Vol. 1 (Stuttgart, Wiesbaden 1983), 114 ff.

154 cited in Peter Kritzer, *Wilhelm Hoegner,* 245.

156 Harold von Hofe, ed., *Briefe von und an Ludwig Marcuse* (Zurich 1975), 75.

157 Wolfgang Koeppen, *Das Treibhaus* (Berlin, Grunewald), 10.

158 Hans von Eckardt, "Es ist an der Zeit!" NZ, 10. 25. 1945.

159 Gerhard Storz, *Zwischen Amt und Neigung. Legensbericht aus der Zeit nach 1945* (Stuttgart 1976), 34.

160 For this and the following, see Jutta B. Lange-Quassowski, "Demokratisierung der Deutschen durch Umerziehung? Die Interdependenz von deutscher und amerikanischer Politik in der Vorgeschichte der Bundesrepublik Deutschland," in *Aus Politik und Zeitgeschichte.* suppl. vol. to *'Das Palament',* 7. 22. 1978, 17 ff.—Also: Manfred Heinemann *Umerziehung und Wideraufbau. Die Bildungspolitik der Besatzungsmächte in Deutschland und Österreich* (Stuttgart 1981).

161 Oskar Vogelhuber, "Erneuerung der Schule," NZ, 2. 15. 1948.

162 c.f. Ulrich Chaussy, "Jugend," in Wolfgang Benz, ed., *Die Bundesrepublik Deutschland. Geschichte in drei Bänden,* Vol. 2: *Gesellschaft* (Frankfurt am Main 1983), 40.—Karl Dietrich Erdmann, "Überblick über die Entwicklung der Schule in Deutschland 1945–1949," *Neue Sammlung,* 3 (1976), 215 ff.

163 O. Haase, "Die drei Quellen der Schulreaktion," *Die Schule,* 3 (1948).

164 "Die neuen Schulbücher," NZ 5. 17. 1946.

165 "Hohere Schulen in Betrieb. Ferien erst im Herbst—Jähriger Unterricht—möglichst ohne Schulgeld," NZ 3. 4. 1946.

166 Martha Maria Gehrke, "Es kommt auf die Persönlichkeit an," NZ 2. 21. 1947.

167 "Höhere Schulen in Betrieb," NZ, 3. 4. 1946.

168 Gerhard Storz, *Zwischen Amt und Neigung,* 30 f.

169 Karl Kietrich Erdmann, "Überblick über die Entwicklung der Schule in Deutschland 1945–1949," 220.

170 To the following: Ludwig Kerstiens, "Die höhere Schule in den Reformplänen der Nachkriegszeit," *Zeitschrift für Padägogik,* 6 (1965), 538 ff.

171 Die Sammlung, 4 (1946), 197 ff.

172 Alfred Döblin, "Reise zur Mainzer Universität," *Das Goldene Tor,* September 1946, 100 ff.

173 To the following: "Berichte aus vier deutschen Hochschulen," NZ, 11. 4. 1945.

174 Hans J. von Goerzke, "Internationale Diskussion in Marburg. Auslandische Professoren vor deutschen Studenten," NZ, 9. 13. 1946.

175 Karl Barth, "Der deutsche Student," NZ, 12. 8. 1947.

176 Alexander Mitscherlich, *Ein leben für die Psychoanalyse. Anmerkungen zu meiner Zeit.* (Frankfurt am Main 1980), 187 f.

177 Karl Jaspers, "Die Verantwortlichkeit der Universitäten," NZ 5. 16. 1947.

178 *Hochland.* (August 1947), 576 ff.

179 "die neuen Volkshochschulen. Übersicht des Wiederaufbaus," NZ, 4. 22. 1946.

180 Ludwig Kroeber-Keneth, "Diskussion um die Volkshochschule," NZ, 11. 8. 1946.

181 Hildegard Brücher, "Ein Wall gegen Hatz und Not. Bericht aus Ulm," NZ, 6. 27. 1947.

182 cited in Andreas Schwarz, "Design, Grafik Design, Werbung," in Wolfgang Benz, ed., *Die Bundesrepublik Deutschland. Geschichte in drei Bänden.* Vol. 3: *Kultur* (Frankfurt am Main 1983), 229.

183 Archive Hermann Glaser, Rotztal.

184 Hannes Heer, ed., *Als ich 9 Jahre alt war, kam der Krieg. Ein Lesebuch gegen den Krieg* (Reinbek bei Hamburg 1983), 104 f. and the following: 119, 129.

185 *Die Sammlung,* 10 (1949), 639.

186 Ulrich Chaussy, "Jugend," 35 f.

187 cited in Ibid., 37.

188 "Jugend zwischen gestern und morgen. Verwhrlosung und Kriminalität der Jugendlichen—Gefahr oder Zeiterscheinung," NZ, 2. 8. 1948.

189 Ibid.

190 "Junge Menschen über ihre Not. Briefe an die Neue Zeitung erörtern ein Generationsproblem," NZ, 4. 1. 1946.

191 Bruno E. Werner, "Hoffnungslose Jugend? Anmerkungen zu einem Diskussionsabend," NZ, 3. 7. 1948.

192 Hans-Peter Berglar-Schröer, "Die Vertrauenskrise der Jugend," *Frankfurter Hefte,* 7 (1947), 696.

193 Cited in Ulrich Chaussy, "Jugend," 42.

194 Michael Theunissen, "Wiedergelesen. Romano Guardini: 'Das Ende der Neuzeit'." *Frankfurter Allgemeine Zeitung,* 3. 3. 1977.

195 Cited in "Ein Gesprach mit dem Schweizer Theologen. Karl Barth sagt: "Ich fühle wie Vater Noah," *Frankfurter Allgemeine Zeitung,* 5. 16. 1964.

196 See Hans Fischer-Barnicol, "Der Glaube als Befreiung. Rudolf Bultmann zum achtzigsten Geburtstag," *Christ und Welt,* 8. 21. 1964.

197 Cited in Hans Fischer-Barnicol, "Der Glaube als Befreiung."

198 c.f. Uta Ranke-Heinemann, "Jesus Christus und die Mythologie," *Die Zeit,* 3. 11. 1983.

199 Julius Ebbinghaus, "Was ist Existentialphilosophie?" NZ, 7. 28. 1947.

200 c.f. Hans Daiber, *Deutsches Theater seit 1945,* 33.

201 Jean-Paul Sartre, *No Exit and Three Other Plays* (New York: Vintage Books, 1949), 108, 121–122.

202 Friedrich Luft, "Berliner Tage mit Sartre," NZ, 2. 5. 1948.

203 See Kurt Rossmann, "Martin Heideggers Holzwege," *Der Monat,* 21 (1950), 236 ff.

204 Theodor W. Adorno, *Jargon der Eigentlichkeit. Zur deutschen Ideologie* (Frankfurt am Main 1964), 14.

205 Albert Camus. *The Myth of Sisyphus and Other Essays,* translated by Justin O'Brien (New York: Vintage Books, 1955), 91.

206 c.f. Helmut Schelsky, *Die skeptische Generation. Eine Soziologie der deutschen Jugend.* (Düsseldorf 1963), e.g., 74 ff.—Karl Seidelmann, *Bund und Gruppe als Lebensformen deutscher Jugend. Versuch einer Erscheinungs-kunde des deutschen Jugendlebens in der ersten Hälfte des 20. Jahrhunderts* (Munich 1955).

207 Also for the following, c.f. Norbert Frei, "Die Presse," in Wolfgang Benz, ed., *Die Bundesrepublik Deutschland. Geschichte in drei Bänden,* Vol. 3: *Kultur* (Frankfurt am Main 1983), 275 ff. Also: Harry Pross, *Deutsche Presse seit 1945* (Bern 1965).

208 Ernst Strunk, "Roman der Produktion," NZ, 3. 1. 1946.

209 Ernst Strunk: "The Story of Production"; *NZ,* March 1, 1946.

210 Norbert Frei, "Die Presse," 280 f.

211 c.f. Harry Pross, "Um Grundkonflikte herumgemogelt. Hat der deutsche Journalismus nach 1945 versagt?," *Süddeutsche Zeitung,* 10. 6/./7. 1979.

212 Cited in Kurt Pritzkoleit, "Das deutsche Pressewunder," *Die Kultur,* 9. 30. 1955.

213 Ibid.

214 Ibid.

215 Eugen Kogon, "Vom Elend unserer Presse," *Frankfurter Hefte,* 7. (1948), 616 f.

216 *Freie Deutsche Presse,* 12 (1948).

217 Norbert Frei, "Die Presse," 295.

218 *Nürnberger Nachrichten,* Number 1 (10. 11. 1945) ff.

219 Hans Wallenberg, "Dank an die Mitarbeiter," NZ, 10. 21. 1946.

220 c.f. Heinz-Dietrich Fischer, *Reeducations- und Pressepolitik unter britischem Besatzungsstatus. Die Zonenzeitung 'Die Welt' 1946–1950. Konzeption, Artikulation und Rezeption* (Düsseldorf 1978).

221 *Der Monat,* 1 (1948), 3.

222 Hans Schwab-Felisch. "'Der Monat'—ein Zeitdokument," *Merkut,* 4 (1971), 407 f.

223 Hellmut Jaesrich, "Das Besatzungskind," *Der Monat,* 241 (1968) 4.

224 Hans Schwab-Felisch, "Der Monat," 405 ff.

225 Hartmann Goertz, "Die Flucht in die Zeitschrift," NZ 1. 13. 1947.

226 Eugen Kogon and Walter Dirks, "An unsere Leser," *Frankfurter Hefte* 1 (1946) 2.

227 Eugene Kogon and Walter Dirks: "To Our Feaders"; *Frankfurter Hefte,* issue 1/1946, page 2.

228 Alfred Doblin, "Geleitwort," *Das Goldene Tor,* 1 (1946) 3 ff.

229 Rudolf Pechel, "In eigener Sache," Deutsche Rundschau, 1 (1946) 1.

230 Hans Paeschke, "Verantwortlichkeit des Geistes," *Merkut,* 1 (1947) 109 f.

231 Heinrich Vormweg, "Literatur war ein Asyl," in Nicolas Born and Jürgen Manthey, eds., *Nachkriegsliteratur. Literaturmagazin 7* (Reinbek bei Hamburg 1977), 203.

232 Theodor W. Adorno, "Auferstehung der Kultur in Deutschland?," *Frankfurter Hefte,* 5. (1950), 471.

233 c.f. for the following: Ingrid Laurien, "Politisch-kulturelle Zeitschriften in den Westzonen von 1945–1949," in Helga Grebing, ed., "Zur Politischen Kultur im Nachkriegsdeutschland. Politische und kulturelle Zeitschriften in Deutschland 1945–1949." (unpublished mss., 1980).

234 Hans Werner Richter, *Briefe an einen jungen Sozialisten* (Hamburg 1974), 113.

235 Heinrich Vormweg, "Literatur als Asyl," 203.

236 Peter Sandmeyer, "Schreiben nach 1945. Ein Interview mit Wolfdieterich Schnurre," in *Nachkriegsliteratur. Literaturmagazin 7,* 191 ff.

237 Hartmann Goertz, "Die Flucht in die Zeitschrift."

238 c.f. Wilmont Haacke and Günter Pötter, *Die politische Zeitschrift. 1665–1965,* vol. 2. (Stuttgart 1982).

239 "Redaktionelle Notiz," *Deutsches Allgemeines Sonntagsblatt,* 10. 1. 1967.

240 "Unsere Aufgabe," *Die Zeit,* 2. 21. 1946.

241 Gerd Bucerius, "'Immer mehr gahalten als versprochen.' Brief an den toten Freund Josef Muller-Marcin," *Die Zeit,* 10. 23. 1981.

242 Gerd Bucerius, "Vom Wesen der Demokratie. Die Qualen des Neuanfangs 1945, gespiegelt in den Artikeln eines grotzen Journalisten: Ernst Friedlaender." To Norbert Frei und Franziska Friedlaender, eds., *Ernest Friedlaender zur Zeit. Leitartikel aus den Jahren 1946–1949* (Munich 1982), *Die Zeit,* 3. 25. 1983.

243 Cited in Hans Dieter Jaene, *Der Spiegel. Ein deutsches Nachrichten-Magazin* (Frankfurt am Main und Hamburg 1968), 25 f.

244 Hans Dieter Jaene, *Der Spiegel,* 29 ff.

245 Hans Bredow, "Der Parteirundfunk im Dritten Reich," NZ, 3. 1. 1946.

246 Cited in Hans Bausch, ed., *Rundfunk in Deutschland,* vol. 3, Hans Bausch, *Rundfunkpolitik nach 1945,* part 1 (Münich 180), 73.

247 c.f. Michael Tracey, *Sir Hugh Greene. Mit dem Rundfunk Geschichte gemacht* (Berlin 1984).

248 Hans Mayer, *Ein Deutscher auf Widerruf, Erinnerungen (I)* (Frankfurt am Main 1982), 337, 353 f.

249 Hannes W. A. Schoeller, "Deutschlands Stimme im Rundfunk," NZ, 3. 31. 1947.

250 To this and the following, Hans Oesch, "Zur Entwicklung der zeitgenössischen Musik. 1945–1950," in *Deutscher Musikrat, Zeitgenössische Musik in der Bundesrepublik Deutschland. I: 1945–1950,* enclosure, 8.

251 Melos, 1 (1946).

252 c.f. Alois Melichar, *Musik in der Zwangsjacke* (Stuttgart, n.p.).

253 c.f. Darl Dahlhaus, Introduction: *Deutscher Musikrat: Zeitgenössische Musik in der Bundesrepublik Deutschland I,* 5.

254 Walter Abendroth, "Die Krise der Neuen Musik. Eine Polemik zur höchst notwendigen Aufklärung eines vertracken Sachverhaltes," *Die Zeit,* 46 (1958).

255 Cited in Hans Daiber, *Deutsches Theater seit 1945,* 113.

256 Hans Mersmann, "Der Hörer der modernen Musik," NZ, 2. 5. 1948.

257 Egon Vietta, "Die stetige Revolution der neuen Musik. Bericht und Bemerkungen zu den internationalen Ferienkursen für neue Musik in Kranichstein, Darmstadt," *Die Kultur,* 8. 1. 1957.

258 H. H. Stuckenschmidt, "Kranichstein, das Schlotz der Neutöner," NZ, 8. 8. 1947.

259 cited in H. H. Stuckenschmidt, "Luft vom anderen Planeten. Notizen über Arnold Schönberg," *Frankfurter Allgemeine Zeitung,* 12. 12. 1964.

260 c.f. Ulrich Dibelius, "Musik," in Wolfgang Benz, ed., *Die Bundesrepublik Deutschland. Geschichte in drei Bänden,* vol. 3: *Kultur* (Frankfurt am Main 1983), 114.

261 Ulrich Dibelius, "Musik," 112.

262 Hans Mayer, "Begegnung mit Paul Hindemith," NZ, 6. 6. 1947.

263 c.f. Fritz Brust, "'Abraxas' von Egk," NZ, 12. 12. 1947.

264 Werner Suhr, "Werner Egks, 'Abraxas'," NZ, 6. 10. 1948.

265 Werner Egk, *Die Zeit wartet nicht. Künstlerisches, Zeitgeschichtliches, Privates aus meinem Leben* (Munich 1981), 398 ff.

266 Ulrich Dibelius, "Musik," 110 f.

267 c.f. Franzpeter Messmer, "Münchner Tradition und Klassische Moderne—der Musikalische Neuanfang," in Friedrich Prinz, ed., *Trummerzeit in München, Kultur und Gesellschaft einer deutschen Grotzstadt im Aufbruch 1945–1949* (Munich 1984), 174.

268 Ernst Bloch, *Das Prinzip Hoffnung,* vol. 3 (Frankfurt am Main 1973), 1249 f., 1258.

269 Joachim-Ernst Berendt, "Der Jazzfan," *Melos,* 24 (1957), 289.

270 Theodor W. Adorno, "Zeitlose Mode. Zum Jazz (1953)," *in Prismen, Kulturkritik und Gesellschaft* (Munich 1963), 132.

271 Ernst Wiechert, "Über Kunst und Künstler," in *Das Gedicht, Blatter für Dichtung* (Hamburg 1946). Cited in Berndt Schmidt and Hannes Schwenger, *Die Stunde Eins. Erzählungen, Reportagen, Essays aus der Nachkriegszeit* (Munich 1982), 47 ff.

272 Doris Schmidt, *Briefe an Günther Franke. Portrait eines deutschen Kunsthändlers* (Cologne 1970), 179.

273 Gerhard Finckh, "Die Suche nach dem 'richtigen' Stil—Kunstdiskussion in München 1945–1949," in Friedrich Prinz, ed., *Trümmerzeit in München,* 113.

274 *Zeitgenössische Kunst I. Moderne Graphik* (Munich, March/April 1946), 5.

275 Friedrich Adama von Scheltema, "Ist der Expressionismus noch junge Kunste?"*Prisma,* 2 (1946), 17 f.—Karl Scheffler, "Die fetten und die mageren Jahre (1946)," (1938), 414 ff.—H. Lüdecke, "Die Tragödie des Expressionismus. Notizen zu seiner Soziologie," in K. Hofer, O. Nerlinger, eds., *Bildenke Kunst 3* (1949), 109 ff.

276 Heinz Trökes, "Der Surrealismus," *Das Kunstwerk,* 8 (1947), 30 ff.

277 Gottfried Sello, "Surrealist furs Leben. Das Gesamtwerk von Heinz Trökes," *Die Zeit* (December 1979).—c.f. also *Akademie der Künste Berlin: Heinz Trökes.* Catalogue (Berlin 1979).

278 Barbara Klie, "Übergangszeit. Drei Phasen der Kunst nach dem Krieg," *Der Monat,* 200 (1965), 100.

279 Cited in Freya Mülhaupt, "' . . . und was lebt, flieht die Norm.' Aspekte der Nachkriegskunst," in, Bernard Schulz, ed., *Grauzonen Farbwelten. Kunst und Zeitbilder 1945–1955.* Catalogue for the exhibition of the Neue Gesellschaft fur Bildende Kunst (Berlin-Vienna 1983), 193.

280 Freya Mülhaupt: "' . . . und was lebt, flieht die Norm'" 193.

281 Ibid., 220.

282 Wilhelm Uhde, "Abstrakte Malerei," *Die Umschau,* 2 (1946), 187 ff.

283 Wieland Schmied, "Zeitgenössische Kunst: Entwicklungen der deutschen Malerei von 1945 bis zu den siebziger Jahren," Universitas, 12 (1979), 1253 f.

284 Franz Roh, "Ein Gespräch über abstrakte Malerei. Zur Ausstellung Willi Baumeister," NZ, 9. 26. 1947.

285 Cited in Gerhard Finckh, "ZEN 49," in Friedrich Prinz, ed., *Trümmerzeit in München. Kultur und Gesellschaft einer deutschen Grotzstadt im Aufbruch 1945–1949* (Munich 1984), 120.

286 c.f. Ibid.

287 Hamburger Kunsthalle, *Kunst in Deutschland 1898–1973.* Catalogue, ed., Werner Hofmann et al (Hamburg 1973), for year 1947.

288 Cited in Freya Mülhaupt: "' . . . und was lebt, flieht die Norm,'" 187.

289 Eberhard Hempel, "Ruinenschönheit," *Zeitschrift für Kunst,* 2. (1948), 76 ff.

290 Freya Mülhaupt: "' . . . und was lebt, flieht die Norm,'" 289.

291 Bruno E. Werner, "Kunst in der katakombe," *Nordwestdeutsche Hefte,* 3 (1946), cited in Charles Schüddekopf, *Vor den Toren der Wirklichkeit. Deustchland 1946–1947 im Spiegel der Nordwestdeutschen Hefte* (Berlin, Bonn 1980), 343.

292 Hans Eckstein, *Maler und Bildhauer in München* (Munich 1946), Introduction.

293 c.f. Doris Schmidt, "Bildende Kunst," in Wolfgang Benz, ed., *Die Bundesrepublik Deutschland,* Vol. 3, 183.

294 c.f. Akademie der Kunste Berlin, *Als der Krieg zu Ende war. Kunst in Deutschland 1945–1950. Ausstellungsverzeichnis* (Berlin 1975), 9.

295 Bruno E. Werner, "Zwischen Kopfschütteln und Anerkennung. Eröffnung der Augsburger Ausstellung 'Extreme Malerei,'" NZ, 2. 3. 1947.

296 Erich Kästner, "Die Augsburger Diagnose. Kunst und deutsche Jugend," NZ, 1. 7. 1946.
297 Hans Sedlmayr, *Verlust der Mitte. Die bildende Kunst des 19. und 10. Jahrhunderts als Symptom und Symbol der Zeit* (Frankfurt am Main 1955), 88, 133.
298 c.f. H. G. Evers, ed., *Darmstädter Gespräch. Das Menschenbild unserer Zeit* (Darmstadt 1950), 150 ff.
299 Siegfried Melchinger, "Struktur, Klima, Personen. Deutsches Theater seit 1945. Ein Überblick," *Theater heute,* 10 (1970), 3.
300 Friedrich Luft, "Triumph der Dorsch," NZ, 10. 7. 1946.
301 c.f. Hans Daiber, *Deutsches Theater seit 1945,* 63 ff.
302 "Köpfe der Woche," NZ, 10. 7. 1946.
303 Fritz Kortner, *Aller Tage Abend* (Munich 1959), 560 ff.
304 To this and the following, see Hans Daiber, *Deutsches Theater seit 1945,* 11 ff.
305 Henning Rischbieter, "Theater," in Wolfgang Benz, ed., *Die Bundersrepublik Deutschland. Geschichte in drei Bänden.* Vol. 3: *Kultur* (Frankfurt am Main 1983), 73.
306 Cited in Hans Daiber, *Deutsches Theater seit 1945,* 26.
307 Bruno E. Werner, "Kritik der Theaterkritik," NZ, 5. 30, 1948.
308 "'Unsere Not, unsere Tugend.' Von der interzonalen Tagung der Bühnenbildner und technischen Bühnenvorstande in Hamburg," NZ, 8. 11. 1947.
309 c.f. Henning Rischbieter, "Theater," 74.
310 Cited in Hans Daiber, *Deutsches Theater seit 1945,* 27.
311 Hans Schwab-Felisch, "Am Ende des bürgerlichen Theaters? Der konservative Grundzug des deutschen Nachkriegstheaters—Dusseldorfer Schauspiel," *Theater heute,* 10 (1970), 49.
312 Thomas Kore, "Hamburger Theaterindrücke," NZ, 2. 14. 1947.
313 Heinz Rode, "Theaterfahrt durch die US-Zone (II)," NZ, 11. 17. 1947.
314 Heinz Rode, "Theaterfahrt durch die US Zone (I)," NZ, 11. 10. 1947.
315 Bruno E. Werner, "Kulturvogel über Trümmern, Kunst und Theater in Stuttgart," NZ, 12. 8. 1947.
316 Dieter Sattler, "Ansprache zur Versammlung der Theater-direktoren, Oktober 1947," cited in Friedrich Prinz, ed., *Trümmerzeit in München. Kultur und Gesellschaft einer deutschen Grotzstadt im Aufbruch 1945–1949* (Munich 1984), 203.
317 Christiane Wilke, "Das mittelgrotze Welttheater. Die Stattstheater in München," in Friedrich Prinz, ed., *Trümmerzeit in München,* 208.
318 To the following, Walther Schmieding, "Kunst gab ich für Kohle. Die Entstehung der Ruhrfestspield. Legende und Wirklichkeit," *Frankfurter Allgemeine Zeitung,* 5. 26. 1977.
319 To this and the following, Hans Daiber, *Deutsches Theater seit 1945,* 77 ff.
320 Wolfgang Pöschl, "Aida ohne Dekorationen. Ein gelungenes Experiment in Kassel," NZ, 11. 15. 1946.

321 Karl Heinz Ruppel, "Das moderne Bühnenbild," *Süddeutsche Zeitung,* (1948).

322 "Unsere Not unsere Tugend. Von der interzonalen Tagung der Bühnenbildner und technischen Bühnenvorstande in Hamburg," NZ, 8. 11. 1947.

323 c.f. Siegfried Nestriepke, *Neues Beginnen. Die Geschichte der Freien Volksbühne Berlin 1946 bis 1955* (Berlin-Grunewald 1956).

324 Gody Suter, "Zürcher Schauspielhaus. Bilanz eines Zuschauers," NZ, 1. 6. 1947.

325 Cited in Ibid.

326 Cited in Hans Daiber, *Deutsches Theater seit 1945,* 8.

327 C. F. Henning Rischbieter, "Theater," in Wolfgang Benz, ed., *Die Bundesrepublik Deutschland. Geschichte in drei Bänden,* Vol. 3: *Kultur* (Frankfurt am Main 1983), 76.

328 To this and the following, Hans Daiber, *Deutsches Theater seit 1945,* 51 ff.

329 Hans Daiber, *Deutsches Theater seit 1945,* 33.

330 Wigand Lange, "Die Schaubühne als politische Umerziehungsanslt. Theater in den Westzonen," in Jost Hermand, Helmut Peitsch and Klaus R. Scherpe, *Nachkriegsliteratur in Westdeutschland 1945–1949,* 23 f.

331 Walther Kiaulehn, "Rückschlüsse auf ein Publikum," NZ, 1. 4. 1947.

332 Bruno E. Werner, "Drei Aufführungen 'Mord im Dom'," NZ, 10. 27. 1947.

333 Troja und der Pazifismus," Zu einer Aufführung in den Münchner Kammerspielen," NZ, 4. 19. 1946.

334 To the following, Wigand Lange, "Die Schaubühne als politische Umerziehungsanstalt," 274.

335 Gunter Groll, "Das magische Theater. Vom Einbruch des Irrationalen in die junge Dramatik," in Alfred Dahlmann, ed., *Der Theater-Almanach 1946/47* (Munich 1947), 252 ff.

336 Wigand Lange, "Die Schaubühne als politische Umerzichung-sanstalt," 28 f.

337 Alfred Kantorowicz, *Deutsches Tagebuch. Erster Teil* (Berlin 1978), 315.

338 Cited in Hans Daiber, *Deutsches Theater seit 1945,* 19.

339 Cited in Ibid., 67.

340 Friedrich Luft, "Die Szene wird zum Tribunal. Berliner Theater-Bilanz," NZ, 4. 12. 1946.

341 Heinz Pauck, "'Drautzen vor der Tur.' Uraufführung in den Hamburg Kammerspielen," 11. 24. 1947.

342 Heinz Pauck, "'Des Teufels General.' Deutsche Erstaufführung in Hamburg," NZ, 11. 21. 1947.

343 For the following: Hans Daiber, *Deutsches Theater seit 1945,* 90 ff.

344 Henning Rischbieter, "Berlin, Deutsches Theater 1949. Brechts Wiederkehr," *Theater heute,* 10 (1983), 20.

345 See, Bernard Zeller, ed., *Klassiker in finsteren Zeiten. 1933–1945. Eine Ausstellung des Deutschen Literaturarchivs im Schiller-Nationalmuseum Marbach am Neckar. Band 2. Marbacher Katalog 38* (Marbach 1984), 167.—c.f. also Bernhard Zeller, ed., *Schau-Bühne. Schillers Dramen 1945–1984. Eine Ausstellung des Deutschen Literaturarchivs und des Theater-museums der Universität zu Köln. Marbacher Kataloge 39* (Marbach 1984).

346 Paul Rilla, *Theaterkritiken,* ed., Liane Pfelling (Berlin 1978), 24.

347 Cited in "Heimkehrer? Texte von Berthold Viertel, Fritz Kortner, Erwin Piscator," *Theater heute,* 10 (1970), 26.

348 Erich Kästner, "Der tägliche Kram," in *Gesammelte Schriften für Erwachsene,* Vol. 7: *Vermischte Beiträge II* (Munich, Zurich 1969), 14.

349 Friedrich Luft, "Die gepolsterte Bank der Spötter, Zur Situation des politischen Cabarets in Deutschland," *Der Monat,* 105 (1957), 33.

350 Jürgen Pelzer, "Das politische Kabarett in Westzonesien," in Jost Hermand, Helmut Peitsch and Klaus R. Scherpe, *Nachkriegsliteratur in Westdeutschland 1945–1949,* 129.

351 Erich Kästner, "Gediche," in *Gesammelte Werke,* Vol. 1 (Koln 1959), 94 f.

352 Ein neues Kabarett, "'Die Schaubude im eigenen Haus'," NZ, 4. 19. 1946.

353 Erich Kästner, "Der tägliche Kram," 99 ff.

354 Werner Finck, "Silversterrede 1945," NZ, 12. 31. 1945.

355 Jürgen Pelzer, "Das politische Kabarett in Westzonesien," 135.

356 Cited in Schauspielhaus Bochum. *Schwarzer Jahrmarkt Anzeiger,* 2. 2. 1975.

357 c.f. Jürgen Pelzer, "Das politische Kabarett in Westzonesien," 137.

358 Cited in Wigand Lange, "Antiamerikanismus und Zensur im Kabarett der Besatzungszeit 1945–1949," *Frankfurter Hefte,* 2 (1984), 56.

359 Cited in Wigand Lange, "Antiamerikanismus und Zensur," 59.

360 c.f. Wigand Lange, "Antiamerikanismus und Zensur," 60.

361 Friedrich P. Kahlenberg, "Film," in Wolfgang Benz, ed., *Die Bundersrepublik Deutschland. Geschichte in drei Bänden,* Vol. 3: *Kultur* (Frankfurt am Main 1983), 359.

362 c.f. Friedrich P. Kahlenberg, "Film," 360.

363 Hermann Kadow, "Kino von innen und autzen," *Frankfurter Hefte,* 5 (1946), 7.

364 c.f. Friedrich P. Kahlenberg, "Film," 362.

365 "Sorgenkinder der Produktion. Zur Filmlage in der britischen Zone," NZ, 6. 30. 1947.

366 Friedrich Luft, "'Und uber uns der Himmel.' Filmuraufführung mit Hans Albers," NZ, 12. 12. 1947.

367 Harald Braun, "Die Bedeutung der 'Filmpause'. Zwang und Zeil einer Fastenzeit," NZ, 11. 12. 1945.

368 c.f. Dieter Krusche, *Reclams Filmführer* (Stuttgart 1973), 157f.

369 Erich Kastner, "Treffpunkt Zürich," NZ, 11. 21. 1947.

370 "Gegenwartsfilm—ja oder nein. Aufforderung zu einer Diskussion," NZ, 1. 9. 1948.

371 Eugen Kogon, "Gegenwartsfilm ja oder nein? Eröffnung der Diskussion. NZ, 2. 26. 1948.

372 "Gegenwartsfilm ja oder nein? Eine Umfrage der 'Neuen Zeitung,'" NZ, 2. 29. 1948.

373 Hans Joachim Goltz. "'Gelenkter' oder 'freier' Buchverkauf?" NZ, 1. 20. 1947.

374 Manuel Gasser, "Fragwürdigkeiten der deutschen Buchproduktion," NZ, 8. 4. 1947.

375 Ernst Heimeran, "Wo bleiben eigentlich die Bücher?," NZ, 9. 12. 1947.

376 c.f. Edith Eiswaldt, "Studenten opferten Lebensmittel-zulage für die Professoren. Studium 1948: Kampf um Bücher, Papier und um Schwerstarbeitzerzulage," *Abendzeitung*, 1978.

377 Eugen Kogon, "Papierknappheit und Verlagsprogramme," *Frankfurter Hefte*, 9 (1947), 873 ff.

378 Marion Vrieslander, "Amerikanische Bibliotheken. Deutsche Leser blicken durch ein neues Fenster in die Welt," NZ, 8. 9. 1946.

379 Peter Härtling, "Die Macht der Verdranger. Ein unbewältigtes Kapitel deutscher Nachkriegszeit," *Frankfurter Allgemeine Zeitung*, 10. 18. 1980.

380 F. C. Weiskopf, "'Denk ich an Deutschland in der Nacht . . .' Die Themenkreise der deutschen Literatur im Exil," NZ, 2. 7. 1947—and "'Die Heimat ist weit. . . .' Die Themenkreise der deutschen Literatur im Exil (II)," NZ, 3. 3. 1947—and "Blick in die Helmat—Blick in die Fremde. Die Themenkreise der deutschen Literatur im Exil (III)," NZ, 5. 9. 1947—and "Hatz, Ironie and philosophische Betrachtung. Die Themenkreise der deutschen Literatur im Exil (IV)," NZ, 6. 12. 1947—and "Märchen aus dunkler Zeit. Die Themenkreise der deutschen Literatur im Exil (V)," NZ, 7. 7. 1947—c.f. also Hans-Albert Walter, *Deutsche Exilliteratur 1933–1950* (Darmstadt und Neuwied 1972).

381 Hellmuth Andersch, "Verlagsaufbau trotz grötzter Schwierigkeiten," NZ, 4. 5. 1946.

382 Gottfried Bermann Fischer, *Bedroht—bewahrt. Der Weg eines Verlegers* (Frankfurt am Main 1967), 221 f.

383 Ibid., 222.

384 Ibid., 225.

385 Ibid., 268.

386 Hans Mayer, *"Ein Deutscher auf Widerruf Erinnerungen (I)"* (Frankfurt am Main 1982), 320 f.

387 Heinrich Vormweg, "Literatur," in Wolfgang Benz, ed., *Die Bundersrepublik Deutschland. Geschichte in drei Bänden*, Vol. 3: *Kultur* (Frankfurt am Main 1983), 50 f.

388 Hans Mayer, "Es rauscht in den Schachtelhalmen ... Irrwege deutscher Lyriker und Verleger," NZ, 4. 7. 1947.

389 Peter Rühmkorf, *Die Jahre die Ihr kennt. Anfalle und Erinnerungen* (Reinbek bei Hamburg 1972), 88 f.

390 Cited in Helmuth de Hass, "Labyrinthische Jahre. H. E. Holthusens Lyrik," in *Das geteilte Atelier. Essays, entstanden in den Jahren 1948–1955* (Düsseldorf 1955) 105.

391 Cited in Klaus Günther Just, "Die deutsche Lyrik seit 1945," *Universitas,* 5 (1960), 517.

392 Rudolf Hagelstange, cited in Hans Günther Just, "Die deutsche Lyrik," 518.

393 Peter Sandmeyer, "Schreiben nach 1945. Ein Interview mit Wolfdietrich Schnurre," in Nicolas Born and Jürgen Manthey, eds., *Literaturmagazin 7, Nachkriegsliteratur* (Reinbek bei Hamburg 1977), 194 f.

394 c.f. Curt Hohoff, "Ernst Jüngers Weg und sein literarisches Werk," *Universitas,* 9 (1954), 970 f.

395 Curt Hohoff, "Ernst Jüngers Weg un sein literarisches Werk," 975.

396 Gottfried Benn, "Kunst und Drittes Reich," in *Essays, Reden, Vorträge, Gesammelte Werke in vier Bänden,* ed. Dieter Wellershoff, Vol. I: (Wiesbaden 1965), 315 ff.

397 c.f. Ernst Niekisch, *Das Reich der niederen Dämonen* (Hamburg 1953).

398 Gottfried Benn, "Probleme der Lyrik," in *Essays, Reden, Vortrage,* 524.

399 Ernst Jünger, *Auf den Marmorklippen* (Frankfurt am Main, Berlin 1980), 68, 119 f.

400 "Der Schreibende und die Kriuk. Hermann Kasack über seinen Roman," *Süddeutsche Zeitung,* (1948).

401 cited in Der Schreibende unde seine Kritik.

402 Erich Pfeiffer-Belli, "Uber die Form und den Gehalt. Anmerkungen zu einigen deutschen Neuerscheinungen," NZ, 8. 1. 1947.

403 Walter Kolbenhoff, "Latzt uns Zeit. Stimme aus der jungen Schriftstellergeneration," NZ, 1. 25. 1948.

404 Hellmuth von Cube, "Wir kennen die Melodie . . .," NZ 2. 1. 1948.

405 c.f. Hugo Steger, "Sprache im Wandel," in Wolfgang Benz, ed., *Die Bundersrepublik Deutschland. Geschichte in drei Bänden,* Vol. 3: *Kultur* (Frankfurt am Main 1983), 15 ff.

406 Hans Habe, *Im Jahre Null. Ein Beitrag zur Geschichte der deutschen Presse* (Munich 1966), 123.—c.f. also Wolfgang Bergsdorf, *Herrschaft und Sprache. Studien zur politischen Terminologie der Bundesrepublick Deutschland* (Pfullingen 1983).

407 cited in D. Sternberger, G. Storz, and W. E. Süskind, *Aus dem Wörterbuch des Unmenschen* (Hamburg 1957). 9.

408 "Gruppe 47. Zusammenschlutz junger Autoren," NZ, 11. 7. 1947.

409 Hans Werner Richter, "Wie entstand und was war die Gruppe 47?" in Hans A. Neunzig, *Hans Werner Richter und die Gruppe 47* (Frankfurt am Main, Berlin 1981), 48 f.

410 Ibid., 52 ff.

411 Ibid., 54.

412 Gunter Eich, *Gesammelte Werke,* Vol. I: *Die Gedichte. Die Maulwürfe* (Frankfurt am Main 1973), 247 f.

413 Hugo Steger, "Sprache im Wandel," 23.

414 Friedhelm Kröll, "Literaturpreise nach 1945. Wegweiser in die Restauration," in Jost Hermand, Helmut Peitsch, and Klaus R. Scherpe, *Nachkriegsliteratur in Westdeutschland 1945–49. Schreibweisen, Gattungen, Institutionen. Literatur im historischen Prozetz,* new series 3, Argument-Sonderband (Berlin 1982), 143 ff.

415 Joseph Bernhart, "Peter Dörfler," in Hermann Kunisch, ed., *Handbuch der deutschen Gegenwartsliteratur* (Munich 1965), 166.

416 Heinrich Vormeg, "Prosa in der Bundersrepublik seit 1945," in Dieter Lattmann, ed., *Die Literatur der Bundesrepublik Deutschland* (Munich, Zurich 1973), 152 ff.

417 Friedhelm Kröll. Literaturpreise nach 1945," 157 f.

418 Gottfried Benn, "Ithaka," in *Gesammelte Werke in acht Bänden,* ed. Dieter Wellershoff, Vol. 6: *Stücke aus dem Nachlatz. Szenen* (Wiesbaden 1968), 1475 f.

419 Gottfried Benn, "Probleme der Lyrik," in *Gesammelte Werke in acht Bänden,* Vol. 4: *Reden und Vörtrage,* 1087 f.

420 Gottfried Benn, "Reisen," in *Gesammelte Werke in acht Bänden.* Vol. I: *Gedichte,* 327.

421 Erich Kästner, "Reise in die Vergangenheit. Wiedersehen mit Dingen und Menschen," NZ, 6. 27. 1947.

422 Cited in Gerhard Hay, "Literarische Positionen im München der Nachkriegszeit," in Friedrich Prinz, ed., *Trümmerzeit in München. Kultur und Gesellschaft einer deutschen Grotzstadt im Aufbruch 1945–1949* (Munich 1984), 219.

423 Hans Mayer, "Vom goldenen Überflutz und vom Papier. Zur Frage der Neuausgaben deutscher Klassiker," NZ, 2. 24. 1947.

424 Albrecht Goes, "Goethegedichte in dieser Zeit," NZ, 2. 28. 1947.

425 Hermann Hesse erhält den Goethe-Preis. Bevorstehendes Erscheinen des zweibändigen Romans 'Das Glasperlenspiel.'" NZ, 8. 30. 1946.

426 Thomas Mann, "Ansprache im Goethejahr," from 25 July 1949 in the Paulskirche in Frankfurt am Main. Cited in Bernhard Zeller, ed., *"Als der Krieg zu Ende war"—Literarisch-politische Publizistik 1945–1950. Eine Ausstellung des Deutschen Literaturarchivs im Schiller-Nationalmuseum Marbach a. N.* Catalogue 23 (Stuttgart 1973), 492 f.

427 Friedrich Sieburg, "Frieden mit Thomas Mann," *Die Gegenwart,* 14 (1949), 16.

428 *Frankfurter Rundschau,* 7. 28. 1949.

429 *Frankfurter Neue Presse,* 7. 30. 1949.

430 Wolfgang Harich, "Das demokratische Deutschland grützt Thomas Mann," *Tägliche Rundschau,* 7. 31. 1949.

431 Karl Jaspers, "Unsere Zukunft und Goethe," *Die Wandlung,* 8. 7. 1949, 584 ff.

432 Leo Spitzer: "About the Goethe Cult"; *Die Wandlung,* issue 7/8/1949, page 548 ff.

433 Theodor Exchenburg: "The Occupation Years 1945–1949"; History of the German Federal Republic in Five Volumes 1. Stuttgart, Wiesbaden, 1983, page 273.

434 Theodor Eschenburg, *Jahre der Besatzung 1945–1949. Geschichte der Bundesrepublik Deutschland in fünf Bänden,* Vol. I (Stuttgart, Wiesbaden 1983), 273.

435 See, "Amerikas Ziele: Ein freies, unabhängiges Deutschland," NZ, 9. 9. 1946.

436 c.f. John H. Backer, *Die deutschen Jahre des Generals Clay. Der Weg zur Bundesrepublik 1945–1949* (Munich 1983).

437 Raymond Dennett and Robert K. Turner, eds., *Documents on American Foreign Relations,* Vol. IX (Princeton, n.p.), 65.

438 Wilhelm Röpke, *Das Kulturideal des Liberalismus* (Frankfurt am Main 1947), 15 f.

439 Ursula von Kardorff, "Knisternde Scheine für die Kinder des Olymp," *Suddeutsche Zeitung,* 6. 20. 1978.

440 "Eine Woche neues Geld. Vom Tag X bis zum Tag X und 6," NZ, 6. 27. 1984.

441 Lambert Schneider, "Neubeginn 1945–1950," in *Rechenschaft uber vierzig Jahre Verlagsarbeit 1925–1965. Ein Almanach* (Heidelberg 1965), 90 f.

442 *Der Ruf,* 6 (1949).

443 Cited in Bernhard Zeller, ed., *Als der Krieg zu Ende war,* 512 f.

444 "Welches war das wichtigste Kulturereignis? Eine Umfrage der 'Neuen Zeitung' bei deutschen Zeitungen," NZ, 2. 15. 1948; 2. 19. 1948.

CHRONOLOGY

The chronology does not provide a systematic overview of all areas of the development between 1945 and 1948. It only highlights certain developments to enable a chronological orientation. It is based on the 1945–1948 volumes of the *Neue Zeitung* and the following publications: Hans Georg Lehmann, *Chronik der Bundesrepublik Deutschland 1945 bis 1981* (Munich: 1981); Wolfgang Benz, ed., *Die Bundesrepublik Deutschland. Politik, Gesellschaft, Kultur,* 3 vols. (Frankfurt: 1983); Theodor Eschenburg, *Jahre der Besetzung. 1945 bis 1949:* vol. 1 of Karl Dietrich Bracher et al., eds., *Geschichte der Bundesrepublick Deutschland* (Stuttgart-Wiesbaden: 1983).

1945

JANUARY. Founding of the *Aachener Nachrichten* as the first German newspaper licenced under American and British control.

FEBRUARY. First union efforts in Aachen with the goal of the refounding of free unions. From the capitulation until the end of the year, hundreds of union organizations are established on a local and regional level.

APRIL. Based on the initiative of Kurt Schumacher, in Hannover the Social Democrats determine to refound the SPD. Suicide of Adolf Hitler in Berlin.

MAY. Unconditional Surrender of the German Forces in Rheims and in Berlin-Karlshorst, May 7 to 9. American President Truman accepts the direction about the main aims of the military government of the USA: Germany is not being occupied for the "purpose of its liberation," but as a "defeated enemy government." Efforts of fraternalization are to be prevented, as well as measures that would strengthen the economy or that would raise the minimal living standard above the level of a neighboring state. Hitler's successor, Fleet Admiral Donitz, is arrested together with the "Executive Reich Government" established by him.

JUNE. The four allied powers take over the supreme governmental power in Germany. They are represented by the Allied Control Council in Berlin, consisting of the commanders in chief. It starts its task in July after the entry of the English and the American troops into the city that was conquered by the Soviets.

Radio Hamburg begins broadcasting under British control. Within a month's time, the stations of Munich, Berlin, Frankfurt, Stuttgart, Cologne and Bremen follow. First edition of the newsreel *Welt im Film,* made by the British-American military government. Berlin: calls for the founding of the KPD, CDU and the central committee of the SPD under the chairmanship of Otto Grotewohl. Western zones: Kurt Schumacher reestablishes the SPD rejecting any cooperation with the communists. Guiding Principles of the Christian Democratic Party that was founded on June 6, from December 1945 on called CDU; postulation of a Christian socialism.

JULY. The Potsdam conference of the Big Three, Harry S. Truman, Joseph W. Stalin and Winston Churchill, since September 28, Clemens Attlee. Germany is divided into four occupation zones and is to be demilitarized, denazified and democratized; areas east of the Oder-Neisse come under Soviet and Polish administration.

AUGUST. *Frankfurter Rundschau* is the first licensed newspaper in the US zone. Allied guidelines for educational policies. Establishment of the welfare organization of the German Protestant Churches. First meeting of the German Catholic bishops after the War in Fulda; demand for the establishment of confessional schools and the publication of ecclesiastical newspapers; objections of the Allied Control Council against automatic arrest of nominal members of the NSDAP and against the expulsion of Germans from eastern areas. A pastoral letter of all Catholic bishops avoids a political valuation of the Nazi years. The four-power agreement of London creates the foundation for the establishment of the International Military Tribunal in Nuremberg.

SEPTEMBER. Founding meeting of the first Protestant Academies in Bad Boll. Anton von Webern is killed in Mittersill near Salzburg by a bullet from a soldier of the American occupation forces. Béla Bartók dies in New York. The US military government founds the states of Bavaria, Wurttemberg-Baden and Greater Hesse. In November, towns and counties receive rights of independent administration. Founding of the DVB in Wurttemberg and of the FDP in November in Bavaria as new liberal parties. In December, they merge to build the FDP under Theodor Heuss. *Totesmühlen* (Death Mills) a documentary film about the concentration camps, opens in the cinemas.

OCTOBER. First concert of the Munich Musica viva. Meeting of the Council of the German Protestant Church. Stuttgart Confession of Guilt. Founding of the Bavarian CSU in Wurzburg with strong federal and conservative alms; affirmation of the "eternal validity of Christian morality;" demand for the intrastate economic, political, and cultural autonomy of Bavaria. The Control Council decrees obligatory and supervised work for all men between 14 and 65 and for all women between 15 and 50.

NOVEMBER. The Control Council endorsed the creation of three air corridors to and from Berlin; the rights of entry on sea and land had only been agreed upon by word of mouth. In Nuremberg, the trial against the main war criminals begins before the International Military Tribunal until October 1946; twelve subsequent trials are directed, among others, against the accused from the foreign ministry, the trusts of IG Farben, Flick, and Krupp, the supreme command of the army, and the SS Institutions.

DECEMBER. News agencies of the British zone are established as German Press Service *(Deutscher Pressedienst).* First meeting of the culture ministers of the American zone. During the course of the year: Reopening of the College for Plastic Arts (Hochschule für Bildende Kunste) in Berlin. Founding of the Association for the Protection of German Writers. Death of Käthe Kollwitz. Karl Hofer becomes director of the Berlin Academy for Plastic Arts (Berliner Akademie der Bildenden Kunste).

Appearances: *Dies irae* by Werner Bergengruen, *Venezianisches Credo* by Rudolf Hagelstange, *Moabiter Sonette* by Albrecht Haus hofer, *Der Totenwald* (reports from the concentration camp Buchenwald) by Ernst Wiechert. Newspapers: *Der Aufbau. Die Wandlung., Die Gegenwart.* Most played new piece: *Leuchtfeuer* by the American Robert Ardrey.

1946

JANUARY. King George VI of England opens the first plenary assembly of the United Nations in the Central Hall of Westminster (London). General Charles de Gaulle resigns from his office as president of France.

At the first postwar town elections in Greater Hesse, the Social Democratic Party receives 41 percent of the votes; in Wurttemberg-Baden and Bavaria, the Christian Democratic Union and the Christian Social Union become victorious. Merger of the liberal state parties into the FDP of the British zone. The Control Council issues a law that permits the criminal prosecution of NS crimes, and the instructions with guidelines for denazification.

FEBRUARY. President Harry S. Truman calls upon all countries of the earth, whose food production exceeds their needs, to unite with the United States in the fight against hunger. The first time in Japanese history, the Japanese Emperor mingles with the people in order to talk with workers. In Bremen, the first inter-zonal consultation between the governors of the American and British states (Länder) takes place.

First conference of union delegates in Greater Berlin. Founding of the DEFA in Berlin (east). Production of the movies *Die Mörder sind unter uns, Irgendwo in Berlin,* and *Sag die Wahrheit.*

MARCH. The "Law for the Liberation from National Socialism and Militarism" in the US zone transfers denazification to German tribunals; all Germans above 18 years are to be examined through questionnaires. Winston Churchill speaks in Fulton, USA of the "Iron Curtain" in Europe and propagates close American-British cooperation. The Allied Control Council in Berlin accepts an industrial plan for Germany that is to permanently destroy the potential of German industry for war without taking away its necessary flexibility for peaceful production. The capacity of the united German raw material and finished goods industry, not including construction, is fixed at about half the prewar level. All of the industrial plants not necessary for peaceful production are to be destroyed or, as reparations, to be transported away.

Nine former PWs meet for a round table discussion in Munich under the sponsorship of the *Neue Zeitung* in order to discuss the future problems of German PWs. Main vote of Berlin's Social Democrats on the merger of SPD and KPD: disapproved.

APRIL. The US zone opens the postal service with foreign countries. First convention of the SPD of Bavaria in Erlangen. Founding of the Socialist Unity Party (SED) in Berlin. County elections in all states of the US zone; in Bavaria and Württemberg-Baden, CSU and CDU receive most of the seats, and in Hesse, the SPD.

The Allied Control Council declares May 1 a national holiday. Regulation for worker councils. In a pastoral letter, the Catholic bishops of the British zone criticize the occupation policies of the Allies and protest among other things against the exploitation of German PWs. The council of the foreign ministers does not reach a consensus regarding the problem of Germany. American Secretary of State James Francis Byrnes demands the merger of the four zones and a peace treaty. Wjatscheslaw Molotow criticizes the Western occupation politics asking for a German central state, a four-power control of the Ruhr District, the "economic demilitarization" of Germany, and 10 billion dollars in reparations. Compulsory merger of SPD and KPD into the German Socialist Unity Party (SED) in the Soviet occupied zone.

MAY. England has to lower bread and cheese rations. Declaration of the council of the EKD (Protestant Church of Germany) and of all church governments, regarding the question of denazification. First postwar convention of the SPD in Hannover; Kurt Schumacher becomes its first chairman, Erich Oilenhauer, returned from emigration in England, becomes its representative chairman.

The representative US Military Governor Lucius D. Clay orders an end to the dismantlings and to the reparations to the Soviet Union which had just begun. The first sentence of the denazification trial court is announced in the court building of Fürstenfeldbruck near Munich. Election of the city parliaments in the US zone.

JUNE. Permission granted for private persons in the USA to send food packages to relatives, friends, and relief organizations in the American occupied zone in Germany. First meeting of the atomic commission of the United Nations. Economic experts of the American and Soviet zones conclude an inter-zonal trade agreement on the foundation of a barter transaction. Eduard Benesch is elected president of the Republic of Czechoslovakia.

JULY. Atomic bomb test at Bikini. The Military Government confers a general amnesty on German youth. In Munich, Stuttgart, and Wiesbaden, the constitutional assemblies of Bavaria, Württemberg-Baden and Greater Hesse meet.

AUGUST. The North German Radio Station begins its program. First international Vacation Training for Music in Darmstadt. Conference of the American military government in Frankfurt concerning youth problems. Great Britain accepts the call of the United States for an economic merger of their zones. The British military government establishes the states of North-Rhine Westphalia and Schleswig Holstein and Lower Saxony in November. The French military government establishes the state Rhineland Pfalz. Limitations on travel between the American and the British zones of Germany are eliminated.

SEPTEMBER. The American Secretary of State James Byrnes announces in a speech in Stuttgart a change in US occupation policies. It wants to help Germany to find an honorable place among the free and peace-loving nations of the world, and to further the democratic, federal and economic reconstruction of Germany. The French demand for the Saarland is accepted. The extent of the areas to be given to Poland is to be eventually determined by a peace conference. Subsequently, Molotow ascertained the Oder-Neisse line as the final German-Polish border. The representative military governors of the American and the British zones raise the food ration in both zones to 1500 calories per day.

The first town elections of the Eastern zone are held in Saxony and Thurungia with the SED becoming the strongest party. The first independent Indian government under Pandit Nehru.

OCTOBER. The International Tribunal in Nuremberg announces the sentence against the 21 principal war criminals and against seven accused organizations. Hermann Goring commits suicide in his cell. Ten of the criminals sentenced to death by hanging are executed in the gymnasium of the Nuremberg prison. The licensed newspapers and magazines in the American zone are permitted to publish information of foreign news agencies. Bomb attack on the tribunal court in Stuttgart. Founding of the Bavarian Party (Bayern-Partei).

NOVEMBER. The American military government expands the authority of German independent administration. Lucius D. Clay sharply criticizes the handling of denazification by German institutions. In a resolution concerning the dietary situation, the state parliament of North-Rhine Westphalia appeals to the Allied Control Council and to the world public. Law on the legal status of civil servants and employees in the public service of Greater Hesse, reforming the professional civil servant of the old style.

First interzonal union conference in Mainz. Visit of the chairman of the SPD (Western zone), Dr. Kurt Schumacher, to England in response to an invitation by the British Labour Party. The German writer Hermann Hesse, who had been living in Switzerland, receives the 1946 Nobel Prize for Literature. Conference in Berlin of the representatives of the radio stations of the four occupied zones.

DECEMBER. With a large majority, Bavaria and Hesse ratify the constitution drawn up by constitutional state parliaments. The American Secretary of State Byrnes and The British Foreign Minister Ernest L. Bevin ratify in New York the American-British agreement about the economic merger of the American and British occupied zones of Germany. The Supreme Commander of the Soviet occupied zone, Marshal Vassili Sokolovski transfers the authority of provincial governments to the newly established state government. In New York, the Secretary of State begins consultations on the peace treaty with Germany. The plenary meeting of the United Nations passes a resolution concerning a general disarmament, the problem of Spain, the reconstruction, and the establishment of an international refugee organization. The trial by jury of 23 SS physicians begins in the large hall of the Court of General Session in Nuremberg. Württemberg-Baden is the first state in the US zone to receive a government in accord with the constitutional guidelines. France establishes a customs border control between the Saar area, belonging to the French zone, and the Western zones, after its attempts to sever the territories left of the Rhine from Germany were frustrated by the other Allies.

In the course of the year: Reopening of the universities of Cologne and Hamburg, as well as other universities. The following novels appear: *The Glass Bead Game* by Hermann Hesse; *Das unauslöschliche Siegel* by Elisabeth Langgässer; *Die Gesellschaft vom Dachboden* by Ernst Kreuder. Among the newly founded magazines: *Der Ruf; Frankfurter Hefte;* and *Nordwestdeutsche Hefte.* Staging of Thornton Wilder's *The Skin of Our Teeth,* first by K. H. Stroux in Darmstadt and then in Berlin. The premier of Carl Zuckmayer's *The Devil's General* staged by Heinz Hilpert in the Zurich Play House, the most frequently played period piece between 1947 and 1950. Exhibition of the Plans for the reconstruction of Berlin. The song *Möwe, du fliegst in die Heimat,* sung by Magda Hein begins the triumph, in German entertainment music, of songs in praise of the homeland.

1947

JANUARY. American President Harry S. Truman accepts the resignation of the former Secretary of State Byrnes and appoints General George C. Marshall as his successor. Protest of the US Secretary of State against the oppression of the political opposition during the preparations for elections in Poland. Peace treaties of the USA with Italy, Romania, Hungary and Bulgaria.

Release of a French plan for Germany that intends a decentralized German federation of states after the end of the occupation. The American and British zones establish the united economic district ("Bizonia"). The French zone merges with the Bizonia in April. First edition of the *Spiegel.*

FEBRUARY. New government in Italy under the Christian Democrat Alcide De Gasperi. The Security Council resolves the establishment of a general disarmament commission. In Nuremberg, the prosecution of 15 National Socialist legal officials begins. The state of Prussia is dissolved by law of the Control Council; it has always been the proponent of militarism and of reaction in Germany.

The CDU of the British zone passes the Ahlen program with the demand to radically reorder the economy with extensive socialization.

MARCH. President Truman asks both the House of Representatives and the Senate to support Greece and Turkey with 400 million dollars. "One of the most noble goals of the United States is the creation of a situation in which we and other nations are able to lead a life free of necessity (Truman Doctrine)." The United States reveals all those parts of the unpublished protocols of the international agreements of Teheran, Yalta and Potsdam in response to the release of the secret protocols by foreign minister Molotov. The congressional committee for the fight against anti-American activities unanimously accepts a report in which the communist party of the USA is accused of being an agent of the Soviet Union. It asks the government to prosecute the communists.

The USA dissolves mandatory military service. Francisco Franco, the Spanish head of state, releases a law for the reinstallation of a monarchy. Secretary of State Marshall proposes comprehensive plans for the economic unification of Germany that include the establishment of a central administration and the issuing of a new currency. Molotov demands the termination of the economic merger of the two Western zones. Before the Military Tribunal in Nuremberg the trial against the industrialist Flick begins.

APRIL. The former commander of the concentration camp of Auschwitz, Rudolf Höss is sentenced to death by a Polish court and executed. The trial against the personnel of the concentration camp of Buchenwald begins in Dachau. The citadel of Helgoland was destroyed. The elections to the state governments in the British zone show the SPD as the strongest party, a majority for the SPD in Schleswig-Holstein and Lower Saxony, and a majority for the CDU in North-Rhine Westphalia. The council of the secretaries of state meets for a last time in Moscow: "No miscarriages, but frustration."

JUNE. Establishment of the economic council of the Bizonia consisting of 52 members, delegates from the state parliaments, and the creation of the central administration. Frankfurt becomes the capital of Bizonia. US Secretary of State Marshall, in a speech given at Harvard University, announces a program of assistance and reconstruction for Europe, in which Germany is included (Marshall Plan). The conference of German ministers in Munich, initiated by the Bavarian Minister President Dr. Hans Ehart (CSU), could not even agree on the agenda. The representatives of the Soviet occupied zone depart on the eve of the conference, due to the rejection of their application to give priority to the building of a central administration for the creation of a united German state.

AUGUST. The plans for new industrial standards for the Bizonia were concluded against protests by the French and Soviets, thus revising the industrial plans of the Control Council. Industry production was to be raised to the level of 1936, the potential of the economy was to be rebuilt and the fatal nutritional situation was to be corrected. Dismantling continued inspite of German protests, but began to slow down. A pastoral letter of the conference of bishops at Fuldau takes the position of the Christian corporative state.

SEPTEMBER. The Minister President of Thurungia flees to the Western zone. Opening of the Leipzig Fall Convention. The Pan American Defense Treaty is undersigned by 20 American republics. The odyssey of about 5,000 illegal Jewish emigrants ends with the arrival of the "Exodus" fleet in Hamburg. The British military government releases the land reform law for its zone.

Founding of the "Gruppe 47." First drawing of the South German class lottery. Start of the soccer season for upper leagues.

OCTOBER. The elections of the Saar district show that 83 percent of the population decide in favor of the parties seeking connection with France. First German postwar foreign correspondent becomes accredited in London.

NOVEMBER. On the occasion of the 30th anniversary of the Bolshevik revolution, foreign minister Molotov declares in his speech in Moscow that there is no atomic bomb secret. Economic accession of the Saar to France. Alfried Krupp is prosecuted in Nuremberg. The directorship of coal mining in the Ruhr valley is placed into German hands.

DECEMBER. The UN committee for human rights passes a declaration in which international human rights are to be fixed legally. The heads of the CDU in the East zone, Jakob Kaiser and Ernst Lemmer, are dismissed, after the Soviet military government ascertains their lack of trustful cooperation. The London conference of the council of secretaries of state is broken off without results. The differences regarding the German question can no longer be surmounted. The points of dissention are: reparations, dismantlings, Marshall Plan, Bizonia, the question of the Oder-Neisse, the peace treaty, and the questions of the German constitution and unity.

During the course of the year: Having been invited by the American Military Government, the architect Gropius comes to Germany for a lecture tour. Wolfgag Borchert's piece *The Outsider* is first broadcast as radio drama, and later introduced in the Hamburg Kammerspiele. Gustaf Gründgens stages *The Flies* by Jean Paul Sartre in Dusseldorf. Ricarda Huch becomes the honorable president of the all German congress of authors in Berlin. Publications: *Dr. Faustus* by Thomas Mann; *Die Stadt hinter dem Strom* by Hermann Kasack; and *Nekyia—Bericht einer Überlebenden* by Hans Erich Nossack. The magazine *Merkur* is founded. Films: *In jenen Tagen* (Helmut Kautner); *Und über uns der Himmel* (Josef von Baky); and *Zwischen Gestern und Morgen* (Haral Braun). The exhibition "Extreme painting" in Augsburg. The first rooms of the heavily destroyed National Germanic Museum (Germanisches Nationalmuseum) can be used again. Founding of the German Art Council (Deutscher Kunstrat e. V.) by artists, publishers, critics and culture producers. Political hits: *Wer soll das bezahlen?* (Who shall pay for that?) and *Wir sind die Eingeborenen von Trizonesien* (We are the inhabitants of tri-zone-esia).

1948

JANUARY. The North-West German Radio Station (NWDR) passes into German hands. During the course of the year, legal foundations are provided for the Bavarian, Hessian and South-West Radio, Radio Bremen and the South-German Radio.

FEBRUARY. Conference of the cultural ministers of the four occupied zones in Stuttgart-Hohenheim. The Max Planck Institute for the Promotion of the Sciences takes the place of the Kaiser Wilhelm Institute. The nonprofit organization consists of 50 independent institutions, research and project groups serving the basic research in the technical and scientific fields and in the humanities.

MARCH. The Soviet military governor destroys the Control Council in protest of the proposals of the London conference of the six powers that aimed at a federal system of government in West Germany and the paticipation of the Western zones on the Marshall Plan, and as protest against the Western Union of Brussels, a five power pact between Great Britain, France, and the Benelux states, largely directed against the Soviet Union. Public criticism by Cardinal Faulhaber on the practices of denazification. Founding of the Bank of the German States (Bank deutscher Lander).

APRIL. The second session of the London conference of the six powers deems it necessary to allow the German people, on the basis of a free and democratic system of government, to restore unity and to increasingly take over the responsibility of government. The military governors should empower the West German minister presidents to call an assembly for the purposes of drafting a constitution. As security provisions, international control of the Ruhr and a military security authority are suggested. First edition of the *Bunte Illustrierte* (first under the title *Ufer*). Upon that follow *Quick* and *Der Stern*.

JUNE. The Warsaw conference of the eight powers (Soviet Union and East European nations) demands a united German democratic government and a peace treaty according to the resolutions of Potsdam.

June 20–21: Introduction of the Deutsche Mark in the three West zones. The Bank of German States, founded on March 1, 1948, receives the right of monetary distribution. Every German receives a head quota of DM 40 and later DM 20 more. The Reich Mark assets are exchanged at a 10:1 ratio; that of salaries, and pensions 1:1. The value of tangible goods stays the same. The public authorities are relieved of all monetary obligations. The ending of the controlled economy, with rations, price and salary controls, as well as inflation due to shortage of goods or hoarding of goods, black markets, and the cigarette currency. The new free market system gradually harmonizes the monetary demand with the supply of goods through an initial price rise. The credit for the currency reform goes especially to Ludwig Erhard, who as the director of the economic and administrative council of the Bizonia eliminates a multitude of price, business and rationing restrictions. The attempt of the Soviet Union to extend the currency reform in the Soviet occupied zone to the whole of Berlin is frustrated by the resistance of the Western powers which introduce the DM into the Western Sectors of Berlin. The Soviet Union responds with a large scale, sea and land blockade against West Berlin and declares the four power administration to be "virtually null." The transport of persons and of goods is interrupted due to "technical difficulties," and the distribution of coal and electricity due to a "shortage of coal." On June 6, the British-American air lift starts, providng West Berlin with food and goods. It is maintained until September 30, 1949.

JULY. The military governors of the Western Allies (Clay, Robertson, and Koening) show the 11 minister presidents three documents in Frankfurt. They propose to call in a constitutional assembly for the founding of a federal state, to examine the borders of the states, and they include guidelines for the relations of the future West German government and the occupying powers. In Koblenz, The West German minister presidents resolve, though reluctantly, to accept the authority granted to them. They propose, however, to replace the constitution with a basic law which is to be drawn up by parliamentary representatives of the states. At a further conference in Rudesheim, under the influence of the Mayor of Berlin, Ernst Reuter (SPD), it is determined that the founding of a West German government does not include the task of a unification of the Reich. At first, it is important to establish a provisional core of a nation. After that, it is possible to reestablish the unity of Germany according to the borders of 1937.

Establishment of the permanent conference of the culture ministers of the states *(Länder)* with a permanent secretariat and permanent special committees. Installation of the United Evangelical Lutheran Church in Eisenach.

AUGUST. A preparatory constitutional assembly of experts, called by the state governments, draws up the guidelines for the basic law of a union of German states on a federal and liberal basis.

SEPTEMBER. The 65 representatives of the parliamentary commission, elected by the 11 West German states (CDU/CSU and SPD with 27 each, FDP/DVP/LDP with 5, the Center, the German Party and the KPD with 2 each), begin the discussions about the basic law, together with five advisory representatives from West Berlin. President: Konrad Adenauer (CDU), Chairman of the respective legislative main committee: Carlo Schmid (SPD). First Assembly of the Catholics *(Katholikentag)* in Main in 1932.

NOVEMBER. The first large postwar strike against Erhard's economic policies. The Magistrate of Berlin is declared retired at a special meeting of municipal councillors called in by the SED, and Friedrich Ebert is thus appointed mayor (East). The former magistrate moves into the City Hall Schöneburg (US sector). The meeting of the city councillors of the majority parties, which had already moved to West Berlin in September because of communist trends, elects Ernst Reuter (SPD) as its mayor (West). This concludes the political and administrative partition of Berlin.

During the course of the year: Founding of Scholarship by the German People (Studienstiftung des Deutschen Volkes e.v.) for the promotion of highly talented students. Refounding of the Association of the German Book Trade. Werner Egks' Ballett *Abraxas* offends the moral sense of the cultural minister of Bavaria; it is removed from the program. Publications: *Statische Gedichte* by Gottfried Benn, the collection of poems; *Abgelegte Gehöfte;* by Günter Eich; *Gedichte* by Peter Huchel; the novel *Die grössere Hoffnung* by Ilse Aichinger; and the magazine *Der Monat.* Films: *Affaire Blum* (Erich Engel); *Film ohne Titel* (Rudolf Jugert); *Der Apfel ist ab* (Helmut Kautner); and *Berliner Ballade* (Robert A. Stemmle).

1949

MAY. On May 8 after the third reading, the Parliamentary Council ratifies the basic law of the Federal Republic of Germany with 53 against 12 votes (CSU 6, Center, German Party, and KPD each 2). Six of 13 representatives of the CSU reject the basic law, because they claim that it inadequately controls the financial system of the states, enables the splitting of parties and does not unanimously stand to the Christian theory of the state. The Parliamentary Council chooses Bonn to become the provisional capital of the federation. Of 62 secret ballots, 32 fall to Bonn and 29 to Frankfurt am Main. After the Approval of the basic law by the military governors and by 10 of the 11 state governments (Bavaria is the exception) it is enacted on May 24.

AUGUST–SEPTEMBER. Elections for the first German Parliament. The first Federal Assembly elects Theodor Heuss (FDP) as President. The first Parliament elects Konrad Adenauer as chancellor with 202 against 142 votes (44 abstentions and one invalid vote). The first government consists of a coalition of CDU/CSU, FDP and DP; the leader of the opposition is Kurt Schumacher (SPD).